# Education, Culture and Values

# Volume IV

The six volumes that comprise the *Education, Culture and Values* series bring together contributions from experts around the world to form, for the first time, a comprehensive treatment of the current concern with values in education. The series seeks to address this concern in the context of cultural and values diversity.

The first three volumes provide a wide-ranging consideration of the diversity of values in education at all levels, and thus represent a framework for the second three volumes which focus more specifically on values education (moral, religious, spiritual and political) *per se*. The six volumes, therefore, bring the fundamental domain of values together with the important issue of pluralism to generate new, fruitful and progressive reflection and exemplars of good practice.

The series will be of huge benefit and interest to educators, policy makers, parents, academics, researchers and student teachers. The six volumes contain:

- diverse and challenging opinions about current educational concerns and reforms in values education
- chapters from more than 120 contributors of international repute from 23 different countries
- conceptual clarification and theoretical analysis
- empirical studies, reports of practical projects and guidance for good practice.

## Volumes I–III:   Values Diversity in Education

*Volume I – Systems of Education: Theories, Policies and Implicit Values* is concerned with the theoretical and conceptual framework for reflecting about values, culture and education and thus provides an introduction to the series as a whole. It is concerned with state and policy level analysis across the world.

*Volume II – Institutional Issues: Pupils, Schools and Teacher Education* considers values and culture at the institutional level. What constitutes a good 'whole school' approach in a particular area? There are discussions of key issues and reports of whole-school initiatives from around the world. Several chapters focus on the vital issue of teacher education.

*Volume III – Classroom Issues: Practice, Pedagogy and Curriculum* focuses on the classroom: pedagogy, curriculum and pupil experience. Areas of curriculum development include the relatively neglected domains of mathematics and technology, as well as the more familiar literature and drama. There is a useful section on aesthetic education.

## Volumes IV–VI:   Values Education in Diversity

*Volume IV – Moral Education and Pluralism* is focused on moral education and development in the context of cultural pluralism. There are highly theoretical discussions of difficult philosophical issues about moral relativism as well as practical ideas about good practice.

*Volume V – Spiritual and Religious Education* distinguishes religious and spiritual education and takes a multifaith approach to pedagogic, curricular and resource issues. The important issue of collective worship is also addressed.

*Volume VI – Politics, Education and Citizenship* is concerned with political education and citizenship. Again chapters from several countries lend an international perspective to currently influential concerns and developments, including democratic education, human rights, national identity and education for citizenship.

**Education, Culture and Values**

Volume IV

# Moral Education and Pluralism

*Edited by*
Mal Leicester, Celia Modgil
and Sohan Modgil

FALMER PRESS
Taylor & Francis Group

London and New York

First published 2000 by Falmer Press
11 New Fetter Lane, London EC4P 4EE

Simultaneously published in the USA and Canada
by Falmer Press, 19 Union Square West, New York, NY 10003

*Falmer Press is an imprint of the Taylor & Francis Group*

Typeset in Galliard by RefineCatch Limited, Bungay, Suffolk
Printed and bound in Great Britain by
TJ International Ltd, Padstow, Cornwall

*British Library Cataloguing in Publication Data*
A catalogue record for this book is available from the British
Library

*Library of Congress Cataloging in Publication Data*
Moral education and pluralism/edited by Mal Leicester, Celia
   Modgil, Sohan Modgil.
       p.     cm.    (Education, culture, and values; v. 4)
     Includes indexes.
     1. Moral education. 2. Multicultural education—Moral and
   ethical aspects. I. Leicester, Mal. II. Modgil, Celia. III.
   Modgil, Sohan. IV. Series.
   LC268.M683   1999
   370.11′4—dc21                                    99–36828
                                                        CIP

ISBN 0–7507–1018–7 (6-volume set)
      0–7507–1002–0 (volume I)
      0–7507–1003–9 (volume II)
      0–7507–1004–7 (volume III)
      0–7507–1005–5 (volume IV)
      0–7507–1006–3 (volume V)
      0–7507–1007–1 (volume VI)

# Contents

# Contributors

**Barbara Applebaum** Assistant Professor of Philosophy of Education, Illinois State University, USA

**David Aspin** Professor of Philosophy of Education, School of Graduate Studies, Monash University, Australia

**James W. Bell** Reader in Education, School of Education, Murdoch University, Western Australia

**James Binko** Professor of Secondary Education, College of Education, Towson State University, USA

**Christopher R. L. Blake** Senior Lecturer in Education, College of Education, Towson State University, USA

**Dwight Boyd** Professor of Philosophy of Education, Ontario Institute for Studies in Education of the University of Toronto, Canada

**Krista Burane** Lecturer in Moral Education, University of Latvia, Latvia

**B. P. Campos** Professor, Faculty of Psychology and Education, Porto University, Portugal

**John Colbeck** Formerly Senior Lecturer in Physics, Goldsmiths College, University of London, UK (d. 1998)

**Gerald Collier** Former Principal of Bede College, University of Durham, UK (d. 1998)

**James C. Conroy** Head of Department of Religious Education, University of Glasgow, UK

**Robert A. Davis** Director of Inservice Education, University of Glasgow, UK

**Anthony J. Grainger** Analytical Psychologist (Jungian), The British Association of Psychotherapists, UK

**J. Mark Halstead** Reader in Moral Education, University of Plymouth, UK

**Terry Hyland** Lecturer in Continuing Education, Department of Continuing Education, University of Warwick, UK

**Carwyn Jones** Lecturer in Sociology of Sport, University of Teeside, UK

**Mal Leicester** Senior Lecturer in Continuing Education, Warwick University, UK

**Mark Mason** Lecturer in Education, School of Education, University of Cape Town, South Africa

**Mike McNamee** Reader in Applied Philosophy, Cheltenham and Gloucester College of Higher Education, UK

**Isabel Menezes** Auxiliary Professor in Education, Faculty of Psychology and Education, Porto University, Portugal

**Augusts Milts** Senior Lecturer in Ethics, University of Latvia, Latvia

**Christyan Mitchell** Professor, Center for the Study of Ethical Development, University of Minnesota, USA

**Celia Modgil** Senior Lecturer in Education, Goldsmiths College, London University, UK

**Sohan Modgil** Reader in Educational Research and Development, University of Brighton, UK

**Darcia Narvaez** Professor, Center for the Study

of Ethical Development, University of Minnesota, USA

**Mordecai Nisan** Professor of Psychology and former Dean, School of Education, Hebrew University of Jerusalem, Israel

**Glyn Phillips** Lecturer in Philosophy, University College of Northampton, UK

**Bill Puka** Professor Education, Rensselaer Institute and Harvard Graduate School of Education, Harvard University, USA

**Ieva Rocena** Lecturer in Ethics, Aesthetics,

Riga Teacher Training and Educational Management Academy, Latvia

**Tony Skillen** Reader in Philosophy, Darwin College, University of Kent at Canterbury, UK

**Nick Tate** Chief Executive, Qualifications and Curriculum Authority, London

**Janis Valbis** Senior Lecturer in Education, Riga Teacher Training and Educational Management Academy, Latvia

**M. B. Wilkinson** Lecturer in Philosophy, Lewes Tertiary College, UK

# Editors' Foreword

This is one volume in a series of six, each concerned with education, culture and values. Educators have long recognized that 'education' is necessarily value laden and, therefore, that value issues are inescapable and fundamental, both in our conceptions of education and in our practice of it. These issues are particularly complex in the context of cultural pluralism. In a sense the collection is a recognition, writ large, of this complexity and of our belief that since values are necessarily part of education, we should be explicit about what they are, and about why we choose those we do and who the 'we' is in relation to the particular conception and practices in question.

The first three volumes in the series deal with values diversity in education – the broader issues of what values ought to inform education in and for a plural society. The second three focus more narrowly on values education as such – what is the nature and scope of moral education, of religious and political education and of political and citizenship education in and for such a society? Thus collectively they consider both **values diversity in education** and **values education in diversity**. Individually they each have a particular level. Thus volumes 1–3 cover the levels of system, institution and classroom. Volumes 4–6 focus respectively on moral education, religious and spiritual education, politics and citizenship education. This structure is intended to ensure that the six volumes in the series are individually discrete but complementary.

Given the complexity of the value domain and the sheer diversity of values in culturally plural societies it becomes clear why 120 chapters from 23 countries merely begin to address the wealth of issues relating to 'Education, Culture and Values'.

*Mal Leicester, Celia Modgil*
*and Sohan Modgil*

# Part One

## Reflections

# 1 Society's Voice

## NICK TATE

What would you say if I asked you whether you valued truth? Justice? Relationships? The community? Your self-respect? According to your disposition you would readily answer that yes, you do value such things, or you would ask suspiciously what I meant by such a question. And if you asked the latter, it would probably be because you took the answers to be so obvious that there would have to be a catch to the question, or because you wanted to know precisely what I meant by (e.g) 'truth'.

But there was no catch to the question when MORI, on behalf of the School Curriculum and Assessment Authority (SCAA), asked 1455 adults a set of similar questions, nor were the words 'truth', 'justice', 'relationships' (etc.) being used in an unusual way. I have no way of knowing how many of those adults asked suspiciously 'What's the catch?' and had to be reassured, but I *do* know that the overwhelming majority of them said that they would agree that they value themselves (84 per cent), their society (94 per cent), their relationships (97 per cent) and their environment (96 per cent). The schools polled agreed even more strongly. In each case 97 per cent of the 1400 schools who answered the questions agreed that they valued these things.

The interesting question then, or so you might think, is not the questions we were asking, but why exactly we were asking them if the answers were going to be so obvious. What exactly did SCAA hope to achieve in asking these questions?

The answer is that SCAA intended to demonstrate, in a society-wide consultation, that the idea – increasingly widely accepted – that because this is a pluralist society we have no common values, is false. SCAA intended, in doing this, to restore teachers' confidence in the teaching of values, to trigger debate about values and to provide schools with a tool by which to elicit the support of parents and the wider community in the important task of promoting society's values, the values that children who will grow up in this society have both a right and a duty to understand. Let me explain.

In January 1996 SCAA held a conference entitled 'Preparation for Adult Life' in response to the concern, increasingly being expressed by parents, governors, teachers and heads, that the emphasis on pupils' academic development triggered by the implementation of the National Curriculum, by the advent of league tables and more generally by concern about standards of academic attainment in our schools, was leading to a neglect of pupils' spiritual, moral, social and cultural development. Delegates to the conference were asked whether they believed this important task was being sidelined, and if so what could be done about it.

The 200 delegates – many of whom were teachers or heads – argued that if this task was being sidelined it was not because schools did not think it important or because schools did not, in fact, promote pupils' spiritual, moral, social and cultural development, but because teachers were unsure about the nature of the task they were being asked to perform, unsure about how, especially given their numerous other duties, they were supposed to go about this task, and unsure about the extent to which they, as opposed to parents and the wider community, should be held responsible for promoting such development. In particular, delegates noted, teachers are often unsure about *which* values, in this pluralist society, they should be promoting.

The fact is that whereas schools have a clear responsibility to promote pupils' academic development, it is much less clear to what extent the promotion of pupils' spiritual, moral, social and cultural development is, ought to be, or even could be, the responsibility mainly of schools. It does not matter, after all, how vigorously a school promotes values if, as soon as children leave the school gates, those children see that these values do not inform the behaviour of the adults who are important to them, or turn on the television and see that they do not inform the behaviour of those in public life. The teaching of values, it seems, is something for which *all* adults have an equal responsibility; this task cannot reasonably be placed wholly upon the shoulders of schools.

Furthermore, delegates noted, if society is asking schools to promote values then it is reasonable for society to say something about *which* values schools are being asked to promote. Society cannot, in the light of its own increasingly pluralistic nature, simply assume that it is obvious which values should be promoted, and that teachers will, by some process of osmosis perhaps, know which values should be promoted. But if teachers are unsure about this, they will lack confidence in the promotion of values: insofar as they feel that they might wrongly be imposing their own values on pupils, they will not instil those values with the confidence that is the sine qua non of good teaching, the sort of confidence that allows room for debate because the teacher has a secure grip on his or her subject matter.

In the light of these concerns, conference delegates recommended that SCAA should set up a body, entitled the National Forum for Values in Education and the Community, and give it a two-fold remit, namely:

1 to decide whether there are any values that can reasonably be said to be common to everyone across society
2 to decide how best society in general, and SCAA in particular, might support schools in the promotion of pupils' spiritual, moral, social and cultural development.

The Forum was convened within a few months as a result of SCAA's asking numerous organisations with a special interest in education or youth, the major religious organisations and a number of organisations with a membership representative of the population at large to nominate Forum members. The resulting body had 150 members who were put in groups of approximately 10–15, each of which met three times (with their discussions being recorded and distributed to the other groups before the next meeting).

The Forum met the first part of their remit by deciding very early on – led by the representatives of the different religious faiths – that there are a number of values upon which everyone in society will agree. These values were pinned down – not without much discussion – in the statement of values that formed the basis of SCAA's consultation (see Appendix, p. 5). This statement, and the agreement achieved in consultation, gives the lie once and for all to the idea that because we are a pluralist society we have no common values. In doing so it provides us with a ready – and empirically justifiable – answer to the question of whose values we should teach in schools (namely: *our* values), thereby providing us with a tool to restore teachers' confidence in what is probably one of the most important parts of their job: the teaching of the values that underpin a cohesive society.

This, then, was why SCAA was asking questions the answers to which seem obvious. The very fact that the answers seem so obvious illustrates, in fact, how odd it was that anyone ever thought that there are no common values.

The very obviousness of the values, of course, has caused some to denigrate the Forum's efforts as just so much 'motherhood and apple pie', so it is necessary to emphasise that the fact that something is obvious does not mean that it is not true. It is also necessary to point out that there are occasions on which the obvious needs to be stated: the very fact that there are people – intelligent, well-educated people – who sincerely ask the question 'Whose values should be taught?', believing that because this is a pluralist society there are no common values, shows that this is such an occasion. Could it be that we have – quite rightly of course – recognised and celebrated our differences for so long, that we have ignored and denigrated the similarities that make these differences, in one very important sense, unimportant?

Not everyone will accept, of course, that the Forum has succeeded in identifying a set of common values, and that the claim that because we are a pluralist society we have no common values has been put to rest. Some critics have suggested, for example, that the Forum's findings are empty because even if we do agree on the values listed, there is no agreement on how these should be applied in behaviour, on their source (God? human nature?), or on how the values should be ordered. Without agreement on these things, it has been claimed, it is simply meaningless to say that there are values upon which everyone will agree.

In responding to these objections, let me first say that the Forum quite explicitly recognised that agreement on values does not entail agreement on the ordering of the values, on the source of the values or on how the values should be applied in behaviour. The Forum, furthermore, was wholly aware of the fact that this means that the statement of values is not and cannot be seen to be the final word on morality.

But then it was never meant to be. It would be quite unreasonable to expect the government's curriculum advisers to solve the problems that philosophers and theologians have grappled with for centuries. It would also be quite unreasonable, and indeed *wrong*, to expect them to pronounce on whether, for example, freedom should be valued more than equality, or autonomy more than life. Not only are these questions not obviously the sort of questions to which an answer *can* be given independently of a particular situation, it is perhaps in learning how to address such questions in particular situations, in learning how to engage sincerely in moral reasoning, that individuals become moral agents in the first place.

The Forum's statement is not intended to be the final word on morality. It is intended to be the trigger for a debate about values. We would like to see the statement being used by schools to stimulate a debate within the school community on what the school's values are, on whether the school should accept the Forum's statement or should construct its own (the consensus achieved on the Forum's statement is good evidence for the belief that any statement a school may construct will not be so very different from that produced by the Forum). We would also like to see schools debating what needs to be added to the Forum's statement (because clearly the values we share are not the only values to which we subscribe) and how the values on which the school finally decides should inform school processes and behaviour. We would then like to see schools use their statement to inform the work that they do in promoting pupils' spiritual, moral, social and cultural development and to elicit support in this vital work from parents, local employers and the local community.

This brings me to the second part of the Forum's remit, which the Forum met by recommending

that SCAA use the statement of values *nationally* in the way that schools might use it locally:

- to restore teacher confidence
- to trigger national debate about values
- to elicit support for schools' promotion of pupils' spiritual, moral, social and cultural development from national organisations of parents, employers and governors
- to structure and support guidance for schools on their promotion of pupils' spiritual, moral, social and cultural development.

The guidance mentioned in the last point should, the Forum recommended, be supported by booklets of case studies (to disseminate some of the very good practice that already exists), a directory of resources, a glossary of terms (to encourage a common language in this area) and guidelines to encourage partnerships between school and community.

SCAA is currently engaged in producing this guidance. SCAA is also approaching national organisations (particularly organisations of parents, governors and employers) to ask them to make explicit their support for schools' promotion of these values and to pledge their active support for schools' work in this area.

Whilst the work of the Forum has not ensured that there can be no moral disagreement, therefore, it has shown us that there is a great deal of moral agreement. And this is of supreme importance to society because if there are values upon which we can all agree then there are behaviours that can, in principle, be justifiably said to be unacceptable. The Forum has shown, in other words, that it is *not* the case that 'anything goes'. And in doing this it has put moral truth back on the agenda.

## Appendix

*The Preamble to the statement of values issued by the National Forum for Values in Education*

The National Forum for Values in Education and the Community was set up by the School Curriculum and Assessment Authority to:

1 discover whether there are any values upon which there is common agreement within society

2  decide how schools might be supported in the important task of contributing to pupils' spiritual, moral, social and cultural development.

The Forum identified a number of values on which members believed society would agree. Extensive consultation showed there to be overwhelming agreement on these values.

The second part of the remit was met by the recommendation that SCAA produce guidance for schools on the promotion of pupils' spiritual, moral, social and cultural development. This guidance, it was recommended, should be structured around the contexts of value, build upon current good practice, encourage rigour and a whole-school approach to work in this area and be supported by booklets of case studies, a directory of resources, a glossary of the terms commonly used in this area and guidelines for community service. It was also recommended that the guidance include suggestions on how the school might involve the local community in work in this area. SCAA was also asked to use the statement of values nationally to instil confidence, trigger debate and elicit support for schools in the vital task of promoting pupils' spiritual, moral and social development. This work is currently being planned.

It is important to note the following points:

- The remit of the Forum was to decide whether there are any values that *are* commonly agreed upon across society, not whether there any values that *should* be agreed upon across society. The only authority claimed for these values, accordingly, is the authority of consensus.
- These values are not exhaustive. They do not, for example, include religious beliefs, principles or teachings, though these are often the source from which commonly held values derive. The statement neither implies nor entails that these are the *only* values that be taught in schools. There is no suggestion, in particular, that schools should confine themselves to these values.
- Agreement on the values outlined below is compatible with disagreement on their sources. Many believe that God is the ultimate source of value, and that we are accountable to God for our actions; others that values have their source only in human nature, and that we are accountable only to our consciences. That statement of values is consistent with these and other views on the sources of value.

- Agreement on the values is also compatible with different interpretations and applications of these values. It is for schools to decide, reflecting the range of views in the wider community, how these values should be interpreted and applied. So, for example, the principle 'we support the institution of marriage' may legitimately be interpreted as giving rise to positive promotion of marriage[1] as an ideal, of the responsibilities of parenthood, and of the duty of children to respect their parents.
- The ordering of the values does not imply any priority or necessary preference. The ordering reflects the beliefs of many that values in the context of the self must precede the development of the other values.
- These values are so fundamental that they may appear unexceptional. Their demanding nature is however demonstrated both by our collective failure consistently to live up to them, and the moral challenge which acting on them in practice entails.

Schools and teachers can have confidence that there is general agreement in society upon these values. They can therefore expect the support and encouragement of society if they base their teaching and the school ethos on these values.

## The statement of values

### The self

We value ourselves as unique human beings capable of spiritual, moral, intellectual and physical growth and development.

On the basis of these values, we should:

- develop an understanding of our own characters, strengths and weaknesses
- develop self-respect and self-discipline
- clarify the meaning and purpose in our lives and decide, on the basis of this, how we believe that our lives should be lived
- make responsible use of our talents, rights and opportunities
- strive, throughout life, for knowledge, wisdom and understanding
- take responsibility, within our capabilities, for our own lives.

### Relationships

We value others for themselves, not only for what

they have or what they can do for us. We value relationships as fundamental to the development and fulfilment of ourselves and others, and to the good of the community.

On the basis of these values, we should:

- respect others, including children
- care for others and exercise goodwill in our dealings with them
- show others they are valued
- earn loyalty, trust and confidence
- work cooperatively with others
- respect the privacy and property of others
- resolve disputes peacefully.

*Society*

We value truth, freedom, justice, human rights, the rule of law and collective effort for the common good. In particular, we value families as sources of love and support for all their members, and as the basis of a society in which people care for others.

On the basis of these values, we should:

- understand and carry out our responsibilities as citizens
- refuse to support values or actions that may be harmful to individuals or communities
- support families in raising children and caring for dependants
- support the institution of marriage
- recognise that the love and commitment required for a secure and happy childhood can also be found in families of different kinds
- help people to know about the law and legal processes
- respect the rule of law and encourage others to do so

- respect religious and cultural diversity
- promote opportunities for all
- support those who cannot, by themselves, sustain a dignified life-style
- promote participation in the democratic process by all sectors of the community
- contribute to, as well as benefit fairly from, economic and cultural resources
- make truth, integrity, honesty and goodwill priorities in public and private life.

*The environment*

We value the environment, both natural and shaped by humanity, as the basis of life and source of wonder and inspiration.

On the basis of these values, we should:

- accept our responsibility to maintain a sustainable environment for future generations
- understand the place of human beings within nature
- understand our responsibilities for other species
- ensure that development can be justified
- preserve balance and diversity in nature wherever possible
- preserve areas of beauty and interest for future generations
- repair, wherever possible, habitats damaged by human development and other means.

## Notes

1  In British law, marriage is defined as 'the voluntary union for life of one man and one woman to the exclusion of all others'.

# 2 Should Moral Educators Abandon Moral Relativism?

GLYNN PHILLIPS

## Thinking about morality

Whether or not it is true that we live in particularly immoral times, there is a generally held view that certain moral values should be taught to the young by, among others, their school teachers. During 1996 Dr Carey, Mrs Lawrence, Mr Blair and Mr Major all lent their support to this proposal. Teachers might not be overly impressed by what these luminaries say, but they might well take notice when they are told similar things by Sir Ron Dearing and Dr N. Tate, respectively the then Chairman and Chief Executive of the School Curriculum and Assessment Authority (SCAA). SCAA has itself published some suggestive ideas about which moral values should be taught to the young (SCAA 1995 and 1996).

In January 1996 Tate produced a paper with the title 'Spiritual and Moral Aspects of the Curriculum' (Tate 1996). The striking thing about this paper is that Tate does not use it to set down his view about *which* moral values should be taught to the young. Instead, he launches an attack on moral relativism, which he claims has undermined 'our surviving moral language' and which has 'the clear implication that the very last thing one should ever be seen doing is to assert that any value is objective and enduring' (para. 14). We ought, he goes on, to replace moral relativism with another view, one which holds that there are moral truths, that some moral truths are 'universal' moral truths, that these constitute 'core values' and that these should be taught to the young.

My hunch is that if, or when, teachers are told that part of their work consists of teaching moral values to the young, the first question they will ask is: 'Which values?', and that will be quickly followed by: 'Why these moral values?' Yet rather than engage with those questions, questions which seem to require answers that sketch out a substantive moral position, Tate has evidently thought it important to address a seemingly quite different kind of issue, one that appears not to ask which moral values are to be taught and learned.

Given his rejection of moral relativism, and his evident support for what we might call a moral truth theory, it seems natural to ask what issue it is that Tate is addressing in these remarks. A way of gaining some illumination on this matter might be to consider some typical responses to moral questions. It is not unusual on applied ethics courses, where consideration is given to issues such as whether abortion is ever morally justified, for students to assert that over such issues, judgements are entirely subjective, or just up to the individual her- or himself, or are judgements which one cannot ever show decisively to be right. Often, the latter point is associated with a contrast between morals and science, with science being held as an example of a discipline or area of knowledge where proof *is* available. And in these not unusual examples, we have, I think, the sort of thing that Tate has in mind. What they exhibit is a way of thinking about morality. A stance is being taken, that moral judgements cannot have any objective basis. The way to think about morality, according to this view, is to eschew any pretence to objectivity in our moral judgements, and to accept that what the individual thinks is the first and the last thing that can be said. It is this view that Tate wishes to contest.

He might also contest the following way of thinking about morality, for the individualist position is not the only one that can be taken. Suppose I hold that some action is wrong, and when asked why I think it is wrong, I reply that it violates some generally accepted moral custom. From this, it looks as though my judgements about what is morally right and wrong are determined by the prevailing moral customs. That is how my moral thinking goes. Now suppose everyone thought that way. Pretty obviously, questions of what is morally right and morally wrong will now vary according to the customs, conventions and what have you of the society in which individuals live. Morality will, on this account, be entirely culturally dependent. Moreover, it seems highly likely that what is held to be morally right by one culture may not be held to be morally right by another culture. What we have here is the thesis of moral relativism.

Moral relativists might agree that moral judgements express a person's moral *beliefs*. What they insist on is that there is some external standard, provided by the cultural conventions, in terms of which the beliefs of individuals can be assessed. In contrast, there are those who might agree with moral relativists that moral judgements express our moral beliefs, but disagree over what makes them right. On this account, moral judgements express our moral beliefs, but the cultural conventions of the society are *not* what makes them right or wrong. This clearly prompts the question of what does make a moral belief a correct one. Suppose, for example, that it is my moral judgement that fox-hunting is wrong. It seems perverse to deny that I am telling you what I morally believe, but what might make this a correct (or an incorrect) moral judgement? Fixing on the idea of me holding a *belief*, a standard account of what a belief is, proposes that to believe that something is the case is to have that mental state in which the world is represented as being a certain way. If I believe that there are elves at the bottom of the garden, 'elves being at the bottom of the garden' is how I represent the world to be. If how I represent the world to be, *is* how the world is, then my belief is a true belief. If how I represent the world to be is not how the world is, then my belief is a false belief.

Is this how we are to think about moral judgements, as a type of belief? If so, it would seem that their nature is to represent something about the world. But what might this be? If I say that fox-hunting is wrong, and if in saying this, I express my moral belief, in what way is this a representational statement? What is being represented by it? We can make sense of the idea that what is being represented in my elf-belief is some possible elf-like state of affairs. When it comes to moral beliefs, however, the idea that something is being represented by

them is more difficult to accept. What, we are inclined to ask, might be represented by the sentence 'fox-hunting is wrong'? Hordes of animal-rightists gesturing at riders seated on horses at a hunt? A fox being pursued across the fields by dogs? These descriptions seem to pick out what we think goes on in fox-hunting, but they fail to pick out what we mean when we tag on 'is wrong'. Perhaps a better idea, then, might be to abandon the notion that moral beliefs are types of *representational* belief, in favour of the idea that they are still beliefs, but ones which are *non*-representational in character. The difficulty is to give a clear account of what the features are of non-representational beliefs. Beliefs still seem to be that mental state which, expressed in words, attempt to capture some feature of how the world is, and if we stick with this, the problem is to make this plausible so far as moral beliefs are concerned. I shall return to this.

Non-objectivist individualism, moral relativism and non-relativistic belief-theory, then, are three of many ways in which we might think about morality. It does look as though these are the three ways which Tate has in mind when he makes his criticisms and sketches his own view. What he is dealing with here is a question in that branch of moral philosophy called metaethics, the question being 'What sort of judgement is a moral judgement?' What I propose to do in the rest of this chapter is to consider whether Tate is correct when he urges us to reject the metaethical theory of moral relativism as a way of thinking about morality. But before doing this, I want to say something briefly about why this is an issue worth bothering with. For it might seem to some to be a peculiarly arcane philosophical dispute, with no practical application at all. Indeed, to develop this point a little further, it might be said that, so far as moral education is concerned, the main task for moral educators is to develop school pupils' thinking about substantive moral questions rather than concern themselves with questions such as 'What sort of judgement is a moral judgement?'.

It seems incontestable that moral educators should aim to develop their pupils' thinking about matters of moral substance. But this cannot be the only task to which moral educators should set their minds. As I have already hinted, when teachers try to develop their pupils' substantive moral thinking over particular moral issues, it is more than likely that young people will make remarks such as 'That's just your opinion', 'There is no right and wrong', 'No moral opinion can be shown to be correct', 'One opinion is as good as another in morality'. These are commonly made remarks. They are remarks about the nature of morality. Indeed, as we shall see in the next section, Tate thinks that these sorts of remarks are symptomatic of a pervasive malaise in our general moral thinking, one that is found in all walks of life including the young. To leave these remarks unaddressed is to risk undermining any further progress that might be made in a pupil's normative moral thinking, for these remarks are often used to block any further discussion. If left unchallenged, they could have the effect of stifling attempts to get serious discussion going on substantive moral thinking. For this reason, then, moral educators too ought to examine the question, 'What sort of judgement is a moral judgement?'

## Tate and metaethical moral relativism

What is metaethical moral relativism? Is Tate right to reject it as an account of the nature of moral judgement?

A standard account of metaethical moral relativism, that is an account of it as capturing the nature of moral judgement, is the view that what makes a moral judgement right is its correspondence with or coherence with the set of values which constitute a culture's values. One recent author (Thomas 1993: 113) regards moral relativists as saying that: 'Moral judgements are nothing but statements of socially accepted norms of conduct (the truth of moral judgements is relative to the norms they report)'.

So, according to this view, if I say that homosexual relations are wrong, what would make this a correct moral judgement, if it is a correct judgement, will be its correspondence with or coherence with some set of generally held values in the culture in which I live, for example, 'single sex relationships are sinful'. The latter makes the former right. Indeed, on Thomas's account, it is what makes the specific judgement a *true* one, though relativists will add that its truth is relative to that culture. It is worth noting that this standard version of moral relativism is one which *denies* that moral judgements are just a matter of individual taste or opinion. The position is that there are culturally held values against which an individual's judgements have to be measured.

Moral relativism as thus understood faces for-

midable objections. For example, relativists seem to have to agree that just because some culture possesses some set of generally agreed values, 'commonly held values' is what 'moral correctness' amounts to. The first objection then is that the fact that there is some set of commonly held values does not in itself make these morally correct. If it did, we would find ourselves agreeing that in, say, a Nazi-type culture, Nazi values are *ipso facto* moral values. But as against this, 'exterminate the Jews, the Gypsies and so on' is the very antithesis of what is morally right. A second objection arises when it is realised, just as bizarrely, that the moral relativist will have to hold that those within a culture who *dissent* from the commonly held values are *ipso facto* morally wrong. Thus, 'exterminating the Jews is wrong', proposed as a dissenting opinion to the main cultural value, is, on this standard relativist's account, a morally wrong judgement.

A third objection arises from the following point. If there are two cultures, one of which holds that exterminating the Jews is morally right whilst the other holds that exterminating the Jews is morally wrong, on the relativist's view of things, *both* positions are morally correct, since each position will be a generally accepted norm of conduct within its own culture. Yet this is to embrace unintelligibility. For now we evidently have to agree both that exterminating the Jews is morally right and morally wrong. Faced with this, a usual move is to say that what is morally right or wrong is relative to the cultural conventions which hold sway, or, as Thomas puts it, 'the truth of moral judgements is relative to the norms they report'. But that just makes matters worse. For now we can ask the relativist whether his own theory, 'that moral judgements are nothing but statements of socially accepted norms of conduct', is itself a theory whose truth is relative to the cultural convention operating in the society in which such a statement is held. If it is, then there is no general ground for accepting it, and someone who did not share the cultural conventions of the relativist would have no reason to accept it. If it is not true relative to the cultural conventions, it must be true, full stop. In that case, the relativist now relies upon non-relative truth to support the truth of moral relativism. If, we might now ask, one non-relative truth is to be admitted, why not others?

It was in the hope of avoiding these difficulties that Bernard Williams (Williams 1981) attempted to present a less problematic version of moral relativism. Williams's suggestion was that a defensible relativist position will be one which accepts that there can be alternative moral belief systems. A person who accepts the moral standards of his or her own culture might nevertheless accept that there can be others who equally accept the moral standards of their own cultures. Williams wants to say that a person who realises that there are diverse moral cultures need not think that their own adherence to their own moral standards is thereby undermined. This would seem to suggest that a person can hold that his or her own moral values are correct whilst noting that there are others in other cultures who would hold that it is their values which are correct. This is clearly different from saying that the values which I hold are correct and the values which they hold are correct. As we noted in the previous paragraph, the latter position generates incoherence is so far as it allows two contradictory moral judgements both to be true. Williams's moral relativist would merely note as a fact that there are other cultures which have different moral standards from one's own, standards which might well be compelling for the people whose lives are shaped by them, but which by their existence do not force a person from some other culture to abandon his or her own commitments to his or her own values. A person can hold, then, that their own, culturally determined, moral values are correct, that other people in other cultures hold their moral values as correct, that one is not thereby compelled to give up one's own moral values just because some other culture has different moral values, and that one can hold that these others, holding their moral values, are incorrect.

Williams's theory might still be vulnerable. Though I am committed to my own culture's values, it is still possible to say that they are morally objectionable. Williams seems not to provide any account of what might justify a person saying this. Perhaps he thinks that such judgements cannot be justified, but in that case we might wonder how it is possible for those within a culture to give any criticism of their culture's values from the moral point of view.

Notwithstanding this point, Williams's position has the advantage that it provides the basis for an important moral principle, namely that we ought to tolerate others' views and lifestyles. How does it do this? Once we grant the cultural variability of morality, the question arises as to what attitude a person from one culture ought to take towards a moral set of standards, different from one's own and located within another culture. Remember that such a person recognises not just that the other culture's moral standards are different from his or her own but also that it is quite possible that he or she could disagree with the other culture's moral standards. Faced with the question of what a person now ought to do, certain choices are apparent. One can mount an attack on the other culture's values – even, perhaps, going so far as to try to suppress them. Or one can decide to govern one's own conduct by the moral principle, 'one ought to tolerate those beliefs and values with which one disagrees'.

A person is not compelled to adopt the principle of toleration. But there might nevertheless be reasons for doing so. One might, for example, be attracted by the idea that if it were one's own moral conventions that were either to be tolerated or attacked, self-interest would incline a person towards toleration. Or one might take the sort of position held by Mill, that variety in moral thinking and practice gives a person extra information on which to develop their own moral positions.

To forestall one objection, this position does not entail toleration of any and every set of norms of conduct. For one could also add that the moral principle of toleration only extends to those cultural norms of conduct which themselves accept the moral principle of toleration. Those who tolerate those with whom they disagree need not tolerate those who are intolerant of those with whom they disagree.

We might conclude tentatively even at this stage of the discussion that Tate's blanket dismissal of moral relativism might lead us to ignore these points about moral variability and might prevent us from seeing that relativism provides an interesting basis for supporting the principle of tolerance, albeit one with the proviso stated in the previous paragraph.

Curiously, Tate does not direct his ire at the standard version of moral relativism. His understanding of relativism is, I suspect, nearer to the idea which I have categorised as individualistic non-objectivism, that is that morality is to be understood as being composed of judgements, whose correctness is determined by the specific individuals making them. 'Ø-ing is wrong', on this account, is a moral judgement the correctness of which is relative to the individual making the judgement. What X thinks is morally right is right just because X thinks so. Let us see how Tate develops this idea. He surmises (1996) that there once was a moral education framework, 'the transmission of a set of rules, precepts and principles . . . the Ten Commandments, the seven deadly sins, the seven principal virtues' (para. 12), but that this has been undermined by 'the spread of an all pervasive relativism'. Relativism, we are told, has even insinuated itself into the old way of moral thinking, the evidence for this being the claimed fact that when people of the older generation give a moral judgement based on the old rules, even they qualify it by saying things like 'But that's only my opinion', 'I don't wish to be judgemental' (para. 14).

Even worse, relativism has got its grip on students, notably trainee teachers. Tate quotes a piece of research from Cambridge by Dr Arnot which found that (p. 4): 'trainee teachers are deeply reluctant to do anything which might suggest that they are imposing ethnocentric, class or gender values on their pupils, as if the truth of a value were always relative to its subject and never universal'. Tate then offers this brief account of moral relativism (para. 15):

> By relativism I mean the view that morality is largely a matter of taste or opinion, that there is no such thing as moral error, and that there is no point therefore in searching for the truth about moral matters or in arguing and reasoning about it.

From even these brief remarks, it is clear that there is more than one position which is being called 'moral relativism'. The first 'relativist' position is that that moral judgements are like the sorts of remarks we make when we indicate what our tastes are: 'I like coffee, you like tea', or, perhaps, 'Modern music is not to my taste'. Now it is not difficult to criticise this account of the nature of moral judgement. If we think that moral judgements are literally like matters-of-taste judgements, we seem committed to thinking that in just the same way that 'It tastes sweet' depends on a certain sort of sensory experience, so moral judgements too depend on some analogue of sensory experience, say a moral experience. Aside from the evident circularity of this view, it appears to posit the existence of a special moral sense. It has to be said that this is a now discredited notion. The existence of a special moral sense seem to defy empirical attempts to locate it and describe it. Yet even if we were to waive this point, the theory runs into a further difficulty. If two people have this special

moral sense, it would appear that when it is stimulated into activity by some event, each person would make the same moral judgement. Yet it is evident that people of similar moral sensibilities can come to different moral conclusions over the same matter.

The second 'relativist' position picked out by Tate is that moral judgements are matters of opinion, a view generally regarded as subjectivism. Yet this in itself is open to a variety of interpretations. One version of this is emotivism, with it roots in Hume's philosophy and its twentieth-century proponents such as A. J. Ayer (Ayer 1946, ch. 6). Rachels tells us (Rachels 1993: 432) that emotivism 'is a theory which says that, in making moral judgements, people are doing nothing more than expressing their personal desires or feelings', Rachels quoting Hume's view that morality is a matter of 'feeling, not reason' in support of this. Standard criticisms of emotivism echo those made of the standard version of moral relativism which Thomas describes. Emotivism permits one and the same judgement to be both right and wrong, if it is the case that two people (or the same person on two separate occasions) disapprove and approve of the same act. A further objection is that whilst X may approve of ø-ing, that is consistent with ø-ing being morally wrong. After all, individuals approve of all sorts of things which are morally dubious. The reverse of this is that sometimes people do not approve of actions which are morally right.

Emotivism can also be said to reverse the usual way we think about morality. It says that to be approved of *is* what it is to be morally right, but as against this it can be objected that it is because something is morally right that it merits our approval. Approval comes after the moral judgement rather than constituting it. We approve of being kind because being kind is, generally, a morally good virtue to display.

Those who hold that moral judgements are expressions of our feelings of approval or disapproval are usually also taken to be agreeing with Hume that so far as morality is concerned, our moral judgements are non-cognitive. That is, they are expressions of that aspect of the human mind which lies beyond our rational capacities. 'What we desire', it will be held, cannot be *subject* to any rational consideration. But this does not exhaust the possibilities of subjectivism. There are versions of subjectivism which reject the view that moral judgements are the expressions of our feelings of approval and disapproval, in favour of saying that a person's moral judgement expresses their *belief* that something is right or wrong, not their feelings. This is *cognitive* subjectivism.

Further analysis reveals that there is more than one version of cognitive subjectivism. There is what we might term 'simple cognitive subjectivism'. This is the view, and I suspect it is the popular version of subjectivism, that when a person, X, believes that ø-ing is right, the phrase 'right for X but not necessarily for Y' is added. It is the term 'necessarily' which provides the trouble here. It is plausible to say that an action is right in some circumstances but not in others. For example, it is right for X to welcome strangers into her or his home but not for Y, if Y is living in the middle of a civil war. But if subjectivism is taken to be the general presumption that an action can be right for X but not for Y, then this too ends in a contradiction, namely that the same action can be both right and not-right. An implication of this position, it should be noted, is that it makes it difficult to defend moral judgements such as 'genocide is wrong', for it appears to mean that it is wrong so far as X is concerned but not so far as Y is concerned.

Just as with the first version of moral relativism, so too cognitive subjectivism can be developed to avoid these errors. One can say that X's belief that ø-ing is right entails that X believes that ø-ing is right whoever holds the belief. How is this still a version of subjectivism? Its subjectivism arises from three further claims, namely that no *conclusive* reasons can be offered for X's belief that ø-ing is right, that X's belief that ø-ing is right based on reasons which have convinced X that ø-ing is right, and that X believes that Y holds that ø-ing is not right (Y's belief too being a belief based on reasons which are not conclusive but are convincing to Y). What this more sophisticated version of subjectivism denies is that there are moral truths.

To fill this account out, we can draw attention to the fact that from time to time people advance reasons for the opinions which they hold. Of course, reasons are also advanced for the true beliefs which we might hold. Yet 'opinion' is often contrasted with knowledge, and this is shown by the fact that whilst we sometimes put down what a person believes by saying 'That's only your opinion' we do not put down what a person claims to know by saying 'That's only what you know'. Insofar as opinions are backed by reasons, nevertheless opinions are not thought of as decisive. They lack some-

thing. Applying these points to our moral thinking, sophisticated subjectivists will claim that moral judgements are the sorts of judgement which can never obtain the status of knowledge, even though they may be supported by reasons. So, whilst 'The train left at 3.30; I saw it' may be thought by most to be a statement of knowledge, 'He made her cry and that's why what he did was wrong' would be held to be a statement of the speaker's moral opinion but not of his or her moral knowledge. If this view prevailed, moral judgement would be thought to be the kind of judgement where it is possible to hold reasons for one's moral opinions, but where in spite of this the status of these moral judgements is not the same as the status of statements about ordinary, empirically discoverable, states of affairs, claims which are accepted on the basis of what a person sees, hears and so on.

Indeed, we might supplement this point by following the spirit of a suggestion made by the physicist Paul Davies (Davies 1984) in his remark that belief in God is a matter of taste. Davies means by this that there are no nor can there be any arguments which would *compel* one to hold such a belief. In similar vein, moral judgements would be judgements for which there are not and cannot be any compelling arguments, even though there can be reasons which are brought forward in support of them. In morality, we might say, the reasons we advance for some moral view *underdetermine* one's moral conclusions.

What are we to make of this theory of the nature of moral judgement? Its general point seems to be that there is a respect in which morality differs from those discourses where we can with considerable regularity decisively establish some conclusion. In morals, the most we can expect is that we decide what we ought to do on those reasons which seem to us to be convincing. We look in vain for a proof that this is so.

There is, I suggest, something in this. It is plausible in those cases where we are faced with conflicting moral duties, each with reasons supporting them but where no set of reasons is decisive. Then, what we judge we ought to do is, in the end, up to us. That is the subjective element in it. We need to be careful, nevertheless, not to overstate this point, and not to say that choice operates similarly in all moral judgements. There would be a temptation to say this in the following case but it is one which ought to be resisted. We have made a promise and then a situation arises which presents other reasons which will defeat that duty, and points us in the direction of some other duty. For example, we have promised to take our children out for the afternoon, but on the way we come across an accident. We can help but only at the cost of cancelling the outing. Most people would accept that the distress of the accident victim takes priority. What we ought to do is clear. Yet the fact that the original duty has been set aside in favour of a new one does not show that choice operates in anything like the same way it does when we have two finely balanced duties. Of course, we do choose to help rather than carry on with the outing, but this is a choice which bows to the compelling nature of helping the accident victim. We know where our moral obligation lies.

It is also worth reminding ourselves that often we take on an obligation, and there are no defeater considerations to move us away from doing what we are obliged to do. Having made a promise, we ought to keep it. Choice does not enter at all.

Perhaps the point which sophisticated subjectivists are really after is an epistemological one, to do with what requirements have to be satisfied for moral judgements to be justified. Whilst we have reasons for keeping the promise we have made – for example, that not to keep it would be to harm the promisee – the reason *does not amount to a proof* that we ought to keep it. Why, the subjectivist asks, should it be thought that moral judgements require a proof before they can be said to be justified? Is not proof out of place here, asking the wrong thing of a moral judgement? We have to be content with something less exalted. Our reasons for doing something do not amount to a proof that that is what we ought to do, and in that sense do not compel us to do what we ought to do. But we still know what we ought to do.

At any rate, this looks like the outlines of an interesting theory about morality. It stresses the importance of choice in certain cases, and it stresses the underdetermination of conclusions by reasons. Ought this to attract the sort of condemnation voiced by Tate? I suspect that he has been tempted into thinking that if we admit that in morality our reasons do not determine our moral conclusions, this forces us to conclude that each moral judgement is as good as any other. Yet even though we cannot *prove* our moral judgements to be right, this does not prevent us from *holding* that they are right, and right for the reasons we cite.

It might nevertheless be objected that this version of subjectivism is still a way of *undermining* any moral judgement. The thought would be that if a moral judgement cannot obtain the status of empirical knowledge, such knowledge requiring proof before claims can be held to acquire the status of knowledge, morality is inferior to statements which can obtain such status. Moral judgements are for ever condemned to be like unsubstantiated empirical judgements, never coming up to the mark. To this the subjectivist can repeat the point that there is no reason to suppose that the standards inherent in successful empirical judgements must be imported into the realm of moral judgements. We might say, for example, that our moral opinions can be supported by reasons, but that there is no further type of reason to use which will convert an already reasoned moral opinion into one which obtains the epistemological status which empirical knowledge has. Morality is just not like that.

## Conclusion

Let me draw the threads of this discussion together. Dr Tate thinks that the moral relativist's way of thinking about moral judgements is objectionable for it gives too much room for individual choice, it appears to set aside the use of argument and reasoning, and it appears to make it impossible to admit that in morality we can make moral mistakes. I have suggested that there are strong criticisms to be made against certain theories which Tate wishes to regard as forms of moral relativism but that other versions of 'moral relativism' survive such criticism. The problematic versions are standard relativism, moral-sense theory, emotivism and simple subjectivism. Williams's version of moral relativism, and what I termed sophisticated subjectivism, may well have instructive points to make about the nature of morality. Williams's version can provide part of the grounds for justifying the moral principle of toleration. Sophisticated subjectivists can help to explain why moral judgements are not like empirical judgements, and do not require proofs before they can be said to be justified. They also give room for the operation of choice in some aspects of our moral thinking. This sort of subjectivism can also rebut the charges, often laid against it, that it results in us conceiving of moral judgements as having to be held in a hesitant, timid way, and that it gives no room for the use of reasons and argument.

Tate wants to say that there are certain moral

standards, certain core values, expressed in terms of moral principles, that everybody should be taught, and taught to keep. These would no doubt include such principles as 'One ought to keep one's promises', 'One ought to tell the truth', 'One ought not deliberately to harm another, unless so doing is in the interests of the person'. But if the education of the school population about morality is to be taken as a serious enterprise, teachers will want to know much more than this. Besides wanting to know which moral principles should be taught, they will want to know what to make of the evident plurality of morality. They will want to know what to make of apparently conflicting moral traditions, and they will want to know what to make of the apparent fact that morality is itself a plural institution, with various moral values or principles which appear to generate moral conflicts and dilemmas. They will want to know something about the sort of thing that moral thinking itself is. Just to rule out moral relativism and subjectivism as having nothing to say in these matters is to set oneself against the possibility that these theories might have something important to teach us in our attempts to understand morality.

## References

Ayer, A. J. (1946) *Language, Truth and Logic*, 2nd edn, Harmondsworth: Penguin.

Davies, P. (1984) *God and the New Physics*, Harmondsworth: Penguin.

Rachels, J. (1993) 'Subjectivism', in P. Singer (ed.) *A Companion to Ethics*, Oxford: Blackwell.

SCAA (1995) 'Spiritual and Moral Development', London: SCAA.

SCAA (1996) 'Consultation of Values in Education and the Community', London: SCAA.

Tate, N. (1996) 'Spiritual and Moral Aspects of the Curriculum', London: SCAA.

Thomas, G. (1993) *An Introduction to Ethics*, Indianapolis: Hackett.

Williams, B. (1981) 'The Truth in Relativism', in B. Williams (ed.) *Moral Luck*, Cambridge: Cambridge University Press.

# 3 A Clarification of Some Key Terms in Values Discussions

DAVID ASPIN

This is a highly significant time to be talking about the nature and places of values in schools and other educating institutions in our modern plural societies. If there was ever a need for educative leadership in values issues there is one now, given the kinds and magnitude of changes and challenges that those societies and their educational institutions are facing. In values matters these changes are so large-scale and their effects in society so manifest that facing them calls for little short of a revolution in our educational thinking and planning. It is towards helping educators make a start on facing the challenges posed in and by the revolution that has accompanied the emergence of modern plural societies that this chapter is addressed.

In his well-known book *The Structure of Scientific Revolutions* (1972) Thomas Kuhn argued that a revolution is experienced when people who are operating within the current major paradigm in any field of enquiry begin to encounter such an array of anomalous phenomena and change that they are no longer able to operate with or from their existing patterns of thinking in order to face the challenge of the new. When that happens, a kind of psychological breakdown occurs. A crisis has come about and in order to cope with this crisis people have, or are driven, to break the mould of the existing form of cognitive operation and to undertake a new approach in their thinking. The change in their circumstances is such that it precipitates a shift into a new form of thinking – a revolution in their paradigm.

It seems to me that a new educational paradigm is now called for, in order that educators might more effectively and realistically confront the challenge of the enormous changes that are occurring widely across the world. Anthony Giddens has recently described their all-encompassing character (Giddens 1995): 'We are at the beginning of a fundamental shake-up of world society, which comes from numerous sources, not from a single source. We do not know as yet where it is going to lead us.'

Not least of the forces driving change is the impulse towards globalisation and internationalisation – the interaction and exchange of economic functions, products, services, ideas, communication and media, culture and knowledge, so that as we enter the twenty-first century we are looking towards a society based upon, governed by and targeted towards the economy of knowledge, the mobility of labour and the increasingly impersonal centripetal forces driving towards the homogenisation of culture. Giddens points out the danger: '(globalisation) is not just an extension of earlier phases of Western expansion. If you could say the West controlled the earlier phases of globalisation, the current phase is one which nobody controls'.

The magnitude of such changes has driven many societies, communities and individuals to a thoroughgoing re-examination of their perceptions and judgements as to what is of abiding importance in social and interpersonal relations, institutions and codes of behaviour at the present time. The nature, form and structure of these changes – amounting, as some people see it, to nothing less than a values revolution – is complex, multidimensional and many-tensioned. These features intensify the influence and exacerbate the effect of a range of change factors on existing educational institutions and agencies. Our growing awareness of the speed and extent of changes in matters of value is a factor in the educational revolution that is already forcing us to subject existing policies, practices, norms and conventions to a radical reappraisal, to see in what ways our present forms and patterns of arrangement and delivery of education might stand in need of criticism or correction, amelioration or even abandonment, so that we might the better accommodate them to the impact of the change factors.

The challenge to education arises from a number of fundamental alterations and transformations. To begin with, there have been considerable expansions in the concepts, categories and bases of values with which we define and frame our principles regulating interpersonal and social relations, in the kinds of problems, topics and issues of value with which modern plural societies are beset, and in the consequent effects of those on the structure, policies and curriculum practices in our educational institutions.

Accompanying such alterations and expansions in the field of values, there have also been major developments in the concepts of knowledge and approaches to understanding and the acquisition of competences of various kinds and in the ensuing remodelling of teaching methods and learning activities and procedures in places in which students and teachers work. There have been almost incredible innovations in modes of communication, information technology and new technologies of learning, which bid fair to challenge existing concepts – perhaps even the very existence – of schools as educating institutions. There have been enormous modifications world-wide in forms of the provision, organisation and management of learning organisations, agencies and institutions, in which our growth and development in the area of values are shaped and framed. Accompanying these is an acceleration in the pace of moves currently being made and set to work to lead us away from the notion of education's stopping at the end of the years of formal schooling and becoming instead a lifelong process in which all can and should engage, in the new knowledge economy and learning society.

At the same time as there have been changes in the substance of what we agree we should teach and how it is to be conceived and delivered across the lifespan, we cannot fail to be aware of changes in the understanding and planning of the various ways in which people learn. The former adherence to a uniform model of knowledge transmission, in which the student was viewed simply as a receptacle, somewhat like a jug, into which teachers didactically pour knowledge, contents and facts until the jug's allocated capacity is filled, has long been rendered inoperable by recent advances in cognitive psychology and metacognition in more

up-to-date thinking about learning. Now it is widely accepted that in order for learning to be effectively secured and integrated into the pattern of the understandings that we already have, it must be student-centred, self-directed, self-internalised and self-monitored. Recent advances in learning theory suggest that students learn best when proceeding under their own steam.

Nowadays in many educational institutions students are coming to stand at the centre of the learning rule. Educators now increasingly accept that students are their own best initiators, arrangers and guarantors of the successful integration of new knowledge and discernment into their existing structures and patterns of understanding and judgement. Today students look much more for personal relevance and applicability in the experiences in which they are required or encouraged to engage, the knowledge they need to assimilate and the competences they are expected to acquire, or in those areas of importance to them in which they realise they are still lacking the necessary information or requisite skills. They are being encouraged to tackle the tasks of the acquisition and mastery of new material or skills in ways that give them greatest sense of fit with the contexts in which they will need to deploy and apply them. They are learning how to monitor their own progress and their learning gains, constantly checking and evaluating, criticising, correcting and extending, as they go along. It is in and by means of such an approach that educators now appreciate learning is made more interesting, relevant and long-lasting.

Teachers' and students' concern for clarity of understanding, security of mastery, relevance, interest and manageability help highlight the central place and significance of values in the curriculum, in teaching and learning activities, in student growth and development. They help us realise that advances in concepts of knowledge and theories of learning are predicated upon the ubiquity of values in all educational undertakings and activities. That realisation has immediate implications for the work of policy-makers, educators and teachers in schools: values stand at the centre of everything they do in the name of education. Teachers' and learners' concern for such values as those instanced above focus the attention on some vital issues, not only with regard to valued principles for pedagogical procedures but also in the content and substance of what is taught and learnt.

Those concerns are clearly exhibited in the

questions, and the search for answers to those questions, that educators, teachers and learners are now increasingly called upon to face. All who have an interest in education and its outcomes are now asking with greater urgency, what knowledge is of most worth; what attainments of knowledge and competence are of abiding importance; which are the values, beliefs and attitudes that future citizens in the plural societies of today and tomorrow should work to acquire; and how desirable development in those values, beliefs and attitudes may be promoted and secured, in a society where values and attitudes are constantly changing, being questioned and revised.

If we are to have soundly based and tenable conceptions of value in modern plural societies, then educators need to be clear as to what kinds of education structures, curriculum content and teaching and learning programmes we should provide in those societies' educating institutions. Most importantly: what implications do new conceptions of value hold for the education and training of educators and educational leaders? These are all critical questions that those who seek to take up leadership positions or teaching responsibilities in such institutions must address.

Values then imbue everything done by schools and all other community agencies and institutions committed to the education of the coming generation. Parents, policy-makers, leaders and teachers in schools, and students as well are all now only too aware of the plethora of values issues with which they are continually surrounded: painful events in Africa, the Balkans and the Asia-Pacific region are daily on their television screens, along with the rise of movements of extreme right-wing nationalism or religious fundamentalism, with all their attendant dangers, as are also the questions arising from newly discovered possibilities of using advances in medical technology to prolong human life, bring it to an end, or use it for purposes for which even rudimentary definitions and classifications, much less moral positions, have still to be developed. In all such cases, teachers have not only to communicate information: they have also to observe and guide the tentative enquiries of younger minds preparing for adult life as they pose the vital questions: 'What ought we to do? By what principles shall we live? How should we determine to diminish human harm and increase human welfare?' (cf. Crisp (ed.) 1996).

Such questions are particularly pressing in a time when societies are increasingly 'plural'. As a result of such factors as immigration, increasing interstate and international mobility of labour, and the growing export and import of different ways of life, modes of community, forms of culture and practices of religion, modern societies, most of which used to be largely homogenous, are now more and more composed of a range of varied constituent groups, cultures and communities. The modern multicultural society will be characterised by a multiplicity of languages, a range of religious beliefs and a variety of cultural practices, that have moved it away for ever from whatever uniformity it was believed to have displayed (a belief more justified by rhetoric than the reality) and towards a new disposition in which a plurality of language patterns, cultural forms and products, and religious, moral and political beliefs obtains. The modern nation-state, perhaps especially in the developed world, is a maelstrom of many cultures, many languages, many forms of life. And such *milieux* embody a plurality of value beliefs, commitments and judgements as to what principles should govern relations between ourselves and others, what norms and standards are worthy of respect and emulation, what precepts should direct and shape our lives and all our main concerns. One of our most pressing educational and community concerns now is to be clear about the morality of pluralism (cf. Kekes 1993).

In this situation, there are some fundamental requirements if we are to help young people to tackle the questions 'What ought we to do? How shall we live?' We might perhaps try to enumerate some of these: the need for clarity, not only about which values are in operation, but what talking about values involves; the need for awareness and appreciation of the ways in which we are all unavoidably enmeshed in and governed by public norms and conventions of conduct in society generally and the communities that make up the social whole; the need for learning how to understand, accept and play according to the rules of the moral game and to come to conclusions that we can be happy to accept and to go along with – and that we are willing to advocate and applaud in the public forum generally. All these forms of awareness, knowledge and skill are called up and are vitally important when we consider some of today's value issues in modern plural societies.

Australia might stand as a powerful contemporary example of the plurality and force of such issues, with its present preoccupation with racial reconciliation, multiethnic tolerance and enabling minority access to the whole range of social and community rights and privileges, the rights and responsibilities of individuals in the case of such issues as euthanasia and abortion, and environmentally sustainable economic development and integration in the Asia-Pacific region. Among and between different groups and individuals considering, discussing and attempting to decide upon these matters, there have been tensions, disagreements and clashes of value, which have extended into the centre of the public realm – in the media, religious and community organisations and into state and commonwealth parliaments. Underlying the attempted resolution of such tensions and dissension lies the larger question: can people, can the state tolerate continuing plurality and difference over such large-scale matters of value, or can some sort of consensus be reached that might help to harmonise and unify the whole community? And – or – is such a consensus desirable? (cf. Stocker 1990 and Griffin 1996).

In attempting to discuss and settle such matters, perhaps we should recognise the indispensable precondition of ensuring that all parties to the issue are generally using the language of values, and the principal terms within it, in roughly the same way. Perhaps the first stage in the process of learning how to deal with and hope to resolve some of the disagreements in opinions (whatever the differences in culture and form of life (cf. Wittgenstein 1953, 1980)) might be to embark upon the search for clarity in our language and thinking about values issues. For we are unlikely to get very far if the language in which we address those differences is, at best, ambiguous, at worst, unknown or misunderstood. If we are to talk about diminishing human harm and promoting human welfare, about systems of ethics and norms of morality, about the difference or similarity between moral and legal questions, about the rules invoked when we use the language of 'ought', we need to be clear about what such terms might mean, about the contexts in which they can be employed, about the norms and conventions that are called into play and the considerations that make certain moves with them decisive. The first part of any process of values education, then, is to get those who are learning to introduce and employ terms, judgements and measures of value to be aware of what they are doing and by what criteria and standards their use

of such terms may be rendered intelligible, plausible and persuasive.

What follows here, therefore, is an attempt to provide some preliminary clarification and characterisation of terms generally found in value discourse. In making this attempt I hope at least to have given educators unfamiliar with philosophical terms and moral concepts in values discourse a possible starting point and some assistance in learning the typical 'rules and regulations' generally operating in value language, to have opened some questions for discussion and perhaps even to have provided one or two pointers on the way forward in such matters. The terms and ideas chosen for clarification have no particular relative order or importance: they are set out in alphabetical order simply for convenience of reference back and forward.

## Clarifying terms used in discussion of moral and values issues

### Attitude

When one speaks of someone's 'attitude' to a thing, one generally refers to strong feelings, deeply rooted feelings or convictions, and psycho-physical orientations towards or away from something they either like or dislike. Reference to an 'attitude' held or taken up by someone implies settled behaviour or a manner of acting on their part, indicative or representative of a particular feeling or opinion about or towards something. Reference to their attitude of mind connotes a settled mode of thinking on their part; a habitual mode of regarding something; a fixed disposition of feeling, liking, approving, desiring; or dislike, aversion, disapproval, revulsion away from something. In ethics some people speak of 'pro-' or 'con-attitudes'; this indicates clearly that attitudes are affective in character, that they are generally positive or negative. There is also often some associated notion that attitudes are to some extent irrational and that this makes them unamenable to rational argument or persuasion. Attitudes are notoriously difficult to change and the problem of attitude change is generally regarded as one of the most difficult in any undertaking of education in general and moral education in particular.

## Action

The carrying out of some process, function, movement or exertion, of which one is consciously aware and which is deliberately controlled and directed towards some end. Together with 'conduct', actions and activity are to be distinguished from mere behaviour, which can be unconscious and not goal-directed. Morality has to do with our actions and conduct towards, and with respect to the promotion of good and the avoidance of harm in the case of, other people: moral action and moral judgement are always 'other-regarding'.

## Axiom

A **maxim** is a proposition or judgement that commends itself to acceptance. In logic and mathematics an **axiom** is regarded as a self-evident proposition requiring no demonstration but assented to as soon as stated; this then functions as a rule or principle determining and guiding intelligible and allowable discourse and judgement in all discourse in the field. There is a sense in which this notion also obtains in ethical discourse. A moral maxim is what is thought fitting in matters of judgement or conduct – a self-evident principle, which all should follow: a well-established, generally/widely accepted or universally conceded first principle of conduct. Some people take or search for such maxims as rules or laws to help them decide and act in moral matters.

Perhaps the best known moral axiom is the famous 'categorical imperative' of Immanuel Kant: he made his test for assessing whether something could be determined to be one's moral duty the application of the principle 'Act only on that maxim that you would be willing to become a universal moral law'; or 'So act as if you were by your maxims a law-making member of the Kingdom of Ends'. This is a formulation of the principle 'Do unto others as you would that they should do unto you' into what Kant called 'the moral law'. Such an axiom leads on to a number of the prime presuppositions of moral discourse and conduct: the principles of liberty, equality, tolerance, respect for other persons, consideration of other people's interests, and so on. These principles are *procedural* not *substantive*.

## Belief

A belief is both a proposition or a statement of an idea or contention as true or existing, and our psychological assent to it and holding of it as true. The important point here is two-fold: one is the *content* of the proposition, the other is the *emotional commitment* we have to that proposition. We make a commitment to a proposition or statement *as true* on various grounds – of some external authority, of evidence, of the force of our own perceptions, memories, intuitions, and so on. But there is always an affective element involved in our assenting to or holding a belief: some proposition, statement or idea is put forward to us (often with some persuasive force) or something occurs to us (often with considerable resonance) and we see it as a notion or claim that can be entertained, assented to, accepted and espoused. Sometimes we espouse such claims or notions with a very firm opinion; this can extend to a state of intense psychological conviction (often someone accepts that something is true almost in spite of the evidence, and this comes close to prejudice). Or it can go the other way and involve the stance of doubt, in which one is extremely hesitant about the strength that one can give to one's claims that something is to be taken as true; in such a case one may be prepared to do no more than merely suspend disbelief.

Beliefs relate to the psychological and subjective elements in our grasp of reality and the ways in which we interpret what we take to be our world. We can share them with other people but not in such a way that we thereby give people our warrant for acting as though what we claim is actually true (that condition is typical of our claims to 'know' something to be the case).

Often reference to our 'beliefs' implies our acceptance, tenure and emotional commitment to some particular set of beliefs. These may be political, social or theological. In this case what is referred to is a set of strongly held commitments that are functions of our most profound and fundamental preconceptions about the nature of human beings, or society, or the divine, and/or the relationships subsisting between them, and the ways in which these commitments define and structure our thoughts, arguments, decisions and actions as a consequence. It is here where we begin to speak of 'faith', 'creed', 'credo' and 'ideology'. All these relate to people's most deeply held convictions about the nature of human beings and the best form of society.

## Conscience

'Conscience' is sometimes taken to be the name of some inner disposition, sense or organ in human beings; it is often associated with the idea of the 'moral faculty', which some people believe all humans have. We do not know whether there is any such thing, however: it is more likely that when we speak of 'conscience', all that is implied is a strong internal awareness of thoughts or actions that we ought, or ought not, to be having or doing. Reference to conscience is a 'façon de parler': phrases involving the word can be interpreted along such lines as the following: 'to have a conscience' is to be sensitive to moral considerations, 'to have no conscience' is not to be sensitive to them; 'to consult one's conscience' is to exercise one's moral judgement, and so on.

## Disagreements in attitudes and beliefs

People disagree in belief when one of them utters a statement or proposition and the other denies it. If what one of them asserts is true, what the other of them asserts to the contrary of that must be false. There can be disagreement in attitude between people who are not asserting any statements or beliefs at all, as when one approves of something the other disapproves of. It is a further question whether moral disagreement (e.g. about abortion or euthanasia) is more a matter of disagreement in attitude or in belief.

## Duty

'Duty' is one of the main concepts in ethics: it refers to acts or activity held to be morally binding on or obligatory to an individual, enjoining upon people that which they ought or are bound to do, carry out, perform. Duty implies clear moral obligation, equally binding on all people and being transformed into one's own personal task and formulated with reference to one's own situation at a specific moment. Acts done out of a sense of duty are typically held to be opposed to acts done out of inclination or beneficence or solely with regard to their consequences and not to their intrinsic moral worth. The concept of duty is closely linked with

other moral concepts characterising the moral activity of the individual, such as *responsibility*, *accountability*, *autonomy*, *self-consciousness*, *conscience* and *motive*.

The interpretation of the origin and nature of duty has been one of the most difficult problems in the history of ethics: the foundations and sources of duty have been sought and found in divine commandments, in the *a priori* moral Law (Kant's 'categorical imperative'), and human beings' natural pursuit of pleasure and happiness (hedonism, utilitarianism).

Critics of these positions argue that, if we derive our duty from divine authority, we are not then being truly moral, personal 'autonomy' being one of the key features of moral conduct; others aver that a position in which 'intentions' are over-riding determinants of the value of a moral act opens the door to a situation in which 'the end justifies the means'. Kant's position rejects both these and elevates 'duty' as the only sure basis of moral action. His ethics are known as 'deontological' in consequence.

## Ethic, ethics, ethical

'Ethics' and 'morals' are often used by people as though they were synonymous or as though the one in some way added to the other. In much lay language there tends to be the notion that 'ethics' equals 'higher-order moral principles', while 'morals' refers to actual patterns of behaviour (often sexual). The point to remember is that 'ethics' is Greek ('*ethos*' '*ethe*') and means the same as 'morals' in Latin ('mos, mores') and for this reason the two can be used more or less interchangeably in ordinary language.

However, there are special uses: in one of them 'ethics' connotes the rules of conduct recognised in certain fields of human activity, professions, vocations and the like, meaning a normative set of principles or morals determining and guiding appropriate behaviour in that field (the 'Hippocratic oath' is a good example of this). In this sense it can often refer to the set of substantive moral principles by which people choose or undertake to live: the Japanese code of ethics that we know as 'bushido', or the 'honour code' at West Point Military Academy, might be good examples here.

In philosophy 'ethics' can also refer to substantive rules of conduct set out and elaborated in the moral system of a particular school or writer, relating to their account of the nature of morals and of the ways in which moral questions should be treated, such as the principles of Epicurean ethics.

Sometimes 'ethics' can mean the same as 'moral philosophy'; at other times it can refer to particular parts of the subject matter of moral philosophy, as when, for example, people distinguish between 'metaethics' (the logical analysis of moral discourse, judgement or action, from a particular philosophical perspective) and 'normative ethics' (particular sets or systems of substantive principles enjoining people how to think, judge or behave when moral questions arise. The Christian ethic would be an example here).

## Moral

The word 'moral' comes from the Latin ('mos, moris', plural 'mores') and meant initially simply the ways in which people behaved. From that developed very rapidly an emphasis upon the ways in which it was felt desirable, right or proper that people *should* behave and this gave the normative dimension to the word that was once merely descriptive (this was also true of 'ethos' in Greek). Thus from this developed an emphasis upon moral guidelines that rapidly acquired the status and force of prescriptions or rules in relation to people's actions, volitions, intentions or character.

Moral maxims or principles are concerned with matters of people's ability to discern and act upon the distinction between right and wrong, good and evil, and with goodness or badness of character, disposition or behaviour traits. They imply a concern for the development of a settled disposition in people to make distinctions between right and wrong in matters of interpersonal conduct and relations and the ways in which such conduct and relationships are and should be regulated.

Moral discourse is now largely concerned with rules of morality and conduct generally, as giving people guidance along the path towards 'virtue': exhibiting a regard for impersonal and universally acceptable standards of perfection (behaviour that admits no criticism or incurs no censure or blame in matters of general conduct).

Moral knowledge and moral understanding (though some people would doubt whether there can be knowledge in matters of morality, since the criteria for what counts as 'truth' are very unclear)

is concerned with our perceptions, judgements, opinions, relating to our ability to discern and make distinctions between right and wrong. Moral education is the attempt to help us develop the power of apprehending the difference between right and wrong and the ability to understand, see the relevance of and apply concepts and terms involving the articulation and bestowal of praise or blame, approval or censure, commendation or condemnation in moral matters. The 'moral law' of which some people speak is simply a connotative term for that body of requirements, obligations and rights, in conformity to which virtuous action consists. People's actions subject to the moral law are those acts having the property of being right or wrong in accordance with the principles enunciated or dictated by that particular principle or set of principles.

Moral philosophy (also called 'ethics') is that part of philosophy generally which treats of the virtues and vices in human conduct, and of the criteria by which we recognise and discriminate between right and wrong; it also treats of the formation of virtuous character, and the ways in which human beings decide how they ought to act, and in accordance with what standards, as well as the springs and origin of such actions. Moral philosophy is concerned with virtue and vice, the rules of right conduct, the excellence of character or disposition as subjects of a study that is analytical and critical, showing by what concepts, criteria and principles people deliberate in moral matters and arrive at their moral judgements and decisions. This is therefore the philosophical study of morals and morality, to be distinguished from scientific or factual studies of moral conduct (e.g. moral psychology or sociology) *and* from the expression of first-order normative moral views.

## Morality and values education

Moral questions are about behaviour, but not simply about behaviour as such, for the question of morality does not arise except in a social and institutional setting. Morality is not concerned with the description or analysis of the way in which people in social and interpersonal settings, relationships and transactions do in fact behave. Morality concerns the conduct of ourselves in relation to other people, and theirs in regard to us, and the way in which we agree between us to regulate ourselves in our interpersonal transactions by adherence to a set of principles. Our agreement to do so rests on our recognition that our interests are preserved and promoted within the nexus of relations and obligations that constitute our lives as human beings.

The commitment of human beings to such obligations is exemplified in our use of language and our development of individual and community relations in the institutional forms of various kinds in which our values and systems of value are embodied. This commitment starts with our birth and increases as we come to maturity. Being the creatures we are, and living as we have to under the constraints of the natural and social conditions surrounding us, we could not possibly survive, much less flourish, without being enmeshed in and having to conform to the customs, conventions and norms of all the various institutions that human beings have established and developed in order to stabilise their identity, understand and control their environment, and endeavour to give some point and purpose to their lives.

The chief of these institutions is language and interpersonal communication. It is in and through these that human beings have found it possible to form and give expression to our sophisticated conceptions of the world and all our main concerns in it, in which the various elements of meaning, truth and value are enmeshed. Our judgements on matters of significance and value are negotiated and settled at the level of the community and in the various forms of relationship, institutions and agencies in and by means of which the life of each community is carried on.

It is not the case that we can simply choose (or not) to 'accept' or to 'play the game' of morality and that this 'choosing' depends in turn upon our 'acceptance' of the institutions in which morality is characteristically exercised. In virtue of the kind of creatures we are and the characteristic form of life we share, and given the ways in which, as fellow constituents in it, we articulate it and elaborate upon it between ourselves, the presence, function and direction of values and regulative principles lie at the heart of the norms and conventions of the various institutions into which human beings, in all our various communities and cultures, are progressively initiated and of which we become bearers and beneficiaries.

That initiation into values and morality, therefore, is concerned with helping us to understand that human life is beset with obligations. One of the aims of this form of life, and of the values education

that gives young people an initiation into it, will be to give us a knowledge of the rules which function in this mode of relating to other people and to seek to develop in us a grasp of its underlying principles, together with the ability to apply these rules intelligently, and to have the settled disposition to do so. For without such an education in values and morality we should be significantly impoverished in our attempt to come to terms with the demands we face in our lives and to exercise our informed choice in order to make that process manageable, tolerable and possibly even enjoyable. In a plural society, where the range of choices is increasingly wide, such an education in the values and morality of pluralism and choice becomes even more important.

Such an education will help to make us see that our life in the different cultures and communities in which we have our being, gain our identity and begin to exercise our choice, is capable of being improved upon, and that just possibly the exercise of our intellectual resources, imagination and creativity can help to add quality to it and make it excellent. An education in values will help us to develop and articulate the reasons which both satisfy us and are open to public evaluation for any particular value judgement or moral decision or for any general moral code that we may make for ourselves or come to adopt, within the institutional framework of our human personhood.

Thus human conduct and action is moral, when it is engaged in consciously and intentionally as part of a whole pattern of behaviour towards other people, in accordance with principles. As such it will be based upon certain beliefs about the rights and duties people have, to do, in some way, with the furtherance of the interests of people in general, the promotion of their welfare and the inhibition or prevention of harm to them. These beliefs will rest upon certain core notions about what constitutes right and wrong – our most basic beliefs concerning the meaning and value of human life and the importance of social and community cultures in sustaining and enriching it – and what one ought to do, as well as an awareness of what 'ought' language, in the realm of interpersonal conduct and social relations, commits one to.

Our judgements and actions in moral matters will spring from a free choice on our part, as mature moral agents, and will be based upon our ability to give reasons for those choices that are relevant and appropriate, capable (in principle, at least) of being judged such by people generally. This means that the moral actions we undertake will be such as can be judged to be *generalisable*: impartial and equally binding on all those who regard such an act as intending to promote human welfare. The latter consideration will mean that the grounds for the action will not be trivial but will really count for something – will have 'a certain magnitude'. They will be held sincerely and applied and exercised with consistency.

Morality is about adopting, justifying, analysing, or applying principles in interpersonal affairs in the world, that are *universalisable, over-riding, other-regarding, action-guiding or prescribing, and significantly related to the promotion of human welfare and the avoidance or inhibition of harm to human beings*. Our attending to these requirements in moral matters is nowhere more called for than in our observance of the various rules and conventions governing all the occasions of interpersonal communication and relations in which we are called upon, as *actors*, to participate.

The point of this argument is that individuals can develop as morally mature and autonomous agents capable of fully participating in society only if they are sufficiently informed, prepared and predisposed. This means that they have some kind of minimum right to health and sustenance; that they have the minimal domestic conditions for perpetuating existence; and that they can engage in communication with others they recognise as equals in having the same rights to autonomy and individual choice as they are aware of developing in themselves, and with whom they can join in discussion, consideration and planning of mutually beneficial modes of action.

On this account, the whole of society and all its constituent groups and communities have a direct interest in securing, providing and safeguarding those conditions and services presupposed by and required for our participation in community life and a society opening up one's freedom to choose and one's equal right to access the goods it offers. This in turn entails the establishment, provision and work of educating institutions, in which people growing towards maturity and autonomy will be helped to acquire knowledge of such goods and services as are offered in and by society, and the ability to make informed choices to avail oneself of them, in ways that will confirm and enhance one's own quality of life and not threaten that of others. These moral values seem to point to one particular

form of social and political arrangement in which such a range of choices and options can be realised and made available to all: that most preferred form of government – the modern plural democracy.

Those who conceive of values education in connection with the maintenance of the rights of all individuals, groups and cultures to a socially inclusive and democratic society are making a point about the nature of the world as they perceive it – as a complex conjunction of aggregations of individual human beings. As Aristotle maintained, 'Man is by nature an animal that lives in groups'; we do not live, indeed we could not start our existence or survive, if we lived alone on desert islands. Personal freedom and individual choice is only possible as an outgrowth of the knowledge and values that other members and groups in society have opened up to us, in all the many and varied modes, styles and settings of culture and value. In this way we can be given some intimation of what choices are available to us in modern plural societies, and we can begin to understand what making choices and calculating the consequences of our choices and actions might mean. For most of us this intimation is first made through our educational experiences, both formal and informal, compulsorily prescribed by others or voluntarily chosen by us, as being in our own interests and those of our community.

Ratz (1986) emphasises the importance of offering such educational experiences to others in a discussion of what he calls the duties of autonomy (Ratz, cited in Bailey 1988: 124):

> There is more one can do to help another person have an autonomous life than to stand off and refrain from coercing and manipulating him. There are two further categories of autonomy-based duties towards another person. One is to help in creating the inner capacities required for the conduct of an autonomous life. Some of these concern cognitive capacities, such as the power to absorb, remember and use information, reasoning abilities, and the like. Others concern one's emotional and imaginative make-up. Still others concern health and physical abilities and skills . . . The third type of autonomy-based duty towards another concerns the creation of an adequate range of options for him to choose from.

It is a paradox of our existence that our autonomy requires the work of other persons. It is given to us and increased by our education; and that requires the learning of language and the transmission of knowledge. Both of these are ongoing social activities and public enterprises in which at least two people must engage in an interaction predicated upon the assumption of the mutual tolerance and regard that is only embodied in the institutions of society. Without the one, there cannot be the other; and without that key institution called education, there can be neither. For autonomy is the flower that grows out of seeds planted and tended by heteronomous hands. For Ratz this point carries a correlative moral implication: on this argument we have a moral obligation, as Bailey puts it, 'to develop and maintain our own autonomy and the autonomy of others' (Bailey 1988: 124). And, as is clear from the argument, this obligation is one that we bear throughout the whole of our lives.

## Ought

'Ought' is a general verb expressing duty or obligation of any kind, strictly used of moral obligation, relating to what is right, good, just, fair, equitable, beneficial to people generally. 'Ought' in this sense should be distinguished from the hypothetical 'ought' of instrumentality or expediency, found in such uses as 'If you want to stay healthy, you ought to watch your diet and take exercise regularly'. 'Ought' used in moral discourse is *categorical* and is used with two implicit features: that the obligation being expressed or undertaken is (1) *prescriptive* – that is, action-guiding – and (2) *universalisable* (or 'generalisable') – that is, relating to everyone in a relevantly similar situation. This verb is found in conjunction with first-order (or 'normative') substantive moral principles such as 'we ought always to tell the truth', 'people ought to keep their promises', 'we ought not to inflict pain unnecessarily', 'we ought to give to charity when we can', and so on.

## Principle

'Principle' comes originally from the idea of 'beginning', 'origin' or 'head of' something; 'principle' serves as the fountain-head and source of fundamental truth and functions as the basis of reasoning and operation in a particular domain (very much like the Greek 'arche' as in 'arche-type'). From this develops the idea of a ruling principle or standard, functioning as an ordinance governing behaviour in a particular realm, and so eventually connoting the rule or code of right conduct to be

followed by an individual or people generally operating in that realm. So in moral matters a principle functions as a general law or rule as a guide to action, or a standard against which particular actions can be assessed. It gives an individual a motive or a reason at the most profound level of moral commitment to guide or lead them to action. When people act 'on principle' they do so out of adherence and commitment to a particular moral axiom or conviction that they hold firmly and will not easily, readily or quickly give up.

## Right and wrong

'Right' actions are those done in accordance or conformity with some standard, rule or principle laying down what is good, just, equitable or morally praiseworthy and worthy of emulation. Such actions are recognised as 'right' by the application of that standard or principle and held up as examples of moral or legal 'rectitude' – what may be seen as correct, proper, fitting or appropriate, as answering to the demands or norms of that which is suitable or required in the particular case or moral situation in question.

'Wrong' or 'bad' actions are those which are morally unjust, unfair, improper, inappropriate, amiss, worthy of censure, blame or condemnation and to be seen as something not to be emulated. 'Evil' acts are those worthy of even stronger condemnation as defining an action or conduct that is vicious, pernicious or in some other way morally odious, insofar as it inflicts damage, injustice or iniquity on people who suffer at the hands of those perpetrating the malevolence involved. In a legal sense 'wrong' connotes violations, transgressions or infringements of the law. Sometimes this involves the invasion of people's rights, to their damage, prejudice or harm; sometimes the claiming, seizure or possession of something, which is unjustified or unwarrantable on legal or moral grounds.

## Rule

The idea of 'rule' is strongly linked with the idea of standard, principle, regulation or maxim, governing individual conduct; it connotes the idea of a standard of discrimination, estimation, judgement or direction. A rule sets up a criterion, test, canon, standard or benchmark by which all actions or products in the domain in which it is regulative are to be measured or judged. In moral matters a rule is regarded as a principle regulating activity, practice or procedure. Here the notion of rule often connotes good order and discipline, conduct, behaviour, manner of acting. The ideas of 'rule', 'standard', 'principle' belong generally to the same cluster of ideas: they function as regulative criteria, benchmarks or ordinances setting up norms and exemplars in the area in which they are established, referred to and applied.

## Standard

A standard is set up in order to present people with an authoritative or recognised exemplar of correctness or perfection that will then serve as a point of reference in matters in which particular qualities, functions or requirements come into play. It provides people with a demonstration of excellence, a criterion, a benchmark, against which they can then measure their own achievements, attainments, performances, activities or efforts to attain to a similar degree of excellence in the class of endeavour in which that standard sets the rules. Generally a standard is viewed as a prescribed object of endeavour, or as the measure of what is correct, appropriate or adequate for some purpose. The standard 'metre' rule set in a wall in Paris may serve as an example here.

## Value

We speak here of 'values' in ethics, as opposed to monetary value or the values of efficiency and effectiveness in delivering a particular product or reaching a particular desired end. In ethics a value can be seen as something which is worthy of esteem for its own sake, which has intrinsic worth. It signifies the 'excellent' status of a thing, object, situation, person, performance, achievement, etc., or the estimate in which it is held, according to its real or supposed worth, usefulness or importance, as 'ex-celling' (standing out from, being above, other things) *in a particular class of comparison with other objects of a similar kind*. Thus to assess the value of something is to consider a thing as being of some worth, importance or usefulness, in a class of comparison in which, by the application of criteria, we rate it highly, esteem it or set store by it. It also relates to the particular principles or standards of conduct by which a person seeks or chooses to live.

Values are to do with matters that take place in the public realm and that we perceive and judge to be matters of importance. We make judgements, which commend or condemn, on matters of importance that take place in the world: values relate to our praise or blame of styles of behaviour, the productions and performances of artists, verdicts of judges, the conduct of politicians, the activities of schools, the policies of economists, interpersonal relationships, occurrences that we experience as a result of the forces of nature, states of affairs in the community, decisions of churches, questions as to people's culture. Such things are part of our thinking and talking on matters of value, our value judgements, and our decisions and actions as to our own and other people's 'good'.

Thus conduct, performances, situations, occurrences, states of affairs, productions, all these are associated with the ways in which we perceive, appraise and are inclined towards or away from such objects, productions, states of affairs, performances, manifestations of conduct. We desire them, we wish to be like them or to possess them, to replicate or emulate them. And we are willing to approve, praise and commend those objects and performances to other people.

We propose to other people that such objects or states of affairs, styles of behaviour, are targets that provide us with standards of excellence that all should aim at, that they are models that can function as guides for our conduct or for our judgement, in ways that all of us could make our own, and commend to other people. Such states of affairs, objects, performances, that we are inclined towards and commend to other people as worthy of emulation, function as norms and criteria of excellence that are interpersonal; they are prescriptive for the generality of the population who we hold can and should experience similar regard for, give similar approval and commendation to the objects, conduct, performances, etc. to which they are applied. These things give us principles to guide our conduct and regulate our lives, and which we can strongly commend to other people to follow.

Values are neither private nor subjective. Values are public: they are such as we can all discuss, decide upon, reject or approve. Value judgements constitute bridges between us as to the ways in which we ought to act, or the things that we ought to admire. Also, values are objective. They are in quite a decided sense 'hard' . They are arrived at and get their life from their status as intersubjective agreements in our community as to what things shall *count as important*. Such agreements are constituted in the institutions that make up our social and communal life. For example: without the institution of banking, monetary exchange and fiduciary trust, a dollar coin is just a brute piece of metal. It is such institutions that give our values their intelligibility and their objectivity. The act of writing a cheque is quite as objective as the action of looking down an electron microscope, because it has meaning, intelligibility that we value, but not only value: it is something upon which we base our subsequent actions. Values are 'hard' in that they are fundamental parts of the fabric of our social relationships. It is in the warp and weft of those social relationships that our judgements of value are articulated, developed, agreed, settled and acted upon. And these objectivities of value are the result of discussion, negotiation and agreement, and are settled at the level of the culture of a community.

## Virtue

'Virtue' was systematically explored by Aristotle, who saw in it the particular 'excellence' of any activity or pursuit. This enabled him to distinguish between 'intellectual excellence' (exhibited in people's intelligence, knowledge and understanding, the chief virtue of which was 'wisdom') and 'moral excellence' (exhibited in the uprightness, goodness, probity and rectitude of people's characters, the virtue of which is seen in the 'practical wisdom' with which they conduct their affairs and relate to other people). The intellectual side of Aristotle's distinction has now more or less disappeared; 'virtue' now relates largely to moral excellence, worth or value in matters of interpersonal conduct; it often also connotes qualities of mind or character held to be admirable from the moral point of view. Sometimes the term is used with respect to a particular domain of human behaviour, connoting chastity, purity or innocence, for example in sexual matters.

## Some practical implications

As I see it, some clear implications follow from the above discussion of moral concepts and terms as to the policies and pedagogical practices embraced and employed by teachers and educators working in our community schools. And these implications flow on from such institutions to the wider social contexts for which their students are preparing.

To begin with, in schools and elsewhere, we need to be clear about the values terms and standards that people so frequently and so widely employ in discussion and decision-making upon matters that have the potential to affect so many members of the community for good or ill. When we talk, for example, about the need for the tolerance of plural sets and systems of value, about the principles underlying race reconciliation, about the moral imperatives enshrined in policies for the treatment of minority ethnic groups, it will be important for us to have some awareness of rights and wrongs, and the principles of procedure to which the use of the language of 'ought' commits us. We need to have some notion of the generalisability and action-guiding character of subscription to such democratic principles as liberty, equality and justice, or the need for human concern and sensitivity underlying such moral principles as regarding other persons as ends in themselves and the application of the 'golden rule'. The foregoing material may be of some use in helping us to get clear about such things and thus avoid ambiguity, misunderstanding or confusion.

Secondly, we need to tackle head on the notion held by some people – perhaps still too many people in education and public life generally – that values are matters of completely subjective preference and individual taste: that a person's values are idiosyncratic. The whole of Wittgenstein's 'public language' argument goes against that notion of subjectivity: we acquire the values of a form of life at the same time as we learn to speak it and learn to play by the rules of the language games that constitute it (Wittgenstein 1953). Now one of the languages that seems to feature in all forms of life is that of obligation and enmeshment in a whole nexus of human relations, social norms and cultural conventions, to which subscription and acceptance is a *sine qua non* of admissibility and progress.

This is to advance the generalist thesis that, by virtue of being born into the human race, people develop conceptions of good, wrong and ought. To be sure, the content of particular injunctions and prohibitions may differ: 'theft' is only a meaningful concept when a major social institution is that of private property; 'murder' is only intelligible when there can be 'lawful' killing; and 'rape' presupposes that other acts of intercourse are 'lawful' . But it is difficult to imagine that such norms as telling the truth, keeping promises and refraining from the infliction of needless pain do not hold for all people, or that such injunctions could possibly be regarded as matters of personal taste and purely private preference. Our values education could spend a deal of useful time on examining whether there is any value content that could be said to be held in common or even shared by the plurality of culture and value systems, and if so what it might be. Other curriculum time could be usefully spent on delineating the value differences and distinctiveness that characterise the various cultural communities constituting that plurality.

Given the centrality of values in all forms of endeavour and activity, we need to underline the important point that education is one of a number of undertakings (law and order, health and welfare, social security and employment services are others) which are shot through with values, which concern a community's aspirations for their young to enter into a future that is better than the one we hand on to them (Warnock 1979). For this reason all stakeholders in education need to be clear that a community's educating institutions and agents are inextricably involved in and irrevocably committed to values education. We therefore need to recognise, support and celebrate the work of teachers in educating institutions: teachers, educators, auxiliaries and all other agents of education are bearers and custodians of a community's culture, traditions and values.

All such people working in education are initiators of young people, not only into the norms and standards defining what is intelligible and permissible in their own cognitive domains, but also into the values and principles that underpin and define what is acceptable conduct in every aspect of the dealings and relations between ourselves and others in that domain and all other domains of human life. This is because education is, as Daveney noted (Daveney 1973), a profoundly moral concept. Engagement in that enterprise therefore calls teachers and all those working in schools to be clear not only about their epistemological commitments as teachers of their subjects but also about their moral responsibilities as educators (cf. Chapman and Aspin 1997).

Given the plurality of values and commitments in modern multicultural societies, we might ask whether it is not reasonable that, as teachers and educators, we should feel any apprehensions about

the notion of imposition in values education in a plural society. Many people, indeed not a few teachers and educators, are anxious lest they be seen to be imposing their own values on others. For my part, however, I believe we should feel less reticent about articulating, expressing and holding to our own values than many people might suppose we should be. There is a sense, in discussion, decision and action with respect to matters of value, in which we cannot do other than follow Martin Luther's example and say 'Here I stand: I can do no other'.

We do not live on desert islands and we do not come neutral to the human encounter, so to speak. When we come to matters of such cardinal importance as multiethnic awareness, racial reconciliation and promoting intercultural understanding, we are not on our own, acting idiosyncratically. As I have said elsewhere in this volume, such matters and values are worked out and determined at the level of the culture of a community. The first part of that community is our own family: we are born into a group which immediately starts talking to us, and behaving towards us, and helping to guide and direct and shape our behaviour, including speaking, feeling, acting and reacting, to certain kinds of stimuli in certain kinds of cases, which more and more resolve themselves into open-ended social situations, calling for flexible but informed, intelligent and sensitive responses on our part. And the family becomes the extended family, the peer group, the school, our particular cultural group, our community, our society. The life of all is permeated by and grounded in values and the value commitments that characterise and define them.

That is life. That is how human beings develop and learn how to interrelate. And sometimes those values, norms and conventions towards which we bring our children up, do not quite look like those in and towards which other people bring up their children. When children become teenagers or adults, some of those different values, different norms and conventions of behaviour, different guides for conduct begin to be questioned and become differentiated and possibly even abrasive – particularly as and when they encounter the plurality of cultures, values and substantive concerns that typify modern communities. It will be part of the growing pains of young people to realise that, on matters they judge to be of cardinal importance, many other people do not only disagree with them but actively oppose their point of view. It is part of their development towards moral maturity to accept that, on such matters, major tensions and disagreements are conceivable and possible.

This is part of the warp and weft of human life. Our growth in awareness of the ways in which we behave in the interpersonal realm could not be other than it is – starting from the communities of whose values, beliefs and attitudes we are repositories and beneficiaries, and then growing onward and outwards from those points that fix us to our cultural and moral identity. In the plurality of cultures we inhabit we have a right to be pleased that this is so, because the children we engender are in a sense bearers of our hopes and values for the better life at some time in the future. We invest our culture and values, which we took over from our parents, into our aspirations for the development in the schools for tomorrow of citizens of the future.

Nevertheless, although we start from such foundations, we do not stay with them all our lives. The values into which we are born and which we embody and express come gradually to rub up against those of other people. At some stage somebody is going to indicate to us that they regard something we have said or done as disgraceful, harmful or demeaning; or they may perhaps evince a milder reaction, still giving the reproof but doing so more mildly. At that point an opportunity of further learning occurs for young people; the growing adolescent might begin to reflect: 'Maybe my parents weren't so right on this as they thought they were. Maybe I should reconsider the ways in which I start to react towards some people'.

These are the realities with which children and young people, parents and educators have to struggle. Differences in values between them can be addressed and may be settled at that point. But the important thing that parents and teachers need to realise about this is that they are not the only educators of the children in their care: they may be the first, but their charges will encounter so many variant, criss-crossing and alternative views of what is important, and a wider range of influences and interactivities later on, that they will be enabled and perhaps encouraged to start taking other considerations into account and making value decisions for themselves, off their own bats, so to speak. When that happens, the process of values education is coming to full flower.

Plato put this well in *The Laws*: he not only made the minister of education the prime minister of the country but he also had the baby's being and exist-ence surrounded by educators from the beginning. This provides a sound basis for the contention that education in values lasts across the lifespan: though teachers in schools during the period of compulsory attendance can help enormously in giving young people the 'right start' (cf. Ball 1993), a continuing commitment to the opportunities for further growth and development offered by lifelong learning will provide the support and guidance that make the development of the individual much less monistic and very much more plural in matters of value, in making value judgements, and in deciding on courses of action or (even if tacitly) formulating principles of conduct, as a consequence.

This plurality of values, value stances, and value conduct I regard as a social and community good, for it provides the context in which all people can develop the virtues of tolerance, respect for other people, and consideration for their needs and interests as if they were our own. Such virtues, or so it seems to me, are presupposed in all further attempts to work out a system of values and principles by which we can regulate our lives and social relations with all our fellow citizens in the global community. I take education as such a moral and community good, since, whatever form it takes, it provides young people with the necessary conditions and information to assist them to take the first steps on the road to moral maturity (cf. Grace 1994 and McLaughlin 1994). And in taking this view, as against those who are inclined to argue for seeing education as merely a commodity which can be bought or exchanged, I am committing myself to the notion of education as one of those public goods that constitute the mortar that binds the bricks of plural communities together.

This is not to say, of course, that these particular public goods must always remain the same. Just because I commit myself to the idea of a particular standard or criterion of value (such as promoting human welfare and diminishing human harm, for example) as constituting a community good does not entail that the content with which I fill out that criterion must always stay the same for me, or for all people. The ways in which different cultures address matters of major moral concern will vary according to their most profound moral presumptions and commitments (cf. Beardsmore 1969; Phillips and Mounce 1970). And, in respect of particular cases and very often over time, these change.

I would think, for instance, that there has been a certain amount of change in the conceptions that people hold of the public goods of health and welfare. There are now considerable differences of view in the beliefs people hold about the quality of life, about being born and suffered to die, about what counts as a dangerous disease, and so on, which acquire especial relevance when one is considering the treatment of people who are, for instance, physically, intellectually, emotionally or psychologically challenged in some way. There is a current dynamism in the debate about such issues, which is moving towards the suggestion that care-givers should give up a major reliance on institutional treatment in such cases and consider other kinds of treatment out in the community or in the home. Such forms of treatment are not only at a different kind of cost to the community, but also require different sorts of values and attitudes in the members of the community that has to integrate such people.

I do not want therefore to imply that the notion of the culture of any community provides an absolute fixed point for all time, in the form of the content that we put into it. When I say that I regard agreements and disagreements about the values we embrace as being determined, set and played out at the level of the culture of a community, I attach to it the assumption that there will be a *dynamism* in that community. Where this is not the case, of course, then the values game changes: at that point values education and its questions becomes, as they say in some places, a whole new ball game. It certainly does not follow from the pluralism for which I am arguing that values, cultures and community will necessarily modify or transmute – though it seems to me highly likely that, in the nature of things, they may well do so.

The version of values education for which I argue, however, presumes a particular view of the dynamism of human cultures and their institutions, which is for me best embodied in the notion of a plural democracy. It is, I believe, such a democracy that guarantees a civil society. If this is not the case, if we are suddenly to imagine or accept that we are operating in an autocracy or a totalitarian state of some kind, then we have to reconsider the standing and value of plurality and the dynamism of a variegated and heterogenous society as marks and features of a civil society. Clearly the views I espouse and propose in the foregoing material are all functions of a particular set of axiological, moral and democratic preconceptions and I make no apology for that. For I believe that in such preconceptions

we see the virtues of pluralism in moral matters exhibited and exemplified.

There are many practical ways and forums in which such preconceptions can be expressed and opportunities for that expression occur throughout the curriculum and in all learning activities. Even a simple lesson in language and vocabulary can play a part in giving life and adding momentum to our growing moral awareness. For example, I once had the good fortune to observe a teacher of English doing an analysis of tabloid newspapers and the way in which their sub-editors composed headlines. She argued that the need to have words of only four letters in headlines had reduced people's capacity to communicate with each other. One always read only of 'Maggie's fury', for example, rather than that 'she was mildly annoyed', 'somewhat disaffected', or even 'a little irritated'. In much media communication, the teacher commented, everything is reduced to that kind of short, compressed, quick print bite. She then invited the class to join with her in an exploration of the economy of the emotion of anger and see how many sophisticated gradations we could produce in our talk about it.

This activity, and the discussion that ensued, served as a lesson in the development of the sophistication of values in communication by which we can make our own talk more articulate and sophisticated, and with which we can more thoroughly make judgements on some of the media reports to which we are constantly exposed and which, without some education in the meanings of and values embodied and conveyed in language, might tend to diminish or even deaden our moral sensibilities. All that particular teacher appeared to be doing was giving an exercise in the extension of vocabulary – but what she was also providing was of course a profound lesson in the ways in which people behave when it comes to things that disturb them and the ways in which they do (and should) handle that disturbance.

Here, then, is an illustration of the ways in which we can put publications in the media to good educational use. All this requires is the imaginative teacher who can propose, for example, that her class should follow her suggestions for engaging in evaluative discussions of all kinds: she might say, for instance, 'Let's all watch an episode of *Neighbours* and then an episode of *Pride and Prejudice* and see what kind of distinctions we can make between them'. Such an exercise would not only enable students to develop some aesthetic awareness but could also encourage them to employ their awareness of whatever differences of style, presentation, character and use of language they found, in attempting to develop and articulate their own value point of view.

Similar examples can be found in other subjects widely across the curriculum – even in such curriculum areas as those of mathematics and the sciences. I still recall one young woman student teaching biology in a girls' school in Malaysia. Her subject that day was gene replication and transmission, as part of a course unit on the development of Mendelian theory. Her case examples were two faulty genes – one that leads to the birth of children with Down's Syndrome and the other that leads to haemophilia. She illustrated these with photographs of afflicted children, in the one case, and with the family tree of Queen Victoria in the other. She pointed out how much difficulty, distress and damage had been caused to individuals and possibly even to nations by the effects of the transmission of such genes. She noted that, nowadays, it was biomedically possible to take measures against further replication. She almost incidentally asked whether taking such action was something that doctors ought to do automatically and what part parents could or should play in making such decisions. This led rapidly to a discussion on major moral and mortal questions of such rigour, seriousness and intensity as I have only rarely been privileged to hear. The teacher had used a curriculum opportunity to broach a matter of value on which a range of opinions was forming – and one in which her students were clearly growing in confidence to express themselves and to endeavour to work out moral principles and the consequences of actions for themselves.

It is part of the work of the good teacher to be doing that kind of thing, adopting that sort of approach, creating and then taking advantage of such opportunities in the classroom and the curriculum all the time (cf. Tomlinson and Quinton (eds) 1990). I rejoice to report on the large number of teachers I have had the professional good fortune to observe espousing this kind of strategy in their lessons. For what they are doing is illustrating their awareness that values and the importance of values education in a plural society occur everywhere in educating institutions and that everything a teacher does in such an institution is nothing less than values education writ large.

## References

Bailey, C. (1988) 'Lifelong Education and Liberal Education', *Journal of Philosophy of Education*, 22. 1: 121–6.

Ball, C. (1993) *Lifelong Learning and the School Curriculum*, Paris: OECD/CERI Publications.

Beardsmore, R. W. (1969) *Moral Reasoning*, London: Routledge & Kegan Paul.

Bridges, D. and McLaughlin, T. H. (eds) (1994) *Education and the Market Place*, London: Falmer Press.

Chapman, J. D. and Aspin, D. N. (1997) *The School, the Community and Lifelong Learning*, London: Cassell.

Crisp, R. (ed.) (1996) *How Should One Live?*, Oxford: Oxford University Press.

Daveney, T. F. (1973) 'Education – A Moral Concept' in D. J. O'Connor and G. Langford (eds) *New Essays in Philosophy of Education*, London: Routledge & Kegan Paul.

Giddens, A. (1995) *Affluence, Poverty and the Idea of a Post-Scarcity Society*, Geneva: United Nations Research Institute for Social Development.

Grace, G. R. (1994) 'Education is a Public Good: On the Need to Resist the Domination of Economic Science' in Bridges and McLaughlin *op. cit.*

Griffin, J. (1996) *Value Judgment*, Oxford: Oxford University Press.

Kekes, J. (1993) *The Morality of Pluralism*, Princeton, NJ: Princeton University Press.

Kuhn, T. S. (1972) *The Structure of Scientific Revolutions*, 2nd enlarged edn, Chicago: University of Chicago Press.

McLaughlin, T. H. (1994) 'Politics, Markets and Schools: The Central Issues' in Bridges and McLaughlin *op. cit.*

Phillips, D. Z. and Mounce H. O. (1970) *Moral Practices*, London: Routledge & Kegan Paul.

Ratz, J. (1986) *The Morality of Freedom*, Oxford: Clarendon Press.

Stocker, M. (1990) *Plural and Conflicting Values*, Oxford: Oxford University Press.

Tomlinson, P. and Quinton, M. (eds) (1990) *Values Across the Curriculum*, London: Falmer Press.

Warnock, M. (1979) *Schools of Thought*, London: Faber & Faber.

Wittgenstein, L. (1953) *Philosophical Investigations*, trans. G. E. M. Anscombe, Oxford: Basil Blackwell.

Wittgenstein, L. (1980) *Culture and Value*, trans. P. G. Winch, Oxford: Basil Blackwell.

## Acknowledgements

I should like to acknowledge the support of the National Professional Development Project 'Values Review Project', based in the Association of Independent Schools of Western Australia, and particularly their Executive Officer, Ms Karen Caple, for my essay on terms used in values discourse and published by that project in October 1996 as *Clarification of Terms Used in Values Discussions*.

# 4 The Meaning of Dominance, the Dominance of Meaning, and the Morality of the Matter

BARBARA APPLEBAUM AND DWIGHT BOYD

A growing body of scholarship has recently focused on revealing the ways in which some groups of people oppress other groups of people in contemporary Western society (Wellman 1977, Katz 1978, Delpit 1988, Young 1990, Essed 1990, 1991, Frankenberg 1993, Goldberg 1993). This focus in recent scholarship can be found in diverse fields of study, but is most evident in discussions of issues involving gender, racial or ethnic membership, and sexual orientation. The resulting literature substantiates the extent to which "pervasive intimations of inferiority" (Bartky 1990: 7) are commonplace. Although rarely defined, often presumed to be understood and, even worse, often employed to refer to different phenomena, the term "dominance" has become a frequent and recurrent theme in this literature. Our primary aim in this chapter is to clarify the meaning of a particular understanding of this notion of dominance as it is found in this critical literature.

Reference to "oppressive" relations among groups often, and appropriately, connotes forms of the use of brute force, shackles of raw power, severe constraints on freedom, conditions of abject poverty and squalor for some, for the benefit of others. These are what we will refer to as "material conditions" of dominance. Whether they are noted in the form of statistics on the frequency of rape or wife battering, reports of police harassment and unjustifiable rough treatment of black youth, "queer bashing" in our public parks, or other similar markers of overt oppression, these material conditions are real and cry out for our moral condemnation. Indeed, they constitute the background against which any other forms of dominance must be seen. Our focus in this chapter, however, is on forms of dominance that are less blatant, harder to see, easier to fall into complicity with, and thus overshadowed by the moral enormity of the more material manifestations. We certainly do not intend, by this restriction of focus, to lessen the moral critique of those material manifestations. Rather, we want to illuminate some more elusive phenomena for the purpose of *extending* that critique in directions that we think warrant equally serious attention. In particular, we want to do this in such a way as to facilitate more attention to this type of concern within the field of moral education, so that discourse within this field will come closer to exhibiting genuine respect for diversity.

These efforts at clarification and critique are aimed, first and foremost, at *ourselves*, because we see the need for them in our own lives, both academic and otherwise. There will be nothing really new or original in our analysis. The conceptual overhead has already been designed and used repeatedly in a wide range of literature. What we are trying to do here is to project a little more light through it and to bring it into focus a little better, so that we – and other members of the moral education community – can see and work with the image more effectively. Our intended audience is, then, primarily those who perceive themselves to be like us in relevant ways and to a degree sufficient to join us in these efforts.

Of course, the two authors of this chapter are certainly different from each other in some ways, some of those being both obvious and potentially significant in the context of our central concern. At the same time, we are also similar in some other ways. Neither these differences nor the commonalities are written in stone. They are not static. Markers of both identity and relative social location are remarkably complex, fluid, and interlocking. However, so that you will have a heuristic starting point both for understanding points of difference between the two of us which will be subsequently used in our analysis and for judging points of possible connection to yourselves and your own location, we offer, in turn, the following rough markers of the positions from which we speak.

First, with regard to Boyd:

- He's white, from a mid-western United States working farm community, one made up almost entirely of people who look like him and his family.
- He was raised by decent, hard-working parents who took their parental responsibilities seriously and lovingly, though seldom demonstrably. They had, relatively speaking, rather conservative political stances and similarly conservative protestant religious beliefs, both of which he has subsequently repented, supposedly.
- He is, although greying at an exponential rate, still relatively able-bodied. But that body is clearly not that of Atlas, or Rambo. It's short, vertically challenged. If he were ever interested in a pro-football career, it would probably have to be *as the football*.
- He's soft-spoken, mild-mannered, reflective, and rarely loses his temper, even at the old, cranky cat. (Well, he does yell at it, knowing that it is in fact completely deaf.)
- As a candidate for surreptitious wife- or child-abuser, he seems to be a non-starter, having never hit another person in anger in his life, even as a child (oh, maybe a tap or two on the older brother's shoulder).
- He's reasonably well-paid, and seldom worries seriously about money. And he would accept *higher* taxes if that would stop the egregious erosion of the social safety net in Ontario being promoted by the current Conservative government.
- He appears not to have blatantly sexist or racist beliefs or attitudes; indeed, he regularly teaches courses on issues directly related to these areas of moral/political concern.
- He is said, and is generally believed, to like women. And some, at least, seem to like him back.
- He's a Harvard-educated, mid-career academic, self-identified with the field of moral education for over 20 years, ex-student of, and strongly influenced by, Lawrence Kohlberg and John Rawls.

- He likes to think of himself as attentive to issues of fairness, justice, and equality, often talking in "dirty Habermasian" language about discourse ethics, the performative attitude, and the like.

With regard to Applebaum:

- She's Jewish (Orthodox to boot), married mother of four, and striving to be recognized as a philosopher of education in the academic world. She has only recently begun describing herself as white and heterosexual in any meaningful sense of the terms – for most of her life, she never perceived these as markers of her identity.
- As an only child whose father was a Holocaust survivor and who was disappointed that she was not a male, she grew up in New York City and was often warned of rampant anti-semitism although she cannot recall ever experiencing it.
- Her gentle, very giving and peace-loving mother has been an underlying influence in her life (although she didn't come to this realization until her mother's death). Caring relationships and the bonds created between people are what she finds of paramount significance and are what contribute to making her life meaningful. She can often feel the pain and joy of her family or friends – sometimes even when they are not outwardly expressing it. Her children tease her when she watches a movie, "Get out the box of kleenex." She smiles in agreement when she hears the 1960's rock group, Jethro Tull, sing "And its only the giving that makes you what you are."
- She is known to take a long time to anger or to take offense. Sometimes, however, she thinks she both forgives and forgets too easily.
- Although she went through a period of rejecting her religious upbringing, in the last number of years she has begun to appreciate and enjoy its value and meaning. Except for the scarf she always wears to cover her hair, she almost looks Christian, or of no religious affiliation – unless, of course, you were to take her out to eat, when you would promptly discover that she adheres to strict Jewish dietary laws. Beer, you quickly learn, is kosher.
- Although she is hopelessly and naturally a romantic, she gets mad as hell when a man treats her as a sexual object only. In such situations, she feels like kicking him where it really hurts. But she is sufficiently gendered and

heterosexually socialized to know that she won't and that she is in some sort of contradictory sense complimented by it.

- As a child she saw her own mother abused and as an adult she cannot bear the degradation and suffering caused to anyone. She morally condemns the horrible "material conditions" of dominance described above. In fact, it was her profound interest in and commitments to morality that have compelled her to return to university to study ethics and moral education after her children became of school age.

So, how is it, we ask ourselves, that this "domination discourse" literature to which we have referred can/does get a grip on us? Is it really directed at *us*? Are we part of what is being criticized? If so, how? And is the charge legitimate? Compared to some, perhaps many, we don't seem to ourselves to be in the nasty camp, actively engaged in supporting the material conditions of oppression noted earlier. We're *bona fide* card-carrying (paperwriting, talk-giving, course-teaching . . . ) *moral educators*, a field that, if anything, can surely be understood as negatively defined *vis-à-vis* those nasties. We *do* both understand that, given the systemic nature of those material conditions, no one, including us, can ever be free of implication or avoid being complicit in ways that permeate the very structure of our lives. And we understand the need to be continuously self-critical about this systemic embeddedness in the material conditions of oppression. On the other hand, we don't see ourselves as out there on the front lines actively promoting, and willingly benefiting from, those conditions. So what, if anything, might we be doing that *could*, on a broader understanding, be seen as a form of domination? And if we can get a clearer picture of what this might be, how are we to understand a moral critique of what we are doing, since it does not seem visibly on a par with the nasties to which we have already pointed? In what kinds of moral harm(s) might we be further implicated?

Two intellectual tasks regarding the ordinary language use of the term "dominance," we argue, facilitate our answering these questions. The first task concentrates on loosening the tight connection between "dominance" and issues of control, ruling, and governing. Successful completion of this task requires a moving away from the focus on tangible and observable behaviors, from the limiting pre-

occupation with individual dyadic relations, and from the exclusive engrossment with "power over." The second task entails shifting our concentration to another, albeit not as prominent, understanding of "dominance," i.e., what is prevailing and most influential. With this understanding in mind and by directing our attention more to social groups rather than individuals, to categories of meaning rather than tangible behaviors, and to a notion of "power to" rather than "power over," we are in a better position to explicate how the more subtle form of dominance works. Moreover, the resulting analysis not only highlights the ensuing harms caused to subordinate group members but also accentuates how dominant group members are implicated in the "taken for granted" benefits and privileges that they enjoy.

## Clarification of focus

Attention to ordinary language, even to dictionary pronouncements about ordinary language use, may be misleading for the sort of clarification task that we have set for ourselves in this chapter. The reason is that the critical literature employing what we are referring to as "dominance discourse" is in fact stretching our ordinary language, asking it to do new work as well as old. This stretching depends on the successful completion of two interrelated intellectual tasks of understanding.

### Task one

The first of these tasks requires a loosening of the tight connection between an ordinary-language grounding of "dominance" in certain forms of interpersonal, relational behavior. We probably all have had more or less direct experience of this basic, ordinary-language connotation. These experiences might vary in intensity and duration, and would include being on both the giving and receiving ends of the behavior, but it is not hard to identify a range of instances within which most people could locate some part of their personal history. They would include, for example, bullying in the school yard, parental constraints on children's freedom of movement and association, school rules on everything from talking in the hallway to dress codes, the courts' dim view of inhaling certain weedy substances, military chains of command, bosses' insistence that certain work be done in certain ways and "on time," etc. This ordinary-language connotation also grounds the more severe material conditions of dominance identified earlier. In all such cases dominance involves, at least, some constraints on the freedom of somebody. However, with regard to the more ordinary forms, the question of whether or not the constraints are justified remains open. In contrast, in cases of what we are calling the material conditions of dominance the constraints are always morally wrong. In both instances, who is "dominant" and whom is being "dominated" are hardly matters of mystery, requiring elevated political consciousness and sophisticated powers of critical analysis. On the contrary, "dominance" here connotes something that can literally be pointed to, seen, felt, easily named, and more or less open to conscious consideration as something that might warrant resistance, if such resistance is deemed prudential.

It is in reference to this connotation that dictionaries synthesize common understandings of dominance in terms of notions of "ruling," "governing," and "control." Indeed, etymologically, this understanding has a firm foundation, with "dominant" stemming from the Latin word *dominari*, which means to rule or govern. There are three interrelated points that we want to highlight in this direction of analysis, anticipating our eventual argument that each of them needs to be modified in order to accommodate the broader meaning of "dominance" that we are primarily interested in illuminating.

The first of these points has already been alluded to in our suggestion that what is being referred to in this common understanding is relatively clear, namely, instances of interpersonal behaviour that are perceived by the parties involved as somehow constraining freedom of action on the part of someone. Sometimes this behaviour is quite direct and immediately experienced, as in bullying in the school yard. Other times it is more indirect, held back as a threat of punitory action *if* other behaviour on the part of someone is not forthcoming, as in an adolescent's risk of being grounded for breaking the rule of getting in before 1:00 a.m., or a corporal's risk of time in the brig for failing to salute a senior officer. Nevertheless, the one "dominating," on this view, does so through some form of tangible and relatively obvious behavior.

The second point of this common understanding that we want to highlight pertains to the social structure in terms of which the identified behavior is being perceived. As suggested by our reference to being on either the "giving or receiving ends," this line of analysis assumes that there are always two relevant parties: *somebody* is doing something (or threatening to do it) to *somebody else*. The "somebody" here must be interpreted loosely: it can refer to particular individuals, as in the bully vs. the "bullee" rolling around in the gravel, or it can refer to collectives of individuals similarly situated in terms of hierarchical relationships, such as privates and generals passing in the street. But the point is that this understanding perceives the structure of the relationship as dyadic: there is always a clearly identifiable doer and done-by, and it is ultimately *individuals* that effect the relationship that is referred to as one of dominance.

Finally, a third and closely connected point concerning the common understanding that needs some more illumination is that there is a certain kind of power that is being appealed to in picking out these kinds of relationships to be predicated by the term "dominance." What is being acknowledged here is the kind of power that can be "possessed" and possessed asymmetrically. It is the type of power that one side of the dyad *has* more of than the other (though the latter is seldom entirely powerless in this sense). It is also the kind of power in which the first side of the dyad can choose the conditions under which it can be *used* in order to effect the desired ends of that first side (especially when those ends are not perceived by the second side to be desirable). Whether through stick or carrot, criticism or cajoling, raw force or just the threat of it, it is something that someone can be said to "wield," and the wielding is done for the purpose of control. In common parlance, it is "power over" (Kreisberg 1992) and it often gives the dyadic relationship a negative connotation to anyone steeped in political discourses featuring putative commitments to individual liberty, autonomy, and equality. Thus, for example, it is in this sense that many poorly paid, overworked, idea-oriented, mild-mannered, ivory-tower-living academics might, with reference to many others in the "real world," legitimately scoff at the idea that they have much power (though we hasten to add that even when such descriptions are accurate, for at least some, e.g., their secretaries, this claim about a lack of power is false).

*Task two*

If we have been successful in loosening the tight connection between an ordinary-language grounding of "dominance" in forms of interpersonal, relational behaviour, we now have room to engage the second task of understanding. What we now need to explicate is another aspect of an ordinary-language understanding that can now be seen more clearly and that suggests a broader understanding of the sort we want to illuminate. Another line of interpretation that dictionaries conflate with the "ruling/governing/control" sense is that of "prevailing and most influential." By looking at alternatives to each of the points of interpretation explored above and examining their difference we can see more clearly another sense of dominance that tends to be overshadowed but is suggested by the phrase "prevailing and most influential."

From our point of view, the most heuristically useful entry point is to examine an alternative to the *exclusive* focus on individuals in the first line of interpretation. One of the strengths of the (individual) dyadic understanding of dominance/power is that it is inherently relational. However, individuals are by no means the only unit of social structure that can be understood in relational terms. The notion of a social group offers, at least on one understanding, a competing perspective to the individual dyadic understanding of dominance/power, one that figures prominently, if implicitly, within the critical literature to which we have been referring in this chapter so far (Razack 1993, Dei 1996). Our understanding of that notion is facilitated by Iris Young's (1990) treatment in *Justice and the Politics of Difference*. For our purposes, we highlight two essential aspects of this treatment which are crucial for any understanding of the type of dominance we are trying to get at in this chapter. These two aspects of Young's treatment of the notion of "social group" concern the connection between social groups and individuals, and the relationship of social groups amongst themselves.

Young introduces the notion of "social group" in order to support her argument that the individual is not prior to the collective but, rather, is constituted by the social group(s) s/he has affinities with. Social groups, she explains,

> are not simply collections of people, for they are more fundamentally intertwined with the identities of the people described as belonging to them. . . . A social group is a collective of persons differenti-

ated from at least one other group by cultural forms, practices, or way of life. Members of a group have a specific affinity with one another because of their similar experience or way of life, which prompts them to associate with one another more than with those not identified with the group, or in a different way.   (Young 1990: 43)

As a unit of social structure, "groups," Young argues, should be understood in contrast to "aggregates" and "associations." In the messy context of ordinary language, each of these is a "group," in the loose sense of a collection of individuals, but the differences among them are socially and politically significant. (And in what follows, we will mark this difference by use of the phrase "social group.")

Aggregates are relatively arbitrary groupings, collections of individuals who are put together into one category for episodic, instrumental reasons, reasons that can change infinitely. Thus we can, if we desire, lump together blue-eyed people, short people, academic people, Kansan people, people who put their left socks on first, and people who happen to be reading this chapter. Beyond our act of lumping, they are likely not even to know that they constitute a collective entity. In contrast, individuals in an "association" *do* know that they can be considered collectively because that is exactly their intention. That is, members of an "association," in Young's sense, are such because they identify with some purpose or aim which they collectively share, as found, for example, in the mission statements of organizations such as the Association for Moral Education or the Philosophy of Education Society. Moreover, because their membership is engaged for their own reasons, members of associations can choose to belong, or not, and even change their minds quite easily.

In contrast to either an aggregate or an association, Young's notion of a "social group" does not start from the assumption that the individual is the appropriate unit of focus, as somehow prior to the collective, and in terms of which the collective must be understood. Unlike aggregates, social groups are not "merely arbitrary classifications of individuals according to attributes which are external to or accidental to their identities" (ibid.: 44). Unlike associations, "Groups . . . *constitute* individuals. A person's particular sense of history, affinity, and separateness, even the person's mode of reasoning, evaluating, and expressing feeling, are constituted partly by his or her group affinities" (ibid.: 45, our emphasis). Although Young's notion of associations acknowledges that groups are defined by specific practices and forms of alliance, the fact that individuals enter into such associations, voluntarily at least in most instances, indicates that the person's identity is considered as prior to and independent of such group membership.

Thus, for Young, social group affinity is characterized by a "thrownness," experienced *as a given*, since "one finds oneself as a member of a group, which one experiences as always already having been" (ibid.: 46). Young emphasizes that her notion of "social group" does not preclude a person having an individual style. Nor does her notion of "social group" negate the possibility that a particular group affinity can be rejected or transcended. She emphasizes, however, that such changes are experienced as fundamental *transformations in one's identity*. Furthermore, this notion of social group as a given does not imply that social groups cannot be redefined but rather that groups are always initially there and only then can they be redefined. As Young notes, "While groups may come into being, they are never founded" (ibid.) for the self is "a product of social processes, not their origin" (ibid.: 41).

In addition, and this point will figure prominently in our subsequent discussion of dominance, a social group cannot be understood as standing independently of other social groups. Groups, according to Young, "are not real as substances, but as *forms of social relations*" (ibid.: 44, our emphasis). A social group "exists only in relation to at least one other group" (ibid.: 43). Clearly explicating what this means is important. Since a collection of people do not see themselves as a "group" (and are not seen by others as a "group") unless they encounter and interact with another group whose way of life is different from their own, one way of understanding that social groups are not independent is to recognize that the notion of "group" becomes coherent only as based upon a notion of contrasting difference. While such a notion of "groups" highlights the need to focus on intergroup relationships, it still allows groups to be viewed as independent entities because the notion of difference it assumes is considered descriptive, empirical and normatively neutral (see Minnow 1990). This is often the notion of groups presumed by advocates of cultural pluralism who deal with race as "simply one more difference on the all American continuum of ethnic diversity" (Rothenberg 1990: 46) and who continue to view groups without any real reference to the nature of their relationships to each other.

Young, however, while alerting us to the need to focus on the relationship between groups, also underscores the nature of the relevant difference upon which such a relationship depends. The independence of groups which Young rejects, we believe, is not merely an acknowledgment of empirical difference, but rather, is based upon the realization that difference is normative and connotes hierarchy. As Paula Rothenberg, in her analysis of difference, explains, "Claims about difference are often difficult to deal with precisely because they are offered under the guise of value-free descriptions yet smuggle in normative considerations that carry with them the stigma of inferiority" (ibid.: 43). Because the concept of difference regarding social groups will always "perform the dual function of implicitly evaluating as 'inferior' what they purport to be describing as 'different'" (ibid.: 47), one social group cannot be understood without understanding another (the norm against which it is evaluated). Thus, "to be a woman" cannot be understood without considering what it means "to be a man." Similarly, understanding what it means "to be a person of colour" or "to be homosexual" cannot be understood without reference to what it means "to be white" or "to be heterosexual," respectively. Young succinctly expresses this relationship between social groups when she claims that for every oppressed group there is a correlate group that is privileged (ibid.: 42).

Moreover, our resulting identities are in this sense multiple (and not even necessarily coherent or internally consistent) and fluid in that, even for the same person, they can entail being both privileged and subordinated in different respects. Although there is a wide spectrum of such groups, always somewhat in flux for any individual, *some* are both relatively stable and constitute more significant markers of personal identity, and are thus of more central concern in the context of understanding claims of dominance. To make this more concrete, the best examples in the case of the authors of this chapter would be the similarity between us in terms of our both being white and heterosexual, and the difference between us in terms of Applebaum's being feminine and Jewish, and Boyd, masculine and "ex"-protestant. The essential point to keep in mind for our concern for unpacking how dominance in the expanded sense operates is that the appropriate unit of focus is not the socially abstracted individual of possible dyadic relation, nor is it the isolated and independent group, but the social group which is differentiated in relation to other social groups and within which individuals are defined.

We want to stress that with this focus on social groups we do not mean to lose sight of the role of the individual, especially regarding issues of human agency and moral responsibility. Rather, our point is to emphasize that without the move to the social-group perspective, the harms and benefits of the critical notion of dominance can be occluded. With this particular notion of "social groups" in mind, with its emphasis on constituting the identity of the individual and on the relational aspects of groups, we can now see how there is an application of "prevailing and most influential" that does not refer directly to things tangible and obvious as suggested by the first interpretation of "dominant." Rather, it refers more to categories of *meaning*, to the various ways that humans have for naming, interpreting, evaluating, and communicating about their lived experience and how these categories of meaning play a role in the differentiation of social groups within a society.

In the quotations that we utilized above to outline her notion of a social group, Young refers quite broadly to "cultural forms, practices, or way of life" as that which serves to differentiate groups, and more specifically, to how an individual's affinity with a particular group shapes "even the person's mode of reasoning, evaluating, and expressing feeling" (Young 1990: 43). The fact that the latter are quite specific, and the former, quite general, suggests that there are probably several different levels at which one could explore social-group differentiation in terms of the notion of categories of meaning. In addition to this problem of relative generality, the vagueness of some of these categories identified by Young, and often referred to in other vague ways throughout the literature, also suggests that a complete specification of the categories themselves and any analysis of their inter-relationships is beyond the scope of what we can accomplish here. We will have to be satisfied with a simple listing of some of the kinds of things that we have in mind when we start to think about how "categories of meaning" are both points of social-group differentiation and potential tools of dominance. Thus, we have in mind:

values
ideals
standards of behaviour
experiential commonalities
modes of discourse
emotional saliencies
structures of social interaction
metaphysical beliefs
narratives of connection
etc.

That these categories may, in some interpretations and/or contexts, overlap each other and become more or less important relative to each other does not concern us as much as simply noting how central they are to human life. Moreover, we are also not so much concerned with the fact that individuals do indeed both express and stretch (or even resist) the content of these categories within which they find themselves embedded (and, partly, constituted), as with the fact that social groups are defined relationally *to each other* in terms of how they give substantive content to these formal categories.

Finally, we need to return, very briefly, to the last remaining of the three points of analysis of the first line of interpretation of "dominance," to the kind of "power" that is picked out. Here we need to see that there are forms of power that cannot be reduced to "power over," to something that someone wields coercively to control another. There is, in addition, another understanding of power which is closer to the etymological source of the Latin word, *posse*, which means "to be able." This stem focuses less on control in the negative sense of constraint effected by someone on someone else, and more on the positive ability to do something, on agency, as in having "power to." Indeed, such a notion of power is explicitly referred to in Thompson and Gitlin's (1995) defense of a feminist pedagogy which creates a space for reconstructed knowledge. Power, for Thompson and Gitlin, is an issue of privilege and entitlements which give certain groups legitimate claims to goods, rights, and services which are denied to other groups. Power, they maintain, "is an entitlement conferred by one's placement within a *system* of hierarchically ordered relationships" (Thompson and Gitlin 1995: 136, emphasis in original). Moreover, as Thompson and Gitlin indicate, power/privilege, although executed through the individual, must be understood as the result of hierarchical group relations. The critical significance of this notion of "power to" for our immediate interests is that it constitutes something which our previously wimpishly described academics do indeed exercise *as a result of* their ivory-tower protection.

## Dominance through meaning

What we have been trying to do so far is to reorient and clarify our focus when we start thinking about how to understand dominance and, in particular, how we ourselves are potentially implicated. What we are now able to see better is that we need to think less in terms of individuals and more in terms of social groups, less in terms of tangible behaviour and more in terms of categories of meaning, less in terms of power as controlling/constraining and more in terms of power as enabling/constraining. We must emphasize again, however, that this is all expressed in relative terms, and for a particular purpose: bringing into better focus something *else* not seen as well as the first side of each of these, but *not* relinquishing the need to utilize the latter where appropriate. If we *do* look in the direction framed by these moves, what emerges is a different picture of dominance and how it works.

Before we articulate our understanding of how it works, as a way of grounding the more abstract discussion we want to mention a few examples of the sort of thing we are pointing to, although we will not attempt either to fully elaborate or to analyze these examples. (Consider them reference points for what follows.)

1 A first example, one quite familiar to most of us actively involved in moral education theory, is the tendency within psychology to construct theories of "normal" development based on the experiences of boys and men (Gilligan 1982).
2 An analogous second example would be the tendency within moral/political philosophy to interpret social interaction in terms of a "public/private" differentiation and to emphasize the public sphere as where the "real, serious" moral activity occurs.
3 A third example, related to both of the first two, is the "double bind" that Jane Roland Martin (1982) so eloquently exposes when women are considered subjects of a traditional liberal education. The educated person as understood in contemporary educational theory, Martin argues, is not gender neutral. In order to be educated a woman must relinquish her own way of experiencing and perceiving the world around her and thus alienate herself from her self. In order to remain unalienated, however, she must remain uneducated. Moreover, it is not that women cannot acquire the characteristics of an educated person but, rather, that when they do, society evaluates them negatively. The traits for which society evaluates women positively, however, are not included in the educational ideal.

4 A fourth, somewhat different, example can be found in Lisa Delpit's (1988) discussion of the ineffectiveness and artificiality of "liberal" white elementary teachers' attempts to facilitate (some) black children's sense of responsibility and autonomy by giving directives disguised as questions (such as "Now, children, don't we all want to wash our hands?"). Delpit maintains that this is a blatant assumption of one culture's experiences as if they were also the experiences of all others. As Delpit relates, the raising of black children can be very different. She recalls the black mother who told her son, "Boy, get your rusty behind in that bathtub," and notes,

> Now I happen to know that this women loves her son as much as any mother, but she would never have posed the directive to her son to take a bath in the form of a question. Were she to ask "Would you like to take your bath now?" she would not have been issuing a directive but offering a true alternative.   (Delpit 1988: 289)

5 Finally, yet a different kind of example can be found in the film *The Crying Game*. If you haven't seen this film, it may not be possible for us to convey this example through words. But if you *have* seen the film, we have *no doubt* that you will remember the scene where, through judicious use of a timely, close-up, anatomically focused camera shot, the beautiful young woman, undressing slowly in front of her male partner with sex clearly on her mind, turns out to be, to the surprise of the partner, a man, and rather unmistakably so. The partner is quite shocked, even revolted. Many, perhaps most, heterosexual members of the theatre audience are also shocked, almost viscerally, by this scene. (Interestingly, though, apparently very few, if any, gay or lesbian members of the audience are surprised at all, because they see the character as a man from the beginning and they anticipate what's coming.)

We will return to some more thoroughly developed examples, ones in which we ourselves feature as main actors, at the end of this chapter. This list, we hope, should however provide enough of a variety of instances that some reference point or points will be established for most people. The general question to which we now turn is "What is happening in situations such as these?" In short, if these are seen as instances of dominance, using the broader notion that we have focused on, how does it actually *work*? And what actually *results* that merits the moral critique to which we have referred? In addressing these questions, it is important to acknowledge that they can never be answered entirely in the abstract, under the assumption that one pattern will fit all. On the contrary, to be appreciated, any instance must be examined in the richness (and messiness) of full contextual detail and historical antecedents. However, we do believe that we can point to the kinds of phenomena to which we need to be attending.

The central idea here is to look for instances of social interaction in which the meaning categories (of the sort listed above) of one social group get normalized or naturalized as an assumed common reference point within a society and those of other groups get marginalized and "othered." These two processes work hand-in-hand; they should be understood as two sides of the coin of the same process.

On one side of this coin what happens might be referred to as a kind of *projection* which utilizes, at a social level, not so much a manifest "power over" as a covert "power to." The particular content of the categories of meaning is projected away from its inherent connection with some social group onto the generalized canvas of "all humanity." Young explicates this process in her discussion of cultural imperialism.

> Cultural imperialism involves the universalization of a dominant group's experience and culture, and its establishment as the norm. Some groups have exclusive or primary access to ... the means of interpretation and communication in a society. As a consequence, the dominant cultural products of the society, that is, those most widely disseminated, express the experiences, values, goals, and achievements of these groups. Often without noticing they do so, the dominant groups project their own experience as representative of humanity as such. Cultural products also express the dominant group's perspective on and interpretation of

events and elements in the society, including other groups in the society, insofar as they attain cultural status at all.   (Young 1990: 59)

Similarly, Bachrach and Baratz (1970) in their discussion of social power refer to E. E. Schattschneider's (1960) notion of a "mobilization of bias."

> Political systems and sub-systems develop a "mobilization of bias," a set of predominant values, beliefs, rituals, and institutional procedures ("rules of the game") that operate systemically and consistently to the benefit of certain groups and persons at the expense of others. Those who benefit are placed in a preferred position to defend and promote their vested interests.   (Schattschneider 1960: 71)

*How* a particular group gets into a position to accomplish such a projection, how it is that they can exercise such "power to," is a question that we will simply set aside here, as we are more interested in accounting for the conditions that come about as a result of their success.

At least two aspects of what we are calling a "projection" are important to recognize. The first aspect is the cloaking of some particular group's preferred content in one or more categories in the mantle of what is said to be "normal" or "natural." It gets portrayed, and largely accepted, as built into reality, not built for and by humans in order to *interpret* reality. It is assumed to be not remarkable, ordinary, available to everyone wherever they are located if they just choose to see reality correctly. The second aspect is that the social group that, in relation to another group or groups, accomplishes this cloaking, *itself* ceases to be seen *as a group*. While the boundaries of other groups, because they are different from the normal, the natural, are thereby highlighted, those of the cloaking group are camouflaged.

Because social groups are defined *in relation to each other*, on the other side of the coin, this projection constructs the content of other groups' categories of meaning not just as different, but as "deviant" – abnormal, unnatural, inferior. The reference point for questions of difference has already been established by the projection and other groups are marked by how close they come to this reference point. But, of course, they necessarily fail. Thus, as Young (1990: 59) says, "given the normality of its own cultural expressions and identity, the dominant group constructs the differences which some groups exhibit as lack and negation." This construction permeates the society and affects all members within it in myriad ways, for example, from images in literature, advertising, and entertainment media, to linguistic metaphors and patterns of language use, to school curricula – including theories and practices of moral education. Moreover, this construction produces a paradoxical reality within which other groups must maintain themselves. On the one hand, their perspective is rendered largely invisible on the major stages of society's reproduction, their patterns of meaning pushed so far to the background that they are seen as undifferentiated, a chorus providing, at best, superfluous background noise. On the other hand, because they can be seen only as lack and negation, they are stamped by this relational identification through a highlighting and stereotyping of this very difference: when noticed, they become marked and named as "Other" (Weis 1995).

## Effects on individuals as members of social groups

If this provides at least an outline of how dominance, in the sense we mean it, "works," what can we see as its results, not only at the level of groups as just noted, but also at the level of what this means for members of different groups, dominant and subordinate? There are a number of consequences both of a psychological and material nature to which we could point, each calling for more elaboration and for more attention as points of moral concern and moral education than can be possibly given here. Yet to give you some idea of the types of harms and injustices dominance generates and how dominant group members are implicated in this injustice, the following consequences will be briefly noted.

There are definite psychological benefits that accrue to members of social groups insofar as their identification is with the relatively dominant. They have immediate access to modes of making sense of their lives that feel comfortable, natural, ordinary because the categories of meaning which they identify with are considered "normal" and the social group with which they have affinity is reflected in a positive manner in society's means of communication. If there is struggle regarding these categories of meaning, it is one of learning how to utilize them effectively, not to comprehend them or to locate

oneself despite them. Moreover, there is a sense in which dominant group members are defined "from within" since there is a felt match between one's self-perceived identity and how others perceive one, and thus little need to engage in what Taylor (1992) has so eloquently captured in the phrase, the "politics of recognition." Furthermore, one is "privileged," in the sense that both this access and match can be taken for granted. One is not forced to see them and how they work to enable, to empower, rather than to frustrate, nor does one perceive the need to critically examine how this might be working differentially for oneself, but *not* for others. And one certainly does not have to place oneself in a position of naming the connection between one's empowerment and others' disempowerment. Insofar as dominant group members see themselves as the norm and what is unremarkable, their dominant group affiliations become invisible and make it difficult to see how they can be implicated in the perpetuation of social harms and injustice.

But insofar as members of some groups gain certain "taken for granted" psychological benefits through dominance, members of subordinate groups suffer certain definite psychological harms. In their case, not only is there no comfortable match between one's social-group identity and the prevailing and most influential patterns of meaning, there is a continual struggle to make room for self-definition that is not alienating. Subordinate group members find themselves defined "from the outside." As Young notes, members of subordinate groups "find themselves defined from the outside, positioned, placed, by a network of dominant meanings they experience as arising from elsewhere, from those with whom they do not identify and who do not identify with them" (Young 1990: 60). The form of the struggle which results from being defined "from the outside" is eloquently captured by DuBois' (1989 [1903]) description of the African-American predicament, but is readily applicable to other social groups as well. Afro-Americans, DuBois argues, develop a "double consciousness" in order to deal with dominance. This double consciousness arises when black people realize that they have learned to see themselves not through their own eyes, but through the perspective of white civilization.

> It is a peculiar sensation, this double-consciousness, this sense of always looking at one's self through the eyes of others, of measuring one's soul by the

tape of a world that looks on in amused contempt and pity. One ever feels his twoness, – an American, a Negro; two souls, two thoughts, two un-reconciled strivings; two warring ideals in one dark body, whose dogged strength alone keeps it from being torn asunder.   (DuBois 1989 [1903]: 3)

Moreover, as Young further explicates, not only do members of subordinate groups struggle with double consciousness, this process of being defined from the outside, but also the image mirrored back to them in society is one of lack and negation. "While the subject desires recognition as human, capable of activity, full of hope and possibility, she receives from the dominant culture only the judgement that she is different, marked or inferior" (Young 1990: 60).

If, as Charles Taylor argues, "our identity is partly shaped by recognition or its absence, often by the *mis*recognition of others," then

> a person or group of people can suffer real damage, real distortion, if the people or society around them mirror back to them a confining or demeaning or contemptible picture of themselves. Nonrecognition or misrecognition can inflict harm, can be a form of oppression, imprisoning someone in a false, distorted, and reduced mode of being. (Taylor 1992: 25)

Moreover, misrecognition *by* others is not the only psychological harm that follows from dominance – *self*-misrecognition is another. Subordinate group members are put in the position where they must internalize the dominant culture's inferiorized images of themselves or, at least, struggle to resist them. In contrast to dominant group members whose group affiliations become invisible and unremarkable, subordinate group memberships become marked by stereotypes and stamped with an essence. These "intimations of inferiority" (Bartky 1990: 7) so permeate society that they are, as Young puts it, "not noticed as contestable" (Young 1990: 59) – not only by dominant group members but by subordinate group members as well. Subordination is made to seem natural and deserved. Like Bentham's model prison, the Pan-opticon, to which Foucault refers in his *Discipline and Punish* (1979), it is the prisoners who disci-pline themselves. There is no need for guards outside the door. Similarly, to the extent that members of subordinate groups internalize the intimations of inferiority which permeate society they thereby "keep themselves down" (Bartky 1990: 22). Finally, although subordinate groups become

marked by stereotypes and stamped with essences, they paradoxically become invisible in that the dominant group

> fails to recognize the perspective embodied in their cultural expressions as a perspective. These domin-ant cultural expressions often simply have little place for the experience of other groups, at most only mentioning or referring to them in stereo-typed or marginalized ways.   (Young 1990: 61)

Such psychological benefits and harms have cor-responding material consequences, of which three illustrations will be outlined here. First of all, since the dominant categories of meaning are embedded in everyday living and decision-making, since dom-inant group norms become universalized as "meas-ures of merit, hiring criteria, grading standards, predictors of success, correct grammar, appropriate behaviour, and so forth" (Scheurich 1993: 7), dom-inant group members are privileged with a certain type of "power to" at the individual level which subordinate group members are denied. One of the best examples of an attempt to elaborate this point that we know of can be found in Peggy McIntosh's self-referential description of the privilege of her "whiteness" in North American society.

> I have come to see white privilege as an invisible package of unearned assets that I can count on cashing in each day, but about which I was "meant" to remain oblivious. White privilege is like an invisible weightless knapsack of special provi-sions, maps, passports, code books, visas, clothes, tools, and blank checks.   (McIntosh 1997: 291)

Secondly, as the specific privileges which McIntosh notes indicate, dominant group mem-bers do not have to struggle with a social world that reflects one's social identity in a negative light. For example, dominant group members are usually able to live in places that they want and can afford; they are able to send their child to a school in which curricular material will testify to the existence of their race; and they are able to turn on the TV or open the newspaper and see people who are like them represented in a positive light. When one has access to such privileges, both in the sense of being comfortable with the meaning-making categories which underlie the criteria of success and of not having to struggle with a social world that reflects one's social identity in a negative light, one has an advantage in attaining material success.

Third, as one's own identification within domin-ant groups tends to disappear from view, all these privileges get perceived by oneself and by others as what one *deserves*, and deserves *as an individual*. As it has traditionally been understood, "individual" here means an abstract entity, a disembodied and autonomous self whose identity as a member of a social group is presumed to be irrelevant to considerations of merit. This is not to deny that there are aspects of individual merit, but rather to point out that individual merit alone does not, cannot, account for the unequal benefits accrued by dominant and subordinate group members.

Conversely, since the criteria of success are based on categories of meaning which are to a great extent foreign to subordinate group members, or at least not necessarily part of the preferred shape of their daily lives, and since subordinate group members must struggle against a negative self-image, their chances of material success in modern society are disadvantaged. Moreover, while dominant group members can assume that they are evaluated as individuals, i.e., persons who merit on their own account certain goods, rights, and services, subordinate group members "must *demonstrate* that they are to be regarded as 'individuals' and not as members of a group" (Thompson and Gitlin 1995: 136, emphasis ours). This unnecessary burden appends additional disadvantages to subordinate group members competing for resources and social benefits. In addition, even when subordinate group members effectively assimilate dominant group norms and when they materially succeed, they often never completely escape their subordinate status in society, as the recent book about prosperous Afro-Americans, *The Rage of a Privileged Class* (Cose 1993), illustrates. In his attempt to understand the anger of middle-class black Afro-Americans, Cose describes instances of black Afro-Americans who, whether they are lawyers, top executives, or professors, still suffer many of society's worst racial indignities.

Not only are subordinate group members unjustly harmed through dominance, the benefits dominant group members derive from dominance, but take for granted, support and perpetuate the status quo in which dominance is concealed. Suggesting ways of eradicating dominance is beyond the scope of this chapter. Yet unless we acknowledge what dominance is, how it works, and how dominant group members are implicated in its perpetuation, many of the unjust harms and inequalities that subordinate groups endure will go unnoticed and will thus continue.

## Back to ourselves: examples illuminated by our analysis

Now all of this must seem rather abstract, a bit removed from where we started. However, we do intend, as we suggested at the beginning, for this analysis to be self-referentially helpful. What sorts of things in our lives are we now in a better position to see with the help of this understanding of dominance? Earlier we noted a range of examples which this understanding sheds some light on, but they were all about other people. We want to bring our concerns back home now, to our own lived experience. Doing so runs the risk(s) of appearing to be engaged in something like wearing our hearts on our sleeves, airing our dirty linen, exhibiting tendencies toward self-flagellation, wallowing in guilt/shame in order to feel better, striving for a self-righteous advantage . . . pick any one of these, or any combination you want. That is not our intention. Rather, we believe that the connection of philosophy to practice must start through personally grounded critical apprehension of practical problems that are seen better as a result of philosophical analysis. Thus, we offer the following two examples.

First, from Applebaum:

Last year, a close friend of mine, who is deeply devoted to Judaism, in many ways more so than myself, but who is also a lesbian and trying to raise a Jewish family in a lesbian home within the Jewish community, was trying to convince me to attend a conference in Toronto about feminism and Judaism. For many reasons, I did not want to attend. However, what I told my friend was that feminism wants to transform Judaism in ways that I am not ready for. For me, I have found that it is better just to pick and choose what I want from Judaism but not try to change the basic foundations. I actually argued to her that I thought it better to just do what you want with Judaism privately, at a personal level, but not to try to change it at its roots. I even went so far as to employ a distinction I often rely on between what I believe Judaism really is and how it is practised in different communities. The Judaism that I respect does not renounce you because you are homosexual, I maintained, it is only the way Judaism gets played out by Jewish communities that excludes. I didn't end up going to the conference but was never comfortable with why not. And one day while reading the critical literature I realized that it is easy for me to argue about picking and choosing what I want from Judaism. I am in a privileged position. I, Barbara Applebaum, heterosexual, married plus four to prove it, am ostensibly accepted in the Jewish community. I can in the recesses of my heart question the basic tenets, pick and choose from the laws and rituals. I have that leverage to make the distinctions that I do. My friend, on the contrary, is ostracized and does not have that advantage. Unless she hides her sexuality as a deep secret, she cannot comfortably go to pray, she cannot send her daughters to Jewish schools without anxious concerns, she cannot go with her beloved partner to Jewish functions. She has to struggle to be on the inside of and accepted by the Jewish community which provides her with things that she both spiritually and materially needs, while I take all that for granted. What I realized was that although as a woman and as a Jew I often see myself in a subordinate social position, in certain contexts and within certain historical periods, I am dominant, indeed. This is one example where my privilege in a particular context blinds me from recognizing what my friend is going through, why what is happening to her is wrong, and how I am implicated in what must change.

Second, from Boyd:

This one is, I believe, particularly ironic. It occurred two years ago and involves, principally, Barbara and me. (I'm the heavy.) According to the OISE bulletin I now teach a course called "Moral Dimensions of Educating within Commitments to Diversity." In fact, it is a spin-off of another course, entitled "Moral Education: Philosophical Dimensions," that I have taught regularly since coming to OISE in 1975, a spin-off that came about through my increasing worry about how to integrate more standard readings in moral education with critical literature dealing with issues of gender, race, cultural diversity, dominance, etc. It also came about because Barbara was working on a PhD thesis on "Respect for Diversity: Its Meaning, Moral Justification, and Educational Implications," and I felt she could really help me with this worry by teaching the Moral Education course with me. She accepted my invitation to co-teach the course, even though I had no funds to pay her for her assistance. The new course was then a direct product of our collaboration around issues of difference, including a number of discussions about how we were personally situated differently in terms of our primary social-group identifications.

We then taught this course together twice. The second time, at the end of the second session (and what I thought of as a good discussion of Young and how difference and dominance is socially constructed), I rather blithely announced both the topic for the next week and the fact that Barbara would unfortunately not be there. When the students asked why, and I mumbled something about Yom Kippur, with considerable tongue-tied embarrassment I suddenly realized what I had done. Despite the fact that I had known for years that Barbara was Orthodox and observed Yom Kippur every year, and the fact that she had mentioned that this year it would conflict with one of the class sessions, I had not even thought about what this meant in the context of the subject matter of the course and our commitment to teaching it together. Nor had I given any thought to the fact that there were likely other Jewish members of the course (including one I knew quite well, the friend featured in Barbara's example).

Now this might be seen simply as a rather crass case of stupidity and forgetfulness. And, indeed, I must confess that on occasion my behavior may very well be so described, and this could be a factor in this case. However, I do not honestly believe that was the whole picture. Rather, I take it to be an example of how my embeddedness in particular social groups and my assumption of the "normality" of norms, values, and expectations of behavior directly shaped my actions. That I was masculine and "the professor" and that the Christianization of Canadian society was something from which I was not alienated (despite no longer having any surface identification with this religion) "allowed" me simply to act, and to feel comfortable with that act (at least for a while). And even if forgetfulness is a factor, it is convenient forgetfulness, fueled directly by these deeper identifications.

## Conclusion

The meaning of dominance as it is utilized in the critical literature has been the preoccupation of this chapter. Understanding this notion requires redirecting attention away from a limiting concentration on individual dyadic relations to an understanding of relationally defined social groups, from a restrictive focus on tangible and observable behaviors to categories of meaning, and from the exclusive engrossment with "power over" to a particular interpretation of "power to." The resulting analysis not only reveals how dominance works but also exposes how dominance, by paradoxically covering and concealing its own footprints and, at the same time, solidifying the imprint, perpetuates unjust harms caused to subordinate group members and obscures the ways in which dominant group members are implicated in these harms.

Merely clarifying the meaning of a term as it is employed in a particular body of literature has not, however, been our primary aim. As should be apparent, there are both epistemological and normative implications of this understanding of dominance which have direct relevance for moral education theory. Our self-referential narratives, for example, highlight one epistemological implication of this understanding of dominance, i.e., that a person's embeddedness in a particular social group is not an irrelevant factor in determining how a moral problem is conceived and whether a situation will be seen as a "moral" one at all. The more general and public examples that we pointed to in the academic domains of psychology, philosophy, and educational theory can now be seen to illustrate one of the normative implications of this definition of dominance, i.e., that there are those who have been unjustly excluded from the enterprise of theory construction. Moreover, theory gets constructed in such a way that "the oppressed group's own experience and interpretation of social life finds little expression that touches the dominant culture, while that same culture imposes on the oppressed group its experience and interpretation of social life" (Young 1990: 60). The understanding of dominance as explicated here shows how the exclusion of some is systemically related to the privilege of others. Similarly, awareness of dominance impacts on moral education theory by demonstrating that the theorist's social/political location is not to be disregarded both in determining the objects of study in theory-building and in who is privileged or excluded in theory construction.

Specifying the myriad ways in which dominance affects moral education theory and what needs to be done is a topic that calls for serious attention. Since dominant group members have generally prevailed in this domain of study, this research will be thwarted so long as moral education theorists do not acknowledge what dominance is, how it works and how they are implicated in its perpetuation. Without this self-reflective awareness, moral education theory will, ironically, stand justly accused of supporting the injustices and inequalities that it aims to eradicate.

## References

Bachrach, P. and Baratz, M. (1970) *Power and Poverty*, New York: Oxford University Press.

Bartky, S. L. (1990) *Femininity and Domination: Studies in the Phenomenology of Oppression*, New York: Routledge.

Cose, E. (1993) *The Rage of a Privileged Class*, New York: HarperCollins.

Dei, G. J. S. (1996) *Anti-Racism Education: Theory and Practice*, Halifax: Fernwood Publishing.

Delpit, L. D. (1988) 'The Silenced Dialogue: Power and Pedagogy in Educating Other People's Children", *Harvard Educational Review*, 58. 2: 280–98.

DuBois, W. E. B. (1989) *The Souls of Black Folk*, New York: Bantam.

Essed, P. (1990) *Everyday Racism: Reports from Women of Two Cultures*, Amsterdam: Hunterhouse.

Essed, P. (1991) *Understanding Everyday Racism: An Interdisciplinary Theory*, London: Sage.

Foucault, M. (1990) *Discipline and Punish*, New York: Vintage Books.

Frankenberg, R. (1993) *White Women, Race Matters: The Social Construction of Whiteness*, Minneapolis: University of Minnesota Press.

Gilligan, C. (1982) *In a Different Voice: Psychological Theory and Women's Development*, Cambridge, MA: Harvard University Press.

Goldberg, D. T. (1993) *Racist Culture: Philosophy and the Politics of Meaning*, Cambridge, MA: Blackwell.

Katz, J. H. (1978) *White Awareness: A Handbook for Anti-Racism Training*, Norman: University of Oklahoma Press.

Kreisberg, S. (1992) *Transforming Power: Domination, Empowerment and Education*, Albany, NY: State University Press.

Martin, J. R. (1982) "The Ideal of the Educated Person", *Educational Theory*, 31. 2: 97–109.

McIntosh, P. (1997) "White Privilege: Unpacking the Invisible Knapsack", in R. Delgado and J. Stefanic (eds) *Critical White Studies: Looking behind the Mirror*, Philadelphia, PA: Temple University Press, 291–9.

Minnow, M. (1990) *Making All the Difference: Inclusion, Exclusion and American Law*, Ithaca, NY: Cornell University Press.

Razack, S. (1993) "Teaching Activists for Social Change: Coming to Grips with Questions of Subjectivity and Domination", *Canadian Journal for the Studies of Adult Education*, 7. 2: 43–56.

Rothenberg, P. (1990) "The Construction, Deconstruction, and Reconstruction of Difference", *Hypatia*, 5. 4: 42–57.

Schattschneider, E. E. (1960) *The Semi-Sovereign People*, New York: Holt, Rinehart & Winston.

Scheurich, J. J. (1993) "Toward a White Discourse on White Racism", *Educational Researcher*, 22. 8: 5–10.

Taylor, C. (1992) *Multiculturalism and the Politics of Recognition*, Princeton, NJ: Princeton University Press.

Thompson, A. and Gitlin, A. (1995) "Creating Spaces for Reconstructing Knowledge in Feminist Pedagogy", *Educational Theory*, 45, 3: 125–50.

Weis, L. (1995) "Identity Formation and the Process of 'Othering'", *Educational Foundations*, 9, 2: 17–33.

Wellman, D. (1977) *Portraits of White Racism*, Cambridge: Cambridge University Press.

Young, I. M. (1990) *Justice and the Politics of Difference*, Princeton, NJ: Princeton University Press.

# 5 From Cultural Patchwork to Rainbows: Tightropes in Values Education

JOHN COLBECK

I want to proceed fairly briskly to a practical question, 'How do you do values education in a context of plural cultures?' I therefore start by defining what I mean by valuing and by educating. I make no claim that these definitions are the only possible ones. On the contrary, in a multicultural world, I welcome plural definitions of such words. I favour competition between plural perspectives (networks of values and beliefs) but, within any one perspective, at any one time, it is desirable to be clear about meanings of words. This requires that, for now, I adopt and declare singular meanings for key words.

My claim is that my definitions of valuing and educating are good ones but not the only possible ones. By 'good' I mean that they are definitions which can promote an increase in valuing of and by people. Valuing and educating can *value-profitably* be seen, in part, in the ways I suggest. I recommend these ways of seeing them, without claiming that the words must always be or ought always to be used in this way. My claim is not a modest one but nor, I hope, too arrogant. Arrogance versus humility describes one of many tightropes we walk. Another tightrope lies between being too serious and too frivolous.

## Valuing

If I value history, I am positively, emotionally attached to history, with reasons. I am disposed to study history for pleasure, for its interest or because I believe that it positively connects with other values. I tend to speak and act favourably in relation to history and to argue its merits. To say that I value history is to say something more reflective and considered than to say only that I like it. Valuing combines emotional attachment with reasoning.

In relation to people, valuing is less passionate than loving, but warmer, more emotional than respecting. It would be strangely cool for me to say that I value my wife, but even stranger to say that I do *not* value her. When loving occurs 'with the heart only' we tend to speak of 'blind passion', without the reasoning element that, I claim, goes with the more settled disposition of valuing. I respect, love *and* value my wife and my children. I can value other people with or without the extra intensity and depth which would come with loving them.

I can respect people's interests, for reasons of morality or justice for instance, when I do not particularly value them, although this raises some problems as to why, with what motivation, I show this respect. The old question 'Why be moral, or just?' is a question about what values motivate us to invent rules which put pressure on us to 'behave as if' we valued others equally, *as* ourselves. An ethics of love or a love of ethics? Both, but I must leave that thread hanging. Tina Chanter (1995) discusses it.

Such is the rainbow variety of human beings that almost anything and anyone can be valued, it seems; i.e. almost anyone and anything *can* be seen as value-able or valuable. The connections between one value and another are so numerous, however, that some things and people have stronger positive connections than others. I value my health highly, for instance, because it has positive connections with almost all my other values. I do not *love* my health, as I might love a person or playing tennis; my reasons for valuing my health are mainly its positive connections with other values. My reason for playing tennis is mainly for enjoyment, but it is also good for my health. Other reasons for valuing tennis may be that it gives me social contact with friends and, possibly, with business or professional colleagues.

A value is a motivating reason for action. In reflection, looking back afterwards, a value is a justifying reason for action. Valuing makes sense of acting.

## Educating

An aim in all action is the attainment of some good,[1] an increase in value. A 'good' action (as for a 'good' definition, earlier) is one that promotes an increase in valuing. An aim in educating is to increase valuing via learning. We select activities as educative according to the degree to which we expect them to lead to an increase in valuing. When we include history in the curriculum, and not skill in mugging old ladies, it is because we believe that the study of history will lead to a greater increase in valuing than will occur by mugging old ladies. The latter may be excluded on the grounds that it leads to, or exemplifies, a narrowing of valuing. An old lady is more important than money. A criminal values narrowly and we devalue him, in a vicious spiral of narrowing (decreasing) values.

This way of seeing educating differs from seeing its aim as to increase knowledge and understanding and from seeing it as promoting development of critical thinking. Increases in knowledge, understanding and critical thinking will be *educative* on this view if, and only if, they lead to an increase in valuing via learning. If either learning or an increase in valuing is absent, we will be failing to educate.

It is a tough criterion, not purely child-centred but child-and-adult-centred equally. It is people-centred, rather than knowledge-centred, critical-thinking-centred or 'thing'-centred. Increases in knowledge, critical thinking and material possessions may or may not contribute towards an increase in valuing. Quite often they do not. Criticism can have negative effects on valuing, leading towards nihilism.

On this view, knowledge, understanding and critical thinking are not valuable *for their own sake* but for ours – *if* they lead to an increase in valuing of and by people. It will be more important, if we choose history for inclusion in our curriculum, that children come to value history than that they learn too much of it – more than they can value.

If we use *de jure* authority to force children to learn things which they *cannot* value, we may pro-

duce a number of negative outcomes: pupils may come to hate all learning and perhaps to hate the 'culture' of adults who impose it on them. In that case, the result will be a *narrowing* or shrinking of their value perspective – an *anti*-educational effect in terms of my definition.

It is not altogether fanciful to suppose that it is *our* failures in educating 'bottom people', at home and at school, which drives some of them into a criminal culture. We then, self-comfortingly, label theirs a subculture. From the experience of being devalued (we devalue their interests), bottom people learn to devalue their society and to behave in ways that cause them to be devalued further. They develop their own culture in *hostility* to that of the main stream. We devalue them; they devalue us.

It is the negative, destructive, value-narrowing hostility which matters. It is a prevalent tendency in human nature to value other cultures as 'sub', or low. It is illustrated in the story of Narcissus – a beautiful youth who so admired his own image in the water that he drowned.

What I am suggesting here is that, when we point the finger at other cultures, including 'our' criminal subculture, we imagine ourselves 'seeing' the other as if through a two-way, half-silvered mirror. We will then 'see' that our finger points, about equally, at ourselves and at the 'other'. We do, I think, see the world through half-silvered glass, projecting our own values onto others in judging them, seeing them in our own terms and not in theirs. We beseech them, as Cromwell did, to bethink themselves that *they* (and not we) may be mistaken. 'Cromwelling' is one aspect of Narcissism.

The imaginative (and real) dodge of a two-way, half-silvered mirror is a method of trying to catch ourselves out in Narcissism. In genuine dialogue with others we may be able to see ourselves and the world more clearly, with less narrowly egotistical self-projection, by combining others' projections with our own. That might be a small start in multicultural educating of ourselves. If multicultural education begins at home, then the half-silvered mirror suggests that we see our criminal subculture as an integral, organic part of our own culture. The subculture reveals, in reflection, faults in the 'high' parts of that culture – often the parts of which we 'top' people tend to be proud.

With my definitions of educating and valuing, the emphasis will be on educating in such a way and to just such an extent as to increase children's internal self-motivation by helping them to value more – more widely and more deeply. An educator who inspires children with an interest in or a love for history will not quite have made herself redundant, but she will have done the most important and difficult part of her job – to inspire in such a way that her children *want* to study history, even when she is not there. Her pupils will have widened their value perspectives. She may also widen her own value perspective, learning, with them, to value their values more than she did.

Using these ideas, a school's success would be measured by asking 'Do pupils value more on leaving this school than they did on arrival?' With a little ingenuity, I suspect that measures of this aspect of 'value added' – added valuing – could be devised.

## Priorities: valuing people

In coming to value X, I add one to the values in my life and thus add one to my reasons for valuing life. I also, by positively connecting myself with X, add one person's value (mine) to the value of X. Things, activities and beliefs acquire value passively in being valued by people. If no one valued gold, it would have no value, only potential for being valued. Without people, there would be no values.

If X is a thing, an activity or a belief, it cannot value me back. In valuing people, however, there is a contingent possibility, even a probability, of being valued back. In coming to value a pupil, I add one to my actively acquired values and also one to her passively acquired values. If, perhaps in response to my valuing her, the pupil values me back (action and reaction are often equal and opposite, not only in physics; if I dislike her she may well dislike me; make a friend, become a friend) she adds one actively acquired value to her values and a passively acquired value to mine. Further, if we establish this value 'rapport', each of us has an opportunity to acquire some of the values of the other. A pupil may 'catch' enthusiasms from a teacher she likes. Her teacher may catch some of her values and also learn from her features of his teaching that were successful. This added value requires no money!

If we are looking for priorities among those 'things' which have greatest potential for leading on to further increase in valuing, then people, as creators and originators of value, are among the strongest candidates. The way to improve a situation is to improve people. The way to improve

people is to value them more. The message is at least 2000 years old but still new.

In contrast to the nihilistic tendency of 'Try to be as value-free as you can' I make a suggestion 'Try to value as much as you can, especially as many people as you can' but not, of course, those things which lead to a decrease or narrowing of valuing. If, as Shakespeare's *Timon of Athens* suggests, valuing gold conflicts with valuing friends, then valuing gold does not lead to an increase of value, overall – another message that is at least 2000 years old, but clean contrary to monetarist philosophy. Money has zero value for its own sake.

## Educating in cultural diversity

Brief as it is, the above discussion is sufficient to consider application of these ideas to educating in valuing in a context of cultural diversity. To a plural thinker, the best way to improve perspectives and cultures is to keep plural perspectives in friendly (games not war) competition with and against each other. We can thus welcome and encourage cultural diversity *so long as it does not lead to hostility.*

The idea has parallels in philosophy of science. For scientific method, Feyerabend (1975) recommends the principle of 'Anything goes', *so long as it increases the power of our theories,* i.e., so long as it is constructive. The phrase in italics imposes severe practical limits on the anarchy of 'Anything goes'. Lakatos' approach in 'Falsification and the Methodology of (plural) Scientific Research Programmes' (1970) (I inserted 'plural') is similar but more positively constructive.

Observing that perspectives, paradigms, theories and 'research programmes' are not abandoned as a result of falsifications or counter-instances, Lakatos claims that 'paradigms' (perspectives would do, I think) are overthrown only when an alternative research programme and its theories are deemed to constitute a 'constructive problem shift'. His 'method' therefore consists in ensuring that, at any one time, there should be more than one, preferably several, research programmes in mutually strengthening, critical competition. Lakatos' early death led to his being seriously undervalued.

We should always regard any current orthodoxy as no more (and no less, either) than the highest, most comprehensive perspective (comprehending most) we have achieved so far – a viewpoint from which we can see furthest, in most different directions. Lakatos' 'method' is very similar to Nietzsche's perspectivism – improving perspectives by setting plural perspectives in agonistic struggle with and against each other in an 'arena'. The method is also similar to the adversarial procedure which we adopt in parliament and in courts of law in order to arrive at truths or best solutions.

## How to avoid hostility?

What I have said so far is naive in relation to cultural diversity. It is precisely cultural and especially religious differences that do lead to hostility. A singular thinker's solution to the problem is, put crudely, 'Convert everyone else to "the" one, true faith – ours'. Hitler and the Pope have this method of thinking in common, although their faiths and methods of arguing are different. I call it 'Titanic', 'mighty, unsinkable ship' thinking.

Where fundamentalists think they already *have* an unsinkable ship, a singular-minded rationalist thinker says, instead, '*Seek to build* a singular consensus (a Titanic) by rational argument, relying on "pure" reason'. Rationalist thinkers do not make the mistake of thinking they have already built a singular, unsinkable ship but they seek, in consensus, to find or build one. In this, I think they mistakenly pursue 'excellence' (instead of improvement) and perfection (instead of 'good enough to go on with' or 'true enough to act on'). Something which is 'perfect' is finished – not always a desirable state.

Plural-minded thinkers' aims and methods are different. They claim that a rationalist's method *depends* on there being two or more perspectives in play. Criticism of one perspective has to be mounted from another. Plural-minded thinkers, because they are sceptical about the unsinkability of 'Titanics', also demand enough lifeboats (little faiths and perspectives) for every passenger. They demand lifeboat drill and practice in racing lifeboats against each other (dialogical argument and games), to develop sailing skills. I leave the metaphor there, incomplete, adding only that a pluralist's aim is more modest and cautious than a singular thinker's. It is still daring enough. We need a 'ship' suitable for travelling uncharted seas and space, into the future. Such a 'ship' (overall perspective or faith) is likely to need fairly frequent modifications – even occasional redesign and rebuilding – to meet changing needs. It needs built-in obsolescence.

In order to avoid ossifying in a static orthodoxy, we need alternative perspectives. This may be difficult in the case of scientific theories such as Einstein's theories of relativity but, since history suggests that alternative, superseding theories are likely to come along, we should be ready, not uncritically, to welcome them.

If we do not equal or excel Einstein we should still be opening-minded towards alternatives (to avoid persecuting the next 'Galileo', who may be a non-intellectual, black woman). In the context of educating, we should try to educate our pupils to be opening-minded towards surprises, 'strange' ideas and people.

In science, it may be difficult to imagine alternatives. In cultural education, the problem is different. In our multicultural society there are, some would say, so many competing perspectives available that we must simplify matters for our pupils to avoid confusing them. It seems that we have to walk, run or dance along a tightrope here between singular or absolute and plural or relative thinking.

I think a modified form of relativism or, as I prefer, plural thinking provides a tightrope between absolute thinking (dogmatism – commitment to a single right answer) and nihilism (no values and no beliefs – an unlivable option). There are now too many versions of 'relativism' for the word to be used clearly without lengthy discussion. In general, '-isms', '-ists' and '-ians' are lazy-minded dodges or oversimple generalisations but, until they are abolished, I use them, reluctantly. Nietzsche, Marx and Jesus said much more important things than Nietzsche-ans, Marx-ists and Christ-ians, their lazy-minded 'followers', ever have. Nietzsche and Jesus both warned against the dangers of 'followers'. They taught that 'following' is not the thing to do. Going on alone is, in the spirit of renewal: 'Ye have heard it said of old time . . . But I say . . .' (Matthew 5:21).

The plural-thinking argument goes something like this: you cannot 'see' without a perspective. Every statement and every question formed as a sentence depends on assumptions. Truths are true relative to a framework of assumptions. It is possible – a concession to singular thinkers here to maintain consistency as a plural thinker – that there are assumptions to which there is no alternative. One particular singular thinker may happen to be right; he may have discovered the only true, bedrock foundation of beliefs and values for everyone, everywhere, for ever. Not only has such a person found 'God', but he knows exactly what s/he said and wants. Jesus and Mahommed, for instance, *are presented by their self-styled 'followers'*, as having such knowledge.

Even if one of these (many!) singular thinkers is right, however, a plural thinker believes that we can only 'prove' his faith, or perspective right by putting it to the most severe test (proving) we can devise. We do this testing by pitting against him, not a doubter but one or more committed opponents of equal skill and sophistication. (That is the function of 'the devil' or of a 'devil's advocate'.) A different aspect of this method is that we are likely to see more completely, all round and 'in' perspective, if we look from several different positions. Visual perspective depends on two eyes. Mind perspectives may need more.

Galileo radically extended our perspective in space-time by *imagining himself as* someone else, somewhere else (with another perspective), looking back on 'our' little solar system (huge relative to any one of us, tiny relative to our universe). He escaped, in imagination only, from his own ego- and geo-centric perspective by adopting another.

If we can manage to see struggles between competing perspectives as a game, instead of a threatening war, we may be able to avoid some of the hostility and fear (but not the hostility that arises in conflicts over territory). For children to take part in this game it seems necessary that they start with some fairly consistent and well-knit network of values and beliefs – values and beliefs which are true enough and good enough to act on, for the time being (which of us has more?). We all do collect such a system of values and beliefs in the process of learning a language at 'mother's knee'. In Europe, our languages tend to be heavily 'male Christian' oriented, for historical reasons.

The perspectives we acquire in learning our languages do, at first, empower us: use of words achieves an enormous economy of effort. Words give us ability to coordinate our efforts with others, for instance – probably one of their earliest functions.

But our language then also moulds and imprisons us, often in a fortress mentality, separating us from those with other languages and cultures. I call this the SLATs effect; specialist languages and trainings empower us within groups but separate us from other groups. This occurs in 'subcultures' within one national culture and, on a larger scale, between nations with different cultures and languages. It occurs between men and women, and between Leavises and Snows.

We collect our values unawares, by subliminal indoctrination, every time we learn a new word; this lack of awareness makes it difficult or impossible to play the perspectives game with others. We have values and beliefs – our *actions* show what they 'really' are – but until we are aware of them we can neither argue for them nor change them voluntarily.

Willingness to change our beliefs and values requires awareness of their origin and fallibility. Objectivity requires awareness of subjectivity. A first task in schools is not to *give* children a perspective but to make them aware of the one they already have (and of its origins in history). I suspect that it is possible for them to learn this from and with each other, in assisted dialogue and in simple writing assignments: 'Things I like', 'Things that are not fair', 'How did I come to feel like that?'

That is, I think, an important place to start – with our own 'now here' (a vanishingly small, 'nowhere' point in space-time) and its history – but where are we going? Towards what end are we working? One answer is 'towards extending people's (value) perspectives in space-time and in as many metaphorical, imaginative "dimensions" as possible'. I name five of these as heart (emotion and feeling), mind (intellect and reasoning), spirit (attitude and élan) and strength (body) for an individual.

The fifth dimension I call simply 'others'. Each 'other' (person) requires respect on all of the four individual dimensions. Another answer to 'Where are we going?' is that we are not working towards any final 'end' (perfection) but rather towards a better way, path, method or spirit in which to travel, or 'go on'. To amend Hamlet, a better question than 'To be or not to be?' is 'How to become, more becomingly, what we already are?' To define the tightrope path that I am recommending, I need to discuss the extremes to be avoided. They define the path. The path is not a straight line but a zig-zag, either side of a fair way, somewhere between a number of extremes.

## Nihilism and its value

One of these extremes is 'nihilism'. Nietzsche called this an abyss. He reached it, in imagination, via critical reasoning. He recoiled from it. 'Nihilism' itself is usually a pejorative label, along with 'indifferent-ism' used by Roman Catholics. Nihilism can, how-ever, be given approving labels such as 'impartial-ity', 'neutrality' and 'pure reason'. Pure? Free of contamination, presumably, by values and emo-tions, seen as distorting 'biases' or 'prejudices' – judging too early – but all judging is 'too early', at some level.

I find nihilism useful as a starting point – an 'abso-lute zero' of values and beliefs to be avoided by any-one who wishes to live or act. I find it, and dislike of it, useful as a justification for advocating moves towards more valuing and more beliefs. It might seem a somewhat negative aim – to move away from nihilism – but it is, however minimal, a start on which many could agree. We need to face the prospect of nihilism, starting from nothing, and go beyond it.

Nihilism and 'nothings' should not be dismissed too lightly. To write these words I had to start with a blank page with nothing on it – an invitation at least to make a doodle on it. Without the blank spaces between and around letters you could not pick them out. The extranothingspacesbetween-words also help. An 'O' is a line with nothing in the middle and nothing round it. A dot needs nothing to surround it. We 'see' by contrasts and contradic-tions – by learning, or seeing what something is *and* what is 'not it'. Like molecules, people need space in which to move and be free to discharge energy.

## Values and commitments

On the other side of that tightrope (opposite to nihilism), commitment, determination and hard, disciplined training are needed for any worthwhile endeavour, from physical gymnastics and ballet dancing to the mental acrobatics required for effective participation in democratic or isocratic (equal rule) speech situations. Speaking and writing well are learned by doing – by trial, error and cor-rection by others. We cannot learn them alone, nor by 'sitting on the fence'. We fall off the fence in *choosing* to sit on it. It moves. We have to get our feet wet and our hands dirty, as children love to do.

Values and beliefs are *necessary* to avoid nihilism and in order to act or live; a life without values is not worth living; it cannot be lived. Values are *desirable* for other reasons (as a means towards liv-ing more abundantly, for instance). Attempts to avoid values and beliefs are moves in the direction of nihilism.

On the far, extreme side of my tightrope lie 'fun-damental', 'absolute' and 'singular' commitments. What is wrong with them? Surely the most effective opponents of Hitler, and those who survived best in Belsens, were those with passionate commitments – committed Jews, Jehovah's witnesses and Chris-tians – rather than liberal philosophers? Well, yes, but the history of people with fundamental com-mitments is a gruesome one, especially when they obtain power. It is aptly parodied, I think, in the witch-queen we call 'wicked' in *Snow White*. The witch asks the mirror on the wall 'Who is the fairest of them all?' When she gets *the wrong answer*, she flies into a rage and determines to kill Snow White.

Historically, people who *know* 'the' right answers have, when they obtained power themselves, called their opponents various names such as 'infidel' to justify massacring them (from crusades to Salman Rushdie), torturing their bodies to save their souls, burning them at the stake. A 'master race' sends members of a 'chosen race' to gas chambers. When 'chosen races' acquire power they drive others from their homes on the West Bank and elsewhere.

When we point a finger at such atrocities now, calling them 'uncivilised' or 'bestial', what does the *two-way, half-silvered* mirror tell us about who is the fairest of them all? Surely the finger will partly point back at us, telling us that such behaviour, far from being 'uncivilised' or 'bestial', is behaviour typical, not of 'beasts' but of the human 'master race' throughout history? Know thine enemy *as* thyself. Is not systematic persecution the behaviour, espe-cially, of those of us who consider ourselves, Narcis-sistically, 'civilised' (city people?) 'masters' and 'better' than the animals? Is not behaviour in cities, greying the green of the earth, noticeably 'worse' than that in the country where we are closer to the animals and the trees?

Ask endangered species of animals and trees for their views on human beings! If cows, or batteried hens, could cull, whom would *they* cull? Which species is most *damagingly* overpopulated?

Where we see (*through* the glass, correctly, I think!) 'fundamentalists' and Hitlers as valuing too narrowly, excluding whole swathes of humanity from their versions of 'morality', the finger seen in the silvered sections points *also* back at us and our own narrownesses. Our morality is *narrowly* restricted to human beings, justifying neglect, mas-sacre, genocide and exploitation of many other forms of life. Not only do we depend on those other forms of life; we have also evolved from them; they are our family, ancestors and cousins. We share elements of DNA with them. Our methods of 'culture' are destructive of our own garden (too much *knowledge* of good and evil). We are on the way towards self-genocide, on a massive scale.

Why should it be seen as 'unflattering' when I suggest that primitive tube-worms and opening- and closing-minded oysters are our ancestors and cousins? Such unpretentious organisms do far less harm (often more good) to the living ecology of space-ship earth than human beings do. We have developed more 'stomachs', so we are greedier! With our 'stomachs' we take in, digest and spew out again, not only air, liquids and food, but also words. Tube-worms do not threaten, as we do, to bring all life on earth to an end. That end, if we do cause it, will be preceded by long drawn-out suffering on a global scale. Compared to the global holocaust which we threaten to prepare by mistake, Hitler's can be seen as a small, warning traffic accident. It will be our children, and our children's children, who suffer if we make hell on 'mother-earth', by mistake, neglecting her.

## Balancing on tightropes hopefully (BOTH)

My typical mode of progress round a golf course provides me with a model for balancing on tight-ropes hopefully. An observer watching me play golf might well conclude that I am at least half-blind. It must look as if I am *feeling* for where the fairway is by frequent trips into the rough and gorse on either side (learning by little mistakes and some big ones). 'If the man could *see*, surely he would go straight?' an observer might say. I don't see, so I use trips to BOTH sides to find out where the 'fair' way is – the fair, 'good enough' way where lies (of my ball) may be good enough and true enough to hit a reasonable shot next time (if only I could 'see').

An acrobat dancing on a tightrope cannot walk straight along it. Watch him. He *feels* for a safe balance by wobbling a little to one side and correcting, wobbling to the other side and correcting again. He *cannot* stand still (try balancing on a bicycle, or on one leg, if you have no tightrope handy). He *has* to move and dance a little, leaning to BOTH sides *alternately* in order to maintain balance.

A singular thinker tends to be locked into an 'either/or' logic. Either Christianity (as if that was singular!) is 'right' or Islam is. Both cannot be right. This logic polarises opinions and is part cause of hostility. Both can, however, quite easily be *equally* right or equally wrong – about half right. The principle of non-contradiction loses much of its force when we recognise that concepts and words in which our questions and propositions are formed are themselves based on assumptions which may be false.

Few statements of interest are either 100 per cent true or 100 per cent false. Even fewer are 100 per cent true for long. Their contradictions are not, therefore, necessarily 100 per cent true or false either. Two contradictory statements can be equally true or false – about half true.

For a large number of true statements it is pos-sible to add 'and vice versa'. 'Our earth goes round our sun' and vice versa (if we treat the earth as viewpoint). 'ESP is all imagination' and vice versa, 'All imagination is extra-sensory, mind's eyes and ears perception (and very real and power-ful, too).' 'Nothing comes from nothing, nothing ever could' and vice versa, 'Everything came from nothing, everything always did.' If everything came from something else, where did *that* come from?

Where *did* we 'come from'? A big bang? One of a series? Did time begin? Where did time 'come from'? Does the idea of 'coming from' make good sense?

These questions are, I think, *intercultural*, although the way I put them is not. They reveal tantalising uncertainties and ignorance. A state-ment may be true in one perspective and false in another, based on different assumptions. Judge-ments of 'rightness' and 'wrongness' are always relative to assumptions. These assumptions are implicitly asserted in any judgements we make. This leads to a form of relativism which I prefer to call plural thinking. We proceed towards plural truths in zig-zag fashion.

Plural thinking and singular thinking are best seen as *methods* of thinking. Singular thinkers tend to use the definite article 'the' in the singular, in indefinite ways: 'the' Bible (others have 'their' bibles), 'the' faith, 'the' world, 'the' sun. Plural thinkers tend to say 'our' bible, 'our' faith, 'our' world and 'our' sun, or to use plurals, recognising that there are many other bibles, faiths and perspec-tives, worlds and suns. They tend to use 'a' rather than 'the': 'A trouble with . . .' rather than 'The trouble with . . .'. Troubles, like problems, seldom come singly. It is surprising how seldom 'the' is necessary or strictly appropriate in the singular. Plural thinkers look for little truths rather than, grandiosely, for 'the' truth. Little truths have star quality.

Determined, experimental commitments to values and beliefs are necessary in order to act effectively. These values and beliefs need to be connected into coherent 'wholes', networks, faiths or perspectives if we are to be strong and to act 'consistently'. But a question always remains. 'Consistent – with what?' An inconsistent Nazi may be preferable to a consistent one.

We find out which commitments are most value-profitable only by trial and error – slowly and over a long time – by pitting one commitment against another, often a diametrically opposite one. The principle is similar to Karl Popper's principle of falsification: we test or 'prove' theories by trying to prove them wrong. If we fail to prove them wrong, we accept them as the best we have, for the time being. We need to balance a principle of non-contradiction with another: 'Contradict on principle, in turn' (COPIT!).

Non-contradiction is needed for strength and consistency *within* each singular perspective. A COPIT principle is needed for improving perspectives by setting rivals against each other.

## Practical recommendations

What are the practical consequences for educating if we want to encourage plural perspectives without hostility? Our aim might be, in the ideal limit, to *extend and develop* the present patchwork of multiple, often conflicting cultures present in our world. (I owe the 'patchwork' metaphor to Morwenna Griffiths, who uses it slightly differently in her excellent book *Feminisms and the Self: The Web of Identity* (1995).) An extension would lead to an even further differentiated (but not fragmented) 'rainbow'. Each individual's different perspective, as an élite of one, would then contribute to a beautiful, integrated whole, rather as each individual brush stroke goes to create an integrated whole in a work of art. For a good 'whole', each individual, different brush stroke matters, as also do the macroscopic 'patches' and larger details in the composition (everyone and everything matters in creating a 'whole').

The macroscopic patches are our many sub-cultures. These, like families, give individuals a sense of belonging, but they also imprison us. We need the ability to go beyond them. Within our species' culture we have British, French, Chinese, etc., subcultures. In one country we have feminists, physicists, philosophers, footballers, Leavises and Snows as subcultures, to name only a few.

Arguably, if we could see it so, we already have something like a moving, rainbow work of art in our multicultural society and world. One task of educating might be to help people to see variety, variation and differences *as* beautiful – *so long as they are not mutually destructive*. All perspectives are not equally valid, but their holders are equally worthy of respect – or valuable. That is one of the trickiest tightropes, I think, to hate 'sins' and 'mistakes', but not those who commit sins or make mistakes. We all do that destructive hating, in different ways, about equally. We *can* love those we disagree with, but it is not easy if we see them as a threat to our egos.

Educating practices which might contribute towards this development would include practice and training in oral dialogue between individuals with contrasting or contradictory views. We would need to demonstrate, in the spirit of games, not war, that opposition between well-matched equals can be both friendly and mutually strengthening. To improve my tennis, I need to play against well-matched opponents.

Dialogues of opposites can be arranged in almost any school subject. Wrong views, deliberately or accidentally presented, can be powerfully motivating to the spirit of enquiry in maths and physics, for instance.

One of my favourite ploys is to defend the 'obvious' view, firmly based on simple observation, that the sun goes round the earth. Pupils (and adults) find the currently conventional view, that the earth goes round the sun, hard to defend. Their frustration generates heated argument. I was once asked by a 12-year-old girl, some three months after the lesson, 'What *was* the answer about why we think the earth goes round the sun?' There is an 'and vice versa' or 'both and more' element to the 'solutions'. All the paths are double spirals or spiral spirals.[2] This opens the door to simple ideas of relativity and reversibility of points of view.

Another useful question, illustrating the need to unpack the assumptions folded into questions, is

'Which came first, the chicken or the egg?' Few adults can deal with it, even now, after years of teaching evolution in biology. Evolution loosens up the idea of nature and extends perspectives in space-time. 'Both evolved together, from earlier forms of life' is often an answer to other 'Which came first?' questions.

Educating is, in part, stirring and surprising people. A lesson is a bridge on which educator and pupil can go to and fro to enter each other's perspective or 'territory'. It is a *reciprocal* dramatic learning experience for both, each trying to equal and understand the other, to exchange hearts and minds, as lovers try to do. I recommend intellectual and spiritual 'promiscuity'! It is life more abundant!

Assemblies provide an excellent opportunity for presenting *friendly* oppositions in brief 'playlets' or debates between, say, a conventional Christian and a Jesus person,[3] a humanist or a Muslim. Drama, exploiting at least four dimensions of space-time, is one of the most powerful means of educating. In Jesus's terms, 'Love your enemy/opponent' or, in Nietzsche's (1954 (1883–5)) terms 'Prove that he (your enemy) did you some good.' The appraisal of such contests, during practical sessions, could be done by a smaller audience. They could be watching out for, on the credit side, 'Point scored without put-down', 'Generosity towards opponent's view'. Negative points might be awarded for hostility, Narcissism and 'Cromwelling' – always seeing the other person as mistaken, not ourselves. (Cromwell is reputed to have said, 'I beseech you, in the bowels of Christ, bethink you that you may be mistaken'.) Several of the dialogues attributed to Socrates, Diogenes the Cynic and Jesus could be presented in this spirit.[4] Pluralism, or perspectivism, is an ideology (system of values and beliefs) or a *method* broad enough to include a number of narrower ideologies struggling with and against each other. The 'game' is like 'king of the castle' between friendly 'kings and dirty rascals'.

As a practical measure, I am experimenting with a two-way, half-silvered mirror between two contestants as a visual aid to 'seeing' the other *as* (I see) myself. In it I can see my own face superimposed on that of my opposite number. If I wag my finger at her, I see my finger also wagging back at me. Judgements (of people) are boomerangs thrown from glass houses. I have had samples made. Preliminary trials are interesting. The experience is weird and new – never seen before – to see someone else *as* me.

## Seeing our world in plural ways

I see these pages as like a patchwork on the way towards constructing, with others, a moving, rainbow work of art. It is not enough only to examine every brush stroke or every patch, nor yet only to stand back and discern 'the' overall pattern of the whole. We have to do both and more – to see from many other positions – in turns.

To extend Nietzche's (1968 (1885/6)) metaphor, 'The world as a work of art that gives birth to itself –', we see and record our world as a *moving* work of art by perceiving, conceiving and re-membering it. In re-membering, we re-construct it to fit into our personal, interpersonal and cultural perspectives. We record the world in our memories, as if on a film which we can run backwards, pause, and run forwards again. Since each of us has different experiences and inheritances, each of us has a different memory-perspective and therefore 'sees' a different 'film' of the world. We agree only in those, fortunately many, aspects in which our experience is shared; sticks and stones and 'objects' are the stuff of 'objective' knowledge. Education, government, culture and religion are not.

Our incredibly flexible minds enable us to differentiate the film record, examining individual 'stills', or snapshots, in fine detail and then to integrate, running the film on to look at larger 'patches', overall patterns and directions of movement (but then losing sight of the details). Old 'stills' may be in black-on-white (snapshots and books), reminiscent of dated, 'either/or', two-dimensional thinking from the era of '78' records. A '78' record was thin, flat and brittle; it had a single spiral track on each of two sides. Stills 'preserve' the past, but by 'freezing' it – as a flat record – in two dimensions only.

Our recording systems have progressed to colour and multitrack, stereo *sound* but, visually, each of our pictures is still taken from a camera in only one place – from one perspective.

We cannot see all sides at once, but we can see many sides in turn, in quick succession, if we move about and change perspectives.

Stereo vision – holographic film-recording in four dimensions – is probably on the way, but *participating* in a lesson, seen as drama, still has a 'live' edge over recorded events. It enables a 'viewer' also to particitpate in, initiate and direct actions, to move so as to 'see' and speak from more than one place and to listen to more than one point of view in *active* dialogue with others. Plural cultures and perspectives improve this drama. To see a moving world somewhere near 'whole', never more than partially but from as many aspects as possible, we need to look in as many ways as possible, from as many cultures as possible, to *begin* to see the rainbow whole. Our world moves on and changes; no static record is ever complete, or perfect. Good art is better, more value-full, than a photograph – it is less cut and dried, more moving and alive.

## Conclusion

There are no conclusions or 'final analyses' in philosophical work. It continually creates itself anew. Loose ends and missing pieces will, I hope and expect, be visible. If there is an overall pattern or thread in what I have written, it lies somewhere in the 'ways of going on' or in methods and metaphors, like dancing on a tightrope and proceeding, zig-zag style, in golf. Or perhaps it lies in something like the plural, moving 'spirit' or 'attitude' which I have tried to adopt and thereby recommend by example.

If I am caught out in Narcissistic arrogance for making recommendations, my defence is that this kind of arrogance is inescapable. Recommendations are implied (because value assumptions are implied) in every action, word, criticism or question. You cannot be 'right' if you never say anything on your own account. It can be wrong to say nothing. I take some comfort from Nietzsche's (1986 (1878)) saying, 'He that humbleth himself wants to be exalted' (for the 'virtue' of humility).

It is arrogant to publish, and no doubt we will be damned for it when we have changed our minds and our mistakes remain, fixed on printed pages like black and white skeletons, 'stills' or 'stiffs' to haunt us in public. But it is not humble to *claim* the virtue of humility in remaining silent: it is irresponsible to say and do nothing if we think we see errors and dangers towards which our collective actions point. Do not publish, also be damned. I cannot stand and watch if a friend seems to me to be rushing headlong over a cliff by mistake, let alone if I think my whole species is doing that, driven by singular consensus, conformity and ego-centric 'common sense'. I may escape a global holocaust, but my children and my children's children may not. If I see and love them *as* myself, and myself *as* them, I too will suffer.

I have tried to point to the dangers of Narcissism (Nazism, 'wicked witch-ism', Cromwellism, elitism – all '-isms') from which I suffer as much as anyone (more than most, under the grand, seductive 'buzz' of doing philosophy as loving wisdom). I have pointed to some ways of trying to be aware of Narcissism in our narrow 'selves'. I have tried to write in the spirit of a child crying 'Cave' to his friends and enemies, caught out playing a dangerous game, and in the spirit of my own two-way mirror. If I have pressed a few warning buzzers, that is enough. I am aware, with something like Rortyan irony, that I may be misdescribing the dangers and the remedies. There will be worthy opponents – friendly enemies – to put me right, constructively.

## Notes

1  I modify the first sentence of Aristotle's, *Nicomachean Ethics* only slightly here.
2  'Spiral spirals' may not be clear. The path of our world round our sun can be seen as a wobbly ellipse, close to a circle, *if we 'fix' our sun*. Adding the movement of our sun itself makes our path into a spiral round our sun's path. Our sun's path, too, is a spiral round our galaxy's path. Similarly, our moon's path is a spiral around our spiral path. What you 'see' depends on how you (think you are) moving – on a perspective.
3  By 'a Jesus person' I mean someone who views Jesus as a man, not as Christ. In *The Lost Gospel* Bernard Mack (1993) presents a view of the sayings of Jesus, based on the lost source material 'Q[1]', as following in the tradition of Socrates and the philosophers known as Cynics. 'Q[1] enjoins a practical ethic of the times widely known as Cynic' (p. 114). If Mack is right, Christianity is not (much) based on Jesus!
4  I have expanded this suggestion about assemblies elsewhere (Colbeck 1995).

## References

Aristotle (1953) *The Nicomachean Ethics*, trans. J. A. K. Thompson, Harmondsworth: Penguin.

Chanter, T. (1995) *Ethics of Eros: Iragaray's Rewriting of the Philosophers*, London: Routledge.

Colbeck, J. (1995) 'Values Education: Save School Assemblies', *NAVET News Values*, 16 (Dec.)

Feyerabend, P. (1975) *Against Method: Outline of an Anarchistic Theory of Knowledge*, London: Verso.

Griffiths, M. (1995) *Feminisms and the Self: the Web of Identity*, London: Routledge.

Lakatos, I. (1970) 'Falsification and the Methodology of Scientific Research Programmes' in I. Lakatos and

A. Musgrave (eds) *Criticism and the Growth of Knowledge*, Cambridge: Cambridge University Press, pp. 91–196.

Mack, B. (1993) *The Lost Gospel: The Book of Q and Christian Origins*, New York: HarperCollins, p. 114.

Nietzsche, F. (1954 (1883–5)) *Thus Spoke Zarathustra: A Book For All and None*, trans. W. Kaufmann in *The Portable Nietzsche*, New York: Viking Press, p. 180.

Nietzsche, F. (1968 (1885/6)) *The Will to(wards) Power* (*Wille zur Macht*) trans. W. Kaufmann and R. J. Hollingdale, New York: Vintage Books, p. 419, aphorism 796.

Nietzsche, F. (1986 (1878)) *Human, All Too Human: A Book for Free Spirits*, trans. R. J. Hollingdale, Cambridge: Cambridge University Press, p. 48, aphorism 1.87.

# 6 The Cultural Desert of Schooling

TONY SKILLEN

It is impossible to discuss 'multicultural education' without examining what these multiplicities are multiples of; it is equally question-begging to embark on such a discussion without an examination of the culture inscribed in our primary embodiment of our conception of 'education': the modern, the contemporary, school. This entails looking, not just at current debates, but at the institutional framework they normally presuppose. I propose to apply my argument to the more specific issues of race, ethnicity and creed. But in my view it would be wrong to ignore the general truth that all education involves interaction and possible clash of cultures, and that, in so far as moral education is the development of the dispositions and capacities of free fellowship, the issues of cohabiting with others, with their differentness and their differences, cut across life's categories from friendship, marriage and work, to broader local, regional, national and transnational relations. In short, you cannot expect to attach whatever is 'educationally correct' regarding specific things like race or gender relations to an otherwise taken-for-granted picture – and then wonder why, for all our efforts, things keep exploding in our faces.

It is hard to conceive of moral education in the absence of commendation and censure or rewards and sanctions. No parent, teacher or even friend could properly do without them. But such practices and responses, to have an ethical impact, function to focus the mind on the action, to effect a rethinking, revaluation, re-feeling of that action. The contractual behaviour policies currently erupting as legal and paralegal documents in schools throughout the realm explicitly work to draw attention to the consequence to the agent of the monitor's response to that action. Indeed, when they are in place and the good behaviour ritually bombarded

with stars, the very disposition to so behave is corrupted by subordination to the disposition to gain reward and recognition – itself a dangerous habit. And when that dangerous habit is conjoined, as it often is, with weekly raffle tickets for virtue . . . or is that a way of teaching that virtue is not necessarily rewarded? But then, in the absence of totalitarian surveillance, the whole thing is a lottery, and part of that mercenary culture. Pretending to confine itself to the externals, to behaviour observable within large-group limitations, the 'new system' not only reinforces but positively inculcates an ethos of appearance management – a virtual morality that at the same time reduces the humanly significant adults in the school and the home to participants in an interactive game of show. (I must not get caught failing to call someone by their 'normal or preferred name' but if I can drop someone else into transgression . . .)

The 'new scheme' at my child's school resembles many other schemes of explicit formulation that have spread among our institutions in recent years; schemes that constitute a veritable 'discourse' of auditing, assessing, monitoring, contracting and controlling that, seeking to bring accountability, to 'professionalise' vocations, in fact render them more like life on a soviet collective farm than in the 'efficient' businesses whose accountancy they ape. But it would be wrong to confine one's critical attention to this respect in which moral accountancy in schools partakes of and reflects wider practices and concerns. For it is not the case that such schemes and policies are just a virus caught by the otherwise healthy body of the school. Misguided and corrupt as the moral accountancy scheme may be, it is a response, and one which might have local benefits, to felt problems, even crises, in schools and their relation to the family and to wider social forces and demands. Indeed, by contractually implicating parents, for years held at arm's length by a teaching profession anxious to assert its territorial domain, the new schemes subvert the notion that education and specifically moral education are, by a kind of definitional fiat, what is done by teachers to pupils in schools. Hence is opened up the whole question of the school's place in social life and of what agencies, practices and processes in social life morally educate us. It is to this question that, with grandiose brevity, I now turn. My aim here is to bring out that my child's school's new scheme is in some ways an appropriate attempt to deal with a situation that cannot really be addressed in the absence of a rethinking of education and specifically of the place of schooling in education.

The contemporary sense of a crisis in schooling (an echo of many such sensings) accompanies a time when efforts are being made to extend the duration of school life. At the same time it is becoming increasingly difficult to recruit people into the teaching profession. The unattractiveness of that profession – illustrated in early retirements and stress-related ailments – is partly a matter of salary and career structures. But these structures are themselves experienced as indices of lack of public respect and esteem for the teacher, a lack of respect and esteem reflected and independently reinforced within the school itself by inattention, rudeness, insubordination, truancy and outright violence. Forking into this spiral is a change in the domestic environment of children: while young children spend more time 'protected' within the walls of their homes, those homes are more likely to have mothers at work and fathers either unemployed or more or less absent, whether from scratch or through marital breakdown. This adds up to what Amitai Etzioni calls a 'parenting deficit' (Etzioni 1993: 104), a phrase which perhaps masks the loneliness, confusion, rage and anxiety of children and on their shoulders when they set off for school. The ideology of schooling always presupposed widespread indifference to its substantial projects: John Stuart Mill in *Liberty* (1859) gave mistrust of parents as the rationale of compelling them to have their children schooled. And domestic deficiencies have always been an assumption of mass schooling. Here from 1874:

> In order to compensate for lack of family nurture, the school is obliged to lay more stress upon discipline and to make far more prominent the moral phase of education. It is obliged to train the pupils into habits of prompt obedience to his teachers and the practice of self-control in its various forms.[1]

But the trend towards contractual obligations on parents to participate in schooling is, in Britain at least, a new level of state intervention into domestic life, an attempt to bolster institutional authority over the child at a time when 'patriarchal' authority is seen to be slipping. With the authority of the state itself at a nadir, we might wonder whether its hand will help. And what sort of a world are we supposed to be exercising all this authority to bring our children up into?

Anyone half awake is aware of dizzying and disturbing changes in the moral environment of which schools are a part. But what gets unattended to in all this are the relatively static categories within which we try practically to reason about moral education. Our dominant conception of school (contrast 'night school', 'language school' or 'riding school') is analytically tied to our conception of childhood as a period of preparatory and protective exclusion from political and economic life – from modern citizenship and modern industry, hence as a time of education for such things. Whereas, in the bad old days, a child might have grown up on the farm learning by watching, imitating and doing what his or her relevant elders did, their ignorance and weakness limiting their capacities (and rendering them open to oppressive exploitation) so that they were at once 'schooled' by the family and progressively participant in its essential activities, the modern child is kept away from the 'adult' world of 'work' within the school and the family, now a sphere of consumption and 'socialisation' rather than of production. And so, whereas Rousseau in his sometimes crazy way tried to think of the nature of childhood in a way that did not presuppose the specific institutions of his time, it seems to me that we continue to think of the child as that-which-gets-educated-at-school and of the school as that-which-educates-the-child. As R. S. Peters's 'Education as Initiation' put it, to think about education is properly a matter of 'considering it from the point of view of the teacher's task in the classroom' (Peters 1965: 89). Nor is this only a failure of conceptual imagination; rather it reflects our implicit subjection to contextual reality: to institutional and socio-economic unshiftables. Hence the quinquennial cycle of radical packages, of toothless bullet-biting, gloved nettle-grasping and sound-bite Great Debates. Philosophers of education used to imagine that they could critically guide frameworks of schooling policy and teaching practice; secure now in the knowledge that we are ignored, might we not enjoy the luxury of irresponsible thought? How's this for an extra-curricular question: what morally educates us for middle and old age, let alone for mortality? What syllabus is that on? Perhaps we could rename old people's homes 'schools'; after all a lot of forgetting goes on there. All of which is a silly way of reminding ourselves that we are, as biosocial beings, always being well or ill-educated, morally and otherwise; that school and home are only part of our upbringing and that we need specifically to question the character of school as an environment of moral and other education.

Schools, like prisons, hospitals and asylums, emerged as architectural institutions with fairly determinate staff practices over the last two centuries or so.[2] Without espousing a Foucauldian assimilation of one to the other, the recognition of their more stable features is useful in reflecting on the failures of countless cycles of New Policies to achieve their 'goals and objectives'. Immanuel Kant, for example, who thought it would have been no loss if Tahiti had been occupied by sheep rather than by its unenlightened native humans (Kant 1991) wrote in *Education* as follows:

> It is discipline which prevents man from being turned aside by his animal impulses from humanity, his appointed end . . . By discipline men are placed in subjection to the laws of mankind and brought to feel their constraint. Children, for instance, are first sent to school, not so much with the object of their learning something but rather that they may become used to sitting still and doing exactly as they are told . . .
> The love of freedom is naturally so strong in man, that, when once he has grown accustomed to freedom, he will sacrifice everything for its sake. For this very reason, discipline must be brought into play very early; for when this has not been done, it is difficult to alter character in later life . . .
> We see this among savage nations who have never become accustomed to European manners.   (Kant 1960: 3–4)

Richard Peters used to say something similar: 'I conceive of the mind of the individual as a focus of social rules and functions relating to them . . . wishes become wants when social standards defining ends . . . and ways of attaining them become

imposed on this autistic amalgam.' (Peters 1965: 107). The school institution thus emerges as immaculately conceived for its moralising role. And so we turn to Emile Durkheim for a filling out of this philosophical programme:

> There is a whole system of rules in the school that predetermine the child's conduct. He must come to class regularly . . . at a specified time and with an appropriate bearing and attitude . . . not disrupt . . . do his homework . . . submit to a host of obligations. . . . It is through the practice of school discipline that we can inculcate the spirit of discipline in the child. . . .
> The morality of the classroom . . . an intermediary between the affective morality of the family and the more rigorous morality of civil life. . . . It is by respecting school rules that he learns to respect rules in general. It is the first initiation into the austerity of duty. Serious life has now begun.   (Durkheim 1961: 148–9).[3]

For Durkheim such regularities were not conceived as mere habituation, nor as Benthamite-Skinnerian patterns of pleasure-pain reinforcement. After Kant they were conceived as modes of introjecting into the child's soul an authoritative conscience, the inner presence in a secular age of the 'god' 'Society' as mediated through the particular school and its maîtres through its, and especially its punitive, rituals: 'The principal form of punishment has always consisted in putting the guilty on the index, ostracising him, making a void around him and separating him from decent people' (Durkheim 1961: 175). He must understand that there is something above him before which he must bow, rules he must obey because they command.

> If we renounce the option of calling upon a divine power, then we must seek another which can play the same role. . . . This power is of course society, society of which we are a part. For, in effect, society stands in relation to its members as a god stands in relation to his followers.   (Durkheim 1995: 30–1).

The constraints habitual endurance of which is integral to the everyday life experience of schooling, then, imply their own dynamic of a certain sort of moral education. Here we are talking, not only of habits, but of a developing sense of 'self' which, through identifying with the institutional icons of social authority and through sensitivity to the moral influence of praise and blame, comes to police itself, or rather those 'impulses' deemed constitutive of an 'autistic', 'barbarous' and unmoralised 'self' with which the agencies of conscience contend: 'Character-traits are internalised social rules such as honesty, punctuality, truthfulness and unselfishness. A person's character represents his own achievement, his own manner of imposing regulations upon his inclinations' (Durkheim 1966: 57).

Enter, then, the school's 'ethos' and its articulation in rules of conduct to supply the content of this developing moral character, to forge within the child authoritative dispositions which, by suppressing impulsive inclinations, will characterise his social conduct. Thus it is 'up to the individual' to comply – the child is held responsible before he is responsible so that he may become responsible. As Nietzsche (1964: 499) darkly put it: 'Men were treated as free so that they might be judged and punished, so that they might become guilty.'

Because school presents itself as a given, and because it is so much part of what we all take to be the natural landscape of growing up, it is able to supply the substance of what it is for the child to be part of 'society', of what it is to be among 'other people', to be 'one among many'. Thus, if we think of such liberal value-headlines as 'respect for persons', 'non-malificence', 'tolerance', 'autonomy', it is likely that we will forget the everyday context within which such values are supposedly being absorbed. Looking again at the New Policy advertised in the letter from school, we are reminded of that context: the room and the corridor, with their imperatives of quietness, slow movement and the need to 'keep hands feet and objects to ourselves' (hence suppressing the very impulses of friendship), not to mention hard work and attentiveness to activities which, as Sugarman says, have 'purposes hard to see'. In moral terms, this substance is a thin one, an etiolated visage of what it is to live, work and play among one's fellows. And the abstract, self-suppressive character of everyday school life's working model of morality sustains itself independently of the heroic or uplifting of assembly addresses or classroom stories and even of the depth and richness of such moral discussion as might be fitted into the classroom timetable. It is therefore little wonder that a tendency to boorish insubordination has been the perpetual accompaniment of official school songs or that the less supervised human density of the playground, with its friendships and enmities, has always been the positive preoccupation of schoolchildren.

That teachers no longer regard it as part of their duty to be in the playground reflects and reinforces its status as extra-curricular time (nowadays being squeezed because of the expense of hiring supervisory staff). But morally speaking, it is, to repeat a dense time, rich in morally relevant and impressive experience for good and for ill. It is a time of self-regulated social activity, which, being at once the expression of inclination and of more or less informal rule-guidedness subverts the moralistic dualities of authoritarian school philosophies. Piaget, indeed, made the marble-ring the front line of his attack on the establishment school and on what he took to be its chief apologist, Durkheim, whom he saw as freezing the concept of morality at an infantile, 'external', 'realist', level:

> All authority comes from Society with a big S; the schoolmaster is the priest who acts as an intermediary between society and the child, and everything therefore rests with the master and the rules are a sort of revelation which the adult dispenses to the child. (Piaget 1932: 364)

Piaget attacks Durkheim's confusion of moral virtue with submission to the 'conscience collective', insisting that children have a natural potential to respect each other, play fair, and to treat each other with generous consideration, developed through their own interactive rule-structured practices, guided, not by 'masters', but by more experienced and recognised wiser heads. Against the 'traditional' model, then, Piaget is recognisably a 'progressive', eulogising the few 'activity schools' and their method of providing an environment conducive to cooperative creative and intellectual activity. This very activity, with its dense mutual negotiation and common effort, fosters the unfolding of children's potential as moral beings. Morality, then, develops as a dimension of social practices and attitudes, with a strength, depth and subtlety commensurate with the activities that have nurtured it. It is not the voice of an authority exercising discipline over submissive activities. 'Community' in this sense is a network of cooperative activity and response rather than the authoritative higher entity monumentally placed atop Durkheim's model of 'community'. Piaget castigated the achievement of the normal school system:

> considering the large number of people who reject all discipline as soon as they have escaped from family and home ties, or who for the rest of their lives are capable only of external discipline and legal morality, it may well be that it is in spite of adult

authority, or certain kinds of adult authority, that the best of our young people sooner or later adopt a disciplined way of living.

If one thinks of the systematic resistance offered by pupils to the authoritarian method, and the admirable ingenuity employed by children the world over to evade disciplinary constraint, one cannot help regarding as defective a system which allows so much effort to be wasted instead of using it in cooperation.   (Piaget 1932: 366)

Piaget is misunderstood as the pre-Kohlbergian inventor of a rigid doctrine of developmental stages; whatever the methodological shortcomings of his empirical method, it was oriented towards a realistic appraisal of the natural potentialities that could progressively be realised by children and he went out of his way to argue that families and schools tended to atrophy such potentialities through authoritarianism, neglect, violence and understimulation. But it must be said that, for all its wonderful display of the spontaneous justice of the playground, the marbles paradigm is damagingly inadequate. As a game, marbles has its limitations, which it to a degree shares with the computer games which now absorb our own children – and which provide in reality a much richer ethical arena than the autistic paralysis of contemporary adult panic mythology – such games require limited teamwork, mutual trust, endurance and initiative. But, more to the point of this chapter, their status as games, and hence as a relieving break from the ardours of real life, vitiate their potential as an alternative paradigm. Indeed that paradigm belongs with a 'romantic' vision of childhood that shares with its authoritarian coercive antithesis the idea of childhood as essentially a 'non-age', a preparation for and protected exclusion from 'real life'. This is visible in its role in progressive conceptions and practices of schooling now under attack from the state as they were under theoretical attack by, for example, British philosophers of education. Whereas the conservative view is of the child as a little savage, a barbarian at the gate, requiring to sculpt himself in accordance with institutional programmes, the Piagetian picture is of the child as a socially playful cub, spontaneously rehearsing with his peers the roles and relationships constitutive of life in a community. Each confines attention to an assumed if differently structured world of the classroom and the playground. The moral and political minimalism entailed by this confinement is illustrated, for example, in the chapter on the com-

munitarian school in Etzioni's *The Spirit of Community*, which rightly asks us to look for a school's morally educative character, not in its moralistic utterances but in 'the set of experiences' of everyday school life:

Are the cafeterias places where students pelt each other with food and noise is overwhelming, or are they civilized places where students can conduct meaningful conversations over lunch? Are the corridors areas where muscles and stature are required to avoid being pushed aside by bullies, or are they safe conduits patrolled by faculty or by students? (Etzioni 1993: 104)

Once he recognised the constraints thwarting his broad socialist project, the pragmatic Dewey tailored his reformist energies, with powerful effect, to reforming classroom styles. But his earlier thinking and the Dewey-School example present a deeper meaning in pragmatism and help to shift the terms of discussion. The Dewey School was a micro-community all right; but it was neither a cage nor a playroom. Hence it realised in a much more serious way the 'activity' values enunciated by Piaget. Democratically devoid of assumptions about the proper activities of children that pervaded the elite progressivists of Europe, Dewey's school was predicated on an assumption of human work as the central social activity. Criticising, as Piaget was to do, the authoritarian conception of discipline as destructive of moral development, Dewey, in 1899, spoke thus of 'discipline':

As regards the spirit of the school, the chief object is to secure a free and informal community life in which each child will realise that he has a share of work to do. This is made the chief motive towards what are normally called order and discipline. It is believed that the only genuine order and discipline are those that proceed from the work that he has to do and his consciousness of the rights of others who are, like himself, taking part in this work. The emphasis in the school upon various forms of practical and constructive activity gives ample opportunity for appealing to the child's social sense and to his regard for thorough and honest work. . . . Hence the emphasis in the school laid upon social occupations, which continue and reinforce those of life outside the school, and the comparative freedom and informality accorded the children.   (Garforth (ed.) 1966: 72)

Moral education, therefore, was something that would be rooted in the early experience of the full gamut of practical life. Whereas Dewey's thinking has come to be seen as associated with dewy-eyed visions of happy classroom group activity at the expense of the sterner tasks of learning, Dewey, in his early years at least, conceived the child's moral environment as one made dense and intrinsically serious by the fact that children had to live and work, not only in classrooms, but distinctively and specifically in laboratories, workshops, farms, gardens and kitchens as well as in art and music studios. Reflection, moral and otherwise, presupposed that rich framework of occupational challenge with its own objective criteria of success:

> 'If wishes were horses, beggars would ride.' Since they are not, since really to satisfy an impulse means to work it out, and working it out means running up against obstacles, becoming acquainted with materials, exercising ingenuity, patience, persistence, alertness, it of necessity involves discipline – ordering of power – and supplies knowledge. . . .
>
> So undoubtedly the little child who thinks he would like to cook has little idea of what it means, or costs, or what it requires. . . . But here too if the impulse is exercised, it runs up against the actual world of hard conditions, to which it must accommodate itself; and here again come in the factors of discipline and knowledge.[4]

The Dewey School, then, is a microcommunity in more than a Durkheimian sense, for it is a microeconomy, an ecosystem with multiple links, themselves the occasion for educative exploration with the world beyond its gates. It is a model of 'education for democracy' by virtue of its own apprenticing practices in the give and take that constitutes democratic justice. By rejecting the dualism of adult–child which reduces childhood to time spent and consumed in a sort of waiting-room for life, Dewey offers the way through the impasse the traditional school throws up against moral education. And by reminding us that the child does not have to be conceived of as a consumer-under-constraint or as an administered beast, Dewey opens up paths that might lead beyond his still circumscribed 'utopia' of the autarchic school environment without our becoming involved in some parody of the travesty of what was supposed to be 'care in the community' for the denizens of another kind of large-scale monster: the asylum for the mentally ill.

Those who detect the odour of Scout-camp burnt sausages or Woodcraft stewed vegetables in all this will not be entirely misled by their nostrils. Although, for financial and especially insurance reasons, school camps are in my experience becoming a rarity, the camping model is in many ways an excellent paradigm of the 'discipline of experience' that Dewey is talking about. When you are camping, with your family for example, you have a micropolis where the give and take, the making and enjoying, the work and the reward, are in palpable contact with each other – and where the antithetical vices of bullying moralism and exploitative idleness are soon exposed. The camp is a place where the value of community is visible; where we contribute, not so much in order to receive as to be a part of a common life.

> Camp is practically inseparable from club. The wise founder of any club will have made mental preparation for camp before ever he opens up his club. It is a platitude, but none the less true, that a week or ten days of camp are more important than the whole of the rest of the year put together. . . . Within a few hours a boy ( . . . ) shows himself – as does the leader and his colleagues – as he really is.[5]

But camps are short – and the one-night school camp can be a nightmare of sleeplessness for elders in charge of children for whom the excitements of extra-classroom life prove 'too much'. Like boarding schools, borstals, sports clubs and families, they are also places liable through their boisterous intimacies to be arenas of perversion and authoritarian or transgressive excess. So it is with life, when deprived of the oxygen of democratic freedom. More durable are practices which are morally educative through being constitutive of social life; of conviviality, through themselves embodying and expressing relationships. These include not only 'Deweyan' activities which, while productive, are so by the deliberate contrivance and protective boundedness of the school garden and kitchen in order that competence, cooperativeness, trust and self-reliance are learned and taught. But such activities include, increasingly with age, activities which are needed 'full stop'. Here I am thinking of community-service activity at social as well as individual levels and also of the intergenerational community level of environmental care and repair. The mark of such activities, at present envisaged as proper only to delinquents, the unemployed and 'Prince's Trust' volunteers among Britain's youth, is that they are constitutive of sociality, of friendship, of fellowship, of community values. They are constitutive of 'good ways of life'. They are also, as it happens, difficult to give account of within the terms of the cash nexus and hence tend to be damagingly undervalued in the amoral working of the market economy and to have become professionally appropriated within the welfare state, whose structures and resources are being gutted by the same processes – democratically endorsed by the reluctance of the 'taxpayer', that moralistic meanie who calls out of the other side of his mouth for something to be done about moral education in our schools. Such work, however democratically orchestrated, requires professional oversight and leadership from elders and (not an identical category) those with more knowledge and experience. It also requires the erosion of the apartheid of age imposed by conventional schooling because it needs people of different ages and strengths to work together, permitting what is atrophied in our schools: the natural processes of leadership and imitation among older and younger. Schoolteachers as well as professionals might be involved in such out-of-gates activity directly, so that there is something to reflect on, discuss and learn from in a classroom situation.

We could pause here to note that Dewey's pragmatist and socialist outlook colours his conception of activity with the shade of a higher utilitarianism, with a preoccupation with the happy cooperative pursuit of shared goals, with 'function-performance'. In the democratic world for which educational experience is to be the exemplary preparation, these 'functions' include many that would have, by Plato and Aristotle and indeed the apostles of 'liberal education' through most of the ages, been deemed 'servile'. Plato's Guardians, after all, were to be kept away from material preoccupations, and Aristotle uses the unthinkable idea that young gentlemen should learn how to cook as a *reductio ad absurdum* of the proposition that a sufficient condition of something's being on the curriculum is that it should entail a useful skill (*Politics*, Book VIII, Ch. 5). Roughly, then, whereas the classical tradition mapped the contrast between the pursuit of things worthy in themselves and the things worthy to be pursued only as means onto the social contrast between the free and the menial strata, Dewey seeks to bring the social classes into the subversively creative friction of learning to make and do things needed as well as valued in themselves. Hence his emphasis, in what after all was a school for a liberal elite's offspring, on mucking out the stables and distributing the manure of social growth. Aristotle's claim that the labour of the body prevents the development of the mind and

vice versa (*Politics*, Book VIII, Ch. 4) bespeaks a philosophy and ideology which it was Dewey's chief mission to counter. Plato's more subtle but associated contrast between free and unfree bodily activity – play, dance and courageous exploit as against labour for lower ends 'necessary' or not (see *Republic*, 7; 536 e) – can, I think, be turned gently against Dewey's excessively 'pragmatist' conception of practices. But a modern conception of 'education for democracy' would need to incorporate the classical wisdom within a non-servile conception of social function as it would have to integrate Dewey's ideas of the place of what William Morris called 'useful labour' into a correction of the classical socio-conceptual dichotomy. Meanwhile we might remember one central piece of common ground among these great thinkers: you learn to become something mainly by doing the things appropriate to being that something.

In contrast, what we see about us today, with interactive activities further choked off in schools as the curriculum is narrowed, is a demand that something called 'morals' be introduced into that curriculum. In January 1997, for example, the Conservative government's Chief Curriculum Adviser, Dr Nick Tate, urged the introduction of 'ten commandments' 'which should not be called into question'. And philosophers of education worry about 'getting moral education into schools' – as if the very moral environment of schools did not have its own transmissive influence and as if teachers, whose authority in their own fields of expertise universally receives such inadequate respect, could come to be regarded as the inspiring sages such 'two extra Rs' programmes presuppose. And as if any thug or vandal could not tell you that bullying and wrecking are wrong, and even why. To hear, on the other hand, reports of teachers as unwilling illiberally to utter moral judgements raises questions about their presumption in requiring the daily attentive presence in their classrooms of their pupils – which 'commandment' does that requirement unquestioningly invoke? What we see here is a fanatical redoubling of expected efforts in a situation where the impoverished conditions of such efforts' success are being increasingly starved. No doubt 'our competitors' are morally outdoing us. Dr Tate attacks teachers' concern to build 'self-esteem' in the absence of real virtue. ('1. Lots of praise and encouragement.') Teachers rightly respond that their pupils, lacking self-esteem, lack the courage to take on tasks and the capacity to appreciate each other. But all this ignores the lack of esteem in children for the tasks they are set and the consequent artificiality of bulk-feeding self-esteem into an unvalued arena. Like respect, esteem entails attention and care; it cannot be doled out. Esteem properly entails recognition of quality, and expressions of esteem are felicitous only when both the judge's perception and the activity are appreciated by the receiver. Otherwise they function as something else: as indices of what will please authority. In the absence of this, neither Skinnerian praise nor Tateful blame can achieve their putative moral objective.

The National Forum for Values in Education and Community, instituted by Dr Tate, was briefly on the verge of commending the idea of 'compulsory community service' to the Conservative government (*Daily Telegraph*, 13 Aug. 1996, p. 1). But what attracted members to the idea was reported as the thought that 'it would be an activity where pupils' performance could be assessed, thus ensuring that schools took it seriously'. Dr Tate cannot see that, far from opening up the community as an arena for the activity of young people and transforming the location of schools in the ethical substance of modern life, this curriculisation of community service would be calculated to turn it into playground fatigue-at-large and a daytime nightmare for ill-equipped and overburdened teachers. By instrumentalising all this into the terms of a term report, the Forum's advisers have infected a notion which needs to be embodied in terms of the intrinsic constituents of the dignity of citizenship with the narrow authoritarianism of the traditional classroom. Thus are even the brightest ideas dulled by the managerial consciousness on which they dawn. Thus do ideas about the development of initiative, cooperation, self-reliance and self-discipline surface as the rationale for promoting the general instituting of school cadets, which some will recall as the parade ground and nursery of all sorts of nastiness. (Of course, my memories are only of Australia in the 1940s and 1950s; British military traditions are no doubt bereft of such boorishness . . . 'Sorry, no squaddies'.)

Teachers have always found the individual-in-community focus of their colleges of teaching a misleading preparation for the disillusioning experiences of classroom management. The reigning powers, making a virtue of necessity, now prescribe that teachers' training be just that, a 'skills' training in delivery-through-management.

This chapter focuses on moral education; but the ethics and substance of enquiry requires its own treatment. Among others, Alan Thomas in two articles for the *Oxford Review of Education* (Thomas 1992 and 1994), amasses considerations that would seem to puncture the illusion that a toughened reactionary regime will suffice to deliver our children well educated into the millennium. Even within their blind vision of an educated mind, the authoritarian backlashers have recipes only for continued disaster. It will remain the university teacher's experience, if she still finds herself in a sufficiently intimate position to ask the student 'But what do you think?', to be met by a look of bemused panic by her well-schooled student. Moral heteronomy and intellectual lifelessness are bound together in the truss of managed passivity.

While government spokespersons and their advisers seek to frighten schools into frightening their pupils with, if not now hell, then some functionally surrogate earthly sanction, philosophers have been excited by the prospect of a genuine introduction into schools of moral education that would be education in a sense deeper than either habituation or indoctrination and imply an enlightened sense of what it is to be a moral being beyond being a tame animal. My argument has been that the school environment is itself too thin a moral arena to provide the basis for the reflective discussion of moral issues projected. Abstracted from rich mutual experience and under the eyes even of a 'non-assessing' teacher, moral discussion can come to be something one is 'good at' independently of how good one is. Within a 'Deweyan' view, on the contrary, where the discussion might arise as reflection on the difficulties, conflicts and lessons of everyday shared activity, the discussors are themselves 'on the line' and the discussion is itself a moral activity requiring mutual respect, mutual listening, a sense of fairness and of common endeavour. That someone might be 'bullshitting' in respect to their own manifest values therefore becomes a genuine issue, not something completely to be set aside as an irrelevance to the issue and argument 'as such'. Ethics, morals, concern our actions and reactions, our initiatives, attentions and responses, and the development of moral judgement is inextricably bound up with this. I have been urging the practical shortfalls of the school as an environment of moral development and treatments of the role in schools of moral discussion may tend to import that poverty. For, morally speaking, it is courage, disinterestedness, patience and mutual trust and attention that mark a good discussion as much as does the content of what is brought up – the dialogue about morality is itself a moral event. And so, as has been emphasised, the form of education implies its own curriculum; discussion entails children learning to take themselves and others seriously in a pattern of give and take that is not only an echo of Piaget's examples of learning through play but is a microcosm of freedom, justice and fellowship. This is to get away from the idea that discussion in this area is a mere deference to the supposed facts of 'multiculturalism' or to the disparity of 'opinions', hence as an exception to the educational rule, where, because truth is held to be uncontroversial, the method of learning through discussion might be deemed by some to be inappropriate. But discussion and its habit takes time; and not to give it that time is to signal a disvaluing both of reflection and of conversation. Where is there space for this time on the school timetable? More fundamental to this chapter's burden: how can we expect children to be moral discussors if their lives as moral agents are so limited as they are by their status as schoolchildren? How are young people, accorded the respect and attention to opinion necessary to moral discussion, to be reconciled with their subject status outside the arena of such discussion? No wonder the promise of 'moral education' is now being delivered in the form of inducement and indoctrination towards conformity. A symptomatic question: how many thought- and discussion-provoking stories suitable for moral discussion concern themselves with school, let alone that tip of school's iceberg which is avowably visible to teachers?

There is an impasse here. Progressivism in schools is under fire from the right; but it is already rendered combustible by the utopianism of thinking that children's natural dispositions and potential could in our era be realised, certainly at a 'mass' level, within the spatial framework of the school and within the temporal context of family life at one end and economic and political life at the other. Politicians and 'traditionalists' seek to echo Durkheim in his transubstantial quest to transfer the mystical authority of the priest to the teacher. But today there is no such authority to be transferred; hence the pathos in the idea of schools regaining the dubious patriarchal dignity they (sometimes) once had. The law-and-order party(ies) could not raise the resources to pay enough staff to police all

that, let alone to offer teachers a salary commensurate with the purported dignity and status of their mission and sufficient to signify to pupils that these people are important figures in society. At the same time, with 'education', for all the moral talk, seen in terms of 'equipping' young people with the 'skills' and 'flexibility' needed to survive in an unedifyingly globalising economy, it is hard for schoolchildren to think of themselves as in anything but a fairly tedious antechamber to an uninviting adult life. What space is there here for the child's idealism to express itself otherwise than in sentimental dreams – to be 'outgrown' ever sooner?

Dr Tate wants schools to be a bulwark against the demoralising and decivilising forces at work in the wider society: inadequate parenting, 'consumerism and pop culture consumerism especially'. He laments teachers' failure, through their own irreligion and 'relativism' to 'transmit' resistance to these forces. At least this shows an awareness of schooling's place as but part of a morally educating environment. But, then, in a way, this has always been recognised and systems of education have normally been prophylactically motivated. For Plato (who by the way supported learning by free play (*Republic*, 536), it was the narrow partiality of family affections that rendered the private home an unsuitable place for guardians to grow up in (*Republic*). Locke (another who opposed the 'public' school as 'ruinous' to young gentlemen) berated the narrowness and soft indulgence of the motherly upbringing offered by his bourgeois contemporaries. 'School' he wanted reserved for 'the children of labouring people' who, by his account, either wandered neglected at large or deprived their mothers of 'the liberty to work'. In either case they were 'an ordinary burden to the parish'.

> The most effectual remedy for this that we are able to conceive, and which we therefore humbly propose, is that . . . working schools be set up in every parish, to which the children of all such as demand relief of the parish, above three and under fourteen years of age, whilst they live at home with their parents and are not otherwise employed for their livelihood by the allowance of the overseers of the poor, shall be obliged to come. (Quick (ed.) 1884: 189–90)

At this 'school' the children were to spend much of their time in industrial work, save on Sundays when they would be obliged 'to be brought into some sense of religion'. 'Spinning and knitting' were to constitute weekday schoolwork – Locke mentions nothing else that will be required. Thus the young would be adequately fed, 'inured to work', 'made sober and industrious all their lives after' and be a minimal burden to parents and parish, 'whereas ordinarily now they are as utter strangers both to religion and morality as they are to industry'.

We have noted already the mistrust toward family life of J. S. Mill, who added in his *On the Subjection of Women* (1869) that the patriarchal home was typically a school of sexist bullying. We need to beware, then, of invoking a 'traditional' world in which, even in the terms of moral conformism, families and schools dovetailed to form a stable unit of moral and civil architecture. And we need to beware of appeals in the name of 'traditional' structures and functions that accompany the mutual buck-passing among parents, employers, public-service professionals, 'the media' and politicians that characterises contemporary 'debate' about civil life and the child's introduction to it. All these institutional persons might be said to constitute a dysfunctional but frighteningly stable 'family'.

But there are changes significant for moral education in family life:

> In the 1960s and 1970s the entire structure of the family has begun to shift. The nuclear family is crumbling – to be replaced, I think, by the free floating couple, a marital dyad subject to dramatic fissions and fusions, and without the orbiting satellites of pubertal children, close friends or neighbours . . . just the relatives, hovering in the background, friendly smiles on their faces.[6]

Although it can never match the electronic speed of capital movement, labour has to flow ever faster to where it is demanded, destroying communities, breaking up extended family bonds and splitting even the nuclear units of children's parents. Female labour – cheaper, casualised, deskillable – has become, as it was in the early days of the industrial revolution, more market-friendly than that of males. In contrast to the 'fallen woman' of Victorian myth and reality, the modern woman is no longer compelled to be attached to a male bread-winner and guarantor of respectability. Divorce and separation are now common – to the extent that every time our nine-year-old finds my wife and me disagreeing, let alone arguing, he is moved in panic to play the Pope. So, in caricaturing brief, we have a situation where, not only is the father's member-

ship and presence problematic; the mother is, with less informal and intimate support than she may have previously taken for granted, in a conflict between her Lockean 'liberty to work' and her need to tend her young children. Or should that read: her need to work and her liberty to be with her children? Yet, at the same time and for many of the same global reasons, children spend more time within this domestic environment, not only as a would-be place of safety and security from the perceived menace of 'strangers', but because they prefer the stimulus of media fictions of anxiety and aspiration to the dullness and social tenuousness of hanging around in streets and parks. Time given to children may be scarce here; but for similar reasons children are expected to make a contribution to domestic life. Children are thus at once infantilised into the habits of domestic passivity and, hyper-conscious of a stressful, violent and cynical adult world, deprived of the active, playful, adventurous and make-believing dimensions of childhood. And when we add the neglect, hostility, violence and abuse that mark so much contemporary home life, it is no wonder that school itself can be a peaceful and attentive interlude to some children and can be dreamt of by some as the treatment for society's ills.

Traditional sexist structures guaranteed that, whereas boys were 'always the problem', girls, identifying with their caring, dutiful and forbearing mothers through the imitative bonds of domesticity, would, whatever the limitations of their moral horizons, be well-behaved in school and attentive to their (at first largely female) teachers. Nowadays, with men making slow if discernible motion towards filling it, women's forced/chosen move from the home creates a relative vacuum in domestic life, exposing girls, in a new way, to the 'hardening' buffets familiar to growing boys. It is in this context that moves to legislate for paternal responsibility and for parent–school 'contracts' (predicated on a dubious promise that school 'training' will be rewarded with a good job) are relevant to the topic of moral education. For, in isolation from a wider social criticism, they promise, once the heat dies down, to do little more than add to the moralistic pressures on failing institutions and on the women that are in their front line. Family life needs the 'space' as well as the time for it to provide the basis of mutual love, trust and significance that are preconditions of good qualities of character. It is right that bringing children into and up in the world is no longer seen as a largely 'private' matter

– Mill saw this. But it is wrong that social intervention in the family is seen as a quasi-police or civil-contract operation, as something to be imposed through surveillance within the crippling dualism of 'society-versus-the-individual' or more 'optimistically' within the terms of the individual parent's 'interest in his and/or her child'. Social life, in other words, needs to open up to families as a natural extension to and natural connection with their domestic life. Here, perhaps, the fact that contemporary 'housing associations' typically include at least in practice an association of households in child minding (it is an insult to what minding is to avoid this derogated cliché), not only to enable parents to work or go out, but more positively in organising and securing facilities for activities for or involving children. 'Neighbourhood' is thus spontaneously institutionalised so that instead of the 'parenting deficit' bringing social accountants unwelcome to the individual front door, it is addressed cooperatively, with, by the way, professional support and backup. Moving in a cross-age space of reciprocity and activity among trusted others, then, the child has some scope to develop virtues, to acquire character through struggling with difficulties. If schools' organisation were such as to flow into and within such democratic structures, how different schools would be. And if families came to think of such associations as part of their life, how different they would be.

The moral suffocation in our contemporary home–school symbiosis demeans young and old alike. Here is a countervailing image, taken from a publication of the National Institute of Adult Continuing Education. It concerns a project in Malvani, a suburb of Bombay:

> This project is just one example of the innovative health education work of the Child-to-Child movement. Children are trained to diagnose and refer common illnesses within the home and community. The inclusion of work which is primarily with children and not adults illustrates the fact that in some societies 'children' have to assume a high level of responsibility early on and are therefore often part of the non-formal education constituency. . . . The peer group methods used are equally applicable to adults, as is the notion of 'lifelong' education, a concept that stresses the importance of seeing education as a continuum linking school, home and community.

Education can be more than just preparation for life in the future; it can also be participation in present life.

Malvani houses 100,000 people. The innovative project, which started in 1978, runs from a health centre in the area, responsible to a Bombay hospital and medical school. The initial purpose was to develop an effective health education programme to reduce the need for curative medicine. The idea of working with children occurred by chance when doctors were running a scheme to provide 4000 children with one nutritious meal daily. They found children to be immensely effective motivators. A team of seven trained health workers and doctors started work in local vernacular and English-speaking schools with 175 10–12-year-old children. They ran two-hour health education classes around a series of defined projects: anaemia, vitamin B complex deficiency and malaria. During the first year they trained as many as 617 volunteer health workers. Classes, which are now twice weekly, are held after school (in India children attend school for half the day), and continue at the health centre with plays, dance, song and charades on health themes.

The educational methods in this project involve children centrally in their learning and are in sharp contrast to other parts of their schooling. They learn the essential facts of a health topic through activity-based approaches, perhaps self-examination or peer-group surveys, and then extend this into the community, using interview sheets with their own and five other families in the immediate neighbourhood. The children keep meticulous records, which are subjected to rigorous monitoring by the team.

Conflict with the traditional school curriculum is a problem. The kinds of task the children are asked to perform are described by Neeta, a 10-year-old:

> We visit our families once a week. We take scales to monitor the growth of babies and seeds and pulses with high nutritional value. We also take the salt and sugar solution ORS (oral rehydration solution) to give to children suffering from diarrhoea, then we check for anaemia, malnutrition and scabies.   (McGivney and Murray 1991: 34–5)

When 'multiculturalism' is discussed, there is regularly invoked a picture of relations among 'communities', perhaps 'ethnic groups' that is analogous to the image of the relation of 'the individual to society' that has been the principal target of this chapter. Just as the moral life of the individual is seen as the regulated non-maleficence of the constrained beast, so the civic interactions of the well-adjusted plurality of 'communities' is seen in terms of the restrained respect for common rules of suspicious engagement – the self-watchful neighbour. This formalism, this consciously 'thin' and 'minimal' regulation, supposedly leaves each community content in the isolated enjoyment of its 'distinctive' 'thick' system of values, traditions, ideals and practices. Thus is fostered the ideal of the national and local state institutions functioning like ideal referees of a contest, with the corollary assumption that the unconstrained 'nature' of these collective entities is to fight in rivers of blood. With that is abandoned the ideal, and educative practices of, a common local, regional, national and international culture that has a density in its criss-crossing affiliation and not only in its supposedly elemental constituents. Whereas, at the moment we have the fiasco of a 'multiculturalism' that supposedly affirms the boy of Afro-Caribbean background sporting his Rasta colours or 'Attitude' caps, the sporting of the British national flag would (rightly) be taken as a white supremacist assertion. Thus the pleasant irony that whereas there is a rich symbolism of 'ethnicity' among minorities inhibited in the sense that here is their home, those precisely who are supposedly very much at home are so devoid of natively nurtured eloquence that they sing 'Swing Low, Sweet Chariot' as their national rugby song. Given Britain's history as a conquering and colonising power, and as a country whose proprietary idioms, images and icons were nurtured in times preceding both its decline from greatness and its large-scale incorporation of non-white immigrants, it is inevitable that its patriotic signifiers would be both nostalgic and, in effect, racially inflected. But such troublesome givens are overlaid by the dominantly abstract discourses of political and civil morality, with its disinterred notion of territoriality and citizenship: contracts of non-maleficence. Thus does a neurotic phobia that national history is nationalistic history and that national geography (– tell me what the main British east-coast rivers are –) is the 'real' home of the natively descendent population inhibit the creative and lovingly critical exploration of this country and its regions' past and present – or future. Such cognitive lacunae are visible also in a literature curriculum whose gutting is mocked in the way 'commonwealth' authors as freely play with their 'imperial' literary texts as commonwealth sports-

people play with their heritage of bats and balls. But these criticisms of the school syllabus and its boring attempt at inoffensive thinness need complementing by the criticism of the cramped arenas of moral education of people who are to make their lives together in places that they might deeply love with a sense of shared, if conflictual and tarnished, times, past, present and future.

A 'multicultured' society that seeks to freeze in place 'hot', 'thick' ethnicities within the frame of a thin and minimalist 'cold' politics of self-interest and mutual 'respect' is a society waiting for the next explosion. A democratic and liberal education in and for the moral life must move beyond these phoney and inefficacious compounds. Educative experience, as the basis and reference point of reflection and imagination, has always been in subtle and sometimes inevitably crude critical and creative tension with given traditions, practices and outlooks. In this sense the very idea of education is 'multicultural'. Protective talk of 'respecting boundaries' blocks from attention the fact that respect and negotiation of boundaries is the very stuff of any enduring relationship, from the most intimate to the most impersonal. That is why the noisy but largely congenial pluralism of the playground or public park is a better model of moral education than the mutual non-interference of the classroom. This is not to deny the value of tolerance, respect or harmlessness; it is to assert that these values have their skeletal place in human intercourse. But in the absence of young people learning together to share and shape their common destiny, to love and understand their common world as the environment of their lives, all the fine rules and sermons and crackdowns will do nothing but hasten the day when things get 'really out of hand'.

## Notes

1 US government publication of statement of 77 authorities, quoted in D. Tyack, *Turning Points in American Educational History*, Waltham, Mass., 1967, p. 325.
2 See for example D. Rothman, *The Discovery of the Asylum*, Boston: Little, Brown & Company, 1971.
3 Barry Sugarman, in his excellent *The School and Moral Development* (London: Croom Helm, 1973), presented this aspect in a less enchanted way:

'Impulse-control and deferred gratification are highly institutionalised in the school . . . further developing these patterns of control on top of the beginning which their families may have made.... [The child is] required to spend most of his time sitting in the required seat . . . not allowed to talk freely or to interact with peers.... Intrinsically attractive activities are supposed to be put aside in favour of others whose purpose is hard to see, but which are demanded by teachers.' (p. 13)

4 J. Dewey (1915 (1900)) *The School and Society*, rev. edn, Chicago: University of Chicago Press, pp. 38–9. In a nonfundamentalist sense, this is my bible, despite its lack of talk of games and sports and make-believe, and for all its earnestness.

5 B. L. Q. Henriques, *Club Leadership*, Oxford: Oxford University Press, 1993, p. 140.

6 Concluding chapter 'Towards the Postmodern Family' in Canadian author Edward Shorter's *The Making of Modern Family Life*, now more than 20 years 'out of date' (London: Collins, 1976), p. 273.

# References

Durkheim, E. (1961) *Moral Education*, London: Macmillan.

Durkheim, E. (1966) *Ethics and Education*, London: Allen & Unwin.

Durkheim, E. (1995) 'The Teaching of Morality in Schools', trans. W. S. F. Pickering, *Journal of Moral Education*, 24: 30–1.

Etzioni. A. (1993) *The Spirit of Community*, New York: Crown.

Garforth, F. W. (ed.) (1966) *John Dewey, Selected Educational Writings*, London: Heinemann.

Kant, I. (1960) *Education*, Ann Arbor: University of Michigan Press.

Kant, I. (1991) *Political Writings*, ed. H. Reiss, Cambridge: Cambridge University Press.

McGivney, V. and Murray, F. (1991) *Adult Education in Development*, Leicester: National Institute of Adult Continuing Education.

Nietzsche, F. (1964) 'Twilight of the Idols', in W. Kaufmann (ed.), *The Portable Nietzsche*, New York: Viking.

Peters, R. S. (1965) 'Education as Initiation', in R. S. Archambault (ed.) *Philosophical Analysis and Education*, London: Routledge.

Piaget, J. (1932) *The Moral Judgement of the Child*, London: Routledge & Kegan Paul.

Quick, R. H. (ed.) (1884) *Locke on Education*, Cambridge: Cambridge University Press.

Thomas, A. (1992) 'Individualised Teaching', *Oxford Review of Education*, 18.1: 59–74.

Thomas, A. (1994) 'Conversational Learning', *Oxford Review of Education*, 20.1: 131–42.

# 7 Manifestations of Relativism and Individualism in Moral Judgments of Individuals: Implications for Moral Education

## MORDECAI NISAN

Discussions of recent trends in people's moral beliefs and values have been based mainly on cultural sources, such as philosophical investigations and works of literature and art, and on sociological findings about general trends in Western society. These data are supposed to inform us about "social representations" which have taken root in people's beliefs and values. However, we may find a large disparity between people's social representations and the application of their beliefs in practice. For example, in the face of a concrete situation a person may wish to discard a relativistic position, even if she apparently shares society's dominant conception to this effect. Consequently, to arrive at an adequate picture of the changes that have occurred in ethical beliefs it would appear essential to examine how people actually apply them – a useful realm might be decision-making in situations of moral dilemmas. An investigation of this kind, besides producing a more accurate picture and sharpening distinctions that may be largely imperceptible at the declarative level, can also illuminate the conditions and boundaries of shifts in attitude. This is a secondary aim of the present chapter. Drawing on the results of some of my empirical studies on moral choice, I will consider people's perceptions of the validity and obligatory nature of moral norms and values. The primary aim of the paper, though, is to reflect on the implications of such changes for moral education.

My point of departure will be two central trends said to inform ethical thinking in recent generations: value relativism and individualism. By the relativistic trend I mean the transition from belief in an absolute order possessing a compelling logic, which leaves no room for insoluble problems, to skepticism about the possibility of such an order, about the validity of values, and about the existence of "rational" solutions to the problems we face. By the thrust to individualism I refer to the shift from the idea that society takes priority in behavioral and value decisions, to the view that priority accrues to each individual's rights, desires, and personal duties. These changes have significant normative aspects, which are discussed in the sociological literature (e.g., Bellah et al. 1985). Here, however, I am concerned with the descriptive aspect: how the changes – in a broad sense – are expressed in the thinking of people in our culture, as manifested in their moral decisions.

It goes without saying that ordinary people do not carry with them an elaborate simulacrum of the changes that have been mentioned, and generally will not be able to describe them, either. Certainly the subtle, complex distinctions made by philosophers (e.g., concerning relativism, Wong 1984) are beyond the ken of the ordinary person. However, there is every reason to expect that far-reaching changes in the cultural perception of ethics will be manifested in the moral judgment of individuals. We will expect to find greater readiness to give weight to personal considerations in the face of moral considerations or considerations of the society at large, and a degree of uncertainty in the existence of a clear, binding moral "truth." The question of whether such trends truly reflect relativism (and individualism) or are also explicable within the framework of conventional moral conceptions, is an open question for philosophical inquiry. Our aim here is to identify changes of this kind, not to determine their exact characterization.

The discussion is based on material collected in recent years by means of interviews and questionnaires in which subjects were asked about their actual and hypothetical behavior in the face of moral dilemmas. These studies did not set out, originally, to investigate the contemporary belief and value system, still less modifications it may have undergone. Their initial purpose was, more modestly, to test hypotheses about judgments and decisions in cases of moral dilemmas and to glean information about the development of moral judgment. However, repeated reading of the material suggests that it can in fact shed light on the perception of values in our society and suggest some useful insights about the changes that have occurred in that domain. Needless to say, neither the findings nor the analysis below make any pretension to describe the "prevailing view" or to present a comprehensive overview of how relativism and individualism may pervade ethical beliefs and values. My assumption is that the arguments to be raised are ingrained in the outlook of a significant segment of the society I am investigating.

If this be the case, the implications for moral and value education may be profound. I shall address that question in the concluding section of the chapter. My central proposition will be that an important anchor of moral commitment today is the individual's personal identity, and that schools can help stabilize that anchor by positing a comprehensive conception of "good" (rather than confining themselves to morality in the limited sense of the term) while also exposing pupils to other conceptions of the good. But before I set forth my thoughts on the subject, and as a background to them, I will present my findings and interpretations on manifestations of relativism (in the next section) and of individualism (in the section thereafter) in people's moral judgment.

## Relativism in moral judgment

The descriptive claim regarding moral relativism holds that perhaps for the first time in the history of Western civilization, relativism in its various guises is accepted (to a certain extent) among the dominant segment of society and not only among a minority group, and is considered legitimate rather than socially deviant. In the past, people may have disagreed about what constituted the good and the worthy; however, they had no doubt that such truths existed and that one should live one's life by their lights. Whereas nowadays it is quite widely accepted that "it all depends on one's point of view" – in other words, it is futile to look for absolute truths, and opinions and values reflect cultural conventions or individuals' mindsets.

The proposition being put forward here is not philosophical but psychological; it relates to the perception of morality and values entertained by individuals in our society. To the philosophical undermining of moral objectivity – an argument as old as the Sophists – it adds the claim that this approach is taking root in ordinary people's minds. We shall call this attitude psychological relativism. By arguing that people accept the undermining of morality, this claim calls into question the possibility of moral education, whether from the cognitive standpoint – education for understanding the good and the right – or from the motivational standpoint, i.e., recognizing and adopting reasons for applying the criterion of the good in decision-making and in concrete behavior.

The claim that individuals take a relativistic view of morality does not accord with the accepted psychological conception of morality (e.g., Kurtines & Gewirtz (eds) 1991). There, morality is perceived as a system of beliefs and attitudes in regard to the good and the right, which are held to possess absolute, binding validity, independent of chance thoughts and inclinations of individuals or even societies. The various approaches to the development of moral judgment all assume the existence in a person of such a perception of the good and the right. Indeed, the primary challenge of the psychological explanations of morality is to account for these qualities of moral judgment, of its being perceived as objective and obligatory. The explanations which have been offered to explain moral development – the emergence of conceptual structures engendered by the attempt to confer meaning on social experience (Piaget, Kohlberg); or the development of a super-ego through identifying with one's parents in a process of resolving an inner conflict (Freud); or the learning and adoption of social norms out of respect for society and its authorities (Durkheim); or through imitation and reinforcement (social learning theory) – all grapple with the most vexatious question about morality. This question is: why do people accept morality as objective, binding truth and therefore behave accordingly, or if they deviate from the moral imperative are filled with guilt or shame, in spite of the fact that these actions and emotions seem opposed to the major driving force of behavior – maximization of individual pleasure and utility. The claim of psychological relativism subverts this accepted picture and calls for a redefinition of morality and indeed of our overall conception of psychic structures. But this is beyond the present subject.

Before turning to examine the manifestations of moral relativism in my studies, I must comment on an important approach to the study of moral development in recent years, which disputes the claim of relativism and ostensibly demonstrates that moral norms are in fact perceived as absolute. I refer to the domain theory of Turiel and his colleagues (Turiel 1983). Their studies suggest that subjects of various ages distinguish between social conventions, perceived as dependent on social agreement, and moral norms, perceived to possess an inner validity that holds at all times and places. Although other studies suggest that the distinction between moral norms and social conventions is itself culture-dependent (Nisan 1987, Shweder, Mahapatra, & Miller 1987), this does not deny the claim that people judge certain norms (which *they* consider moral) as absolute rather than relative.

However, this understanding of the findings on the distinctions between morality and conventions is disputable. It is necessary to distinguish between the perception of behavior as intrinsically bad in a pragmatic sense and in a morally binding sense. Norms such as "Thou shalt not kill" or "Thou shalt not steal" are indeed perceived from the outset as possessing a "reason" independent of time and place. But this perception may involve acceptance of their pragmatic logic and still not carry a sense of personal obligation. The norms I have mentioned, perhaps in common with all norms judged as absolute, involve harm to human welfare or to justice, and such harm is indeed not time- or place-contingent. So it is not surprising that both children and adults perceive such norms as possessing absolute validity, independent of social convention; they also will hold (in fact, will agree with the prevailing norms) that such actions should be outlawed. But we should distinguish between evaluation of behavior as deleterious to human welfare, and as such intrinsically "bad," and its second-order evaluation, following reflection (not necessarily at this moment), as personally binding.

This distinction between the "pragmatic," inherent in the act, and reflective, inferred by the individual, senses of obligation seems to be important for understanding psychological moral relativism. The distinction between morality and conventions shows that in first-order evaluation, which is related to the pragmatic level, the typical moral norms are

indeed perceived as non-contingent. However, the claims about a relativistic view of morality refer to the reflective rather than the pragmatic perception of obligation. If we imagine an artificial separation between a stage of the (immediate) perception of an act's moral content and a stage entailing its reflective evaluation, we can say that after an act is perceived immediately as "bad" (because it harms people's welfare, for example), it is still left to the individual to evaluate the full meaning of that initial perception. Relativism can follow from that second-order evaluation. One may decide that one's immediate perception of the act as bad has no binding force. If the judgment is not accompanied by a personal commitment, it does not carry an obligation. It will be perceived as one of several considerations. When this happens, the moral norm has lost two of its central features: its strong obligatory status and its over-riding of all other considerations. These may be taken as manifestations of psychological relativism.

Such a devaluation in the status of moral considerations emerges in some of my research, in which I investigated a phenomenon I called "limited morality" (Nisan 1985, 1993). In these studies I was concerned with breaches of morality. Using interviews and questionnaires, I reconfirmed what has always been known: that people permit themselves to violate moral norms in order to satisfy personal needs. However, and here there may, after all, be something new, I also found that in many cases people do this believing, even calculating, that such deviations from the moral norm do not make them bad. In other words, these departures from the norm are not due to error, weakness of will, or the deliberate jettisoning of morality; rather, people feel that they possess a sort of sanction or right to stray occasionally from the moral way. In my research I posited the thesis of the "moral balance," according to which people take the liberty of straying from the norm when they feel satisfied that overall they maintain an "acceptable" moral balance, based on their commissions and omissions over time, and do not seek to attain moral perfection.

Two points in regard to the phenomenon of limited morality should be stressed here: first, people's perception that they are "allowed," occasionally, to violate a moral imperative; and second – this follows from the first point – their positing of a personal interest as possessing a "legitimate" status *vis-à-vis* the moral consideration. For example, students who insist that cheating on exams is morally indefensible empathize with a student who cheated if they are told that the exam was critical for his future (as opposed to a situation when the exam is not thus characterized). As this example shows, for many "ordinary" people moral norms have lost their absolute force and may be subordinated to other considerations, including personal interests. It will be noticed, however, that this attitude does not reflect a "psychopathic" discarding or ignoring of morality, but exists, supposedly, "while staying within the realm of morality." Subjects who expressed attitudes along these lines or reported moral deviations they themselves had committed not only defined themselves as "moral people," they also revealed that it is important for them to be moral. Yet, as they see it, moral norms do not possess absolute force, necessarily over-riding other considerations. They are amenable to the individual's evaluation as to the weight they carry in behavioral decisions. This approach acknowledges the special status of morality: people apparently consider it more important to maintain a moral balance than to maintain other "balances." The point is that the decision about how to act whenever a moral consideration arises is left to the individual and is not seen as coerced by any sort of authority.

Another facet of this form of relativism, less blatant but no less meaningful, is the reaction of students to dilemmas that represent a conflict between two important values, such as between morality and personal fulfillment (Nisan 1993; an example I used: a scientist who has to decide whether to go abroad on a longed-for sabbatical in a first-rate research lab, leaving his elderly, infirm parents on their own). Confronted with such quandaries, students will frequently say that there is no single solution, that every person has the right to decide according to his or her considerations, that the answer depends not only on the values one upholds but also on personal circumstances. Such responses present an attitude radically at odds with the Enlightenment conception of a well-ordered system of values, in which every problem has an attainable solution (Berlin 1990). Our subjects' responses effectively challenged every aspect of that outlook. Yet they also presented a positive alternative: in place of the "right" solution we now have the personal solution, the individual's private choice. The less "relativistic" version of this conception is that the choice is an individual one

because every person's situation is different and general solutions are not possible. The more relativistic version is that everyone has the right to solve the problem as they wish and that personal choices have their own validity and force. Subjects presented both versions in the reasons they gave for their decisions.

We are thus faced with two manifestations of relativism in people's ethical judgment: one involving the status of morality, the other its validity. The first assails not the validity of moral norms but their status. The inner logic of commandments such as "Thou shalt not steal," which derives from what is perceived as basic conditions for social existence and welfare, is not refuted by skepticism. However, even moral imperatives which possess solid inner logic and are not held in doubt by people, are not considered obligatory in a full sense. Not only have they lost their special status as over-riding all other norms and considerations (those which are not part of the moral realm), they have also lost their "hard" obligatory dimension. Although their sheer quality may still endow them with a distinctive status, they may be rejected in the face of non-moral considerations. If so, their status is relative to other considerations, and at the same time, as noted above, relative to personal circumstances, including what I called the individual's moral balance. However, we should reiterate that even in this manifestation of relativism morality receives a special status, revealed in the wish to preserve moral identity or moral balance. Moreover, there appear to be norms ("don't kill") which people accept as possessing an almost absolute force, which to violate would be unthinkable, and which apparently repel any possible "relativistic" approach by the force of their pragmatic logic or social status.

The second manifestation of relativism, which is related to the more frequent use of the term, involves the justification and validity of values. This expression of relativism applies mainly to norms and values which lack clear intrinsic or pragmatic logic. These are usually social and personal values associated with the concept of the good, and involving one's flourishing and development; however, they may also be values associated with doing harm to other individuals or to society as a whole. Here, relativism is manifested in questioning the actual validity of the accepted values and not only their status or social weight. People are often willing to countenance and legitimate a position that rejects an accepted value, their point of departure being that the value in question rests on a personal foundation and that in such cases everyone has the right to decide individually and act accordingly.

Still, even this expression of relativism does not reflect a nihilistic approach which denies outright the existence of valid values. In most cases, it takes the position that different, even opposing values, are valid according to individual choice – a sort of ethical pluralism, which does not necessarily imply ethical relativism. When subjects say that certain decisions are justified or "legitimate" they are, after all, acknowledging that some sort of justification or legitimacy, hence also validity, exists with respect to the decisions and their underlying values. This validity cannot be anchored in an "objective" foundation, for that would leave no room for the multiplicity of parallel "valid" values, which are not altogether mutually compatible. It must be a different sort of validity (discussed in the following section).

To sum up this section: an analysis of responses to moral dilemmas reveals an attitude which we can call limited psychological relativism. On the one hand, "not everything goes": the validity of norms or values possessing necessary inner or pragmatic logic – those that are a precondition for the existence of interpersonal relations and for the maintenance of society – is recognized. However, even these norms have lost their strong obligatory and overriding status. On the other hand, with respect to norms and values of other types – those lacking a clear pragmatic logic, those relating to social or personal good and not involving acute harm to others or to society – a readiness exists to question the absolute nature of their validity. Yet, even that questioning does not cut the ground from under values in general. The responses of subjects in the interviews suggest a new type of legitimacy and validity. It is that type of legitimacy which underlies the concept of ethical pluralism: the view that different and incompatible values and norms may be valid for different people.

## The individualist thrust in moral judgment

The sweeping, multiple-faceted thrust toward individualism in the modern era has been discussed extensively in various areas of the social sciences (e.g., Bellah et al. 1985). Here I am limiting myself

to some of its manifestations in making judgments about moral dilemmas. We should keep in mind that such a restrictive approach may cause us to lose sight of the broad view of individualism as a comprehensive orientation (for a discussion from the psychological standpoint, see Markus & Kitayama 1991) as opposed to its more limited manifestations.

Relativism and individualism in moral judgment are intertwined. The absence of transcendent, absolute truths, combined with an instrumental approach to society, makes man himself "the measure of all things." Human beings, with their needs, traits, consciousness, inclinations, and will, become the sole source and criterion for conferring meaning and direction on any evaluation. Of course, anthropocentrism is hardly a recent innovation, but as some thinkers suggest (see, for example, the discussion by Sandel 1982), the individualistic trend has developed lately to an extreme level, granting decisive weight to personal, subjective will, in contradistinction to objective reason. This is the sense of the individualism I will address in this chapter: ascribing importance to the individual's will, as opposed to demands made by society or, ostensibly, by abstract principles.

The manifestations of individualism in the realm of value judgments can be depicted as laid on a continuum, which extends from insistence on the individual's freedom in the face of society's tyranny, through granting individuals the status and right to please themselves and express their will when confronted with social or moral demands, to a kind of positive individualism in which the individual is not only entitled but also duty-bound to give expression to his or her personal will. The sequence seems almost circular, the two ends connecting at the point where one's personal will makes demands that supersede the necessity inherent in rational and moral principles.

The starting point of the continuum matches the findings of Nucci (1981) on children's distinction of a domain of personal autonomy – behavior (such as choice of clothes, games, and so forth) which both children and adults consider exclusively within the individual's purview. Nucci's claim of universality for this distinction may be too sweeping, but his findings do seem to shed light on an important dimension of human perceptions, including those of children. Even if we agree with Nucci that such a domain is intrinsic to every culture and is a precondition for the development of personal autonomy, it is hardly disputable that not only the scope of the phenomenon but equally its depth and meaning have sharply intensified in the modern era. The right of children to decide what to wear, what to read, or even what games to play, which Nucci's subjects take for granted, is hardly self-evident to children in an ultra-Orthodox community in Israel (Nisan 1987) or to Indians in the study by Miller, Bersoff, & Harwood (1990). Indeed, the very meaning of personal autonomy appears to have changed over time. There are grounds for believing that Nucci's findings on children's perceptions (Nucci 1981) reflect the liberal, individualistic approach which emphasizes individual rights and limits the area amenable to intervention by the state or any other social instance.

Further along the continuum we shall place the findings of the studies on "limited morality" described above. If man is the measure of all things, people have the right to give priority to their own personal needs and inclinations. Thus, we find that people consider it their legitimate right to prefer personal over moral and social considerations. Nor do these personal considerations include only what psychologists call "self-actualization" – activities that bequeath greater meaning to life (Maslow 1970); they also encompass ostensibly lower needs, such as material interests. The egotism and Narcissism that some researchers found in the "culture" of the 1970s (Lasch 1975) were and remain unique in that their espousers consider them the individual's right and not socially deviant, acceptable values and not the abandonment of values, self-actualization rather than escape – for, after all, society does not take precedence over its constituent individuals. The individual's goals and wishes, including hedonistic desires, come to occupy a central place in the considerations that guide life.

In my studies of limited morality, subjects who were asked to accept or evaluate decisions referring to specific dilemmas often acknowledged the existence of valid moral norms. But nevertheless, as described above, they held that the individual's right to personal satisfaction is not self-evidently subject to social norms. Their conception is that one's "life" takes precedence over such norms, and by "life" they mean far more than mere physical existence: the term embraces everything that renders existence meaningful for the individual. They can, therefore, imagine situations in which the will to ensure meaningfulness justifies the violation of certain moral norms: The reasons they present recall the claims made by Williams (1981) on the

status of a personal project in human life (although, of course, they were far from his explicit analysis). The individual insists on the right to self-preference. This attitude constitutes an astonishing change from the traditional view that moral and social imperatives take precedence a priori over personal desires and inclinations.

Perhaps, though, the most fascinating manifestation of the new individualism is found at the end of the continuum described above: in the shift from the idea that individuals have the right to satisfy their wishes when they conflict with social norms, to the attitude that it is one's duty to remain true to oneself and let one's personality express itself. Individualism, then, no longer only confers rights and freedom, it also presents a demand: to preserve and be faithful to one's personal identity.

If man is the measure of all things he is expected, in this conception, to demonstrate stability and consistency – to uphold the "measure" itself. This is of course not a new expectation, but it reaches a new height of intensity when man is the criterion by which all else is measured. It is in fact the expectation of authenticity (Trilling 1972; Taylor 1989). It recalls dissonance theory and other consistency theories but differs from them, at least in terms of their prevalent version. The consistency which is supposed to inform authenticity is not such as is required to preclude contradiction and disruption in human activity, or to uphold one's rational image. These problems can also be resolved by changing people's attitudes or even their self-perception (Festinger 1957); whereas the expectation of authenticity is based on sustaining the individual's identity. To modify attitudes and self-perceptions is to diminish authenticity, not sustain it. A deviation from authenticity does not necessarily affect the effectiveness of behavior or induce irrationality. It does, however, entail a feeling of falseness and betrayal of identity, and this needs to be rectified in future behavior which will make manifest and give expression to one's identity.

The expectation, in a normative sense, that a person will be authentic found expression in my studies on identity and the perception of the desirable or worthy. In them I presented dilemmas of the following kind: Danny, a 16-year-old, is deeply interested in astronomy. An important, one-time lecture on the subject, which Danny wants to attend, will clash with a football game which he would also like very much to see. He must make up his mind between the two events. Do you think Danny should attend the lecture? How strongly do you think so, and why? A second group of subjects was presented with a similar dilemma, the only difference being that Danny was said to take "some interest" in astronomy. The findings showed that when astronomy is described as a substantive component of Danny's identity he is expected to attend the lecture – the perception is that he ought to go – to a greater degree than when astronomy is said to be only moderately important for the child. These findings apply to boys aged 16–17 but only slightly to the 11–12 age group. The former were also more inclined to explain their responses in terms of the need to be true to oneself. The development of the self and of identity during adolescence (Damon & Hart 1988) generates a center of gravity that carries a kind of obligatory feeling to sustain systemic stability and balance, to maintain the self as a good person.

Apparently, then, making man the measure of all things entails a price or obligation. Granting people the right to behave as they wish and not subordinating them to society's expectations brings in its wake a counter-obligation: they are expected to respect their personal will and be true to themselves. It is important to note that the right and duty involved here lie in the individual's own perception; they do not emanate from "external" judgment. Thus, even in the case of one's rights and duties vis-à-vis oneself, individuals are not free of the inner logic that informs the language of rights and duties. Faithfulness to one's identity is required in order to justify the supposed elevation of identity to a normative status, as we have described. If you do not respect your personal identity – are not faithful to it – there is no justification for giving it greater weight than other considerations. (One can, of course, conceive of a more extreme form of individualism, without any such commitment; in which the commitment is, as it were, to the absence of commitment. In our study we were not able to distinguish between such a nihilistic type of commitment and the absence of a commitment characteristic of 11- and 12-year-olds, caused by lack of crystallized perception of identity.)

Granting personal desires priority requires us to clarify their nature, which leads to a distinction between a person's different kinds of desires: those that are more oneself (part of one's identity) as against those that are less oneself, that are related to uncontrolled needs or external pressures and influences, and thus give less expression to an individual's distinctive identity. A frequent statement in the reasons adduced by our subjects is: "If this is so important to him, then let him be true to himself," or "If he doesn't go to the lecture he is a wimp."

The findings on the individual's duty to personal identity corroborate Taylor's (1989) claim about the (normative) expectation regarding authenticity, i.e., behavior that gives expression to one's true self and identity. They underline the influence and weight that the need for authenticity carries for decisions and behavior of our contemporaries. This supposedly closes the circle of individualism in which the individual is held to be the basis, the point of departure, and the criterion for all our considerations. In addition to the first sense of individualism, which is entailed in becoming detached from external authority, be it transcendent or social, so that priority accrues to the individual's projects and rights, another sense also took shape: a view of the individual as possessing a relatively stable inner core, comprising identity, substance, and will, which, in turn, entail continuity, self-affirmation and self-expression, and faithfulness to self. Individualism in this sense finds in the individual – in one's identity – the basis for investing norms and values with validity, while also engendering its own norms of behavior.

The concept of balanced identity, which I drew on to explain decisions made in cases of moral conflict, is apt here. It suggests that one principle that informs decisions in such conflicts is sustaining a balanced identity, ensuring that all the values which are cardinal to one's identity will receive satisfactory if incomplete expression. This principle holds that people feel obliged to give expression not only to the moral aspect of identity, but also to other components, including personal interests. The liberty people allow themselves to commit a moral deviation need not necessarily reflect a temporary forsaking of morality; it may be a response to an identity demand. People aspire to be at one with themselves (to a sufficient degree) in overall terms, across calculations of time and of the values they cherish; from that aspiration evolves the demand people make of themselves to be faithful to the components of their identity.

# Reflections on moral education in our era

The manifestations of relativism and individualism we found in the judgments of ordinary people reflect very concretely the confusion that afflicts individuals who must make moral choices without absolute norms to draw on and before they have developed methods for dealing with such decisions. If in the near past the realm of "dilemmas" was confined largely to situations in which two moral considerations of a similar weight were in competition, it now appears far broader: situations in which a moral consideration is in competition with an important personal consideration may also be perceived as dilemmas which have no self-evident solution. On the face of it, this situation (taken as also reflecting a philosophical inconsequence) reduces the justification for and the possibility of moral education. Yet, by the same token, it also reinforces the need for such education. It is arguable that precisely the newly broadened realm of moral dilemmas and the absence of accepted rules for their resolution necessitates society's guided intervention in order to help youngsters find their way through the maze of moral choices.

An important point to be considered in deciding whether moral education is justified concerns the scope of society's influence on the individual's values. The manifestations of relativism in our subjects' judgments, as described above, go a long way toward supporting the argument about the preponderant importance of culture in shaping beliefs and conceptions which determine people's actual decisions in moral dilemmas. The schools, as part of the culture, and indeed as institutions that seek to inculcate culture in the next generation, cannot absolve themselves of responsibility in this sphere: not only because parents and children alike expect them to address the issue, but more pointedly because not to provide moral education is to send a distinct message about the status of morality. It is a message of extreme relativism, holding that the realm of values is not amenable to rational examination and is beyond the purview of "established" culture. In an age of psychological relativism, whatever its extent, that message is taken as a positive attitude on the part of the schools, rather than as a consequence of the position that schools should avoid intervening in this sensitive area. Moreover, in this age of communication, if formal education avoids addressing values it is knowingly abandoning

children to the implicit, and at times unintended, messages conveyed by the mass culture. The least we might expect from the educational system, therefore, is to develop awareness of and sensitivity to values and to ethical messages (including hidden messages), while at the same time exposing pupils to values which are not transmitted by the dominant consumer culture. That minimum can be conceived of as part of the schools' central cognitive task, i.e., to give their pupils a wide-ranging, open presentation of human culture with its rich diversity of values and the different conceptions it has developed for deciding in dilemmas of values.

However, do educators have a basis for adducing ethical messages of any kind? The findings we described above – loss of strong obligatoriness and overridingness of moral considerations; acceptance of different conceptions of the good as equally valid; recognition of the legitimacy of personal considerations, including hedonistic considerations, in making value decisions, and acceptance of personal solutions for moral dilemmas – may discomfit the moral educator who wishes to transmit a clear ethical message. Indeed, at first glance we seem to have nothing that can serve as an anchor for moral obligations. However, as we saw, a closer look at the findings turns up several points that may lead to the emergence of a renewed model of moral education.

First, a primary aim of moral education is to develop moral thinking, as it has always been. In general, as noted, people acknowledge the pragmatic validity of moral norms. This perception may stem from the (non-contingent) intrinsic meaning of the behavior in question (gouging the flesh) or from the (contingent) meaning conferred on it by social conventions (suitable attire at a wedding). Both sources of validity, the intrinsic and the social, are based on and indicate the pragmatic nature of the norms. As said before, the loss of respect for social norms does not entail a denial of their value in human life (including their symbolic value). Indeed, both children and adults, even as they question the sanctity of norms in general, acknowledge the pragmatic value of many norms, including some that derive from one's social ties to a group. Recognition of the pragmatic validity of norms develops out of day-to-day experience, but this does not mean that it is outside the purview of moral education. Moral thinking, the development of which is one of the components of moral education, is supposed to help children see and understand considerations which are not clear at first sight concerning the pragmatic validity of norms. The relativistic thrust in the perception of morality has not affected the need to develop moral thinking – to bring about a distinct, complex conception of the considerations and consequences involved in making moral decisions.

Second, moral education must develop second-order evaluation. As pointed out, the pragmatic validity of moral norms is insufficient to endow them with obligatory force; it only posits them as one more consideration to be taken into account by the individual. Indeed, as said above, moral norms have lost much of their potency and no longer override other considerations a priori. Children may recognize the pragmatic "badness" of cheating on tests, but why should they not cheat anyway, when they consider the great utility of that course of action? This question encapsulates the great challenge of moral education. The more diminished the impact of transcendental or social sources of authority, the greater the need to ground the obligatory force of norms on second-order evaluation (Frankfurt 1971): that is, on a reflective evaluation leading the person to view the antisocial act as "undesirable" or "unworthy" from the individual's point of view. This will ensue from reflection on the pragmatic value of norms and from extracting their relevant meaning. As suggested above, that kind of evaluation will invest the perceived norm with a claim on the individual, and will make it relevant to her view of herself.

As I see it, one important challenge of moral education today is to induce pupils to make that evaluation. Relativism and individualism of the sort described above, and in particular the loss of valid bases for evaluation, "draw" people to behave in a manner directed largely by first-order evaluation, which by its nature is based on a consideration of immediate utility. In contradistinction, moral education should have as one of its central goals to encourage reflective, second-order evaluation. This is in any case an essential occupation of the schools, particularly in teaching subjects related to culture. Such teaching offers a model for second-order evaluation: by making an evaluation (these works are worthy of study), by adducing criteria for making evaluations, and by using those criteria to evaluate works of culture. Education to make evaluations is thus a central element of every curriculum. I am suggesting that it be honed and developed deliberately to encompass issues of morality and values (the problem of the criteria that should inform

evaluations is a subject for separate discussion). Taking a cognitive-developmental approach (Kohlberg 1984), I believe that pupils who acquire experience in making second-order evaluations will no longer be able to do otherwise; henceforth they will be "condemned" to pause and reflect on the immediate factors influencing them – in the realm of values as in the realm of aesthetics and in more practical realms. (Of course, this does not apply to quasi-automatic behavior such as is impelled by schemata that have developed while this behavior was being assayed.)

Third, moral education must deal with the development of identity. After a person has made his evaluations as to the desirable and worthy, there is a need for a motivational anchor so he or she will not be swept up in a sea of utilitarian considerations. The discussion above pointed to a possible anchor, whose importance has grown in recent times. As we saw, people who permit themselves to deviate from morality nonetheless accept its validity as their point of departure; they aspire to be good, even if not saintly. The displacement of the good from its preferential position, as conferred on it by God or by society or by "reason," has not affected – at least not in the concrete judgments obtained in my studies – the recognition that we can judge good from bad and that the good possesses a cognitive and motivational status that urges its realization. We saw also that subjects who display tolerance for limited moral violations and are ready to accept different conceptions of the good and different decisions for moral dilemmas, nevertheless seek to sustain their identity as good people. They do not cast off the burden of the good. These attitudes, as found in our studies, provide a basis for moral education anchored in personal identity, in the way people perceive and define themselves.

The judgments that turned up in our studies confirm the claim that moral skepticism has heightened the need for self-definition, for a conscious conception of self-identity. They also underline the role of identity in directing behavior. A conception of identity furnishes people with a compass to guide their decisions. It engenders, as noted, a need to sustain and be faithful to one's identity, to the point of considering it a duty (not necessarily in a strong sense) to give expression to its central components. The sense of having a duty to one's identity develops during adolescence, parallel to a questioning of prevailing norms (Nisan 1996). Adolescents come to recognize their obligation to their identity, to the ideals and the projects they consider essential aspects of their selves. Identity, then, will "suggest itself" as an anchor for different types of commitments undertaken by adolescents, whether chosen by them from the outset (e.g., to an ideal) or adopted post factum as dictates of fate (e.g., to the nation). This situation holds out a tremendous prospect for moral growth driven by self-examination and the building of one's identity.

Fourth, moral education must address conceptions of the good. Morality which is motivationally grounded in identity suggests morality with a somewhat different thrust from what we usually have in mind when thinking about morality. I will call the identity-grounded morality "morality of aspiration," as contrasted with "morality of duty" (following the discussion and terminology of Fuller 1970). "Morality of aspiration" is an outgrowth of the desire to be good (or "good enough"), as opposed to "morality of duty," which is grounded in the obligatory validity of moral principles. The danger in a morality of aspiration lies in its "flexibility" – the obligation that springs from the aspiration to be a good person is not absolute and leaves an opening for moral concessions. On the other hand, it is ego-syntonic, perceived as part of one's self, and undertaken, if one may say so, more wholeheartedly and on a foundation of personal harmony.

The morality of aspiration (related to the virtue approach in moral philosophy) posits different educational demands from the morality of duty. True, it does not omit the need to transmit and clarify moral norms: the aspiration to be a good person cannot overlap moral judgments of right and wrong, such as those associated with human welfare, justice, and so forth. However, the morality of aspiration goes beyond moral norms in the limited sense of the term "moral." The aspiration to be good, to be "sufficiently at one with oneself" and to be true to one's identity, cannot be confined to prohibitions against harming human welfare and society. Necessarily, it encompasses personal and social good, and as such implies moral education in the broad sense of the term. This may clash with the liberal approach that objects to the intervention of schools or the state in people's "perceptions of the good," on the ground that this belongs to the private domain of each individual. But if the schools want to present identity models and foster commitment to one's own identity, they must address a broad range of values, beyond not infringing on rights; values are a core element of identity.

Fifth, and pursuant to the above, moral education should confront pupils with the need to commit themselves to a complete value system. Education anchored in identity does not end with the presentation, however distinct and complex, of different conceptions of the good and the desirable or worthy. A central element of identity is commitment to a conception of the good, and perhaps the schools are not exempt from dealing with this. This cannot remain at the cognitive level of analyzing values and one's commitment to them; pupils should come to make a concrete commitment. Can schools truly forge such a commitment? I want to suggest that beyond activities such as community volunteer work, a school should propose a commitment to a comprehensive conception of a worthy life. School offers many pupils their only chance to explore *commitment* to a value system. The idea of school presenting an ideal, or a comprehensive conception of the good, may shock many readers and seem to contradict a pluralistic conception of the good. Is it not in fact reductionist indoctrination that will encourage intolerance? Recent history makes such dangers appear tangible, unfortunately. We have learned that ideological education may succeed "too well." However, the education for the good that I envisage is fundamentally different. In a pluralistic society even a school with a defined educational vision can and should present an open posture, in which the pupils are made aware of and exposed to other conceptions of the good. Moreover, present-day students are (and should be) aware that they are in a period of moratorium in which they can examine how the vision of the school compares with other visions. In addition, it is reasonable to expect that the "skepticism" mentioned above will help prevent children from being closed to other ideas at an early age. The experience of attending a school committed to a vision of the good but with an open posture can provide a model of comprehensive good which enables and stimulates the pupil's aspiration to achieve a whole identity; and this will be accomplished without any narrowing of horizons or promotion of intolerance, while the pupil remains aware of the individual's duty to make a choice and commitment.

Sixth, moral education must address the individual's commitment to the group and develop its positive potential. In the morality of aspiration, which is based on preserving and expressing identity, commitment to the group, including commitment to the culture, will be given significant weight. Group affiliations are undoubtedly important elements of identity, which elicit the individual's faithfulness to their symbolic and concrete expressions. Cultural or national identity is not only an important element of a person's identity, but also a bridge between personal identity and society. In addition to enriching the individual, cultural identity constitutes a meaningful basis for commitment to higher-order values. Now, the demands of the group may conflict with the demands of universal morality. Faced with this issue, educators cannot avoid a philosophical clarification; indeed, they should seize the opportunity to discuss the relationship between loyalty to one's identity and a universal conception of morality (see Tamir 1993). In a study of distribution of resources, we found, as expected, partiality toward group members over strangers, but we also found that this partial form of distribution was accepted only when based on fidelity to one's identity (as opposed to hostility toward others). Similarly, we found that commitment to the group may be adopted and justified by people on the basis of universal considerations, and not necessarily – as some psychological research makes us believe – on the basis of their disavowal. Moreover, subjects distinguish between situations in which partiality is acceptable (e.g., because of a feeling of solidarity) and those in which it is not acceptable (discrimination stemming from hostility to others). The dangers latent in loyalty to the group are well-known in our world, but it would be wrong to ignore not only the weight and potency of such loyalty in people's lives, but also its potential positive elements. Indeed, it is precisely the dangers inherent in loyalty to the group that make it imperative to address the issue. The educator must carefully guide loyalty to group identity within the framework of the pupil's attempt to achieve a balanced identity.

## Conclusion

Claims that a relativist and individualist orientation has taken root in the domain of values raise doubts about the possibilities of moral education in its traditional form. An examination of reasoned responses to moral dilemmas suggests a far more encouraging picture. Moral norms are indeed losing their special status as possessing absolute validity and overriding every other sort of consideration. On the other hand, people develop conscious self-definition which entails an aspiration to self-improvement and faithfulness to one's identity. This self-definition also serves as a basis for commitment to the good and the worthy. That commitment rests on the will to be good and at one with oneself (to an "acceptable" degree) and to give expression to one's identity. An important aspect of the development of identity is the tendency to make (second-order) evaluations of behavior in the past and future in terms of its "worthiness." Such evaluations are not without a natural "anchor." One of their important bases is the "pragmatic" meaning of different kinds of behavior, including the meaning that originates in social conventions. Another basis for the perceived validity of values may be personal elements in one's identity, particularly those bearing a distinctly individual character (e.g., an abiding interest in astronomy). These bases enable people to accept a multiplicity of values.

Formulating more radically some of the trends that emerged, we would say that morality's absolute validity is replaced by commitment to personal identity; respect for society is superseded by an acceptance of its expectations and norms on the basis of their pragmatic meaning; morality based on prohibitions and obligations gives way to morality based on the aspiration for human flourishing; and belief in "objective" moral meaning yields to moral meaning dependent on society and on particular conditions.

These developments provide the foundation for moral education based on the development of second-order evaluations and a commitment to one's identity: education directed toward a broad, committed conception of the good. The schools can and should be central agents of this educational process. Faced with the rising tide of instrumentalism and consumerism, the schools should be able to put forward a model of second-order evaluation – a model which will go beyond the declarative level and find expression primarily in the ethos that guides the community and directs the school experience.

## References

Bellah, R. N., Madsen, R., Sullivan, W. M., Swidler, A. and Tipton, S. M. (1985) *Habits of the Heart: Individualism and Commitment in American Life*, New York: Harper & Row.

Berlin, I. (1990), *The Crooked Timber of Humanity*, London: John Murray.

Damon, W. and Hart, D. (1988) *Self-understanding in Childhood and Adolescence*, Cambridge: Cambridge University Press.

Festinger, L. (1957) *A Theory of Cognitive Dissonance*, Stanford: Stanford University Press.

Frankfurt, H. G. (1971) "Freedom of the will and the concept of a person," *Journal of Philosophy*, 68: 5–20.

Fuller, L. L. (1970) *The morality of law*. New Haven: Yale University Press.

Kohlberg, L. (1984) *Essays on Moral Development, Vol. 2: The Psychology of Moral Development*, New York: Harper & Row.

Kurtines, W. and Gewirtz, J. L. (eds) (1991) *The Handbook of Moral Behavior and Development: Theory, Research and Application* (vols. 1–3), Hillsdale, NJ: Lawrence Erlbaum Associates.

Lasch, C. (1975) *The Culture of Narcissism: American Life in an Age of Diminishing Expectations*, New York: Norton.

Markus, H. and Kitayama, S. (1991) "Culture and the self: Implications for cognition, emotion and motivation," *Psychological Review*, 98: 224–53.

Maslow, A. H. (1970) *Motivation and Personality*, 2nd edn, New York: Harper & Row.

Miller, J. G., Bersoff, P. M. and Harwood, R. L. (1990) "Perceptions of Social Responsibilities in India and in the United States: Moral Imperatives or Personal Decisions?" *Journal of Personality and Social Psychology*, 58: 33–47.

Nisan, M. (1985) "Limited Morality: A Concept and its Educational Implications", in M. W. Berkowitz and F. Oser (eds), *Moral Education: Theory and Application*, Hillsdale, NJ: Lawrence Erlbaum Assiciates.

Nisan, M. (1987) "Moral Norms and Social Conventions: A Cross-cultural Comparison", *Developmental Psychology*, 23: 719–25.

Nisan, M. (1993) "Balanced Identity: Morality and Other Identity Values", in G. Noam and T. Wren (eds), *The Moral Self*, Cambridge, MA: MIT Press.

Nisan, M. (1996) "Development of the distinction among the 'desirable', morality and personal preference," *Social Development*. 5: 219–29.

Nucci, L. (1981) "Conceptions of Personal Issues: A Domain Distinct from Moral or Social Concepts", *Child Development*, 52: 114–21.

Sandel, M. J. (1982) *Liberalism and the limits of justice*, Cambridge: Cambridge University Press.

Shweder, R. A., Mahapatra, M. and Miller, J. G. (1987) "Culture and Moral Development", in J. Kagan and S. Lamb (eds), *The Emergence of Morality in Young Children*, Chicago: University of Chacago Press, pp. 1–33.

Tamir, Y. (1993) *Liberal Nationalism*, Princeton, NJ: Princeton University Press.

Taylor, C. (1989) *Sources of the Self: The Making of Modern Identity*, Cambridge, MA: Harvard University Press.

Trilling, L. (1972) *Sincerity and Authenticity*, Oxford: Oxford University Press.

Turiel, E. (1983) *The Development of Social Knowledge: Morality and Convention*, Cambridge: Cambridge University Press.

Williams, B. (1981) *Moral Luck*, Cambridge: Cambridge University Press.

Wong, D. B. (1984) *Moral Relativity*, Berkely: University of California Press.

# Part Two

## Curriculum Dimensions

# 8 Developing a Values Framework for Sex Education in a Pluralist Society

## J. MARK HALSTEAD

Sex education is one of the most contentious areas of the curriculum, and public disagreements about methods and approaches are widespread. In 1994, for example, there was extensive media coverage when it came to light that during a sex education lesson for 9- to 11-year-olds in a Leeds primary school a school nurse had answered questions about oral sex and 'Mars bar parties' and had involved the children in role-playing an extra-marital love triangle (Meikle 1994). But the ensuing arguments about the appropriateness of this approach were about much more than content and method; they pointed to serious disagreements about the aims of sex education and the underlying values. The nurse concerned, and the parents, teachers and governors who supported her, stressed the need for openness and honesty in answering children's questions (Burstall 1994), whereas many of those who complained about her approach, including some parents and politicians, gave higher priority to the preservation of children's innocence (White 1994).

There is a wide diversity of views about the aims of sex education. For some, sex education is primarily about safer sex, and the effectiveness of a sex-education programme may be judged in terms of the extent to which it leads to increased condom use (Harvey (ed.) 1993). For others, it is about reducing teenage pregnancy (Massey (ed.) 1995: 8), or encouraging sexual abstinence among young people (Lickona 1991, ch 18, Kilpatrick 1993, ch. 3), or helping people to satisfy their sexual needs (Harris 1971: 9), or increasing understanding and acceptance of 'differences in sexual norms and practices' (Sex Education Forum 1992), or developing an appreciation of 'the value of stable family life, marriage and the responsibilities of parenthood' (Department for Education 1994: 6), or empowering young people by increasing their knowledge about sexuality (Massey 1990: 136–8), or enjoining 'chastity and virginity before marriage and faithfulness and loyalty within marriage' (Islamic Academy 1991: 8), or developing a greater sense of style, satisfaction or fun in sexual relations (Wilson 1965: 145, Jones 1989: 57), or encouraging responsible sexual decision-making (Went 1985: 19–20).

Behind these disagreements about aims lie incompatible and conflicting values. I am using the term 'values' to refer to fundamental convictions and principles which act as general guides to behaviour and decision-making (Halstead 1996a: 5). Conflicting values in this sense lie at the heart of the current dilemma facing teachers of sex education. On the one hand, they acknowledge that schools reflect and embody specific frameworks of values in their teaching, organisation and relationships, and they recognise the need to be open about the values on which sex-education programmes are based. On the other hand, they are faced with a greater diversity of values in the sexual domain than ever before, as a result of the glamorisation of sexuality (Reppucci and Herman 1991: 130 ff) and the changes in sexual norms, values and behaviour that have occurred in many sections of society over the last 30 years (Thomson 1997: 258 ff). It is not just (as it is sometimes represented; see, for example, McKay 1997) a debate between restrictive and permissive sexual ideologies; it is more that when it comes to opinions about sex people inhabit different worlds, speak different languages, hold incompatible and widely divergent values. For Nick Fisher's pocket sex guide (1994) to have some 'street-cred' among its target readership, it was inevitable that its direct and unpatronising language would be condemned as 'smutty' and 'distasteful' by the then Health Minister Brian Mawhinney. We inhabit a plural society, not simply in the ethnic sense, but in the more fundamental sense of a society made up of diverse groups with widely divergent beliefs, values and worldviews. What is more, there is a large number of pressure groups, each with a different agenda, and each often talking at cross purposes with the others, vying for influence in sex education. However convinced teachers of sex education are of the profound importance of the topic for schools, they thus face an uncertainty about what values should underpin the planning of sex education and what values, if any, should be taught to children. The result is that until recently the topic of values in sex education has been largely neglected.

This chapter seeks to respond to this neglect, and is divided into three parts. The first disentangles and examines four distinct debates which are carried on about sex education in relation to values. The second part explores the main sets of values which are commonly put forward as an appropriate foundation for sex education. The third argues that planning for sex education at the school level must begin with a discussion of underlying values by all interested parties, so that a values framework can be developed which has the support of the majority of the school community, though the agreed framework may vary from school to school. However, the needs of minorities who do not agree with the dominant framework of values should not be neglected, and multicultural education provides some principles which could help sex education to respond to the values pluralism in contemporary society.

## Four debates about sex education

### Should it be taught in school at all?

Opposition to sex education in schools comes in three main forms. First, there is a group of mainly right-wing thinkers who claim that contemporary sex education subverts the law or that it encourages behaviour which results in outcomes (including teenage pregnancy and sexually transmitted diseases) which are a drain on the public purse (Whitehead 1994, Phillips 1995, Whelan 1995). Secondly, there are some parents from religious groups (notably Muslims: see Halstead 1997a) who perceive the values being transmitted to children in sex-education lessons in school as so far removed from those of their own faith that they prefer to exercise their legal right to withdraw their children

from sex education lessons and teach them at home or in the place of worship instead. Pressure groups promoting conservative family values have sometimes reached the same conclusion, arguing that sex education is in much safer hands if it is left up to parents (cf. Reiss 1995: 373–4). Thirdly, as already noted above, it is sometimes argued that young children have a natural innocence which may be prematurely lost as a result of lessons designed to raise their sexual awareness (Collyer 1995: 27–9).

In reply, the proponents of sex education in schools argue strongly against all these claims. First, they point to research which suggests that sex education does not encourage students to become sexually active at younger ages (Marsiglio and Mott 1986, Baldo et al. 1993) and that if young people are educated in the correct use of condoms this will reduce both teenage pregnancy and the spread of sexually transmitted diseases (Berne and Huberman 1995). Secondly, they point out that though parents are normally the most natural and most important sex educators of their children, they are not always in the best position to understand the influences to which their children are subject as they grow older and therefore may not be able to meet all of their specific needs (see Halstead 1997a: 325 ff). Thirdly, they argue that to abandon sex education in schools would not in itself guarantee the preservation of children's innocence, for even very young children pick up a lot of information about sex in the playground and through informal interaction with their peers, though the learning may be haphazard and inaccurate. Parents can have little control over the values to which the children are exposed in this way. Television is also a major source of sexual knowledge and values (Ward 1995), making accessible to children 'the secrets that adults used to keep to themselves' (Adler 1994: 43), and even if parents restrict the access of their own children to television, they cannot prevent them from talking to other children who have more ready access. In fact, Archard suggests that the 'supposed sexual innocence of children is largely contradicted by the known facts' (1993: 40). The answer is not necessarily to attempt an even tighter control of everything the children see and hear; as Collyer (1995: 28) points out, the quality of innocence should not be confused with ignorance. The sexual abuse of children is more likely to thrive where they are kept in ignorance about sexual matters. Formal sex education can respond to these challenges not by trying to protect children from the influence of peers or television but by developing their ability to reflect critically on the sexual values to which they are exposed in the broader society and to deconstruct the sexual messages of television and advertising. Indeed, developing the capacity for such critical reflection is what education is centrally about.

The proponents of sex education in schools also point to very widespread support for school-based sex education among parents and others in the UK (Allen 1987, Health Education Authority 1994) and elsewhere (Kenny and Orr 1984, Marsman and Herold 1986), though this general support may mask considerable disagreement about what values, if any, should underpin sex-education programmes.

## Should it be value-free or value-laden?

It is sometimes suggested that in view of the strong disagreements over underlying values, the only acceptable approach to sex education in our society is a value-free one. On this view, sex education merely involves imparting knowledge to children about biological aspects of the human body and human reproduction. The approach assumes that 'facts' are separable from 'values' and that whereas sexual 'facts' should be taught by the school nurse or biology teacher, sexual 'values' are the responsibility of the parents, or the place of worship, or of the child herself (if 'values' are viewed as personal matters which should not be 'imposed' by anyone: cf. Warnock 1979: 89). The main problem with this approach is that it is in fact impossible to impart knowledge without at least an implicit values framework – but if the values are left at the implicit level, and there is no systematic reflection on and discussion of the values involved, then children are more likely to develop their values in a haphazard manner. Indeed, it is not uncommon for the values which pupils develop in school to be different from those the school intends (cf. Halstead 1996a). If children are not given direct guidance and help in school but are left to pick up their values as and when they can, this may leave them open to manipulation at the hands of those less concerned for their well-being than the school is. This suggests that it should be a high priority for the values of the school to be explored and articulated, rather than left within the hidden curriculum, so that teachers may have more confidence in offering guidance to pupils. Recent research suggests that many student teachers consider themselves inadequately prepared to teach values, and lack confidence in this area (Arnot 1996). Yet over 10 years ago Lee (1983) warned of the dangers of 'the ostrich position', which involves a refusal to take on contentious issues or to discuss the conflicting and confusing emotions and values that sexual matters generate.

We are thus faced with a potentially paralysing vicious circle. Attempting to teach sex education in a value-free way seems to imply that values are optional, subjective or relative. As we have seen, it also leaves children more vulnerable to the influence of their peers, the media or the hidden curriculum as their values develop. Most parents do not want this, and would prefer schools to offer clear guidance to children on values until they have the maturity to make their own moral choices. Indeed, it is implicit in what has been written so far that values are not only an important part of sex education, but the foundation on which all planning of practical work must be based. But there remains considerable disagreement over what values should underpin sex education policies (whether at the level of the individual school or at a broader level – though the DFE (1994) has offered *some* guidance here), and over the place of values in the actual teaching of sex education.

## Should health-related values take priority over educational values?

Sex education initiatives may derive from concern about public health or education, and these two sources may generate quite different approaches. The health-based approach aims to put pressure on young people to change their behaviour for medical (but not for moral) reasons; Morris (1997) calls this the 'utilitarian-missionary' approach. The educational approach teaches people to resist external pressure and to develop their own moral values. A health-oriented approach may view sex education as a way of tackling risk-taking behaviour and achieving official health-policy targets, such as halving the rate of conception among girls under the age of 16 in Britain by the year 2000 (Department for Health 1992). Research by the Health Education Authority, the Terrence Higgins Trust and other health organisations suggests that any health campaign which is perceived to offer moral guidance or even to have 'educational' goals is unlikely to have credibility among targeted groups of young people

(Selwood and Irving 1993: 88–98). Thus non-judgemental, explicit, even raunchy, comics like *Smack in the Eye* and *Hang on, Just a Sec* have been used extensively to develop AIDS awareness and promote condom use. There is a similar self-conscious avoidance of moral guidance in safer-sex posters produced by the Health Education Authority and others (carrying messages like 'Isn't it time *you* got into a condom?' and 'Don't stutter and blubber, give him a rubber') and in popular sex guides such as *Your Pocket Guide to Sex* (Fisher 1994) which sets out its approach to morals under the heading 'Human Beings are Sexual Animals': 'It's all perfectly natural. As in all areas of human activity, people want to make rules about sexuality. The truth is, there are no rules' (p. 4). If a health-oriented approach shows any interest in the values and attitudes of young people, it is usually to discover whether there is any correlation between sexual attitudes and practices which increase the risk of exposure to HIV/AIDS (cf. Ford 1991).

From an educational point of view, however, sex education cannot operate with values different from the whole educational enterprise. It is essentially a moral activity, concerned with the balanced development of the whole person and with the development of particular attitudes, skills and personal qualities. A recent legal case in America (Brown v. Hot, Sexy and Safer Productions, Inc. 1996) illustrates the difference between educational and health-based approaches to sex education: two students claimed that they had been humiliated and intimidated by the explicit nature of a health-oriented assembly presentation which involved suggestive skits, simulated masturbation and 'lewd language' (Zirkel 1996). The promotion of 'responsible sexual behaviour', a dominant motif in contemporary sex education in Britain as in other Western countries (Reiss 1995: 377–8), may be seen as a combined approach. The phrase has strong health connotations, and has come to be linked with the use of condoms, because it draws attention to the irresponsibility of passing on sexually transmitted diseases and of initiating unwanted pregnancy. However, it also encompasses a number of liberal educational values such as respect for others, honesty and non-exploitation in sexual relationships, while leaving many of the decisions about the practicalities of sexual behaviour up to the individuals concerned (Howe 1990: 116–18).

## Should schools promote 'enabling' rather than 'absolute' values?

A number of advocates of sex education (Lenderyou 1995: 54 ff, Ray and Went (eds) 1995: 27, Thomson 1997: 265 ff) have recently argued that the sort of values which schools should promote in sex education should be 'enabling' or 'process' values rather than 'prescriptive' or 'absolute'. 'Enabling' values are positive, inclusive values like tolerance, equal opportunities and respect for difference, and empower children to make full use of their individual freedom and choice. Thus they tend towards a philosophy of neutrality and relativism, recognising as equally valid a wide diversity of sexual beliefs, values, practices and identities. By contrast, the prescriptive values approach is always controversial. It is often associated with religious or conservative perspectives, involving such values as an emphasis on 'the idea of accountability to God' (Islamic Academy 1991: 4). In the USA abstinence-based sex-education programmes such as *Sex Respect* and *True Love Waits* have had a significant impact over the last 10 years (Eisenman 1994, Natale 1995). Liberal critics have sometimes dismissed the promotion of abstinence as a form of 'unethical manipulation' (Massey 1990: 138). Lickona, on the other hand, attempts to justify a pro-abstinence approach by emphasising the need for young people to internalise values such as self-control and protection against damaging emotions such as loss, guilt, betrayal and the feeling of being used (1991: 354–5). Cultural values (such as beliefs about marriage and family life, or romantic love, or the importance of sexual pleasure) may equally be presented in a prescriptive manner. The circular issued by the Department for Education in 1994 acknowledges that children might come from cultural backgrounds that do not reflect the values it presents as appropriate for sex education, including self-restraint, dignity, sensitivity, loyalty and fidelity, and advises teachers to avoid causing offence and to help such children feel a sense of worth, while at the same time to helping them 'to raise their sights' (DFE 1994: 6). Even this tentative guidance, however, has proved controversial, and Wringe (1994), for example, has called into question its emphasis on 'the value of stable family life, marriage and the responsibilities of parenthood' (ibid.).

The 'enabling' approach is initially seductive because it seeks to avoid controversy and confrontation in a pluralist society. But is it really possible to teach sex education in this way? First, we must note that the neutrality would not extend to rape, child abuse or the exploitation of others. There are certain fundamental values on which our society is based (such as human rights, equality and respect for persons) which would be undermined if a neutral attitude were adopted to such actions. Secondly, there are certain qualities of character which are highly valued in our society which teachers are not expected to be neutral about. Few parents, for example, would want their children to be free to choose between caring and not caring, being responsible or irresponsible, being sexist or non-sexist. These values and qualities of character could in fact be used as a starting point for developing a values framework for sex education. When we turn to second order values, it is clear that the wisdom of adopting a value-neutral approach to sex education and encouraging children to make moral choices for themselves before they have developed the maturity of judgement and breadth of knowledge, understanding and perception to do so with confidence is certainly open to question. Children need moral guidance, confidence and a stable base for their own lives if they are to grow into mature and responsible adults, and this is unlikely to be achieved through a value-neutral approach.

It no longer seems an impossible task for schools to identify a set of substantive values on which at least a working agreement can be reached. By a working agreement I mean something less than full consensus, since the latter is unlikely ever to be achieved. I mean simply 'a moral framework which suits most of the pupils and their families in the schools most of the time' (Lenderyou 1995: 51). The final section of this chapter focuses on ways of achieving this working agreement through democratic discussion, and also examines ways of taking account of the distinctive beliefs and values of those who remain outside this working agreement. But before this we must attempt an analysis of the various values which play a part in current approaches to sex education, so that they can be set into some kind of order.

## A categorisation of values in sex education

The values that underpin contemporary sex-education programmes, whether taken for granted or openly stated, fall into six main categories.

## *Socio-economic values*

Values relating to population control, public expenditure and the provision of social welfare undoubtedly underpin sex-education policies at the macro level. In recent debates in the media and in parliament young single mothers have been portrayed as a growing burden on the welfare state and links have been suggested between absent fathers and growing crime rates (Helm 1993, Phillips 1995), though these claims are highly controversial and research shows that higher levels of teenage pregnancy are generally associated with 'poverty, unemployment, low self-esteem and lack of hope for the future' (Selman and Glendinning 1996: 203). An appropriate way forward is likely to involve not the restriction of access to welfare favoured by some politicians but more effective education combined with social support and increased employment opportunities. One of the basic assumptions underlying sex-education programmes, however, is that such education can reduce adolescent pregnancy and thus alleviate the social and economic problems that have been blamed on teenage sexual activity (Reppucci and Herman 1991: 129).

## *Health-related values*

For some, health is '*the* overriding value in people's lives' (Howe 1990: 117) and the reduction of risk-taking behaviours such as exposure to disease is the central goal of sex education, particularly in the post-AIDS era (Reiss 1993: 127–8). Indeed, as we have already seen, it is seen as so important by many people that anything which gets in the way of the 'safer-sex' message (such as moral guidance or advice) is discarded as more of a hindrance than a help. However, health-related values may encompass not only such negative goals as avoiding risks to health, but also more positive goals which go beyond the physical dimension, including a concern for psychological and emotional health and well-being.

## *Values related to liberal education*

These centrally include personal autonomy, the development of choice and decision-making skills, self-determination, a rejection of manipulation and indoctrination from any source, and control over one's own life and body (Reiss 1995: 9–11, Halstead 1996b). They also include rational moral values, such as respect for others, personal responsibility, non-exploitation of others and the avoidance of sexist attitudes and unjustified discrimination (Spiecker 1992); civic virtues such as self-respect, self-esteem, honesty, trust, friendship and decency (White 1996); and the values which underpin legislation in the sexual domain, such as the protection of children from corruption and abuse, the preservation of the public interest through legislation against pornography and perversion and the protection of individual rights, including freedom from invasive behaviour (DFE 1994: 20–1).

## Children's and young people's values

In the past children's needs, wishes and values have been largely defined by the experts in child development. Any of the following might be highlighted: pleasure and personal fulfilment; abstinence and self-control; intimacy and affection; assertiveness and critical awareness; the knowledge of one's sexual identity; character development; the capacity for loving relationships. However, Thomson warns of the danger of 'leaving the experience and voices of young people out of the debate over values in sex education', so that 'the debate becomes a battle between different adult groups over their preferred vision' (1997: 267). In recent years there has been a greater willingness to listen directly to children (John (ed.) 1996), who may themselves put greater stress on values such as empowerment, openness from adults, reassurance, freedom from embarrassment and anxiety about sex, emotional security and ways of coping with stress and feelings of vulnerability. A survey of 16–24-year-olds in the South-West of England identifies, perhaps oversimplistically, two sexual philosophies among young people: 'relationship/romantic' and 'casual/recreational' (Ford 1991). It seems likely that much sex education currently takes inadequate account of the dominance of the idea of romantic love in many young people's thinking; a phrase like 'once they (children) are old enough to want to have a sexual relationship' (Lenderyou 1993: 87) makes questionable assumptions about the way that young people take their first steps towards sexual experience.

## Cultural values

In one sense *all* values are cultural products, but certain sexual values and practices stand out as clearly belonging only to specific cultures – for example, arranged marriages; particular family structures; the virtue of abstinence; the acceptability or otherwise of certain forms of sexual behaviour; conceptions of childhood as a time of innocence; the mystification and romanticisation of sex; the exploitation of sex in advertising; pornography; and notions of body image. In a multicultural society where different cultural values exist side by side, disagreements inevitably arise over whether schools should transmit cultural values at all, and if so, which ones (see below).

## Religious values

Religions continue to have an important influence on the way people behave sexually, though they contain a huge diversity of sexual values, and there is rarely consensus on values even within a single religious tradition. Some traditions see marriage as a religious duty for everyone, whereas others see celibacy as an equally valid (or even superior) lifestyle. Some traditions find homosexuality totally unacceptable (cf. Halstead 1998), whereas others urge acceptance as the only response which is in keeping with religious principles (Lenderyou and Porter 1994: 41–2). Some traditions are certainly more prescriptive than others. Many traditions celebrate religious virtues such as purity, chastity, fidelity and self-discipline, but others have argued for a new vision of sexual relationships which is free from the 'patriarchal' attitudes and assumptions of the past (Thatcher 1993, ch 1). Many traditions would also probably emphasise the importance of love as the basis of meaningful relationships, the importance of the spiritual dimension in sexuality and the importance of seeing sexuality as a gift from God.

Of course, these six categories are neither mutually exclusive nor clear-cut in the distinctions they make, but the list does serve to draw attention to the complexity of the values frameworks which underpin sex education and to the nature of the disagreements which were discussed in the first part of the chapter. As we have seen, there are disagreements between conflicting values within the categories as well as disagreements about how the values should be interpreted. There are further dis-agreements over whether all the categories are equally valid, and if not, over which should take priority. However, it is hoped that the categorisation may prove a useful tool in discussions about values in sex education at the school level.

## Negotiating values for sex education in a pluralist society

This section argues that in their search for a work-ing agreement schools must embark on a demo-cratic discussion of values, and concludes by focus-ing on those outside this working agreement and discussing how far schools can and should take account of the needs, beliefs and values of those who do not share the emerging consensus. It is clear that values can no longer be left at an implicit level. Previously values were deeply embedded in the taken-for-granted worldviews of teachers and were shared or taken on trust by parents. This worked quite well when society was more homo-geneous – or when people were less willing to chal-lenge the dominant white middle-class values. But now there is a need for values to be made explicit, so that schools can be more accountable, especially in a pluralist society (Nias 1981). Schools can no longer simply relay the dominant values of society to children uncritically. Nor can they hide behind claims about meeting children's needs, because the concept of needs is by no means self-explicit; much hinges on the values of the people who define the needs (cf. Halstead 1988: 26 ff). Nor can schools expect all the answers to be provided by central government. In Britain the Department for Educa-tion has offered a certain amount of guidance, but has also made it clear that it is the responsibility of the individual school to ensure that its sex educa-tion is 'set within a clear framework of values' (DFE 1994: 6).

So how should a 'clear framework of values' be developed, especially when, as we have seen, there are so many disagreements over values? The first step in resolving the problem of conflicting values in sex education, I suggest, is for schools to embark on a process of discussion about values with all interested parties, including governors, teachers, community leaders, parents and pupils. Such dis-cussions will have a four-fold purpose: they will enable individuals to think through and become clearer about the values which they may simply have

taken for granted in the past; they will bring dis-agreements to the surface; they will enable the school to be confident in its knowledge of the values of parents and others when planning for sex-education; and they will help to generate decisions about which values should take priority in the con-text of the particular school. In this way the school will be able to develop a justifiable set of coherent and consistent values on which there is a working agreement and which can act as the basis for developing a sex-education policy.

The democratic discussions proposed here will involve a careful examination of values with a pos-sible link to sex education and of the conflicts that exist between different sets of values. This may take different forms. For example, the process may start with an examination of the school's existing policy for sex education, as recommended by the Depart-ment for Education (1994: 23) and Ray and Went ((eds) 1995, ch. 2). Or the discussions may be based initially on a particular text or set of texts which are considered by the school to present an expert view or to encapsulate up-to-date thinking about sex education. Or the school may attempt a systematic examination of the full range of possible values, as outlined on pp. 89–90 above.

If school policy is based on the outcome of the kind of democratic discussion being recommended here, it will undoubtedly result in a diversity of provision. Three main patterns of provision may emerge.

1  Many schools will doubtless opt for the open, liberal, secular values which underpin most of the resources currently being produced for school-based sex education. I have attempted a brief summary of these values elsewhere (Halstead 1997b). They include an emphasis on partnership and equal opportunities; an open approach which does not advocate any one lifestyle and avoids prescriptive values; the promotion of sexual health in its broadest sense; the development of self-esteem, tolerance, assertiveness, informed and responsible sexual decision-making, communication and negoti-ation skills, respect for and sensitivity towards others, and awareness of rights; the avoidance of unwanted sexual experience, the reduction of guilt, anxiety and embarrassment, and the rejec-tion of sexism and exploitation. The philosophy underpinning this approach has been set out more fully by Lenderyou and Porter (1993).

2  Many other schools (and not only church schools) will opt for a broadly Christian framework of values, with a strong emphasis on traditional cultural values. Church schools may wish to begin with the guidance offered by their own denominations (see, for example, for Church of England schools, Brown 1993, and for Catholic schools, Catholic Education Service 1994). County schools where the majority of pupils belong to a particular culture or faith may similarly wish (legitimately, in my view) to give much more weight in the planning of sex education to the values of that particular tradition.

3  A smaller number of schools (including, for example, those with a majority of Muslim pupils) may seek to base their sex education on a more prescriptive framework of values, often linked to the teaching of a specific denomination or religious group. Of course, this could only occur if the school's right is recognised to base sex education on a substantive set of values in line with the wishes of the majority of parents and other interested parties.

Such diversity of provision should be quite acceptable within a multicultural society so long as certain conditions are met: (i) children must be prepared for citizenship of the broader society (this will include teaching about the values of equal opportunities and individual rights); (ii) they must be given information about other values and ways of life than their own; and (iii) the needs and interests of those children who belong to minority groups which do not share all the values of the school must not be neglected (Halstead 1995).

However, the last point raises a central question of policy. How *should* schools respond to minorities who share neither the open, liberal, secular values that are dominant in many state schools nor the broadly Christian and traditional cultural values which are also widespread in both church schools and state schools? I have in mind not only certain Muslim groups but also some sections of the Sikh community in the West, some Hindus, some black Christians and some Orthodox Jews as well as some evangelical Christians. Of course it is recognised that there are other minorities such as gays and lesbians who may have special needs and interests in relation to sex education, but these have been dealt with extensively elsewhere (see, for example, Khayatt 1994, Cavicchia 1995, Lind and Butler 1995, Ray and Went (eds) 1995, ch. 11) and will not be discussed in detail here. It is also recognised that in the more open system described above there may be a small number of schools where the boot is on the other foot in that sex education is based on a prescriptive framework of values linked to a particular denomination or religious group. In such schools there might be non-believing minorities whose needs would also have to be met. But at present the children whose beliefs and values are least likely to be taken account of in the planning and delivery of sex education in state-funded schools are those who belong to cultural and religious minority groups. Such groups may, for example, place strong emphasis on values such as the preservation of family honour or obedience to divinely ordained rules relating to sexual behaviour. So the question which must now be considered is how schools should cater for Sikhs, Jews, Muslims and others who have values different from those currently being promoted implicitly or explicitly through sex-education programmes.

One possible response is that the needs of children do not vary according to the beliefs and commitments of their parents (since, it is claimed, *all* children need to be free to distance themselves from the culture of their parents and to make autonomous decisions about their own commitments and life plans) and that education therefore can and should become a common enterprise for the children of all groups in a pluralist society. On this view, it is not the role of state-funded education to protect the distinctive cultural or religious identity of any minority group (cf. Halstead 1995: 266–7). In line with this view, Beattie and Meredith argue that sex education 'should not violate the convictions of the *majority* of the population', but 'cannot be made the servant of minority interests' (quoted in Massey 1990: 135–6). The problem with this approach is that it leaves minority cultures vulnerable to gradual corrosion as a result of sustained exposure to the liberal values of the majority, and is a recipe for social conflict. Crude majoritarianism may not be the best approach to democratic decision-making, in sex education as in many other areas of life.

In my opinion, multicultural education provides an appropriate framework for sex-education policy to take account of the distinctive values of religious minorities. There are two distinct senses of multicultural education (Halstead 1988, ch. 8). The first refers to those aspects of education which are considered appropriate for *all* children if they are to be adequately prepared for life in a pluralist society. The second refers to the attempt in schools to respond positively to the religious and cultural requirements and sensitivities of children and parents from minority groups, as far as this can be achieved without contravening fundamental educational objectives. Both dimensions can be applied to sex education. First, the sex education of all children in a pluralist society must include knowledge of that society, including its law on sexual behaviour, its fundamental shared values (such as freedom, equality, truth, justice, respect, caring and responsibility), and the diversity of other beliefs and values in the society. Knowledge of diversity is an important part of preparation for participation in society even if the diversity is not represented in the composition of the particular school. It is an important way of tackling prejudice and encouraging social harmony, and it can also provide an escape route for those who feel trapped within the culture of their parents or community. The sex education of all children must also include the development of appropriate attitudes, such as *acceptance* of the law, *commitment* to the fundamental values and *tolerance and respect* for the diversity of beliefs and values. The second dimension of multicultural education requires schools to demonstrate respect for the religious and cultural beliefs of minority groups. This includes ensuring that where the distinctive beliefs and practices of minority groups are taught, they are taught accurately and sensitively. It also includes not inculcating in children values which contradict those learned at home and internalised as part of their cultural or religious identity, and not putting children in the position where they are expected to act contrary to their own deeply held beliefs.

It is often maintained that respecting the religious and cultural beliefs of minority groups may conflict with other equal opportunities issues, particularly those relating to sexual orientation (Walkling and Brannigan, 1986, Thomson (ed.) 1993: 7). However, the two dimensions of multicultural education set out in the previous paragraph do together provide a way out of this dilemma. For example, the first dimension requires that children from faith groups which condemn homosexuality should none the less learn about it as part of their preparation for life in a pluralist society, just as lesbians and gays need to learn about religious views on sexual identity (Halstead 1998). In each case accurate and sensitive information should be pro-

vided, and in each case children must learn the need for the toleration of diversity in a pluralist society (Reiss 1997). Such toleration implies a conscious decision not to interfere with behaviour of which one disapproves (see Halstead 1996c). However, if schools go further than this and encourage children to *celebrate* difference (as is sometimes recommended: see Thomson 1993: 10, Lenderyou 1995: 54), this is in danger of conflicting with the second dimension of multicultural education. For asking committed Jewish, Muslim or Sikh children to *celebrate* the existence of something their religion condemns is asking them to change their beliefs; in just the same way, lesbian and gay young people will find it extremely difficult to *celebrate* the fact that a central part of their personal identity is subject to such condemnation.

A multicultural approach to sex education, especially in the second sense of multicultural education, is likely to involve making a number of changes to sex-education programmes in order to demonstrate respect for the beliefs of religious minorities and to avoid offence. Some examples from Muslim beliefs and values will illustrate this point. The main anxieties that Muslims have about sex education fall into three categories (Halstead 1997a). First, some of the activities and materials used in sex education offend against the principle of modesty and decency. Secondly, contemporary sex education tends to present certain behaviour as normal or acceptable which Muslims believe is sinful. Thirdly, sex education is perceived as tending to undermine the Islamic concept of family life. If a school is committed to multicultural education, this means that it should listen to such anxieties and explore ways with the parents of adapting its sex-education policy to take account of their views, so long as the changes do not 'undermine the integrity of the programme and the entitlement of other pupils' (Ray and Went (eds) 1995: 45). Such adaptations might include any or all of the following:

- Providing single-sex classes as the norm for sex education, and ensuring that classes are taught by a teacher of the same sex. This would avoid putting Muslim children in the position where they are required to discuss intimate issues about sexuality with members of the opposite sex outside the family, in contradiction to the Islamic expectation that each sex should feel a 'natural modesty' in the presence of the other (Noibi 1993: 57).

- Checking materials used to ensure that they are not considered immodest, indecent or sinful by parents or pupils. Looking at photographs or videos of fully naked bodies or the explicit enactment of sexual relations would certainly offend against the principle of modesty and be unacceptable from a Muslim point of view. Looking at sexually provocative pictures or even 'watching people kissing on TV' is also considered sinful (D'Oyen 1996: 78).
- Ensuring that the Muslim perspective on marriage, children and family life, pre-marital and extra-marital sexual relations, permitted and forbidden sexual practices, family honour, homosexuality, masturbation, contraception, abortion and other key issues in sex education, is given equal respect and prominence alongside other perspectives.

Such changes would help to ensure that the values and beliefs of Muslim parents are not being ignored, and similar (sometimes indeed identical) adaptations would help to demonstrate responsiveness to other minority faiths, the aim being in each case that as far as possible no young person should feel excluded from the school's provision on the grounds of religious belief. The legal right to withdraw children from any or all parts of a sex-education programme, except for those elements which are part of the National Curriculum, as granted in Section 241 of the 1993 Education Act, must be retained as a safety valve, but if schools are willing to adapt their approach to sex education to take into account the beliefs and values of minority groups and to ensure that no children are being required to act against their religion, then it seems likely that the right to withdraw will be exercised less frequently. In any case, such an approach is required by the principles of freedom, justice and equality of respect in a pluralist democratic society.

# References

Adler, J. (1994) 'Kids Growing up Scared', *Newsweek*, 10 Jan.

Allen, I. (1987) *Education in Sex and Personal Relationships: Research Report no 665*, London: Policy Studies Institute.

Archard, D. (1993) *Children: Rights and Childhood*, London, Routledge.

Arnot, M. (1996) 'Education for Citizenship: The Concerns of Student Teachers in England and Wales', seminar discussion paper presented at the National Symposium 'Education for Adult Life', SCAA, London, 15 Jan.

Baldo, M., Aggleton, P. and Slutin, G. (1993) *Does Sex Education Lead to Earlier or Increased Sexual Activity in Youth?*, Geneva: World Health Organisation Global Programme on AIDS.

Berne, L. A. and Huberman, B. K. (1995) 'Sexuality Education: Sorting Fact from Fiction', *Phi Delta Kappan*, 77. 3: 229–32.

Brown, A. (1993) *Sex Education: Guidelines for Church School Governors*, London: The National Society.

Burstall, E. (1994) 'Cheers and Tears over Candid Nurse', *The Times Educational Supplement*, 1 Apr. p. 5.

Catholic Education Service (1994) *Education in Sexuality: Some Guidelines for Teachers and Governors in Catholic Schools*, London: CES.

Cavicchia, S. (1995) 'Lesbian and Gay Issues in Sex Education', in D. E. Massey (ed.) *Sex Education Source Book: Current Issues and Debates*, London: Family Planning Association.

Collyer, J. (1995) *Sex Education in Primary Schools: A Guide to Policy Development in Primary Schools*, London: Forbes Publications.

Department for Education (1994) *Education Act 1993: Sex Education in Schools* (circular number 5/94), London: DFE.

Department for Health (1992) *The Health of the Nation: A Strategy for Health in England*, London: HMSO.

D'Oyen, F. M. (1996) *The Miracle of Life: A Guide on Islamic Family Life and Sex Education for Young People*, Leicester: Islamic Foundation.

Eisenman, R. (1994) 'Conservative Sexual Values: Effects of an Abstinence Program on Student Attitudes', *Journal of Sex Education and Therapy*, 20. 2: 75–8.

Fisher, N. (1994) *Your Pocket Guide to Sex*, Harmondsworth: Penguin.

Ford, N. (1991) *The Socio-Sexual Lifestyles of Young People in South West England*, Bristol: South Western Regional Health Authority.

Halstead, J. M. (1988) *Education, Justice and Cultural Diversity: An Examination of the Honeyford Affair, 1984–85*, Basingstoke: Falmer Press.

Halstead, J. M. (1995) 'Voluntary Apartheid? Problems of Schooling for Religious and Other Minorities in Democratic Societies', *Journal of Philosophy of Education*, 29. 2: 257–72.

Halstead, J. M. (1996a) 'Values and Values Education in Schools', in J. M. Halstead and M. J. Taylor (eds) *Values in Education and Education in Values*, London: Falmer Press.

Halstead, J. M. (1996b) 'Liberal Values and Liberal Education', in J. M. Halstead and M. J. Taylor (eds) *Values in Education and Education in Values*, London: Falmer Press.

Halstead, J. M. (1996c) 'Liberalism, Multiculturalism and Education: A Review Article', *Journal of Philosophy of Education*, 30. 2: 307–13.

Halstead, J. M. (1997a) 'Muslims and Sex Education', *Journal of Moral Education*, 26. 3: 317–30.

Halstead, J. M. (1997b) Review of books by D. E. Massey and L. Scott, *Journal of Moral Education*, 26. 3: 368–71.

Halstead, J. M. (1998) 'Should Schools Present Homosexuality as an Acceptable Alternative Lifestyle? a Muslim Perspective', *Cambridge Journal of Education*, 28. 2: 49–64.

Harris, A. (1971) 'What Does Sex Education Mean?', *Journal of Moral Education*, 1. 1: 7–11.

Harvey, I. (ed.) (1993) *Condoms across the Curriculum*, Cambridge: Daniels Publishing.

Health Education Authority (1994) *Parents, Schools and Sex Education: Summary of Main Report*, London: HEA.

Helm, T. (1993) 'Find your own Homes, Lone Mothers to be Told', *Sunday Telegraph*, 16 Dec.

Howe, K. R. (1990) 'AIDS Education in the Public Schools: Old Wine in New Bottles', *Journal of Moral Education*, 19. 2: 114–23.

Islamic Academy (1991) *Sex Education in the School Curriculum: The Religious Perspective*, Cambridge: Islamic Academy.

John, M. (ed.) (1996) *Children in Charge: The Child's Right to a Fair Hearing*, London: Jessica Kingsley.

Jones, R. (1989) 'Sex Education in Personal and Social Education' in P. White (ed.) *Personal and Social Education: Philosophical Perspectives*, London: Kogan Page.

Kenny, A. and Orr, M. T. (1984) 'Sex Education: An Overview of Current Programs, Policies and Research', *Phi Delta Kappan*, 65. 7: 491–6.

Khayatt, D. (1994) 'Surviving School as a Lesbian Student', *Gender and Education*, 6. 1: 47–61.

Kilpatrick, W. (1993) *Why Johnny Can't Tell Right from Wrong*, New York: Touchstone (Simon & Schuster).

Lee, C. (1983) *The Ostrich Position: Sex, Schooling and Mystification*, London: Writers and Readers Publishing Cooperative.

Lenderyou, G. (1993) *Primary School Workbook: Teaching Sex Education within the National Curriculum*, London: Family Planning Association.

Lenderyou, G. (1995) 'School Sex Education, Faith and Values', in D. E. Massey (ed.) *Sex Education Source Book: Current Issues and Debates*, London: Family Planning Association.

Lenderyou, G. and Porter, M. (1993) 'A Secular Perspective', in R. Thomson (ed.) *Religion, Ethnicity and Sex Education: Exploring the Issues*, London: National Children's Bureau.

Lenderyou, G. and Porter, M. (1994) *Sex Education, Values and Morality*, London: Health Education Authority.

Lickona, T. (1991) *Educating for Character: How our Schools can Teach Respect and Responsibility*, New York: Bantam.

Lind, C. and Butler, C. (1995) 'The Legal Abuse of Homosexual Children', *Journal of Child Law*, 7. 1: 3–9.

McKay, A. (1997) 'Accommodating Ideological Pluralism in Sexuality Education', *Journal of Moral Education*, 26. 3: 285–300.

Marsiglio, W. and Mott, F. L. (1986) 'Impact of Sex Education on Sexual Activity, Contraception Use and Premarital Pregnancy among American Teenagers', *Family Planning Perspectives*, 18: 151–4, 157–62.

Marsman, J. and Herold, E. (1986) 'Attitudes toward Sex Education and Values in Sex Education', *Family Relations*, 35: pp. 357–61.

Massey, D. E. (1990) 'School Sex Education: Knitting without a Pattern?' *Health Education Journal*, 49. 3: 134–42.

Massey, D. E. (ed.) (1995) *Sex Education Source Book: Current Issues and Debates*, London: Family Planning Association.

Meikle, J. (1994) 'Mars Bar Lesson Revives Sex Debate', *Guardian*, 24 Mar. p. 2.

Morris, R. (1997) 'Myths of Sexuality Education', *Journal of Moral Education*, 26. 3: 353–61.

Natale, J. A. (1995) 'The Hot New Word in Sex Ed', *The American School Board Journal* (June): 18–24.

Nias, J. (1981) 'The Nature of Trust', in J. Elliott et al. (eds.) *School Accountability: The SSRC Accountability Project*, London: Grant McIntyre.

Noibi, D. (1993) 'An Islamic Perspective', in R. Thomson (ed.) *Religion, Ethnicity and Sex Education: Exploring the Issues*, London: National Children's Bureau.

Phillips, A. (1995) 'Teen Mums: The Whole Story', *Independent*, 13 Jan.

Ray, C. and Went, D. (eds.) (1995) *Good Practice in Sex Education: A Sourcebook for Schools*, London: National Children's Bureau.

Reiss, M. J. (1993) 'What are the Aims of School Sex Education?', *Cambridge Journal of Education*, 23. 2: 125–36.

Reiss, M. J. (1995) 'Conflicting Philosophies of School Sex Education', *Journal of Moral Education*, 24. 4: 371–82.

Reiss, M. J. (1997) 'Teaching about Homosexuality and Heterosexuality', *Journal of Moral Education*, 26.3: 343–52.

Reppucci, N. D. and Herman, J. (1991) 'Sexuality Education and Child Sexual Abuse Prevention Programs in the Schools', in G. Grant (ed.) *Review of Research in Education 17*, Washington, DC: American Educational Research Association.

Selman, P. and Glendinning, C. (1996) 'Teenage Pregnancy: Do Social Policies Make a Difference?' in J. Brannen and M. O'Brien (eds.) *Children in Families: Research and Policy*, London: Falmer Press.

Selwood, S. and Irving, D. (1993) *Harmful Publications: Comics, Education and Disenfranchised Young People*, London: Art and Society Ltd.

Sex Education Forum (1992) *A Framework for School Sex Education*, London: National Children's Bureau.

Spiecker, B. (1992) 'Sexual Education and Morality', *Journal of Moral Education*, 21. 1: 67–76.

Thatcher, A. (1993) *Liberating Sex: A Christian Sexual Theology*, London: SPCK.

Thomson, R. (ed.) (1993) *Religion, Ethnicity and Sex*

*Education: Exploring the Issues*, London: National Children's Bureau.

Thomson, R. (1997) 'Diversity, Values and Social Change: Renegotiating a Consensus on Sex Education', *Journal of Moral Education*, 26. 3: 257–71.

Walkling, P. H. and Brannigan, C. (1986) 'Anti-sexist/Anti-racist Education: A Possible Dilemma', *Journal of Moral Education*, 15. 1: 16–25.

Ward, L. M. (1995) 'Talking about Sex: Common Themes about Sexuality in the Prime-time Television Programs Children and Adolescents View Most', *Journal of Youth and Adolescence*, 24. 5: 595–615.

Warnock, M. (1979) *Education: A Way Ahead*, Oxford: Blackwell.

Went, D. (1985) *Sex Education: Some Guidelines for Teachers*, London: Bell & Hyman.

Whelan, R. (1995) *Teaching Sex in Schools – Does it Work?* Oxford: Family Education Trust.

White, C. (1994) 'Tackling the Sex Education Class Barrier', *Telegraph and Argus*, 14 Apr. p. 32.

White, P. (1996) *Civic Virtues and Public Schooling: Educating Citizens for a Democratic Society*, New York: Teachers College Press.

Whitehead, B. D. (1994) 'The Failure of Sex Education', *The Atlantic Monthly* (Oct.): 55–80.

Wilson, J. (1965) *Logic and Sexual Morality*, Harmondsworth: Penguin.

Wringe, C. (1994) 'Family Values and the Value of the Family', *Journal of Philosophy of Education* 28. 1: 77–88.

Zirkel, P. A. (1996) 'Hot, Sexy – and Safer?' *Phi Delta Kappan*, 78. 1: 93–4.

# 9 Moral Imagination and the Case for Others

## M. B. WILKINSON

> I cheated in the final of my metaphysics examination: I looked into the soul of the boy sitting next to me.
>
> Woody Allen

In a previous paper (Wilkinson 1999), I outlined the basis of a possible universal ethic based upon the envisioning of possible futures. If such a universal ethic is possible, then there is scope for moral education which can speak with confidence, while fully respecting cultural traditions. It would be helpful, I hope, to summarise some of my earlier conclusions.

Ethical life takes place within a metaphysical context. Much modern debate about ethics has tried to eschew any metaphysical assumptions, and to talk only about the language of morals. This seems to me a fundamental error, not least because living morally presupposes a world in which we experience, live and act. To think about anything, as Husserl often remarked, is always to talk about something. That there is something is presupposed. The twentieth-century philosopher has tended to avoid anything which can be called metaphysical since the onslaught of logical positivism and the linguistic concerns of Wittgenstein and his followers.

To do this was an understandable reaction against the idealist philosophies of nineteenth-century thought. But it should be noted that the most famous assault on metaphysics, in *Language, Truth and Logic* (Ayer 1946), actually directs all its attention to questioning the possibility of transcendental metaphysics, and makes from that the assertion that: 'The arguments which we use to refute them (those who indulge in transcendent metaphysics) will . . . be found to apply to the whole of mataphysics.' This assumption may be questioned (Lejewski 1986) on many grounds, but for present purposes, one consideration will do.

Metaphysics may be defined as the study of what exists. Now, it may well be that there could be things unknowable to human minds, of which we cannot coherently speak. But it does not follow from this that we can say nothing of what exists. There are two possible approaches to metaphysics, called, for convenience, the 'ontological' and the 'cosmological'. Cosmological metaphysics concerns a theory of the whole – God, the universe, spirits and so on. Ontological metaphysics is a piecemeal concern: it tries to determine what we can be fairly sure there is, without claiming completeness. Whether the former is possible is a question we may leave to one side: the second certainly seems a reasonable enterprise, involving no necessary commitment to dreaming of the transcendent. For the purposes of ethical discussion, the second path, the ontological, seems to me sufficient.

I propose one basic metaphysical proposition, with one sub-proposition:

*Proposition 1*   There exist at least material objects.
*Proposition 2*   Among material objects there are sentient, reflective and self-directed objects, called 'persons'.

These propositions seem modest enough, even banal, but they are, I think, sufficient for the construction of a universal ethic. I know of no culture which would deny either of the propositions, though most would want to supplement them with other postulates about existing entities. But if these are sufficient metaphysical principles to construct at least a minimal ethic, which can be taught and agreed across cultures, then, using Ockham's Razor (the principle of parsimony, that the simpler explanation is always to be preferred) there is no need to multiply entities beyond necessity.

These propositions seem to me intuitively grasped. As babies we become aware of a world of objects even before we can name those objects: we try physically to grasp them, and our first words are attempts to name objects. We quite quickly learn that there are at least two types of objects, those which are insensitive and those which react to us.

We also find in babies a primitive valuing function: they like some sorts of things and dislike others. Indeed we like certain kinds of things even before we learn their nature: to love or hate appears to be a primitive function of mind, as Brentano pointed out (Chisholm 1986). If we are feeling scholarly, we can add that this function has evolutionary value: survival depends to a considerable extent on fearing and disliking certain kinds of things and seeking others. (There is no need, for the moment, to raise the crucial question of why we have these responses: it is sufficient to observe that these appear universal.)

As we grow, these functions become more sophisticated. We become aware of two things: of ourselves as centres of consciousness and of the possibility of choice. At first it may be only a belief that if I scream loudly enough I may receive (desirable) attention. But I learn that I can, up to a point, influence my surroundings, but also that there are limits to that influence. I can summon the attention of my mother, but I cannot remove from my room that black grate which so frightens me, because I can make out its brooding presence even in the dark. I continue to value and to loathe.

Later still I learn that I can think in a connected way. In particular, I learn to remember – in doing so I sense a continuity in myself – and also to imagine. I can imagine that black grate as a malevolent presence, but I also discover in myself the capacity to imagine possible futures. When I scream, I do so because I can imagine that someone will come, and the presence of my mother is preferable to the loneliness of my room. My actions create reactions, and so I learn the interplay of persons with each other, reinforcing my vague awareness that the two metaphysical propositions are grounded in reality as it is known to me.

It should be noted that I cannot demonstrate that what I claim to be the process of learning and growth is really so. I can adduce the empirical evidence of my sensory evidence, and my observation of the behaviour of babies: other than that, I can

only assert a fundamental belief that my observation will be found to be shared.

Throughout this description, there is the underlying assertion that as persons we are always active. We are not in agreement with some traditional philosophers who appear to treat the mind as simply a receptacle of sensation. We do not, I think, habitually find ourselves as simply observers. We are in action, always. Even when I react to a situation by doing nothing, that doing nothing is my action. And it is a chosen action. There is a sense in which I am obliged to choose, as the existentialists have rightly pointed out. To be a choosing, acting person is a condition of my being. Of course, there was a point at which my choices were so unconsidered as not to be worthy of the name, and if I suffer certain types of brain damage, or become senile, I may again find myself incapable of true choice. But by the term 'choice', I mean considered activity.

It is to considered action that we apply the term 'moral': an action by a baby or a lunatic or someone suffering from senile dementia we cannot properly describe as moral or immoral – at least since Aristotle *Nichomachean Ethics* we have desisted from attaching moral opprobrium to the actions of the incapable. From this it follows that the field of conscious action is the realm of the ethical.

Now, if it is in the field of conscious choice that we are moral or immoral, it is essential to outline the conditions of moral choice.

## Moral choice

In the sixth book of the *Nichomachean Ethics*, Aristotle famously develops – with a psychological insight and vocabulary far beyond that of his teacher, Plato – an account of the place of prudence and moral judgement in assessing circumstance and determining particular moral actions. But behind his analysis there lies a presupposition which he does not explore, the faculty of imagination. But the idea of imagination is implicit in weighing possible outcomes: one must be able to picture those outcomes before they can be prudently weighed. Without the ability to imagine there are no possibilities before the mind. The ability to imagine is the precondition of moral reflection: if we lack imagination there is no possibility of the ethical life – what characterises the thug is the failure of the moral imagination.

At least since Hume, it has been a commonplace

among philosophers to deny the possibility of deriving a statement of value from a proposition about the facts of the world: facts about the world are described in terms of the verb 'to be', moral imperatives in terms of the verb 'ought', and the latter, it is held, are not formally derivable from the former. As I claimed in an earlier paper (Wilkinson 1998) this has led philosophers to a profound pessimism about the possibility of finding any factual justification for ethical principles. And this, in turn, has led to the modern scepticism about the justification of morals. I believe this scepticism to be misplaced.

A consideration of the nature of a moral choice is helpful here. Let us suppose that a neighbour asks me to help him to erect a new garage. What he has presented me with is a choice of two possible futures: a future in which I am helping him to build his garage and a future in which I am not. These futures are describable in factual terms, in terms of the verb 'to be'. I am being asked to imagine those possible futures and to select one rather than the other. Nor is my choice simply a matter of 'plumping' for one rather than the other: it is a real choice because I can give reasons for those options. I can choose to help because, as a matter of fact, I like my neighbour (coveting neither his wife nor his ox), because I know he cannot manage alone, or because I have nothing better to do. Against his request, I might consider my future relations with him, my awareness of my total lack of rapport with the inanimate, or a host of other reasons, such as finding doing nothing a splendid occupation. But there is only such a choice because I can envisage these futures. In part, the quality of my eventual choice will be determined by the accuracy of my imagining. If I am unrealistic in my picture of my capabilities then it is more likely that I will embark upon unrealistic behaviour, such as volunteering for the most technically complex work, with predictably dire results.

On a technical note, it is worth stressing how this analysis avoids the is/ought problem. When I say 'I ought to help my neighbour', this is translatable as 'At a future point, either it will be true that I am helping my neighbour or it will not be true that I am helping my neighbour, and it is true that I prefer the former state of affairs'. But in saying this, I appear to leave untouched the question of why the former state of affairs is preferable. We may observe that it is a condition of the human mind to prefer certain kinds of activities, but we are also aware of the shifting nature of our preferences: what seems desirable activity today, in abstract, might seem highly undesirable when faced tomorrow by the pieces which are to be reassembled as a garage. Nevertheless, it is possible to argue that some of my problem is the consequence of poor original imagination, in that in my enthusiasm to be a good neighbour I neglected fully to picture what was actually involved in the task. Equally, my mental picture of myself and my abilities might have been unrealistic, as might have been my neighbour's belief that I was capable of giving the assistance required.

But even if all this is true, there is still something missing from the analysis: the reason why it is worthwhile to help my neighbour. We need at least one moral principle, which states roughly that it is proper to seek the good of persons. I am reluctant to formulate such a principle more precisely, partly because I do not seek to add another to compete with existing moral precepts – I am not arguing for a new morality, but seeking common ground – but also because this seems to me to be the common feature of many, perhaps all, current models of ethics, from Christianity's 'Love thy neighbour' to Bentham's 'greatest good of the greatest number' and Kant's second form of the categorical imperative. In other cultures, this idea may be found in the Chinese subordination of the self to the wider family or community group and may be discerned elsewhere. Indeed, the concept is presupposed in the very idea of an ethic: it is the precondition of the desire to be moral.

If this is true, it is suggestive in that it leaves open the precise cultural expression of the principle while allowing the principle itself as a common basis for discourse. Underlying such an analysis is a presupposition of a value for humanity, even a version of natural law, not with theological overtones, but simply based on the natural human facts of altruism, sympathy, loyalty and concern for others, which one finds natural to all cultures. That this is so may be determined empirically, I think. (Even the philosopher's exception of the Ik, who appeared to have no ethical norms, may be questioned, Battersby 1978.) There is nothing intellectually imperialist in assuming that the wish to do good is universal: and if good is only so when it is experienced as such, then it is good for a person or persons, as persons are the only inhabitants of the earth capable of experiencing it as moral action. (Whether an animal could be counted in this sense as a person is a separate question: I leave open the separate and essential enquiry about whether all or any animals are capable of such experience – even so, we may legitimately argue that cruelty to animals is profoundly damaging to the persons who perpetrate that cruelty; it is not good for persons to be callous, as doing so suggests an infirmity of the moral imagination.)

Given the desire to do good as such, for the sake of persons, and the concept of moral imagination, it may be that we have sufficiently described the preconditions of the moral life. How this conception is translated into action, indeed how it may be taught, requires us to probe these concepts further.

## Content of the moral imagination

From what I have said so far, it follows that the moral imagination involves the ability to imagine conceivable outcomes, with as much accuracy as possible. But outcomes occur within the context of the world: any discussion of these cannot be isolated from the contents of the world in which they happen. (We may note, parenthetically, the extent to which most of us possess only the haziest idea of the contents of the world: this raises important educational issues – by eschewing metaphysics in our teaching we do disservice to the possibility of clear thought.)

My proposal, given the huge variety of ontologies available, is to develop a model for the moral imagination based upon the two metaphysical propositions outlined earlier, that there exist at least material objects, and that among these objects are the sentient experiencing objects we call persons. This model is extremely productive for the purpose of defining the moral imagination and is likely to achieve almost universal acceptance. I repeat that this model rules out no further possibilities: it neither affirms nor denies God or anything else, and so remains culturally open.

In the nineteenth century a crucial observation was made by Franz Brentano (Chisholm 1986) on the nature of human thought. He recognised that we cannot picture an abstraction. For instance, if I think of the abstract notion, 'justice', the mental pictures before the mind are particular: I may think of courts, judges, the figure with the scales over the Old Bailey, or fairness of behaviour. What I cannot do is to have a mental image of the abstraction – I can envisage only instances in which the abstraction

is embodied. This particularity is central to an understanding of the imagination. If mental pictures are always particular, then it follows that so too will be the moral imagination.

This has far-reaching consequences. The Polish philosopher Tadeusz Kotarbinski, acknowledging his debt to Brentano (Kotarbinski 1966a), developed the metaphysical thesis known as reism, or in its later form, concretism. This philosophy, technically described as unicategorial pansomatic ontologism, is more severe and more controversial than I need for present purposes. Kotarbinski asserts that the sole constituents of reality are material objects: I am content to say that there are at least physical objects, ruling out no further possibilities. In doing this, I intend to avoid the errors which can creep into understanding and discourse from an assumption of the real nature of abstract entities.

The point can be simply made. If we consider any adjective, such as 'blue', we can see its use in a variety of contexts: 'the sea is blue', 'the book is blue', and so on. A moment's thought will indicate that it is impossible to separate the blueness of a thing from the thing itself: that which is blue is always a blue something. And yet in our language, we do make such a separation, as for instance if I say, 'blue is my favourite colour'. In this sentence 'blue' functions as a noun, the subject of the sentence. But it names nothing, serving only as a convenient linguistic term for all the instances which are described adjectivally as 'blue'. The technical term for such an abstraction is an 'onomatoid' – something which functions as a noun but designates no entity. It is a feature of the human mind, however, to have an almost superstitious belief that a name must be the name of something. Throughout philosophical history we find examples of this error, from Plato, who having words for beauty, goodness and so on was led to posit the ideal forms for things in themselves, to those who having words for unicorns and phoenixes were led to ask what kinds of things these might be, to designate them as belonging to a class of fictitious objects, and then exhausted themselves in trying to define a fictitious object. A similar phenomenon can be found in those who have spent fruitless hours trying to determine what sort of thing 'nothing' might be (a something called 'nothing' is surely a contradiction in terms).

We may note that there is a parallel process with gerund forms. There is no such thing as 'running' apart from the objects which run, nor can we imagine running apart from someone who runs. The same is true of moral terms, such as 'justice'. We may properly describe a person as 'just' in accordance with certain criteria of ascription, and the incidences of his behaving justly we may conveniently call 'justice', but it does not follow that justice in itself exists apart from those things we call just. Religious believers instinctively recognise this when they speak of the justice of God – which is the justice of something, and not a free-floating form. Yet we may remember how frequently we use terms such as 'love' (think of earnest teenage conversations, mostly embarrassing, on the meaning of true love), 'loyalty' (beloved of managers everywhere), 'trust', as if any of these things had reality outside the individual instantiations of them. We overlook our total inability to picture any of these things, and yet their picturing is always particular. Kotarbinski (1966b) has suggested the importance of freeing the humanities of these onomatoids: most people, I suspect, are unaware of how much our discourse presupposes them. There is an error in assuming that relationships somehow exist apart from those things which are related, or that 'caring' can be separated from those persons who care. Errors about forces of history depend on a similar kind of ontological mistake, as if there could be revolution somehow independently of those who are revolutionary. Much reification occurs in discussions of economics, social sciences, management theory and elsewhere.

And yet, moral activity takes place always in the realm of the particular. It is this person who needs my help, that particular suffering which needs alleviating. Moral demands are always concrete, even if not always immediate. The relief of the starving in Africa is the relief of concretely hungry persons. Any resolution of suffering begins with the particularity of this suffering. If it is to be understood, that understanding is necessarily in the context of actuality: to know in abstract what hunger is is not the same as the understanding of this person's hunger.

We are aware of this from experience. We can ignore general appeals to our charity, but not so readily refuse the individual whom we know and who appeals directly for our help: the particular beggar affects us far more, even if we do not give, and feel guilty, than the abstract request to give to the homeless. Fund-raisers for charity are aware of the special force of the television pictures of suffering persons: we imagine the pain of an individual in a way that we do not recognise the human reality behind the statistic of several thousand hungry.

Conversely, indifference follows when we do not picture the individuality of pain. The person who says 'they are only Jews' is blind to individuality: he lacks the moral imagination to see beyond a distinguishing and collective feature. The thug who delights in beating old ladies is one who sees age as something contemptible, and lacks insight into the lived experience of the personhood of someone else. We may add to this point, the second form of Kant's categorical imperative, that we should so act as to treat people always as ends, and never as means only. As William Temple indicated (Temple 1934), this has particular value in creating a moral outlook. In the realm of economics, production exists for consumption: immorality creeps in when persons (consumers) are manipulated, such as by creating an artificial shortage, for the sake of profits. We see in history how often persons have been used for the sake of an ideal: Lenin, Hitler and others have been manipulators of this kind. Lenin was perfectly capable of ordering the shooting of fifty innocents to make a point, and publicly stated that any behaviour was acceptable for the sake of the revolution (Lenin 1968). Ideals are surely for persons, not persons for ideals.

If this is true, then it follows that the central task for the moral imagination is the right understanding of persons. This is why I have insisted upon the person as object in the world, rather than an abstract humanity. Sartre mocked the cult of humanity, referring to the person who looks at the phenomenon of flight and exclaims that 'Man is magnificent' (Sartre 1973). This is rather the attitude of the young student who says that we know so much more than Aristotle, as if we were somehow born with the wisdom of the ages and do not each have to learn what we can. That I know of things that Aristotle could not does not mean that I know more than he did. Humanity is nothing but the persons who make it up. There is a truth in Margaret Thatcher's infamous 'There is no such thing as society' if she meant that there is no abstract society and no society separable from the persons who make it up. One cannot abstractly do good for society other than the good of particular persons.

The difficulty of understanding persons is a special one. Some philosophers have doubted that we can ever know the existence of other minds: certainly I cannot know other minds as I know my own. There is a sense in which Descartes' attempt to know the fullness of reality from 'I think therefore I am' was misplaced. Nothing else can ever be as real to me as I am to myself. It will lack that experienced inwardness. In any case, reality is a comparative matter. If I ask 'Are ghosts real?', I am not asking if ghosts are as real as I am to myself: I am asking if they are contents of the world as chairs and tables are. To ask whether something is real is always to ask 'Is it as real as *x*?'. I have been content to use as the criterion of reality the material objects of the world. Nevertheless, there is a special mystery about others. It is a commonplace that this mystery is concealed by language. I think I understand another because we share a language. I know that my friend and I describe the same colour patches as 'blue', but I have no idea what his inward experience of blue may be. I have reason to suspect it is different from mine, if, for instance, he praises a newly painted room and describes its beauty with pride while I find it perfectly vile. The same is true with tastes: we can both describe the taste of sardines, yet he finds the taste a delight, while I do not. The privacy of pain has often been remarked: a nurse has no idea of how a hypodermic needle hurts me, nor can I describe that inward experience. (A revealing comment was made by the late Frederick Leonard in an article published on his reaching 80, of the indignity of old age: 'Others will always know better what's good for me. Their feet will know where my shoes pinch' (Leonard 1982), which, of course, is precisely what they cannot know.) It is that inability to imagine that inwardness of others which seems the impenetrable barrier to the full moral imagination for which I have argued.

But the barrier may not be as impenetrable as at first appears. A potent clue is to be found in the work of Josiah Royce. His moral insight is worth extended quotation. In response to the question 'What then is our neighbour?', Royce says:

> We find that out by treating him in thought just as we do ourselves. What art thou? Thou art now just a present state, with its experiences, thoughts and desires. But what is thy future Self? Simply future states, future experiences, future thoughts and desires, that, although not now existing for thee are postulated by thee as certain to come, and as in some real relation to thy present Self. What then is thy neighbour? He too is a mass of states, of experiences, thoughts, and desires just as real as thou art, no more but yet no less present to thy experience now than is thy future Self. He is not that face that

frowns or smiles at thee, although often thou thinkest of him only as that. He is not the arm that strikes or defends thee, not the voice that speaks to thee, not that machine that gives thee when thou movest it with the offer of money. To be sure, thou dost often think of him as if he were that automaton yonder, that answers thee when thou speakest to it. But no, thy neighbour is as actual, as concrete as thou art. Just as thy future is real, though not . . . [yet] . . . thine, so thy neighbour is real, though his thoughts never are thy thoughts. Dost thou believe this? Art thou sure what it means? This is for thee the turning-point of thy whole conduct towards him. What we now ask of thee is no sentiment, no gush of pity, no tremulous weakness of sympathy, but a calm, clear insight.   (Royce 1965)

This, surely, is the true voice of the moral imagination, recognising a special nature in others. Appreciating this requires going beyond either assuming that his description is exhausted by terms for his race, class, social standing, colour, sex, height and so on, or beyond a simplistic view that he is really just like me. It is that his thoughts are as real to him as mine are to me, though shrouded from me by appearance. It is not the case that if we disagree about politics or religion we are both as right as each other – that would be the sloppiest type of cultural relativism – but it is the precondition for understanding his sincerity. Understanding what my religion or politics might mean to me has the potential to inform me of the depth his can possess for him, which means that I am less inclined to dismiss his views as simply misguided or trivial. Thomas Nagel (1986) has pointed to the way in which our search for understanding requires a tension and search for both subjective and objective aspects: there is a danger in the age of science that we exhaust understanding by a series of psychological, sociological, economic and biological descriptors, and yet we are all fully aware that a total description of ourselves in these terms would not add up to a total description of the experienced 'I'. Russell rightly indicated the distinction between knowing all the truths about something and knowing the thing itself (Russell 1970). The moral awareness involves above all the sense of that inwardness of persons; this, as Royce rightly says, is the beginning, 'the turning-point of thy whole conduct'. Morality involves sensitivity as a precondition: being moral is not exhausted by a study of precepts, because its field is always particular. Moral judgement is not the conclusion of a process but a prelude to appropriate action. And action is always particular.

This is why I have insisted upon the particularity of the imagination. If, as I think, the sphere of the moral lies not in the general but in the specific and individual, it is necessary to recognise its situationalism. Aristotle, supremely, emphasised the particularity of moral judgement (*Nichomachean Ethics*); in our own day, the subject has been explored in depth by Joseph Fletcher (1966) and William Temple (1944). We recognise in our experience the way in which following a given precept in all circumstances leads to actual harm. Someone who always told the truth would be a monster: there are occasions when silence or even a lie is the right thing for the good of persons. If a brute asked me to tell him the way to his intended victim, I would argue that my lie was not morally understandable in the circumstances, but absolutely the right thing to do. I could not make such a decision if I lacked imagination to see the consequences of putting him on the right path: that imagination is the precondition of right judgement. It is impossible to do good for persons without some ability to see possible (future) goods.

If, however, I can envisage possible futures, then it is possible to make some types of factual judgement. I can think of several possible futures that seem to me undesirable. I can conceive of political circumstances under which I do not want to find myself, and individual life patterns, such as being deaf and without music, which I consider undesirable. Nor is this undesirability simply a matter of emotion. I can give particular factual reasons why I would find myself unable to flourish under totalitarianism or when deaf: I can name experiences which I have always enjoyed which would be impossible under those circumstances. In a wider sense, I am able also to give factual reasons, based on actual descriptions of known behaviour among large numbers of dispossessed, why homelessness hurts not only the homeless but all of us. I can show historical instances of the consequences, and I can demonstrate the reality of actual harms to persons, both in terms of security and property. Such a judgement is as factual as one about the state of the economy or the likely consequences of a multiple road crash. The car designer makes judgements about the possible future safety of his vehicle in just such a way, and it is no more nor less factual than mine about human good. Designing a safer car presupposes the moral principle that it is good not to harm persons. Of course, this judgement does not have the mathematical certainty of the answer to a correctly worked equation, nor are we always correct in our predictions of possible futures, but we can only be as precise as the subject matter will bear (Aristotle, *Nichomachean Ethics*). And, like the car designer's, the moral judgement is capable of refinement and improvement in the light of experience, reflection and planning.

## Moral education

The question arises whether the moral imagination provides sufficient basis for formulating an appropriate system of general moral education. By itself, it seems a necessary precondition, and it could be sufficient condition provided that we do not simply encourage imagination, but also explore the conditions of imagination. There is an important difference between moral imagination and fantasy, just as there is in art between the uncontrolled and the disciplined imagination.

What distinguishes the moral imagination is first that it is conditioned by context. Moral decisions, I have insisted, do not occur in a vacuum but when faced – as we all are – by the conditions of life as lived. Robert C. Solomon has pointed to the artificiality of management games as a tool for developing management skills, on the grounds that the game lacks the particularity of the situation in which real decisions are made, often in competition with other demands (Solomon 1992). The idea that moral imagination can be developed by role-play alone seems mistaken. Of course the reading and discussion of literature awakens awareness of possibility, by encouragement of understanding and sympathy, just as history, economics and sociology can he better understood by treating forces not as abstract but as the consequences of human behaviour (Schama 1989). More valuable still is the sense of the organisation of the school as community: this is itself a teaching device in which there are the advantages of structure and a degree of security within which decisions have a context. This context is available throughout the school day and is not restricted to a special subject of moral education. Such an approach requires exploration and discussion as well as command.

The exploration of the possibilities of the moral imagination requires awareness of conditions and limitations, if it is not to end in wishful thinking. If the end is activity, then it is crucial to see what can be encompassed, to learn what is in my power alone, what requires assistance and what the constraints of aspiration may be. One of the hardest steps, when faced with endemic poverty, is to recognise that the fact that I cannot do everything does not imply that I can do nothing. To do something is a small alleviation and a potent example. Pyramids were built one block at a time. This emphasises again the value of particularity, the general pious hope giving way to the actual.

The first limitation that must be faced is the universal condition of death: anything I do is bounded by the brevity of time. There is – it is widely recognised – a tendency today not to speak of death, as if it were too difficult a topic for the young, a shameful secret to be avoided. And yet the young thug who takes life casually is one who has never thought what it means for this person to be killed. A death is seen as a piece of cartoon fantasy and not the particular end of the universe. It is difficult to counteract a culture which treats death as a kind of crime caused by lax living. Magazines are full of health advice – do this and you will not die of that – which draws a veil over the inescapable point that if I do not die of that, I will die of something else. There is a cast of mind that is baffled when someone dies – 'but she did not smoke and always took lots of exercise'. Death becomes also something that happens to someone else. The young will sometimes say that they do not mind dying at 70, which is translatable as 'I do not mind dying then', concealing from themselves that death is always now: whenever I die, it will be in the present. Nor is realism about death morbid. If the moral life is about living, it must involve realism about the precariousness of that life.

Another factor, which requires exploration in greater depth than I have space to give, is the affective nature of the moral imagination. Imagination is not a purely intellectual process: it is coloured by feelings. Among those feelings are likely to be those of affection. In any culture, there is a disharmony when the dominant colouring of the mental recreation of the world consists of hatred and resentment. This is the universal mark of dysfunctional and anti-social behaviour. A well-functioning person sees life as one which is unavoidably social, involving mutual ties. Aristotle (*Nichomachean Ethics*) recognised the significance and value of civic friendship in providing social cement to the polis. A more rule-bound modern approach has been inclined to overlook this aspect of political life (Schwarzenbach 1996), yet a moment's reflection reveals the need for recognition of mutual dependence as a condition of flourishing. Simple human limitation means that there are things I cannot do alone, for which I need assistance. To receive that assistance – at least after the first few years of life – I have to provide a measure of reciprocity (Gewirth 1979). In saying this, we are going beyond merely arguing that to demand my rights but not to grant them to others involves me in logical inconsistency (Nozick 1981): I am saying that the conditions of life become incomplete. I owe duties to others not simply because it is in my self-interest to do so, but because all will ultimately be better off. If, as I have suggested, moral imagination is the basic condition of moral thought, with a Roycean conception of the inner reality of the other, then it follows that the affection I may have for myself is envisioned as part of the other.

Such an argument breaks down if we lack self-love: lack of self-esteem is a potent source of contempt for the other. To avoid this it is necessary to educate understanding of the self and our uniqueness. This, I tentatively suggest, is best achieved when I recognise that my insight is of a universe, the only universe I can know, seen from my vantage point. G. K. Chesterton argued against suicide precisely on the grounds that we do not kill ourselves – we kill the universe. It is a crime against being. This privileged view is not only the potential richness of my life but it is the unique gift I can give to others. There is a tendency for all of us to see others in the third person – 'X is a pupil, and pupils see things like this' – forgetting that the pupil's experience is necessarily first-person and unique. But it is unique in community with other first-person perspectives. This is why it matters so much that we should try to hold in balance unique individual needs and those of community. It is the microcosmic nature of the class in the broader society of the school which should enable the possibility of maintaining at least a rough-and-ready training in the dual aspect of individuality. To concentrate only on the individual is to miss part of the essence of that individual – the extent to which the person is defined by the possibilities created by others and their situation. Concern for the community is not necessarily a watering down of unique personhood: it is part of its condition. Good teachers are instinctively aware of these tensions and possibilities, but good practice expands when we render possibilities explicit.

A further condition that needs exploration is trustworthiness. This is potentially difficult to achieve, in that we all have from early life experience of the trust that is misplaced and the bitterness of disappointment. But a kind of trust is the precondition of thought. We take it for granted that the floor will remain solid beneath our feet; only sophisticated analysis of the problem of induction teaches us how much of an act of faith that trust is. But some things are always taken for granted if we are to make any intellectual progress. The problem is that people prove less trustworthy than furniture. Of itself, this need not be altogether unfortunate – the fickleness of persons is tribute to unpredictability: a reminder that persons are not just things. Inspection of our own inconstancy is vital to self-knowledge as well as reminding us of the nature of the conditions within which moral imagination works: people will not always behave as we confidently predict. When trustworthiness is found, we value it the more and see more clearly its positive advantages. Many mutual activities in education are aids in developing not blind trust but awareness of the potentiality of possible shared bonds.

The limitations of trustworthiness are valuable in developing sound attitudes towards loyalty. Loyalty is a deep instinct: managers of a certain stamp love to appeal to it, usually as a plea to ignore their own errors. But loyalty is not virtuous. It may be a precondition of virtue, but it can, when thoughtlessly given, lead to all kinds of evil. Loyalty, it is often said, has to be earned. More to the point, it needs to be reflective if it is not to be a blind acceptance of the dishonourable. Only by discernment of persons and situations can we determine with any certainty the proper objects of loyalty. Critical awareness is therefore a central activity, too often overlooked.

Underlying each of these points about the moral imagination is a central educational concern: the need for teaching to be underpinned by considerations of ontological metaphysics. As teachers, we cannot hide from the need to be clear about what there is in the universe, a concern for what life and thought are about. Aristotle's concern for meticulous detailing of the physical content of the universe is the necessary starting point and the benchmark of significant thought. We need to ask not simply what a word *means* (a question often asked of students), but what kind of thing it is about. (A. J. Ayer argued (Ayer 1946) that when we ask for a definition of something, we ask for its verbal definition only: we ask for equivalent words. This seems untrue in many cases. If a child asks 'What is a hippopotamus?', he is asking 'What kind of a thing is a hippopotamus', not 'How do you define a hippopotamus?', and I may answer him not by a verbal definition but by pointing to a thing in the world, and saying, 'That's a hippopotamus!' – my 'definition' is one of demonstration and recognition.) Only with this kind of analysis can we define the content and limits of the imagination.

The benefits of ontological analysis in the course or education are incalculable. A good example can be found in the teaching of accountancy. Any system of accountancy is designed to provide measurement of wealth, but that measurement is wholly conventional, whether in terms of historic cost, replacement value or some other factor. The figure on the balance sheet is not the reality it measures but only a model, for conceptual purposes, of one aspect of it. Yet most accountancy teaching, in my experience, restricts itself to technical questions of how to prepare accounts: it does not deal with the reality it represents. One sees often in business the trend of treating the balance sheet or the bottom line as if it were the whole reality that matters, when it is only a picture from one angle of a living organisation. A great deal of the immorality of much business practice flows from a failure to recognise the distinction. Learning the difference between accountants' reality and the world's reality improves not only moral standards but the self-understanding of the discipline. Thought about the nature of reality would prevent at least some errors in any subject.

Therefore it seems that a potent source for the content of moral imagination would be the widespread development of philosophy as a school discipline, but this would need to be a philosophy based not on the arid search for verbal meaning but on the contents of the world: in short, on metaphysics. This metaphysic must consider not only the nature of things but the developing, complex, subtle, acting, thinking, imagining and feeling entities, persons in an intersubjective realm of persons.

I have tried to emphasise that the moral imagination is above all practical, and the potential for it is universal. It is impossible to begin to think accurately about the world if we have no sense of its common nature. Only by reflection on the world as it is knowable to us can we determine our vision of our place – and that of others – in it. That is why we must look beneath cultural difference to the underlying vision that we dwell in a communal experience of being born, growing and dying, together with other sentient persons. It is in that common fate that we find the basis of something to say, each to the other.

## References

Ayer, A. J. (1946) *Language, Truth and Logic*, London: Victor Gollancz.

Battersby, C. (1978) 'Morality and the Ik', *Philosophy*, 53. 204: 201–14.

Chisholm, R. M. (1986) *Brentano and Intrinsic Value*, Cambridge: Cambridge University Press.

Fletcher, J. (1966) *Situation Ethics: The New Morality*, Philadelphia: SCM.

Gewirth, A. (1979) *Reason and Morality*, Chicago: University of Chicago Press.

Kotarbinski, T. (1966a) 'The Development Stages of Concretism', *Gnosiology: The Scientific Approach to the Theory of Knowledge*, Oxford: Pergamon.

Kotarbinski, T. (1966b) 'The Humanities without Hypostases', *Gnosiology: The Scientific Approach to the Theory of Knowledge*, Oxford: Pergamon.

Lejewski, C. (1986) 'Logic, Ontology and Metaphysics', in S. G. Shanker (ed.) *Philosophy in Britain Today*, London: Croom Helm.

Lenin, V. I. (1968 (1920)) 'The Tasks of the Youth Leagues' *Selected Works*, Moscow: Progress.

Leonard, F. S. (1982) 'The Bonus Years', *Choice* (Oct.).

Nagel, T. (1986) *The View From Nowhere*, Oxford: Oxford University Press.

Nozick, R. (1981) *Philosophical Explanations*, Cambridge, MA: Harvard University Press.

Royce, J. (1965) *The Religious Aspect of Philosophy*, Philadelphia.

Russell, B. (1970) *The Problems of Philosophy*, Oxford: Oxford University Press.

Sartre, J.-P. (1973) *Existentialism and Humanism*, London.

Schama, S. (1989) *Citizens*, London: Viking.

Schwarzenbach, S. A. (1996) 'On Civic Friendship', *Ethics*, 107. 1: 97–128.

Solomon, R. C. (1992) *Ethics and Excellence: Cooperation and Integrity in Business*, Oxford: Oxford University Press.

Temple, W. (1934) *Nature, Man and God*, London: Macmillan.

Temple, W. (1944) *Christianity and Social Order*, London: Macmillan.

Wilkinson, M. B. (1999) 'Against Cultural Relativism', *Values in Education and Cultural Diversity: Vol. 1*, London: Falmer Press.

# 10 Value Conflict and Fair Play, and a Sports Education Worthy of the Name

MIKE McNAMEE AND CARWYN JONES

'Hypocrisy', wrote De La Rochefoucauld, 'is a tribute which vice pays to virtue.' The educational critics of sport could scarcely imagine a more fitting object for the duc's words. For, while few cultural practices have provided the English language with richer moral metaphors than sport ('playing the game' only being the most famous), few bring with them such tawdry disavowal of their vaunted ideals. For every one great sportsman or woman there seem to be dozens who flout the rules, abuse officials, take and offer bribes, or wilfully set out to dismember the very opposition who make the contest possible. The very idea of espousing the language of education here seems anathema. But the myth persists; it refuses to lay down and die. And so it seems worth trying to distinguish fact from fiction in the history of sports and their educational legacy. In this chapter we take to task a certain social psychological approach to the questions of value conflict and fair play in sports and argue that its adoption of a formalist framework in sports and in ethics is highly problematic. We also open up the moral educational potential of sports by drawing attention to the richer ethical sources of their informal framework.

## Values in sport: conflicting positions

Sociologists of education have often traced the variety of attitudes and beliefs that people have taken up in amateur and professional, elite and recreative sport and attempted to show how they differ in and between these groups with respect, for example, to age, gender and social class. Functionalists have argued that cultural practices like sport operate in societies as do the living organs that contribute to the health of the body. In complete contrast, sociologists of a Marxist and neo-Marxist persuasion have traditionally regarded sports as potent negative ideological forces that serve to divert the working classes' attention from their parlous and exploited state. Moreover, anti-racist and feminist scholars have held up sports as pernicious conservative forces that promulgate and maintain racist and sexist dispositions.

In addition to the disparate accounts from sociological perspectives, psychologists have attempted to ascertain the values that people purport to find in engaging in different sports in order to see where their motivations lie. Behaviourists argue that the values people develop in sport are no more than the socialising effects of the prevailing environment. Freudians may view sports as practices that enable aggressive and proto-sexual acts motivated by life and death instincts and the pressures of society.

Whatsoever their aspirations, these social scientific enquiries, and others besides, aim to achieve the same thing: to characterise and evaluate the attitudes and behaviours of people in appropriate contexts. What they cannot do, and perhaps ought not aspire to, is settle particular questions about the goodness and badness or rightness and wrongness of the different attitudes and behaviours, or the more abstract questions about what it is for something to be right or wrong, good or bad in sports. To do so requires *philosophical* reflection of a certain kind which we will attempt to instantiate in this chapter.

We first offer a brief account of sports education. We then provide an account of a psychological project concerning values in sport, and critique the particular, cognitivist, picture they espouse. Finally we allude to a richer account of valuing in sport derived from the idea of virtue, or character, that is generated in and through the ethos of sports.

## A sports education worthy of that name

In Britain, at least, during the 1960s an important terminological difference arose in educational circles. What was previously referred to as 'physical training' or 'physical conditioning' or (rather more pejoratively) 'physical jerks' came to be known as 'physical education'. The difference was, of course, more ideological than one might at first sight think. Teachers of the 'new' physical education wanted full-blown educational status and the respect that was accorded to it (Kirk 1988). Yet, as many commentators observed, the title 'physical education' was indicative of a claim rather than a guarantee of the truth that what went on under its name was actually educational. If a detailed linguistic analysis of the 'physical education' were required it would doubtless begin by distinguishing the several meanings that the term is used to convey. There are at least three of these. First, 'physical education' is used to refer to a collection of activities such as athletics, gymnastics and games that are taught in schools. Secondly, it can refer to an academic course of study that comprises various disciplines such as biomechanics, pedagogy, physiology, philosophy, psychology and sociology. Thirdly, it can refer to the profession of people who, through such knowledge, teach those activities. The three are closely related, but for the purpose of this chapter it is the first sense which is taken as paradigmatic. Yet under that heading 'physical education' there is no unifying principle. What binds them together is historical contingency (Kirk 1992) rather than any tight conceptual coherence (Reid 1996, 1996a, Carr 1997, McNamee 1998).

For the purposes of this argument, we refer to the more limited conception of activities which fall under the heading sports that can properly be considered educational. This allows us to dismiss such activities as dance and outdoor pursuits that fall under the heading 'physical education' but which represent and embody activities of considerably different nature and logic. We do so under the heading 'Sports Education' first introduced in the USA by Siedentop (1990) though we are not committed to his particular picture of it. We will presume an account of education along the lines of Peters's (1996) classic account of education as initiation – though, again, we are not thereby committed to the full-blown, intellectually biased, account of liberal education he developed. We are drawn to his more general picture of education comprising an initiation into inherently worthwhile pursuits which are constitutive of a given culture. So by 'sports education' we refer to the morally acceptable initiation into a range of pursuits that are logically characterised as ritually derived rule-governed activities, engaged in by humans that employ embodied capacities in the attainment of the excellent performance of codified versions of basic motor actions typically in the form of a contest (McNamee 1996). Such contests form part of the culture in which they reside, both reflecting its dominant norms and, to a certain extent, shaping those norms also. So, whether indeed sports are educative might not be thought to rest solely upon empirical claims as to the moral status of competitors but rather to their potential to open up portions of a society's cultural heritage (whether we now, perhaps, must think in less local and more global terms is a moot point).

We have elsewhere claimed that some of the most prominent social scientific investigations of moral *development* in sports (e.g. Bredemeier and Shields 1995) are methodologically and theoretically flawed. In particular we have focused on the failure of cognitively biased social psychologists to appreciate the role of perception in moral judgement and action (Jones 1998) and have argued that the developmental paradigm of Kohlberg and Haan cannot unproblematically be applied to sports. We will focus now on a pervasive, yet subtly different psychological approach to the moral status of sports which attempts to examine the value priorities of young sportsmen and women.

## Psychological investigations into values in sports

Lee (1988, 1993) and Lee and Cockman (1995), in common with many social scientists (e.g. Bredemeier and Shields 1984, 1986), believes that there is a tangible decline in the standards of behaviour in sport. The kind of behaviour that Lee refers to is most visible in elite sports like soccer due to the constant glare of the television cameras. Good and bad conduct is clearly visible in glorious technicolour, slow motion and close up. Lee's specific concern is the apparent decline in the exhibition of sportsmanship and fair play in youth sport. This, however, is not unconnected to the general decline in standards of behaviour in elite sport. Lee argues that an unquenchable thirst for sporting success is cultivated and nurtured by the media, by elite athletes and even the government. Given the prevailing atmosphere it is no surprise, according to Lee, that a win-at-all-costs attitude is adopted by the coaches, teachers and the young athletes themselves. Winning, he argues, is valued above all else; educational benefits, enjoyment and fair play are at best 'also-rans'.

Lee (1995) aims to examine the veracity of the claims for decline through a psychological examination of the moral standards in youth sport represented by the participants' values. Essentially the question for Lee is 'Why is unfair play increasingly chosen as a viable option in sport?' Lee argues that identification of the prevalent cognitive priorities or values which provide the basis for decision-making in youth sport may provide answers to this question. Following Rokeach (1973), Lee chooses the concept of 'value' as the most significant notion to investigate because he believes that values 'are central cognitive constructs by which people organise their lives' (Lee 1995: 61) and that, following Schwartz (1992) they represent clear indicators of present and future behaviour since 'they guide selection or evaluation of events' (ibid.). Particular patterns of behaviour are manifestations of particular motivational priorities which incorporate a person's values. Moreover, with respect to moral behaviour, the identification of the motivational priorities or values is even more important because it is the motivational or intentional set within or before the act that identifies its moral status. At the risk of oversimplification, what Lee proposes is that the difference between the fair player and the cheat is a difference in their chosen value priorities.

Lee (1995) draws upon Rokeach (1973) and Schwartz (1992) for theoretical support for his psychological account of values in sports. Neither Rokeach or Schwartz offers a normative or substantive account of what is worthwhile (as might be offered by a philosopher of values, education or sport), rather they offer a description of a behaviourally antecedent cognitive construct. To reiterate, the most important feature of a value for Lee's project is that it directly guides and influences action in concrete situations like sport, thus making a legitimate subject for researching action in sport.

Again following Rokeach (1973), Lee proposes that a value is a kind of proscriptive or prescriptive belief. Holding a value means that a person believes that a certain state of affairs ought to be or ought not to be the case and will act to make it so.

Another characteristic of a value according to Rokeach is its stability: the relative unit of a person's character or personality can be described partly in terms of their values: values can be likened to the glue that holds together a person's identity over time in spite of their varying physical attributes. Rokeach also argues that values are limited in number: one value may give rise to a number of different attitudes and behaviours. The value of honesty, for example, may inform or influence a person's attitude towards any number of given objects or situations. Condemnation of theft, lying, deceit and cheating may all be manifestations of the value of honesty. A final and more controversial aspect of Rokeach's account of values is that they are universal in nature. A limited number of values are recognised, if not always shared, by everyone. This conclusion is reached by Rokeach through a combination of empirical investigation and theoretical postulation. Given the purported nature of a value adopted from Rokeach, Lee (1995: 63) argues that:

> the construct of values permits the development of a strategy to examine the nature of fair play which depends on the application of general principles of conduct which supersedes the immediate demands of the situation. These principles guide the decision-making process and hence influence the expression of attitudes and behaviour in specific situations.

To play fair according to Lee is to play in accordance with the requirements of certain principles, specifically moral principles. Lee (1995) argues that concerns about sportsmanship or fair play arise when the principles of sportsmanship are violated, for example when someone cheats by feigning injury, seeking to gain an unfair advantage. He cites Fraleigh (1984), who argues that only moral principles can rightly serve as guidelines for right action in sport. Only through the application and implementation of moral principles, rather than of sport conventions or one's own self-interest, can right action in sport be guaranteed. Moral principles, unlike certain conventions or self-interest, are universal and impartial; their application neither favours nor prejudices any one player or team at the expense of another. These formal criteria of equality and impartiality characterise moral principles such as justice. For Lee moral values are the embodiment of these moral principles. To exhibit the value of sportsmanship is at the same time to act in accordance with the moral principles of justice and equality. The rules of sport are similar in nature to moral principles: they serve to ensure the equality and fairness of the contest. By breaking the rules and gaining advantage the fairness of a contest is lost and essentially a moral principle, that of fairness, is violated. This view of fair play in sport is called the 'formalist' account and is discussed later.

In order to identify the kinds of values that underpin unfair or immoral behaviour in sport, Lee (1995) conducted semi-structured interviews with young football (soccer) and tennis players. The kinds of values that guide their decision-making in sport are purportedly revealed in their responses to certain hypothetical dilemmas. If a respondent showed concern for fair play in preference to rule-breaking strategies in a given dilemma, this was taken to reflect the value of 'sportsmanship'. Similarly, if a respondent showed a strong concern for winning rather than fairness-reasoning, such an attitude is said to be characterised and motivated by the value of 'winning'.

In his analysis of the discussions and responses, Lee identified 18 value categories. The data was interpreted in a manner that suggests the validity of theoretical stance that a relatively small number of universal values are responsible for behaviour. One value category already mentioned is 'sportsmanship'. Comments such as 'It is always important to play fair and respect the decision of the referee' were taken as evidence for the value of sportsmanship. The most commonly expressed value was winning (95.4 per cent). There was also a high value placed on enjoyment (89.7 per cent), and similar, though not quite as strong, was the concern for sportsmanship (83.9 per cent). These statistics do not reflect any particular individuals' value priorities since they do not attempt to examine which value would be prioritised in any given situation. Given that the sample is representational, however, they do seem to indicate that the young soccer- and tennis-playing population values winning *and* sportsmanship. These results as they stand reveal little about the *causes* of the growth in unsporting behaviour; in fact they may call into question Lee's initial concerns.

The central problem for Lee's view that the values of and in sport are on the decline only becomes apparent when individuals are asked to prioritise their values against some previously existing set of data (which he never presents). Although many have expressed a concern for fairness, the fact is that if Lee's initial observations about the decrease in fair play are true, sportsmanship is *not*

prioritised in concrete situations. Lee draws upon Schwartz (1992) for a possible explanation. Schwartz's conception of a value is similar to that of Rokeach (1973). In contrast, however, Schwartz argues that values guide the selection or evaluation of behaviour. The most important facet of Schwartz's theory for our present concerns is his idea that individual values are *grouped* together according to the similarity of the motivational goal they represent. For example, the values of honesty, responsibility and helpfulness are similar in their motivational natures, so much so that Schwartz groups them together under the category of 'benevolence'. Just as certain values have an affinity with similar values, others are said to conflict with each other. The values in the benevolence group conflict, according to Schwartz, with values such as ambition, influence and success which collectively form the category of 'achievement'.

Lee (1995) suggests that the relationship identified by Schwartz between groups of similar kinds of values highlights a fundamental problem in sport. If the values of winning and sportsmanship are assimilated into a general value category they are seen to be in conflict with each other. The value of winning resides in Schwartz's category of achievement along with values such as ambition and success, whereas the value of sportsmanship resides in the category of universalism along with values like social justice and equality. Lee (1995: 72) argues that:

> In the terminology commonly in current use in sport psychology this conflict represents that between desirable social and moral values, and competence – whether it is more important to be fair and display sportsmanship or to win the contest at whatever cost.

Essentially Lee's work accomplishes two preliminary tasks: first he provides empirical support to the belief that competitors' values are the main influence on moral decision-making in sport; secondly, he provides empirical support to the belief that sport, by its very nature, embraces a value conflict, namely between winning and playing fairly. The outcome of this value conflict is increasingly the prioritisation of winning resulting in a decrease in fair play. Having purportedly established certain causal factors in the decrease in fair play in youth sport, Lee's next task is to prescribe a remedy. Lee intimates towards this but does not develop an account of what a value education in and through sport might look like. He does, however, suggest that one of the important factors is the role of exemplars. Teachers, coaches and especially the behaviour of elite sportsmen and women all influence the value priorities of the young. Currently, if Lee is right, their influence is problematic: they exemplify unfair rather than fair play.

In the present context, there are two important and related issues that need clarifying in relation to Lee's work. We will phrase them in terms of two questions. First, is the value concept as discussed by Lee the most fruitful concept to use given his concern with the alleged rise in unsporting conduct? We shall call this 'the problem of characterising value in sport'. Secondly, is Lee's utilisation of a formalistic framework to characterise normative standards of fair play and sportsmanship to which participants ought to comply, sufficiently rich for him to prove the claim of moral decline? We shall call this 'the problem of a formalist framework of values in sport'. The answer to the former question demands both psychological and philosophical examination. The answer to the latter requires a socially and historically situated ethical investigation.

## The problem of characterising value in sport

The concept of 'value' as employed by Lee is primarily a cognitive construct that guides decision-making in the direction of the motivational goal that it represents. If we take honesty as an example, the value of honesty will guide decision-making in the direction of the outcomes that represent the goals of honesty, not to lie, not to steal, not to cheat and not to deceive. According to Lee (1995: 63) values are 'general principles of conduct which supersede the immediate demands of the situation. These principles guide the decision-making process and hence influence the expression of attitudes and behaviour in specific situations'. To view values this way provides important methodological leverage. First, a value as a central, general and stable construct allows the researcher to pass comment on a quality of the given subject under scrutiny. The profile of a person's values is not a mere snapshot or glimpse of the way they behave at any given moment but is rather a pattern from which we may make inferences about their character or personality. A snapshot of a person's values in this or that act

gives information of the here and now whereas a picture of their values is contextually independent. Attitudes and behaviour may be fairly sensitive and contextually dependent but values are not. Given these points, researchers can gain access to a person's values without having to be present at any given time when these values are expressed. If values are stable, it is fair to assume that a response given today which is informed by a certain value, will be repeated in decision-making at some point in the future. Secondly (and crucially, given Lee's understanding of the normative nature of the research), Lee argues that access to the motivational antecedents of behaviour is imperative because any comment on the moral status of a given act cannot be implied from observation of that act alone: 'the simple observation of a morally questionable action does not necessarily indicate any morally reprehensible motivation' (1995: 58–9). Lee's identification of values through surveys or interviews is intended to fulfil this last criterion: to ensure that merely observed behaviour is inadequate since a criterion of adequacy for normative explanations of sports values necessarily requires knowledge of the antecedents of that behaviour (i.e. the motivating value set).

There are numerous problems with Lee's concept of value, of which we will limit our discussion to two. The first question is whether or not the concept of value as described by Lee has any utility in assessing moral action and moral actors in sporting situations. The important issue here is the stable and context-independent nature of values and the assessment procedure that relies on accepting them as such. To ask someone in the sanitised environment of an interview what they believe they would do in a given situation, or what they believe ought to be done in a certain situation, and infer from their responses that their action in a specific situation will comply with their prediction requires an unacceptable leap of faith. To verbally profess one's commitment to honesty is different and not always related to behaving honestly in certain circumstances. To accept that what one says is an accurate prediction of what one will do requires a significant investment of confidence in the primary role of cognition in behaviour. This problem is accentuated by Lee's particular methodology for the following reasons. Value priorities are revealed in hypothetical dilemmas by identifying the primary motivation in decision-making. The situation is stripped of the time constraints, the environmental pressures and the general atmosphere of a sporting contest that would influence decision-making. Indeed without such knowledge of such factors we can scarcely make sense of the interviewees' posited values. This problem is compounded by the lack of ecological validity in the methodology. The identification of a value priority, such as fairness, could be supported by the opinion of the coach and spectators, the research participants' disciplinary record and the actual conduct of that player in the same or similar contexts. Only this kind of richer information would tell us whether a player not only values fair play but is also disposed to play fair. It is the disposition to play fair, not to foul, and to conduct oneself with dignity and respect (and so on) on the sports field that is important, not simply a verbal endorsement of the values of fair play. We therefore argue that an examination of sporting action should start with an identification and examination of players' dispositions rather than values.

A value expresses a kind of belief that something ought to be the case, or that a certain state of affairs is desirable. Yet it is a different matter to be disposed to act so that this state of affairs becomes the case. The kinds of dispositions that concern us in sport are virtues like magnanimity and generosity (Keating 1964). The list can be easily supplemented by courage, fairness, honesty, reliability, tenacity, trustworthiness, and a host of other traits definitive of a good person (Pincoffs 1986). And these characteristic traits – some moral, others aesthetic or merely functional – are all required for excellent sports and need to be instilled through habit and more explicit educational strategies by the sports educator. So the difference between a value and virtue goes far beyond a semantic distinction. For Lee (1995) a value serves as a kind of context-independent action-guiding rule, while for other researchers (such as ourselves) committed to a picture of moral or value development a virtue will more closely resemble

> some sort of standing disposition to perceive and/or think and/or feel and/or behave in certain characteristic ways in certain situations – which situations are partly designated or defined as situations of a certain kind by the standing disposition(s) in question. (Flanagan 1991: 277)

And this, we illustrate below, will depend crucially on the educator who will nourish a specific picture of how that sport is to be played in relation

to its shared and partially definitive cultural norms and values – its ethos.

The second part of the above quotation further illuminates the difficulty with Lee's uncritical adoption of the value concept respectively from Rokeach and Schwartz. In order for a value to provide a guide to action, a person must be faced with a situation that requires a decision. In the case of sport, Lee argues that when one is faced with a kind of moral dilemma or conflict, the value that is prioritised will influence behaviour in those circumstances. Such an account presupposes that these dilemmas or conflicts are universally self-evident. Different kinds of behaviour might result only if there is a difference in value priorities. We argue that this is not in fact the case. Yet the way in which a person behaves depends as much on the way they perceive a situation as on a judgement or decision they may make in light of the situation they may face (Blum 1994, Flanagan 1991). In sport, for example, if a player has to make a decision between two alternatives, to play fair or to cheat, then the fact that these alternatives are open to them already tells us something about their character. Right action is as much to do with being sensitive and aware of what is required, seeing and understanding what is required, as choosing a particular course of action in any given situation. To comment further requires a fuller explication of the formalist normative framework adopted by Lee.

## The problem of a formalist framework of values in sport

To know what is required in sporting situations is to return to the second question posed on p. 107. To suggest that sporting behaviour has declined suggests that some kind of standard of acceptable behaviour in sport is not being adhered to. Properly to understand the educational task, how children *ought* to behave in sport, requires an examination of the rules and standards that govern participation in sport. What is required is not a formalistic account of conduct in sport (which is necessarily thin in order to be universalistic) but a richer, more context-sensitive account of sports and their moral atmospheres in and through which moral and immoral conduct can be understood and evaluated.

In recognition of the importance of understanding sports' ethos, D'Agostino (1981) develops the formalist account that sports are defined exhaustively by their rules. He stipulates that: 'By the ethos of a game I mean those conventions determining how the formal rules of that game are applied in concrete circumstances' (1981: 7). What is most important to understand here is the target of D'Agostino's argument. Logically, it is said that the rules of a game define it. If a person breaks those rules then, logically, they are not playing the game. Of course, it is often said that this is grossly counter-intutive. Given that so much of sport is contained by acts of rule-breaking it seems nonsense to argue that these actions are not part of the sport. By introducing the notion of an ethos over and above the mere existence of game-defining rules D'Agostino captures the commonsensical distinction between the permissible and impermissible, the acceptable and the unacceptable. The formalist thesis that the rules define the game only serves to distinguish game-playing from non-game-playing behaviour. A player may break a rule in a manner that is deemed by the appropriate population as acceptable; this is how they play the game; this is how they interpret the rules. Moreover, the ethos determines unacceptable behaviour – that which should disqualify the person as a player of the game.

Two revisions of this thesis are recommended. In the first instance, we should avoid a formalism that D'Agostino fails to recognise in his own thesis. He presupposes the analytical account of sporting games as rule-governed practices. While this is true it is incomplete in respect of its analytical reductivism. To interpret a game merely as a system of rules is to ignore its social and historical situatedness. Viewing sports as practices (McNamee 1995) in and through which the virtues are learnt, shared and reinforced, allows us to consider those particular forces that shape an understanding both of the formal rules and the ethoses of sports and their antecedent forces. This allows for a much richer recognition of the sources of value in stories, myths, facts, technical factors, coaching styles, spectator involvement, media representations and so forth. A sports education worthy of its name must consider and critically evaluate these sources in order to initiate pupils into the best that the practice has to offer. Secondly, and closely related to this point, is the recognition that an ethos is never likely to be merely the conventional interpretation of the rules. There are two sub-points here that need to be brought together. First, one should not expect homogeneity among these norms and values

though there is likely to be some measure of convergence. Secondly, among these disparate forces not all will be dominant. There will be patterns of dominance and passivity over time and place. Sports just are played differently in different cultures. And it is precisely the educational dimension here that demands critical selection and reinforcement.

As far as research-related considerations go, part of the challenge of the empirical research in this area is to tease out the relative strength of the different sources of the ethoses and to distinguish the multiplicity of norms and values that are contested over by different agents and agencies. A final challenge is then to contextualise these ethoses normatively in respect of fair play. To accept these points is to cede both theoretical and methodological ground. In the first instance it will be necessary to observe research participants in the appropriate settings. This, of course, does not entail the disavowal of questionnaire- or interview-based methods but rather emphasises their incompleteness. The triangulation of data, so commonly employed in participant observation and ethnographic methods, will be an invaluable methodological commitment that will ground data in an ecologically valid manner. Theoretically, it will be clear that researchers must eschew the formalist framework of morality as a thin system of universal rules or principles impartially applied. Instead they will recognise the value of local and particular norms and action-guiding reasons. Again, there must be iteration between those inescapably general notions of respect for others, not harming them, and so on, but notions must be understood from within the contexts of sports (the constitutive and regulative rules) and with a proper recognition of their ethos. At this point, one might reasonably ask either how such a sports education would differ categorically from a socialisation therein and/or whether a critical inititation into sports practices is possible. Such points are, perhaps fortunately, beyond the scope of this chapter (cf. Morgan 1998, Roberts 1998). A brief elaboration of the idea of a sports ethos, of which values in sport will be both cause and component, is now necessary.

The ethos of a sporting practice, then, is the relatively shared interpretation of the basic norms, rules and values justifying and regulating the engagement in that game among its members. An ethos must first incorporate some relatively common ideas of what it is that constitutes a good sport played technically and tactically well. Secondly, an ethos will comprise a relatively common interpretation of the rules of the sport played in a morally acceptable manner. Thirdly, ideas of the good player and of the values virtues which are being cultivated in and through that very sport are required to constitute the inescapably personal dimension of an ethos. Finally, there must be a recognition of the fact that an ethos extends beyond the lives of the participants themselves. So a complete account of a sports ethos will include all the foregoing considerations in addition to the relatively shared understanding of the roles and limits of officials, coaches, administrators and spectators (Loland and McNamee 2000).

It will be clear then that any social scientific account of values and their inevitable conflict in cultural practices must move beyond both the methodological and the theoretical limitations that we have pointed out. Specifically, we argue for philosophically sophisticated accounts of ethics and sport generally (McNamee 1995) and for a picture of values in sport that is grounded in the specific ethos of given particular practices in contrast to the thin, universalistic, formal framework.

## Concluding remarks

When Peters argued in his classic treatise (1966) that a formal criterion of education was that such knowledge as is possessed by the educated person should not be inert but rather should characterise their way of acting in the world, he drew attention to a crucial point – whether it is formal or ideological is not of great import here. It is precisely this idea that sports educators must bring to children if the range of sporting practices is to be introduced to them in a manner that will be the bedrock of a lifetime's committed engagement. It will furthermore be their duty to open up and make desirable the significant joys and attendant frustrations that come from the pursuit of excellence within the frameworks of sport, formal *and* informal, and to initiate them critically into that aspect of the culture which sporting practices instantiate. To do this upon a sound scientific and educational footing requires that investigations into values in sport must be theoretically and methodologically richer than many psychological enquiries have heretofore been.

## References

Blum, L. (1994) *Moral Perception and Particularity*, Cambridge: Cambridge University Press.

Bredemeier, B. J. and Shields, D. L. (1984) 'The Utility of Moral Stage Analysis in the Investigation of Athletic Aggression', *Sociology of Sport Journal*, 1: 138–49.

Bredemeier, B. J. and Shields, D. L. (1986) 'Moral Growth among Athletes and Non-athletes: A Comparative Analysis', *Journal of Genetic Psychology*, 147: 7–18.

Bredmeier, B. J. and Shields (1995) *Character Development and Physical Activity*, Leeds: Human Kinetics.

Carr, D. (1997) 'Physical Education and Value Diversity', *European Physical Education Review*, 3. 2: 195–205.

D'Agostino, F. (1981) 'The Ethos of Games', *Journal of the Philosophy of Sport*, 8: 7–18.

Flanagan, O. (1991) *Varieties of Moral Personality: Ethics and Psychological Realism*, Cambridge, MA: London: Harvard University Press.

Fraleigh, W. P. (1984) *Right Actions in Sport*, Leeds: Human Kinetics.

Jones, C. (1998) '*A Philosophical Critique of Selected Social Scientific Research into Values and Moral Development in Sport*', unpubl. doctoral thesis, University of Wales, Cardiff.

Keating, J. W. (1964) 'Sportsmanship as a Moral Category', *Ethics*, 75: 25–35.

Kirk, D. (1988) *PE and Curriculum Study*, London: Croom Helm.

Kirk, D. (1992) *Defining Physical Education*, London: Falmer Press.

Lee, M. (1988) 'Values and Responsibilities in Children's Sport' *Physical Education Review*, 11. 1: 19–27.

Lee, M. (1993) 'Moral Development and Children's Sporting Values', in J. Whitehead (ed.) *Development Issues in Children's Sport and PE*, Bedford: Bedford College of Higher Education Press, pp. 30–42.

Lee, M. (1995) 'Value Foundations of Ethical Decisions in Children's Sport' in A. Tomlinson and S. Fleming (eds) *Ethics, Sport and Leisure: Crises and Critiques*, Brighton: CSRC.

Lee, M. and Cockman, M. (1995) 'Values in Children's Sport: Spontaneously Expressed Values among Young Athletes', *International Review for the Sociology of Sport*, 30. 3–4: 337–52.

Loland, S. and McNamee, M. J. (2000) 'Sport, Fairness and Play: Plural Values and Shared Ethoses', *Journal of the Philosophy of Sport*, 27.

McNamee, M. J. (1995) 'Sporting Practices, Institutions and Virtues: A Critique and a Restatement', *Journal of Philosophy of Sport*, 22: 61–82.

McNamee, M. J. (1996) 'Values', *Encyclopedia of World Sport*, Amherst, MA: ABC Clio, pp. 1123–8.

McNamee, M. J. (1998) 'Education, Philosophy and Physical Education: Analysis, Epistemology and Axiology', *European Physical Education Review*, 4. 1: 75–91.

Morgan, W. P. (1998) 'Ethnocentrism and the Social Criticism of Sports: A Response to Roberts', *Journal of Philosophy of Sport*, 25: 82–102.

Peters, R. S. (1966) *Ethics and Education*, London: Allen & Unwin.

Pincoffs, E. L. (1986) *Quandaries and Virtues: Against Reductivism in Ethics*, Lawrence: Kansas University Press.

Reid, A. (1996) 'The Concept of Physical Education in Current Curriculum and Assessment Policy in Scotland', *European Physical Education Review*, 2. 1: 7–18.

Reid, A. (1996a) 'Knowledge, Practice and Theory in Physical Education', *European Physical Education Review*, 2. 2: 94–104.

Roberts, T. (1998) 'Sporting Practice Protection and Vulgar Ethnocentricity: Why Won't Morgan Go All the Way?', *Journal of Philosophy of Sport*, 25: 71–81.

Rokeach, M. (1973) *The Nature of Human Values*, New York: The Free Press.

Schwartz, S. (1992) 'Universals in the Content and Structure of Values: Theoretical Advances and Empirical Tests in 20 Countries', in M. P. Zanna (ed.) *Advances in Experimental Social Psychology*, Vol. 25, New York: Academic Press.

Siedentop, D. (1990) *Sports Education*, Leeds: Human Kinetics.

## Acknowledgements

This chapter arises out of collaboration of the International Fair Play Research Network. We are particularly grateful for the insights of our colleagues and especially to Scott Fleming, Sigmund Loland and Per Nilsson.

# 11 Learning Moral Commitment at University in a Plural Society

GERALD COLLIER

## Probity in public life

An endemic problem in every human society is the abuse of power by those in positions of authority, from the governments of advanced Western countries (CSPL 1995) to those of small ex-colonies, from senior executives of multinational corporations to leaders of trade unions or local government councils. The initial assumptions of this chapter are accordingly the following: first, that probity in public life is – given food and shelter – the most fundamental of the predicaments facing a modern society; second, that since universities form the apex of the educational system in most countries, it is essential to examine the ways in which such institutions are likely to influence their students' moral outlook (CIHE 1990, Steadman et al. 1994); and third, that the foundation of that probity is a firm adherence to a small constellation of moral values, namely truthfulness, the dependability of one's word, moral courage, sense of fair play, law-abidingness, concern or respect for other persons, concern for the common good (White 1990, Pelikan 1992, Grace 1995). The first three elements may reasonably be summed up in 'integrity'; an expectation of some stable practice of such values is the basis of a climate of trust (Giddens 1991). These assumptions call for elucidation in several respects.

## Moral values pursued in their own right: an Aristotelian view

First, it is necessary to clarify the use of the slippery word 'values' in this chapter. It will be assumed that the central concept is that of 'valuation', of setting a value on some object or mode of behaviour; it is seen as an active process, a disposition towards action, possibly as a driving force. In the present context our main concern will be with moral values, that is, values to which a sense of obligation is attached.

A further distinction is important: between – on the one hand – adherence to a particular moral value because authority or convention says so, and – on the other – adherence to that value because it is seen as 'right' or 'good' in itself, and the 'oughtness' derives from the 'rightness' of the action. It is in this sense that Aristotle argues: the individual 'chooses the action for its own sake' (1955).

Societies vary greatly in the extent to which ordinary citizens, whether as parents or in workplaces, depend on coercive methods for instilling, or for securing conformity with, the values to which they themselves adhere. In many English households there is little formal instruction in how to behave; the spoken word tends to take the form of apparently casual remarks, while the children pick up from their parents and other older people what to do and how to do it. They become honest or generous because that seems a natural way to behave among those people, and in doing so, see that these are in themselves 'good' or 'right' ways to behave, and in some way satisfying. That is, the children absorb from the surrounding culture the 'natural' way to behave (the word 'culture' being used here in the sense of the web of customs, meanings, relationships and values which characterise that community). In another community, however, the adults may give systematic verbal instruction on moral principles and impose a strict system of rewards and punishments to secure conformity. If the element of coercion is severe, the values may become compulsive and a source of prejudice

(Adorno et al. 1950, Triandis and Draguns 1981). Yet, in spite of this, many individuals may grow up under such a regime and still discover for themselves that honesty or generosity is good in itself.

One more preliminary point needs to be made. The extraordinary multiplicity of human cultures makes it hard to credit the general validity of any values (Bloom 1987, Squires (ed.) 1993). If we cannot 'prove' the 'validity' of such values as were listed earlier (MacIntyre 1985, Squires 1993), we have to look for another basis for adherence to them. A valuation is not to be seen as a proposition about what exists or what occurs: propositions can in principle be checked for validity against evidence; but a valuation cannot be presented in a factual form which can be tested against evidence (see, for example, Janik and Toulmin 1973). To find a backing for a moral value we have to turn either to a religion, or to a tradition, or to a belief in its validity in its own right, as 'good' or 'right' in itself. In short, if we are personally concerned in depth with practical problems in the real world – whether genocide in Rwanda or corruption in governments – we are 'forced out of equivocation back into open commitment to certain political principles and values' (Soper 1993: 21). There are indications here in Soper, and in other chapters of the same book (Squires (ed.) 1993) of a clear leaning towards belief in the validity of certain values in their own right. And so, as Weeks writes (1993), 'The key question is whether it is possible to find a common narrative standard by which we can come to terms with different ways of life, whether we can balance relativism with some sense of minimum universal values'. Clark (1983b), Hodgkinson (1991), Grace (1995) and others have emphasised the centrality of value issues in the administration of universities and schools. In the present context, however, we are concerned with the 'minimum universal values' that may sustain probity in public life, and the conditions of their promotion in a university.

## Potential moral influence of a British university

I have argued elsewhere (Collier 1997; cf. Douglas 1986, Barnett 1992) that in British higher education the ethical influence of the institution operates mainly through the climate or ethos that pervades the culture of the department (Becher and Kogan 1980, Clark 1983a, 1983b, Williams and Blackstone 1983) or institution. The day-to-day responsibility for running the institution as a whole lies with the vice-chancellor and his/her senior colleagues – the 'senior team' – while the responsibility for the departments/professional schools/ 'faculties' in 'new' universities – rests with the corresponding 'senior teams' of those bodies.

The senior teams are involved in four areas of activity: the provision and administration of a 'code of law' for the institution; the provision of teaching and of facilities for research and study; the management of innovation; and personal contacts with colleagues and students. The authority structures of the institutions vary considerably, from the more hierarchical to the more participatory, according to the history of the institution. Whatever the structure, however, it is argued that the code of law must be adequately promulgated and the system seen not only as fair and open but as 'transparent'. It is furthermore argued that the teaching should not merely be competent in preparation and delivery, but should exert a persistent pressure towards the articulation of assumptions and the development of critical judgement (Barnett 1992).

With regard to innovation it is suggested that the scale of change, planned or unplanned, has been, and will continue to be, unpredictable in its impact. It is assumed, moreover, that students arriving in the institution at the age of 17 or 18 will have already acquired some conception of the values of integrity and so on, with some disposition towards the practice or rejection of such values. Hence it is assumed that, if teaching is incompetent, or the handling of infringements of the institution's regulations inadequate, or the members of the senior teams give, through the multiplicity of personal interactions with others (Burke 1794, Layder 1994), no firm impression of integrity, then there will be a tendency for the student culture to reject such values (Becker et al. 1968. Collier et al. 1974) if the institution claims to stand for them.

The above framework of assumptions defines in a summary and somewhat simplistic manner the way in which the culture of a British university is likely to make an impact, positive or negative, on the ethical dispositions of its students, in the sense specified. That is, it presents a modest 'ideal type' picture of a traditional institution.

## Role of reasoned analysis in a plural society

Many, perhaps most, human societies in the late twentieth century are 'plural', not merely in the sense of having regions or social-class communities noted for their recognisable cultures, but in the stronger sense of having minority groups marked by conspicuously different racial traits, or language, or other special characteristics. What has to be borne in mind is the depth of attachment of many members of such groups to the distinctive features of their cultures, and the strength of their identification with them. It is enough to note the Muslims in Bradford or Birmingham, the Afro-Caribbeans in the USA, the whites in South African society under the apartheid regime, the French in Canada, or for that matter the protest groups for animal rights in Britain.

If we concede that our major objective must be to foster the development of 'enduring dispositions' towards behaviour marked by the values listed earlier, it still remains important that students should learn to distinguish moral judgements based on a sense of what is right in itself from those based on unchallenged custom or fashion, or derived from a coercive training in earlier years. They need to learn, too, to distinguish between 'good faith' and 'bad faith', between 'genuineness' or integrity of relations between people and some 'mask' that cannot be trusted; to distinguish the underlying dominant values of an individual or a group from those which are most loudly proclaimed. The usual assumption made by academics in such circumstances is that they should set up a new course of lectures accompanied by seminar discussions among 20 or more students. These, however, suffer from a fatal flaw: they consist largely of the interchange of generalisations about behaviour. The only way to learn the distinctions and discriminations outlined above is by the analysis of concrete cases (Collier 1974, 1988, 1993, Collier (ed.) 1983): to cite random examples from across the humanities: the forces at work in the abdication of King James II in 1688; the chain of perceptions and values behind Emma Woodhouse's sudden discovery of her love for Mr Knightley; perhaps even the complex of conflicting values implied by Margaret Thatcher's decision to take military action against Argentina in 1982; perhaps even a probing of the integrity of Becket in T. S. Eliot's *Murder in the Cathedral*, or of the character taken by Henry Fonda in the classic film *Twelve Angry Men*. Students need to be engaged at some depth if they are to learn *how to find* the evidence that will guide their interpretation; or, to use other phraseology, the learning process requires an 'existential' quality, of significance for living; it involves *both* a search for objective, documentary and other concrete evidence *and* a search for unvoiced 'body-language' clues (Collier 1993).

Haydon (1995) presents some acute comments on various approaches to value issues through the analysis of the moral basis of 'liberal democracy'. However, if the arguments advanced above carry any weight, they imply that in this field too it is of some importance that students' discussions should start from concrete cases, such as perhaps a case study of a county council's development plans; or a university council's handling of a 'discipline' case; or an episode from Trollope's prime minister series; or even a section of *Watership Down*. In any case, students will need to study specific episodes from several historical, political, literary and/or other sources if they are to begin to clarify their own moral priorities.

In a contemporary Western society one kind of minority group may be composed mainly of disaffected but fairly intensively educated individuals, another may consist of students brought up as strict Muslims. If a tutor wishes to embark on such work it will be necessary to select materials for analysis which have an immediate reality for the students, yet lend themselves to the searching out of motives: that is, the characters must be sufficiently fully developed, and of such authenticity as to command the respect of both teacher and students; and the material needs to be part of a coherent course of recognised standing. The very substantial advantage of basing such courses on outstanding authors – Shakespeare, Dickens, Austen – is that the potential profit from examining the characters and situations offered by such authors is so great; as of course is also the case with materials within other disciplines that offer equally rich evidence for study and analysis. But if members of minority groups such as those mentioned above are included, an exclusive focus on British material may be fatal. It may be more practicable to find suitable current films or fiction: but in the selection of such materials a certain sceptical wariness is needed, since highly charged responses may lie close to the surface of a seminar discussion. Films of classics can also usefully offer illuminating contrasts with the originals (Collier 1974, Collier (ed.) 1983).

Many students are quite unaccustomed to such work. The strongly instrumental approach to degree-level study traditional in some technical colleges in Britain (Pitt 1974) does not favour the kind of interchange described above. Seminar groups of 20 or more students may not yield much in terms of developed insight. However, the division of the class into sub-groups ('syndicates') of 3–5 students, with suitably designed exercises to be taken up by the students, may yield more satisfactory results (Collier (ed.) 1983, Collier 1990, Crook 1994).

A further aspect of such work requires attention. Kohlberg (1976, 1986) has offered evidence indicating that young adults are unlikely to respond positively to such values as those listed earlier unless there is a certain climate of relationships in the university. Kohlberg refers to this as the 'moral atmosphere' of the community, that is, its 'justice structure', the trustworthiness of its authorities and a certain climate of mutual trust and concern (1976; cf. Garbarino and Bronfenbrenner 1976, Collier 1993). If this is absent, a tutor may well find any such work counter-productive. The grim events of 1971–5 at North London Polytechnic, a college of over 5000 full-time students, illustrate how far a disaffected and highly organised minority can go towards wrecking the work of a department (Jacka et al. 1975).

Even if the conditions are favourable, a further problem still has to be resolved: that of assessment. Courses which have no recognition in the assessment procedure are apt to be disregarded; courses of the kind outlined above can easily be killed by a conventional formal essay-type examination. It is possible to devise alternative methods of assessment (Collier (ed.) 1983) but tutors would need to ensure that students fully understood the new pattern.

Whatever styles of teaching and examining a university adopts, the transition of 'enduring moral dispositions' into settled convictions involves more than the reinforcement of existing dispositions and more than academic study, however 'existential' that experience may be: it requires a degree of critical reflection on one's personal life and the realities of one's aspirations and priorities (Perry 1970). These are private matters and cannot be forced; the time required may be measured in years.

A further implication is relevant. There have been many complaints in recent years that the study of literature, and indeed of the humanities, has lost its way (e.g. Bloom 1987). If the arguments so far presented in this chapter have any force, they surely imply that no area of study stands in greater need of development than the exploration of the values implied, the motives operating, in all those human situations of great literature: the basis of adherence to those values, their origins in human relationships, in psychological events, in sociological contexts, the effective priorities among them, and the implications we may see in them for our own situations (Collier 1997).

## Coda

The principal object of the reasoned analysis described above is an understanding and appreciation of the very different ways in which individuals are attached to their dominant values, and the subtle but fundamentally more far-reaching, and to this author more beneficial, influence of those values which are believed in and pursued for their inherent rightness. This holds good even if, in the course of such analytical probing, students who are curious to uncover the predominant sources of their own private values and outlook, may come to understand the network of economic and political power structures and social forces which operate to maintain the value system in which they have been reared. In generating such an understanding, however, their probing will probably also have revealed how deeply rooted in their own souls certain altruistic values are, an abiding passion for social justice perhaps, or an immutable belief in selfless love, or in inner integrity. These may be bedded with an array of egotistical demands and desires, but whatever the individual's place in a plural society may be, well-conducted explorations of well-selected material in a suitable climate may be expected to yield useful results.

## A contrasting type of university culture

A marked contrast is offered by France. The explosions of the student world in May 1968 took their origin in the civil rights movement in the USA in 1964 alongside the popular resentment of the Vietnam war; they were most savage, however, in France, and the extraordinary shockwave gave rise to intensive discussion at every level as to how the higher-education system in France might, or should, or could be reformed. General de Gaulle, as president, appointed Edgar Faure to be minister of national education, to design a new pattern of higher education and steer it through parliament; the result was the Loi d'orientation of 1968, which introduced certain radical changes (Bourricaud 1982).

The higher-education system in France has for a long time been marked by three distinctive features. First, university professors are civil servants, proposed by committees of peers but appointed by the minister under strong civil service protection, with almost impregnable powers. The professors in any given subject may well meet in Paris to design the curriculum for their subject for all universities. One of the main objectives of the student representatives in the negotiations for the 1968 legislation was to establish the participation of students and junior staff in the running of the universities. They had some success in this respect, but a precautionary regulation was also inserted, to the effect that, if the proportion of students voting fell below 50 per cent, their representation would be correspondingly reduced.

A second feature of the French system is that universities have no monopoly in either teaching or research. Alongside the universities stand the 'Grandes Ecoles', for which entry is via competitive examination and which, having immense prestige, attract many of the ablest individuals of their generation. Moreover, research is largely directed and funded by the Centre National de la Recherche Scientifique (CNRS). Hence a third feature of the system: universities have little scope for developing as distinctive independent institutions planning and running their own distinctive lives of teaching and research. Because access to courses is so liberal, and because so much of the curriculum is decided on a national basis, a large part of the teaching is delivered to very large numbers of students in vast lecture halls. Certain modifications have been introduced since the 1968 legislation without affecting the broad picture.

It becomes clear that the idea of a university basing its structure on the collaborative working of fairly small teams of colleagues in the sense outlined for a British university is foreign to French thinking. Thus the ethical influence of the culture of relatively small units is less likely to develop. This does not of course preclude the close collaboration of colleagues on professional matters, or for that mat-ter of students following the same courses. But even the School of Mines at Nancy – one of the smaller Grandes Ecoles, visited by the present writer in 1964 to make enquiries about the restructuring of the curriculum (Walters 1964) – was according to the principal set on its new programme by quite a different approach. The principal and vice-principal worked out the new system between them and then, interviewing all staff individually, asked them to accept and implement it.

Insofar as France is a plural society, with fairly sharp divisions on racial and religious lines, the higher-education system appears to make no special provision for this. In any case, many teachers at these levels will regard the emphasis on philosophy at the baccalaureate stage as giving sufficient attention to ethical development in the student population.

## Conditions in the Third World

Turning to the Third World, we find a great variety of situations: plural societies in many forms. In general, the first universities in the Less Developed Countries (LDCs) (Lewis 1977) have been established by occupying powers, which exercised a fairly tight control over the selection of expatriate academic staff and of students, with the object of excluding 'subversive' individuals with disturbing ideologies. In the British case (Pratt 1977) the ethos and the selection of teachers and of curriculum were congruent with the values of the colonial administration. These institutions sent out graduates capable of forming the civil service of the British regime. In many cases they had followed courses steeped in the literature and visual arts of the West. Hence to a considerable degree these graduates were cut off from the indigenous culture, while having absorbed fragments and flavours of our listed values without having lived among them. Radical alien ideologies were often introduced at or after independence by individuals who had gained their qualifications in countries other than the previously occupying power.

In some LDCs there were long-standing tensions between different tribal groups, with the 'danger that racial or other antagonisms would be so strong as to lead to the destruction of any ordered government' (Sierra Leone, Rwanda) (Ten 1975). In some cases (Singapore, Malaysia) the different cultures had not only different cultural outlooks and values but different political and religious allegiances (Singapore 75 per cent Chinese; Malaysia 51 per cent Malays, 36 per cent Chinese; in Malaysia Islam is the state religion), and furthermore expatriate lecturers imported yet other ideologies – academic Marxists, capitalist economists, followers of Newman. In Singapore the government introduced very tight control over access and curriculum (Ten 1975). It is difficult to see our listed values receiving effective attention among the competing ideologies.

On the other hand many LDC governments regard their universities as instruments through which they may provide a vital service for their country: offering courses on their own language and culture (Pratt 1977); on the economic, political and cultural problems facing them, and the ways in which these can be handled, involving staff and students in the trial and assessment of proposed solutions, and thereby also generating a pride in, and attachment to, their own society (Soedjatmoko 1977). In some regions, however, the heads of these institutions, being accustomed to unquestioned authority, have alienated student opinion and stirred up a rejection of the university's experimental projects, along with the ideals that inspired them (Lewis 1977).

Alongside such purposes the government may also be looking to the universities as standing for an element of rational thinking in a society dominated by oral traditions of superstition (Pratt 1977), and indeed having among its expert staff a body of highly experienced and competent individuals well placed to contribute their expertise outside the boundaries of the university, and exercising an influence parallel to that of the senior teams in a British university as sketched above (Soedjatmoko 1977).

As regards the values of integrity and so on listed earlier in this chapter, in many LDCs these values will be interpreted in quite a different way from the way this author interprets them (cf. Douglas 1986): there will be no precise translation of the abstract phrases used, though there may well be recognisable equivalents in some form. The 'code of law' for the institution is likely to be very different; the nature of the bonds that bind the community together may be very different (Montefiore (ed.) 1975). The influence of the activities of the 'senior teams' or senior staff members may be closely similar to those outlined earlier; on the other hand, as we have seen in South East Asia, these influences may be diluted, or reinforced, or counteracted, by a variety of other forces arising from political or economic or cultural pressures.

In short, it would be perilous, in an essay of this kind, to do more than note the broad structure of potential moral influence of a university which appears to emerge from the work of Kohlberg and his associates, alongside the practical work under way in Britain (CIHE 1990, Steadman et al. 1994, CSPL 1995, SCAA 1996) and the developments in reasoned analysis (Collier 1974, Collier (ed.) 1983, Haydon 1995) given that our primary aim must be to foster the growth of 'enduring dispositions' towards behaviour marked by our listed values, pursued in their own right, and eventually developed into settled convictions.

# References

Adorno, T. W., Frenkel-Brunswik, E., Levinson, D. J. and Sanford, R. N. (1950) *The Authoritarian Personality*, New York: Harper.

Aristotle (1955) *Nichomachean Ethics* (II, iv) trans. Thomson, Harmondsworth: Penguin.

Barnett, R. A. (1992) *Improving Higher Education*, Buckingham: Society for Research into Higher Education and Open University Press.

Becher, T. and Kogan, M. (1980) *Process and Structure in Higher Education*, London: Heinemann.

Becker, H. S., Geer, B. and Hughes, E. C. (1968) *Making the Grade: The Academic Side of College Life*, New York: Wiley.

Bloom, A. (1987) *The Closing of the American Mind*, New York: Simon & Schuster.

Bourricaud, F. (1982) 'France: The Prelude to the Loi d'orientation of 1968', in Daalder and Shils (eds) (1982).

Boyer, E. L. (1987) *College and the Undergraduate Experience in America*, New York, Harper & Row.

Burke, E. (1794) *Letter on a Regicide Peace*.

Clark, B. (1983a) 'Governing the Higher Education System' in M. Shattock (ed.) *The Structure and Governance of Higher Education*, Guildford: Society for Research into Higher Education.

Clark, B. (1983b) *The Higher Education System*, Berkeley and Los Angeles: University of California Press.

Collier, G. (1974) 'Experiments in the Exploration of Values', in Collier et al. (eds) (1974).

Collier, G. (ed.) (1983) *The Management of Peer-Group Learning*, Guildford: Society for Research into Higher Education.

Collier, G. (1988) 'Higher Education and the Critique of Values', *Journal of Moral Education*, 17. 1: 21–6.

Collier, G. (1990) 'Syndicate Methods', in N. Entwistle

(ed.), *Handbook of Educational Ideas and Practices*, London: Routledge.

Collier, G. (1993) 'Learning Moral Judgement in Higher Education', *Studies in Higher Education*, 18. 3: 287–97.

Collier, G. (1997) 'Learning Moral Commitment in Higher Education?', *Journal of Moral Education*, 26. 1: 73–83.

Collier, G., Wilson, J. and Tomlinson, P. (1974) *Values and Moral Development in Higher Education*, London: Croom Helm.

CSPL (Committee on Standards in Public Life) (1995) *Standards in Public Life* (Nolan Report), London: HMSO.

CIHE (Council for Industry and Higher Education) (1990) *Towards a Partnership: The Humanities for the Working World*, London: CIHE.

Crook, C. (1994) *Computers and the Collaborative Experience of Learning*, London: Routledge.

Daalder, H. and Shils, E. (eds) (1982) *Universities, Politicians and Bureaucrats*, Cambridge: Cambridge University Press.

DFE (Department for Education) (1991) *Higher Education: A New Framework*, London: HMSO.

Douglas, M. (1986) *How Institutions Think*, Syracuse, NY: State University of New York Press.

Garbarino, J. and Bronfenbrenner, U. (1976) 'The Socialization of Moral Judgement and Behaviour in Cross-Cultural Perspectives', in T. Lickona (ed.) *Moral Development and Behaviour*, New York: Holt, Rinehart & Winston.

Giddens, A. (1991) *Modernity and Self-Identity*, Cambridge: Polity Press.

Grace, G. (1995) *School Leadership*, London: Falmer Press.

Haydon, G. (1995) 'Thick or Thin? The Cognitive Content of Moral Education in a Plural Democracy', *Journal of Moral Education*, 24: 53–64.

Hodgkinson, C. (1991) *Educational Leadership*, Albany, NY: State University of New York Press.

Jacka, K., Cox, C. and Marks, J. (1975) *Rape of Reason*, London: Churchill Press.

Janik A. and Toulmin. S. (1973) *Wittgenstein's Vienna*, London: Weidenfeld & Nicolson.

Kohlberg, L. (1976) 'Moral Stages and Moralization: The Cognitive-Development Approach', in T. Lickona (ed.) *Moral Development and Behaviour*, New York: Holt, Rinehart & Winston.

Kohlberg, L. (1986) 'A Current Statement on Some Theoretical Issues' in S. Modgil and M. Modgil, (eds) *Lawrence Kohlberg: Consensus and Controversy*, London: Falmer Press.

Layder, D. (1994) *Understanding Social Theory*, London: Sage.

Lewis, W. A. (1977) 'The University in Developing Countries: Modernization and Tradition', in K. W. Thompson, B. R. Fogel and H. E. Danner (eds) *Higher Education and Social Change, Vol. 2: Case Studies*, London: Praeger.

MacIntyre, A. (1985) *After Virtue*, London: Duckworth.

Montefiore, A. (ed.) (1975) *Neutrality and Impartiality*, Cambridge: Cambridge University Press.

Pelikan, J. (1992) *The Idea of the University*, New Haven: Yale University Press.

Perry, W. G. (1970) *Forms of Intellectual and Ethical Development in the College Years: A Scheme*, New York: Holt, Rinehart & Winston.

Pitt, V. (1974) 'Polytechnics: Moral Education?', in Collier et al. (eds) (1974).

Pratt, R. C. (1977) 'Universities and Social Values in Developing Countries', in K. W. Thompson, B. R. Fogel and H. E. Danner (eds) *Higher Education and Social Change, Vol. 2: Case Studies*, London: Praeger.

SCAA (School Curriculum and Assessment Authority) (1996) *Education for Adult Life: The Spiritual and Moral Development of Young People*, London: SCAA Publications.

Soedjatmoko (1977) 'Higher Education and Development: An Overview', in K. W. Thompson, B. R. Fogel and H. E. Danner (eds) *Higher Education and Social Change, Vol. 2: Case Studies*, London: Praeger.

Soper, K. (1993) 'Postmodernism, Subjectivity and the Question of Value', in Squires (ed.) (1993).

Squires, J. (ed.) (1993) *Principled Positions*, London: Lawrence & Wishart.

Steadman, S., Eraut, M., Cole, G. and Marquand, J. (1994) *Ethics in Occupational Standards, NVQs and SVQs*, London: Employment Department.

Ten, C. L. (1975) 'Politics in the Academe', in Montefiore (ed.) (1975).

Triandis. H. C. and Draguns. J. G. (1981) *Handbook of Cross-Cultural Psychology, Vol. 6: Psychotherapy*, New York: Allyn & Bacon.

Walters, S. (1964) 'University Reform: A Case Study from France', *Universities Quarterly*, 18. 2.

Weeks, J. (1993) 'Rediscovering Values', in Squires (ed.) (1993).

White, J. (1990) 'The Aims of Education', in N. Entwistle (ed.) *Handbook of Educational Ideas and Practices*, London: Routledge.

Williams, G. and Blackstone, T. (1983) *Response to Adversity*, Guildford: Society for Research into Higher Education.

# 12 Personal, Social and Moral Education in Latvia: Problems and Prospects*

KRISTA BURANE, AUGUSTS MILTS, IEVA ROCENA AND JANIS VALBIS

## The need of a system of personal, social and moral education (PSME) in Latvia – a state in transition

### Special role of PSME for a state in transition

In Latvia as in many Central and East European countries the historically unprecedented transition from the so-called socialist system to a free and democratic society is taking place. Transition like this involves essential changes in the consciousness of the people – their views, systems of values, attitudes and relations. For this transition to proceed faster and more successfully a purposeful education of the members of society is necessary, beginning at school level. It requires a radical transformation of the education system, especially in the PSME field.

Although the official communist propaganda advocated the basic principles of humanity – freedom, fraternity, equality, human dignity – in reality a double morality existed – one for the ordinary people and another for the privileged party elite. Education was dominated by indoctrination in official communist dogmas within a strictly authoritarian system. The 'communistic upbringing' of young people blindly believing in the rightness of the socialist system as the only just social system was considered the main task of education.

After the restoration of independence in Latvia reformation processes started in the education system, aimed at bringing it into line with the democratic education systems of other free countries. The most radical changes were and still are needed in the PSME field, but at the same time this is the most difficult part of the education system to change. Radical transformations are necessary in

*This chapter was originally written in 1996.

the contents of education and it is a difficult task to change teaching styles and approaches formed in the long years of occupation. In fact, a new system of PSME is needed and its formation must be preceded by analysis of the existing situation in society and in the education system.

### Factors influencing the values of the population of Latvia

Unfortunately at present we cannot speak about a unified system of shared basic values in the society of Latvia, for a number of reasons.

1 The older generation of Latvians still have recollections, probably idealised ones, about democracy and its values in the years of independent Latvia (1918–40). During the subsequent long years of soviet occupation many Latvians identified these values with the national values of Latvian people.

2 The double morality of the soviet system has remnants in the consciousness of the people, who heard and viewed on the TV screen official communist ideology propagating the principles of freedom, human rights and equality, but suffered from the manifestations of totalitarism in their real everyday life. This promoted the devaluation of normative moral values and a decline in the role of general humanistic values.

3 The influx of Western ideology based significantly on pragmatic and utilitarian values and bringing in many features of democracy and market economy, together with popular culture which sometimes indirectly propagates violence, crime and cruelty.

4 The weak influence of religion on the values system of society. Although Christianity was

introduced in Latvia in the twelfth century, nowadays there are no strong religious traditions in the majority of population, partly due to the long years of dominating atheistic propaganda.

When analysing the dominant values in Latvian society it should be kept in mind that Latvia is a multiethnic, multicultural state whose ethnic composition was intentionally formed by the soviet occupational government through genocide against Latvians and by bringing in hundreds of thousands of people from Russia and other soviet republics. As a result Latvians now constitute only a little more than half of the population (55.1 per cent) and people of other nationalities 44.9 per cent (Russians 32.6 per cent, Belorussians 4 per cent, Ukrainians 2.9 per cent and others 5.4 per cent) (UNDP 1996). This must be compared with the situation at the end of World War II, when 88 per cent of the population were Latvians. The majority of immigrants live in towns. Therefore in the six largest towns of Latvia, including the capital Riga, Latvians constitute the minority, more than 50 per cent of the inhabitants have Russian as their first language and there are more pupils in Russian-language schools than in Latvian-language ones.

Although Russian was not formally declared the state language in Latvia during the soviet years it was actually the official language used in all social institutions. This resulted in the gradual russification of society and the Latvian language came close to extinction. To stop this process the Latvian language was declared the only state language after the restoration of independence.

## Values systems of the main groups

In terms of the principal values systems the society of Latvia falls into two major groups.

1   People identifying themselves as Latvians are generally united around the ideal of a free and independent Latvian state. This ideal was formed in long years of occupation, when human rights were violated and everybody was submitted to psychological, economic and even physical pressures. Almost two thirds of Latvians consider their national identity as their main collective identity. In their consciousness general human values and ideals assumed national form and the belief emerged that the restoration of independence would bring about freedom,

justice, equality and also welfare. Nevertheless the first five years of independence and the concomitant radical changes in economics resulted in a significant reduction in living standards for the majority of people. This caused disillusionment in national ideals and a corresponding dropping of allegiance to some important values. This is rather dangerous for the younger generation as it creates in some of them nihilistic attitudes towards the relations between the state (society) and individuals in respect of freedom and responsibility. Two opposite tendencies are popular among young people: to educate themselves and devote their future activities to Latvia; and to study abroad so as to be able to live and work in developed foreign countries.

2   People of other nationalities differ in their values orientations depending on the cultural heritage they identify themselves with. In recent years many national minorities have activated their cultural life and national schools, so enhancing their human self-consciousness and orientation towards general human values.

Unfortunately many of the immigrants brought into Latvia by the soviet government belong to marginal groups within society – they don't identify themselves with any ethnic group and don't recognise any national cultural heritage. They can be considered as representatives of the imaginary 'soviet people' oriented mainly towards the Russian culture. In the system of practical russification in Latvia they had no need to respect the Latvian culture and language so they did not even try to become integrated into the Latvian environment. Now, when Latvian is the only official state language, they have lost the privilege of using only their native Russian language and many of them feel uncomfortable and even hostile to the independent Latvian state with its ideology of democracy and human values. Many immigrants live in Latvia only because of the economic advantages, partly received as illegal heritage from the previous system which was governed significantly by Russian-speaking persons.

The economic difficulties of the transition period put great strain on the everyday life of the majority of people – about 60 per cent of families can balance their family budgets only with significant efforts, 15 per cent of families have got into debt and only about 10 per cent of families have no material problems. This means that problems of material welfare and social security are dominant also in the values hierarchy of the society.

In the social perspective the economic difficulties hinder the emergence of the middle class which is usually the promoter and bearer of the main social values, the founder of a uniting values system for the whole society. This is one of the reasons why it is difficult to implement in Latvian society the main democratic values – freedom and responsibility, fairness, mutual trust and empathy, initiative and participation in social affairs.

## Need for development of the PSME system

It is acknowledged that the development of society can be influenced by moral and educational means. Nevertheless these can be effective only if included in the general system of legal, political, financial and economic reforms, as in the values hierarchy of individuals material and ideal values are tightly interwoven. The formation of a new values system aimed at integrating society must anticipate and project the model of the future society.

Education at all levels is of utmost importance for this and the school system is one of the basic parts of it. Unfortunately after throwing out the 'communistic upbringing' of our schools' curricula we have not yet replaced it with a new system of PSME. Teaching and learning at school is dominated by acquiring knowledge and skills, and little attention is paid to values education and character development. These problems are separately dealt with in several subjects and in the overall work of the school but there is no unified system of PSME.

On a larger scale we must create a system of PSME for the whole society, starting from the family and pre-school education institutions and ending with continuous adult education including the so-called third-age education. Nevertheless we consider PSME in schools the most important, taking into account its organised character and the possibility for society to influence it and reform it in its own interests.

PSME is essential for social integration, in particular by developing multicultural awareness and reducing manifestations of ethnocentrism. We can consider as a positive sign the tendency of more and more bilingual and Russian-speaking families to educate their children in schools in which Latvian is the language of instruction. Correlated PSME in all schools will further reduce the barriers between Latvian- and Russian-speaking communities.

## Aims and tasks of PSME in schools; main forms of implementation

### Aims of PSME

In the draft plan for the new Education Act (MESL 1996a) now in the process of endorsement by the Saeima more weight has been placed on the all-round development of character. This can be seen from the fact that three of the five main tasks of education deal with it:

- to promote the development of knowledgeable, skilled and well-bred, mentally and physically developed active personalities
- to promote the growth of self-determined, competent, conscious and responsible members of a democratic society
- to promote the development of persons creatively mastering and enriching national cultural values and those common to all humanity.

Of the 10 basic principles of education included in the draft of the Act, six directly concern the development of moral and spiritual qualities and individual socialisation. These are the principles of humanity, democracy, professionalism, individualisation, national identity and virtue. They apply to all aspects of the educational process: contents, methods, relations and attitudes, etc.

At present there are no official detailed documents (such as a framework curriculum) defining the direction and aims of PSME in schools. In the draft of such a document now under consideration in the Ministry of Education and Science the aims in the values and personal education field have been formulated using as the prototype the Swedish curriculum Lpo 94 (SMES 1996). The school shall strive to ensure that all pupils:

- develop the ability to consciously adopt an ethical standpoint based on humanistic principles, values, knowledge and personal experience, and behave and act according to generally accepted norms
- develop self-confidence and self-esteem – confidence in their abilities and powers and certitude in their actualisation, awareness of their uniqueness and prospects
- develop a sense of responsibility for their action and behaviour

- develop the ability to evaluate thoroughly and critically their knowledge, skills and attitudes, to set aims for their improvement and to control this process
- develop themselves as useful members of society – cultivate understanding, respect, tolerance and empathy towards other people, ability to work together in existing groups and to join new ones
- develop themselves as honest and just persons able to act in accordance with the principles of humanism and law
- develop their characters – purposefulness, will-power, persistence in reaching pre-set aims
- stand up against manifestations of violence and humiliation, provide help and support to other people
- take care of the local environment and nature in general.

Some of the aims can seem contradictory – to develop self-respecting and self-confident personalities on the one hand and to cultivate understanding, respect and tolerance towards other people on the other. Our teachers, with their 'inherited' rather collective thinking and authoritarian style of teaching, often give priority to the formation of community and setting common interests, at the expense of developing independent, non-conformist personalities. We think that the development of self-confident, strong personalities should be given priority because a person with sufficiently high self-esteem

- is able to set high goals and to reach them
- has positive attitudes to the environment
- is ready to take a risk and to assume responsibility
- is tolerant and open to cooperation without sacrificing his/her principles.

In order to succeed in this work the school must change from the present orientation towards the cognitive aspect of education with the teacher as information source and 'pusher' of learning to learner-centred education aimed at the all-round and harmonic development of the personality. Of the four pillars of education formulated in the report of the commission of UNESCO, 'Education for the XXI Century' – *learning to live together, learning to know, learning to do* and *learning to be* – greatest emphasis should be placed on the first (Delors 1996).

## PSME at school

Work has been started in Latvia to develop a new concept of the contents of the basic (nine-year) education, giving more weight to PSME. The existing system of subjects and time division in periods will be retained as the basis with (presumably) one integrated PSME subject aimed at providing the main contribution to the moral and social development of the personality and the formation of harmonic individuality. The new Norwegian core curriculum for comprehensive schools can serve as a good example (DKKUF 1996).

Nevertheless PSME cannot be reduced only to a particular subject – the corresponding problems and questions should be studied also in the framework of other subjects in the form of cross-curricular themes. This requires the development of special guidelines and methodological materials for the teachers of these subjects.

In PSME the school ethos and the psychological climate of the school and of the class are of great importance. The process of socialisation starts with activities in the class and school community. That is why the preparedness of teachers for this work is essential. The main factor determining the success of PSME is doubtless the personality of the teacher – his/her professionalism in the widest and best sense of the word. In Latvia each form-master(mistress) devotes about one tenth of his/her working time and efforts to PSME work with the pupils in his/her form. One period per week is included in the schedules for common activities with all pupils of the form. This is a significant resource for PSME, but in many cases the work lacks purposefulness and efficiency.

Consequently, the PSME system proposed by us includes the following four main elements:

- integrated PSME subject(s)
- cross-curricular PSME themes
- general educational influence of the school
- PSME activities of teachers, especially the form-masters(mistresses).

## Situation and problems in the PSME field

Now let us have a closer look at the situation and the related problems. We agree with Rossiter (1996) that the best solution, if we take into account the scientifically grounded tendency towards the integration of learning, would be one integrated PSME subject based on general human-istic values and principles. It should include moral values and norms, laws and rules of social life, secur-ing the quality of human coexistence. Moral, social and legal matters are inseparably interwoven in our life so it is reasonable to study them as one subject. Such an approach has been adopted in Lithuania, with one subject somewhat arbitrarily called 'Eth-ics' extending through the whole schooling time from grade 1 to grade 12 (LRSMM 1994). Of course, the contents are arranged so as to take into account the age of the pupils, with a spiral structure approaching the same themes several times at successively higher levels.

It is clear from the beginning that a subject like this cannot be taught and learned by the traditional methods used in conventional subjects. It must be based on active forms of learning – discussions, role-plays, projects, contacts with outstanding people, etc. The affective aspect of learning is very important for the internalisation of moral and social values, and for developing empathy and other human qualities.

In Latvia we still don't have the concept and pro-gramme of integrated PSME. Nevertheless the first steps have been made. In 1994 'White Lessons' were introduced as one period weekly in the elem-entary grades (1–4) to acquaint children with the worldview and traditions of Latvian people associ-ated with the changes of seasons and using native folk songs, fairy tales, riddles and beliefs. This programme

- helps to acquaint children with the national cultural heritage
- develops the thinking and communication skills of children, and forms awareness of the unity of man, nature and the world
- develops human values and qualities such as goodness, love, fairness, dignity, empathy, self-awareness, etc., using ethical values of the folk culture.

Starting in 1995 a 35-hour 'Civics' course has been introduced in grade 9. This course deals with the principles of democracy and the fundamentals of the functioning of state and society. A virtues-education course is under development for grades 5–7.

Even when an integrated PSME subject exists, discussion of values issues should not be excluded from other relevant subjects. To make this process efficient, scientifically founded and thoroughly elaborated guidelines for the main cross-curricular themes must be developed for teachers. They must be well correlated with the syllabus of the main PSME subject to exclude unnecessary overlapping but to secure deeper and wider study of the main concepts. This additionally emphasises the need for a unified PSME system in schools.

The class and school communities are the first collectives (after the family and kindergarten) where children learn the skills of living and working together. Here they acquire the first experience of democratic participation, forming common atti-tudes and sharing tasks and responsibilities, solving conflicts, etc. The highest level of socialisation involves various forms of pupils' self-government and other organisations.

Latvian schools have rich traditions of nurturing national cultural heritage – generally high levels of musical education in schools allow school choirs to reach nearly professional standards and thus the regular song and dance festivals for schools are very popular. They bring together in Riga thousands of singers and dancers from all over Latvia, giving them unforgettable aesthetic, social and emotional impressions.

Also school traditions often include various forms of musical and dramatic performances, teach-ing the pupils persistence in achieving satisfaction in common work and its results, developing skills of cooperation, and learning to respect their own national cultural heritage and the cultures of other nations.

## The work of teachers (form-masters or mistresses) in the field of PSME

### Guidelines for teachers in the PSME field

At present the traditions of teamwork are not yet popular with the Latvian teachers and they work mainly individually. This means that PSME work is done mainly by the form-master or mistress (FM), who have this as their official paid duty. Other teachers participate in PSME according to ability and inclination while teaching their subjects and taking part in the school's common activities. In the future all teachers and other school personnel will become more and more involved in PSME, so new guidelines have been formulated as follows. All who work in school:

- cooperate to develop a sense of togetherness

and solidarity among pupils, as well as a sense of responsibility for people outside the school environment

- care for the spirit of solidarity in the school
- actively counteract any acts of oppression or violence in school.

The teachers:

- respect every pupil's personality and organise the work according to the principles of democracy
- ascertain and discuss with the pupils the basic values of Latvian society and their influence upon the actions of individuals
- openly discuss various current topics, ideas and problems
- together with pupils develop regulations for work and participation in the group
- cooperate with the family in the education of pupils and explain the norms and rules of the school as the basis for the school's work and cooperation with the community.

## Specific role and tasks of the FM

As there are only a few schools in Latvia having professional school psychologists and counsellors the FM must not only play the main role in the personal education of pupils but also be adviser, friend and consultant in many personal matters. His/her ability to create a warm and sincere working climate and a spirit of cooperation and mutual support determines significantly the outcomes of learning and the efficiency of PSME in particular. The spiritual and cultural development of pupils is one of the main areas of concern for the FM, along with essential life skills in the elementary grades.

Probably the two main functions of the FM are leadership and coordination. To perform them well it is necessary to know the pupils as closely as possible, and also to know their families because successful PSME work requires close cooperation with them. The coordination function is essential in organising various projects and other activities involving several teachers and community representatives.

The modes and methods of work of the FM can be very different – from discussions and various psychological games to meetings with exemplary individuals, thematic parties, visiting theatre performances, museums, excursions, etc. The FM is the initiator and stimulator of positive class traditions – collective birthday parties, visiting sick classmates, etc. – as well as the organiser of participation in all-school activities – various festivities, sports events, competitions.

As many important issues of PSME are not included in the official subject syllabi very much depends on the work of the FM and their creative and responsible attitude towards their duties. Unfortunately in the process of teacher education there is little practical training in this area and it takes time and effort in practical work to gain enough experience. More active support is needed from the educational authorities in the form of methodological and teaching materials like those provided for PSME in British schools (Hitchin and Riviere 1995).

## Teachers' code of ethics

To succeed in PSME based on humanistic and democratic principles and values it is necessary that all teachers share these values. Therefore we reckoned it worthwhile to formulate the teachers' code of ethics (TCE) defining the main moral values and personal qualities of teachers (MESL 1996b). (Two of us, A.M. and J.V., took part in the task group developing the draft.) The basic principles and values included in the TCE are the following:

- professionalism and collegiality
- freedom and responsibility
- truthfulness and fairness
- respect and self-esteem
- delicacy and sensitivity.

The TCE suggests how these principles and values should be actualised in the everyday work of teachers and their relations and common work with pupils, colleagues, parents and other people. The first comments on the draft of the TCE are generally positive and now the task group will edit the final version to be submitted for endorsement by the Ministry of Education and Science.

We think that the TCE must not be regarded as just another instruction or regulation but as an impetus for starting thorough discussion about the moral and psychological climate in the school, and for reaching a common understanding and sharing of the main values. We envisage that a poster with the text of the TCE signed by the teachers will be displayed in each school and everybody – including, of course, pupils – will be able to follow how the principles are observed by the teaching staff. An obvious requirement here is that an analogous pupils' code of ethics is placed nearby – such codes have been drafted and are implemented in many schools in Latvia.

## Problems of teachers' pre-service and in-service education

The existing system of teachers' pre-service education is aimed mainly at their development as personalities and professionals in teaching particular subjects. Relatively little attention is paid to prepare them for PSME work, in particular in the role of FM. Usually there is one course, 'Theory and practice of education (upbringing)', which is not sufficiently supported by practice in schools. Therefore it cannot be expected that young teachers will be good FMs and will contribute significantly to PSME.

When new subjects like 'Civics' are introduced it is impossible to rely on teachers having been trained to teach these subjects in teacher-education institutions. That is why the in-service education system is necessary. The same is true for the education of teachers for the new PSME subject(s) and the preparation of teachers for their work as FM in the new situation.

The present system of in-service education of teachers is not well suited for such a task because its organisation is based mainly on courses required by the teachers and offered by various educational institutions. Besides this the number of courses financed by the state budget is relatively small and the teachers' salaries are too low to support their in-service education.

## Adult education

### Family education and support centres

Any normal education (including PSME) starts in the family, whatever it is. Unfortunately in previous years and still now the education in our schools does not prepare young people for family life. As a result family education is very often wrong and sometimes even harmful. The resulting conflicts and psychological traumas can deform the child's personality and the educational faults of the family

are not easy to correct in the course of further education.

Therefore it is important for society to educate parents, especially young ones, in institutions where experienced psychologists, educators and health-care specialists can give consultations on various aspects of family education. In the Riga Pedagogical Higher School a Family Education and Support Centre has been established with the following main tasks:

- to promote the awareness of the family as a value, to restore the confidence in the family as the most significant factor of human development
- to educate parents and parents-to-be in the child's development and family-life problems
- to support the development of equal, safe and benevolent relations in the family, to provide help in overcoming individual and family crises
- to provide families with pedagogical and psychological knowledge for the development of children's personalities and actualisation of their potentials
- to serve as the base for the training of students in family education.

The centre will be the first link in a network of prospective centres in all regions of Latvia. The functioning of such centres is particularly important now because the number of pre-school education institutions has decreased significantly and a high percentage of children do not receive organised pre-school education.

### Public universities and other forms of adult education

In the pre-war independent Latvia public universities were the favourite mode of popular enlightenment. Now this form of non-formal adult education is experiencing a revival and at present seven public universities are functioning in various parts of Latvia. Not all of them are directly oriented towards PSME, but the very participation in the process of education is of positive value from a PSME perspective.

Many other forms of adult education, including the requalification of unemployed people, are also making an indirect contribution to PSME. Taking into account the relatively high level of unemployment, courses for the unemployed are important for their social support and raising their level of social activity.

## Conclusion

Agreeing fully with the view of education as 'an indispensable asset in the attempt to attain the ideals of peace, freedom and social justice' (Delors 1996) we would stress that it is PSME that most fosters harmonious human development and plays a special role in the creation of a better society. Therefore the development of PSME in schools and in society in general is of the utmost importance.

In Latvia work has been started to reform the contents of education so as to give more weight to PSME. It is important that all aspects of education of the character (spiritual, cultural, moral and social) are treated within a common integrated framework curriculum as they are inseparable in the person's development and life. In the specific ethnic situation of Latvia it is important that the new content takes this factor into account and aims at the integration of different social groups and the creation of a civic society.

Much has to be done in the field of adult PSME. TV is used now for language acquisition and for entrepreneurial (economic) education but there are few programmes devoted to the spiritual, social and legal aspects of personality development. Although the number of Internet users is growing rapidly, it is still small and the educational potential of the Internet is not efficiently used.

Of course, PSME cannot be regarded as the panacea for curing all social ills and as a means of achieving universal economic welfare. Nevertheless it is very important for development of the society and that is why coordinated efforts are needed to foster it at all levels. The present chapter is aimed at giving impetus to this work.

## References

Delors, J. (1996) *Learning: The Treasure Within*, Report to UNESCO of the International Commission on Education for the Twenty-first Century, 237 pp. Paris: UNESCO.

DKKUF (Det Kongelige Kirke-, Utdannings-og Forskningsdepartamentet) (1996) *Laereplanverket for den 10-Arige Grunnskolen*, 357 pp. Oslo: KUF.

Hitchin, P. and Riviere, D. (1995) *More Dilemmas: Real-life Problem-solving Exercises for Personal, Social and Moral Education at Key Stage 3*, 122 pp. Lancaster: Framework Press.

LRSMM (Lietuvos Respublikos Svietimo ir Mokslo Ministerija) (1994) *Lietuvos Bendrojo Lavinimo Mokyklos Bendrosios Programos*, 357 pp. Vilnius: Leidibos Centras.

MESL (Ministry of Education and Science of Latvia) (1996a) Education Act. *Izalitiba un Kultura* 1, 13–19 (in Latvian).

MESL (Ministry of Education and Science of Latvia) (1996b) Teachers' Code of Ethics. *lzglitiba un Kultura* 28, 8 (in Latvian).

Rossiter, G. (1996) 'The Moral and Spiritual Dimension to Education: Some Reflections on the British Experience', *Journal of Moral Education*, 25: 201–14.

SMES (Swedish Ministry of Education and Science) (1996) *The 1994 Curriculum for the Compulsory School System*, 26 pp. Stockholm: SMES.

UNDP (United Nations Development Programme) (1996) *Latvia Human Development Report*. Riga: UNDP, pp. 21–61.

# 13 Inclusive Moral Education: A Critique and Integration of Competing Approaches

BILL PUKA

## Character and culture

Character education has enjoyed a meteoric rise in the field of moral education. It is now clearly dominant. The character program is twofold: to nurture moral virtues and to promote moral literacy – the basic knowledge of right, wrong, and value. Six methods are key: (1) instructing students directly in certain basic values and ideals, (2) establishing behavioral codes and enforcing them, (3) telling stories with moral lessons, (4) modelling desirable traits and values, (5) holding up moral exemplars in history, literature, and current-day communities, extolling their traits, (6) providing in-school and community outreach opportunities (service projects) through which students can exercise good traits and pursue good values.

This diversity in moral content and function promotes cultural and psychological diversity as well. It spans a variety of favored ethical orientations. And each component can be pursued in particularly eclectic ways. Morality tales and exemplars can be chosen, for example, that are particularly beloved in the various cultural traditions.

Over several decades the character approach stood on the sidelines while alternative programs (values clarification, moral discussion) had their day. Now, in claiming to tackle urgent problems plaguing urban youth, character education has moved front and center. It is touted as the only direct and decisive approach available for addressing student drug and alcohol abuse, youth crime and gang violence, teen pregnancy and risky promiscuity. Approaches such as values clarification or moral discussion are held to be too indirect and intellectually remote to change actual behaviors and motivations on these issues.

## Pros and cons

In concept, character education easily encompasses the competing emphases on moral reasoning, valuation, and socialization (cultural transmission). It deals with the full gamut of moral traits, proclivities, interpersonal orientations, and practices. It is also far more personally compelling and inspiring than these more limited approaches, featuring live personalities and their interesting features, not abstract concepts or general principles. Thus it can pique the peculiar interests of different groups, motivating them. The character approach does not merely consider how to think about moral issues or values, but how to feel, act, and relate to others in everyday practice.

To critics, character education seems limited by psychological individualism and its cultural boosters. Virtues appear to be personal traits nurtured within each individual, not features of groups or relationships. But any serious attempt to nurture virtues must rely heavily on social relationships and settings. Good character comes of good relationships and of ongoing participation in group practices. It is habituated activity of institutionalized sorts. And it can only be expressed in such ongoing relations and practices. In fact, personal virtue is a relational trait – a trait *of* friendships and communities themselves, and members within them. And it comes tailored to its varied social environments. Consideration, courage, or honesty take quite different forms in different cultures. A virtuous person is skillful in tailoring self-expression to such contexts.

Through its mere conceptual diversity, character education can offer "something for everyone." It can provide some moral place for each cultural group to belong and find their preferred values reflected. And it can help each group appreciate the other's preferred values and orientations, even trying them out in practice.

Still, in practice, the character-education approach has a sordid past with which advocates misguidedly claim continuity. It retains dangerous affiliations with indoctrinative practices and partisan ideologies – often mean-spirited, moralistic ideologies. Leading character advocates are dismissive of alternative moral ideologies and approaches. Where the character approach might learn from these traditions, and accommodate them, it is instead hostile and condescending. This is especially true of cultural traditions that depart from the explicit affiliation of character education with Western, Judeo-Christian values. Leading character advocates vaunt this tradition as not only superior to alternatives, but validly generalizable across non-Western subcultures (Bennett 1988, Wynne and Ryan 1993).

Though the values-clarification and moral-reasoning approaches focus more narrowly, they provide a moral "something for everyone" as well. Students' diverse values are to be noted and taken seriously in both approaches. All are to be reflected on and discussed together, respecting each viewpoint and seeking bases for accord. Yet values clarification and moral discussion are successfully designed to avoid the partisanship and indoctrination problem to which character education proves vulnerable. Clarifying values does not involve deciding on the right values. Reasoning and discussion allows challenge and disagreement with the "established" position. It allows any sorts of values and principles a chance to win the day or find parity among alternatives.

The problem with these two approaches, from a diversity perspective, is that they *merely* allow. They do not directly speak to each value alternative, affirming its distinct orientations and providing them a distinct place. In being accepting or respecting of all, they are indifferent to what is preferable in each. They tolerate rather than affirming or making way for. Values clarification thus slides into relativism. But so does the values and virtues side of moral reasoning or discussion. In attempting to be fair-minded and even-handed to all morally credible turns of mind, it lets highly positive ideals, values, and virtues slip from special notice, failing to credit their higher-mindedness. Minimalist and begrudging values should be *protected* equally, perhaps, but they should not be rated or promoted equally.

Still, more pointed alternatives that uphold certain values, even a sizable range of values, raise clear problems. They cannot help but show favoritism toward valuers, de-emphasizing or excluding the pet values of some. Consider current criticism by "ethical carers" of the so-called justice reasoning or theme itself, prominent in the moral-discussion approach. Its attempted neutrality among competing values is claimed to veil a favoritism toward peculiarly masculinist, individualistic, and judgemental values. Neutrality itself becomes such a partisan, one-sided value for critics. But with justice, this sort of bias is correctable. A misuse of the justice concept and its design is at issue, rationalizing underlying interests. By contrast, the popular caring theme in ethics cannot help but favor traditionally feminine, relational, and interpersonally sensitive traits. Personal styles that go heavy on bravura, personal assertiveness or aloofness are morally endangered on such themes – and overly so. (Much style is simply style, and should not define moral responsibility or adequacy.) Stoic personalities and subcultural styles cannot measure up on care's "dialogical" standards. (Norwegian and Icelandic styles are "responsively challenged" here, for example.) Nor can the earthy, jostling style of some ethnic subcultures that equate "talking" with arguing. (Italo-American, Irish-American, and working-class Jewish subcultures are well-publicized examples.)

Arguably, caring is designed to be partisan in these ways and with good reason. Its aim in posing this side of the value picture is to complete a formerly one-sided one. Add caring to justice and we have true non-partisanship – not passive non-partisanship (neutrality) but proactive cross-partisanship. This point might be well-taken if there weren't a less partisan way to go, for example, correcting justice biases, and if so many moral themes and sub-themes were not left out. Where is the place of moral honor here, which is so central to many cultures' ethics? Where is the overarching virtue of integrity for that matter, or the more pagan moral values of lustiness, or wit and jocularity? Ethical caring is mostly serious and sensitive. It talks problems out, empathizing with others' pain, problems, and worries. Some care theorists claim that it also involves the sharing of joy. But consult the "empirical data" on care research. Consult your images of sensitive souls, *responsively* sharing the joy of others. Do bawdiness or jocularity come to mind? Do you imagine loud and inebriated groups singing and dancing at raucous parties or weddings?

To what extent can we craft a properly inclusive and virtuous approach to moral conceptualization that simultaneously sees to the *moral* inclusion of social and psychological differences? To what extent can we formulate a moral integration of competing moral themes and pedagogies that builds on their clearest strengths, using each to overcome each other's weaknesses and limitations? This is the attempt here – to provide each moral-education approach a prominent place, and also keep it in its place to provide the others space.

## Diversity and inclusion

In my view, cultural diversity is an overestimated value in moral education and should be approached eliptically. Partly this is because other diverse influences are stronger – local ethnic, family, and peer socialization, and psychological type. It is also because some of these diverse but complementary influences are of greater moral relevance or validity, along with some common influences. Diversity perspectives egregiously underestimate the difficulties we face in achieving key aims of morality: mutual understanding and accord over values and cooperation in their implementation. Admittedly, it would be nice to "let a thousand flowers bloom" in moral thought. This is a creative, fulsome ideal. But it is a primarily intellectual and ideological one, nice in theory. In practice, we already have more moral perspectives than we can handle – *far* more. On many key social and interpersonal issues we are plagued by stultifying moral disagreement, hostile contention, and mutual alienation.

Our failure to agree on a broad range of crucial issues has spawned a widespread proclivity toward value relativism and cynicism in American and European society. Among other detrimental effects, this proclivity marginalizes morality in daily practice. In the face of intractable roadblocks to effective relations – to getting on with the business of life – we simply go around. Moral issues start to be seen as intolerable annoyances, even embarrassments to be skirted. (We typically apologize for showing moral virtue – "Oh it was nothing; I got a lot out of it too" – yet proper humility could be expressed in so many less morally expensive ways.) In daily life we take the "moral point of view" more often to show social outrage or personal pique. Or

we shop morality for windowdressing when our pragmatism seems too crass and needs sprucing up.

Inclusion is the key, I suggest, not diversity. And inclusion is most key in the negative – opposing the perennial injustices of ethnocentric bias and their distorting effects on moral outlook. On the positive side, inclusion affirms people's heartfelt commitments and the sense of identity that goes with them. But this has the dire side-effect of legitimizing misguided beliefs and their horrific practices. Cultural examples include mutilation (clitoridectomy), cruel retributivism (amputation for theft, castration for rape), extreme racism and sexism, and classist inequality. Ethnocentrism itself is a defining value of most traditional cultures, legitimizing discrimination against immigrants or foreigners. As many well-meaning "diversity advocates" have come to realize, affirming the de facto ethics of most cultures and subcultures is an exercise in injustice. Egregious sexism is perhaps its most pervasive form.

## Opposing approaches

### Paths to virtue

There is an almost eerie similarity in the way most character-education presentations begin. A distinctive failure scenario is attributed to "other approaches," which the author has tried, then rejected. The superior assets of character education then follow. Past presentations of my own role-models program in moral education ('Be Your Own Hero') have begun precisely in this way, despite my unfamiliarity with the character-education literature. I offer a thumbnail sketch, emphasizing the American experience.

### Part I (of scenario): the failure of moral education

Each time American society decries the decline in American values, it calls on schools to provide courses in ethics. Ethics as a field is dominated by moral philosophy. And as a moral philosopher I am constantly trying to answer that call.

For 15 years I've supplemented philosophical ethics with moral psychology. The purpose is to open motivational pathways for my students between conceptual understanding of what is right and actually doing it. Primary helpers in my efforts have been Aristotle, Kant, Mill, Kohlberg, Gilligan, and Noddings. But often I have felt more impeded than helped by these mentors and the tools they provide.

*Moral philosophy* supplies us with general theories of obligation. Most often cited are utilitarianism, individual (natural, libertarian) rights, social-egalitarian justice, Kantian respect for persons, and moral perfectionism. Put commonsensically, the leading principles of these theories are: "Act always to maximize overall social benefit;" "Guarantee equal unimpeded liberty for each individual;" "Promote the equal distribution of economic opportunity;" "Render each person equal regard for their self-determining traits and potentials;" "Contribute to the maximum development of socially desirable traits and their expression."

Unfortunately, grasping these principles provides little direction on what to do, and basically no inspiration for doing it. Such principles chart the general limits and parameters in which acceptable moral aspirations should fall. But they pose no actual options for acting on them. "Maximize the good, yes, that's the point," we note. "Do what's best for everyone in the situation, of course. But what sorts of things actually maximize the good?" The *morality* of respect also isn't obvious: "It's obvious that we shouldn't step on people or stand idly by while they succumb to dire oppression or deprivation, but what are the positive, substantive conveyances of moral respect and on what basis do we merit or owe them?" Failing to answer such questions is somewhat of a drawback since we look to such principles for guidelines to action.

Worse yet, the principles of ethical theory are locked in bitter conflict. Each alternative implies that its competitors are flawed – indeed, that they oblige us to do wrong. In practice, for example, maximizing social welfare and oppressing unpopular minorities often goes hand in hand. So does respect for individual property rights and gross economic inequality. What then is ethics telling us – first, to contradict ourselves, then to ferment injustice more systematically?

When I assign students the task of applying egalitarian justice or utilitarian principles to a moral dilemma, they have much more trouble than when they address the dilemma directly via common sense. This is not much of an educational recommendation for theoretical principles.

*Applied Ethics* improves little on "pure" ethics.

No applied theory resolves the direct conflicts among theories being applied. Indeed, there is no applied ethical theory period. And non-applied principles are not fine-grained enough to address particular issues. Thankfully, these inadequacies have been skirted through a shift in educational focus. Applied ethics classes address problems and dilemmas directly, using the *methods* of moral philosophy, not theories. Such methods include conceptual analysis, comparative interpretation, and justificatory argumentation. But the diversity of such analyses and the conflicting arguments raised in debate foster a moral hopelessness in class. As all theories can be "ripped apart," so all moral problems can be "debated forever." At least this is the students' impression. Any argument for one side can be countered with arguments for the other; moral dilemmas cannot be resolved (Hoff-Sommers 1991). Students conclude that ethics is futile, yet another ironic lesson for moral education to teach.

Moral philosophy is a collegiate enterprise. But the major approaches to pre-college moral education also seem woefully incomplete, indirect, and unreliable.

*Moral socialization* (social learning) transmits the prevailing social norms and conventions of our society to students. It simultaneously reinforces the internalization of this ideology. But its relativistic, conventional depiction of morality fails to distinguish morally basic and shared values from non-moral and arbitrary ones. It does not transmit our achieved understandings or justifications of values. Nor does it nurture the competences to work these rationales out and apply them to varied situations. Its message is predominantly, "We believe this; so you believe it also." As a result, students are objectionably indoctrinated in this approach. Luckily, some students eventually see through the aura of objectivity surrounding socialized norms. But this only engenders a socially resentful form of egoism. Relativism sets in with a rejection of moral conformity, sensible or not. Reckless amoralism often results (Kohlberg 1984, ch. 1).

*Values clarification* seems woefully limited by design. Hitler was very clear about his values and about the values of non-Arians; so what? The last impression moral education should create is that all values are primarily matters of personal perspective, or all principles matters of preference or taste. If we are not confused and vague about them, they are all tolerably fine. Obviously, making views comparably explicit doesn't make them comparably valid. Yet in helping students become more aware of their values, and tolerant of their value differences, values clarification fosters just these impressions. Questions of which clarified values are worth holding are left virtually untouched in this approach.

Yet suppose this approach fostered a clear-sighted evaluative take on values, assessing which values best rate. The results would still be inadequate. Even the most thorough conceptual understanding is but one step toward becoming a good person and treating others well.

*Moral discussion* (dilemma discussion) helps sophisticate reasoning about morality. More specifically, it develops the ability to support one's viewpoints with arguments and justifications, comprehending others' supporting rationales as well. Obviously, arguing for viewpoints is not the end-all of moral reasoning or understanding. Indeed, it can frustrate thoughtful understanding, jumping to speak before it hears. In practice, rational argument typically pushes a partisan side, to win, rather than truly investigating the case for each side to find tandem strengths.

Obviously, most moral *debates* cannot be won – at least not by children in a class session or two. Thus moral-discussion strategies also impress students with the futility of ethics. Ironically, they may foster precisely the sort of relativism that they originally hoped to combat in values clarification: "Any viewpoint can be argued or criticized on a comparable level."

Again, reasoning leaves out moral perception, imagination, and a host of interpersonal skills. Working alone, or out of step with these competences, it can set moral thought and action awry. And obviously, good moral reasoning, understanding, or knowledge is light years from moral knowhow or action. Kohlberg's research on moral development, from which the moral-discussion approach derives, is itself plagued by this judgment–action gap.

Often Kohlbergians point to a sizable (70 per cent) correlation between judgment and action, boosting the promise of the moral-discussion approach. But this gets matters backwards. Moral action is primarily what we're after. Advocating an indirect approach, which nurtures reasoning to ferment action, requires us to justify every percentage-point of *non*-correlation. Otherwise, we should "train" actions and their effective motivations directly, explaining as we go.

Consider a worse problem. Hypocrisy and rationalization are two of the biggest socio-moral problems we face. Cognitive-moral development, if anything, exacerbates them. The tools of good justification are the tools of good rationalizing and self-deception as well. Yet no account is offered in this approach of the difference. Nor are safeguards provided to prevent the insidious undermining of moral choice and character by these self-justifying influences.

On the flip side: Kohlbergian research places many of the most morally exemplary individuals at "low levels" of moral reasoning – Stages 3 and 4 (Kohlberg 1982, ch. 9, Colby and Damon 1992). Exemplary lives seem to draw from a well of naivety. Moral saints oversimplify problems and are over-optimistic toward solving them. They also show a quaint literalism in interpreting moral directives. As several "moral heroes" expressed matters to me: "The golden rule says to love one's neighbor as oneself, so I do." Such literalism is obvious in the life of Mother Teresa and in Christian helpers of Jews during the Nazi Holocaust (Oliner and Oliner 1988). It is obvious in the scores of "creative-altruism" interviews analyzed by Colby and Damon (1992). Is more sophisticated reasoning, then, clearly more boom than bust for moral education?

All the major approaches to ethics and moral education share two questionable notions. First, in each, morality and moral character are seen as relatively delimited parts of life, personality, and action. Second, these parts stand off to the side of the real business of life. We see this every day in commonsense conversation also when speaking of "the moral dimension," a typical footnote to our practical decision-making concerns.

Depicting morality through its borderline cases, at the extremes of life and death, bolsters this misimpression. Kohlberg's moral-discussion dilemmas and the dilemmas typically taken up in applied ethics show this tendency. Even in daily life we typically cite abortion, euthanasia, or capital punishment as the burning "moral issues" of our time. It is our common mistake here to equate the substance of moral phenomena with what is "interesting," "challenging," or "puzzling" in thinking about them. How we treat each other day to day – whether we really listen to each other, whether we speak to each other civilly, whether we show some support, being there for those close to us – this is the stuff of morality, continually kneaded in our everyday interactions.

## Part II (of scenario): the hope of educating virtue

Faced with such limited ethical tools, one seeks alternatives. In my own case, the bitter conflicts among ethical theories led to a search for eclectic, accommodating ethical theories. I evolved an eclectic ethic, The Right Mix, which breaks rival views down into combinable portions and integrates them piece by piece. The aim here is to promote complementarity rather than the holistic hegemony of one view over all rivals, excluding piecemeal assets. To deal with the over-generality of moral principles and the narrowness of education programs, I adopted morally non-distinctive approaches to choice and action. (Such approaches typically are thought of as psychological, practical, or spiritual rather than moral.) Featured here are classroom trainings in Rogerian counseling methods, "arts of loving," meditational techniques, "self-help" methods ("ten ways to a happier relationship"), and pop-music videos. ("If you want to make the world a better place you've got to look at yourself and make a change.")

But the most promising approach I've discovered – the approach that "puts it all together" – is ancient ethics. Originally, ethics dealt with the art of living well or flourishing, which includes being well. The "good life" involves perfecting our potentials and traits and integrating them in character – true "integrity." The truly integrated character naturally expresses itself in social participation. (We are social beings blessed with social selves.)

"Good-life" ethics are found in Plato, Aristotle and the Confucians, as in the major religions. In these traditions, moral exemplars and their virtues are the chief means of modeling, explaining, and motivating ethical behavior, also of justifying and educating it. Exemplars come primarily in individual form (Buddah, Jesus, the Sage, the Mother, the Godhead), but also as couples (Rama and Sita, Arjuna and Krishna) and groups (utopian societies, communities of saints).

Using exemplars in moral education provides refreshing directness. We need not foster conceptualizations that *might* eventually yield correct judgments, nor abilities that might someday become excellences. We need not hope that these contribute a bit in future to desirable moral practices. Rather we pose the question, "Would you like to know how to be ethical?" Then we reply, "Here is how: these people are how. These are living, hol-istic embodiments of moral excellence – beautiful variations on the beautiful theme of goodness." We help students notice. "Here is how very good people think and feel. Here is how they perceive other people and look out on the world. This is what makes them tick. Here is how they stay motivated and committed and how they got that way originally."

Through exemplars or character education we can show students why people find fulfillment in what seems to others pure drudgery and sacrifice. We can observe with them how these good people put their beliefs into practice – and practice well, not just well-intentionally. We can show moral "saints" being good friends, parents, children, and citizens. Then we suggest, "Perhaps some of their ways are ways for you. Let's see."

Students find it especially enlightening to notice how everyday saints eat, how they approach personal hygiene (a big issue for Gandhi), and how they have fun outside their "mission" (e.g., rollerblading). Studying actual people, living actual lives, reveals the flaws and hypocrisies typical of saints. This deflates hero-worship and brings heroic accomplishment within reach. Other main virtues of exemplar education are notable also.

*Personal identification.* Exemplary individuals are personally interesting, accessible, and understandable. Their qualities are gripping, moving, and inspiring. We care about their "principles" because *they* care about them, and because they show the personal consequences of following them.

*Holistic integration.* Exemplary *people* are morally holistic, showing all the aspects of moral thought and behavior – psychological, spiritual, autonomous, habitual, traditional, socialized, ritualized, individualistic and relational, skilled and artful. (They contrast sharply here with principles and codes.) What theorist would have de-emphasized creative perception and imagination in ethics, empathy or emotion, if attention remained focused on moral *persons* in life and action?

*Functional embodiment.* Moral exemplars show morality in *action*, not just *being*. They let us see moral tenets actually functioning in daily life, with virtues. Thus they bridge, in their person, the great gaps between theory and application, abstraction and particularization, good judgment and good action.

*Comportment.* Exemplars reveal the many nonmoral resources that go into moral development and behavior. They expose the underrated link between inner virtue and outward style. This involves speaking in gentle tones, or raucously good-humored ones, being considerate in the little things, and being warm and friendly, not just phil-anthropically grand. Exemplars link ideals to practi-calities, the good to the beautiful, and moral char-acter to personality generally.

Some of the exemplar's assets for education extend to character education as a whole. However, that approach emphasizes particular virtues, not their integrated expression in whole lives. Exem-plars are the centerpiece of my own educational program, "Be Your Own Hero: Careers in Com-mitment", which combines exemplary role-models with community service. In the following section I outline its components.

## Dismissiveness and its remedy

Dissatisfaction with so-called "liberal" approaches to moral education has turned character advocates dismissive. The foregoing failure scenario is indica-tive. A notable exception here is Thomas Likona (1983, 1988, 1992), who tries to combine char-acter and cognitive-moral development. (Obvi-ously I am trying to become an exception myself here.)

There is an irony in such exclusionary tendencies since they show a clear lack of virtue. To ignore the obvious strengths in approaches one rejects is not only unreasonable and imprudent, but arrogant and dishonest. It lacks respect for the enduring and committed efforts of colleagues in a noble cause. And it deprives one's students and audiences of their discoveries. Unfortunately, such dismissive tendencies are not accidental in the current character-education movement. They symptomize ideological and moralistic biases that mar edu-cational practice. Luckily, they can be remedied. Proceeding inclusively, character education can accommodate alternative approaches. There is nothing inherent in the approach that excludes them. Or, if one pleases, the competing approaches can be integrated on a comparable footing, with character education merely contributing its proportionate share.

### *Reclaiming values clarification*

There is a long literature of complaints caricaturing values clarification as a self-absorbed and mindlessly relativistic enterprise. Seen critically, this approach invites students to vent personal preferences – "I like this, you like that" – to little moral effect. "You do your thing, I do mine" is not the lesson in toler-ation, much less responsibility, that moral educa-tors should aim to teach. For older students, already pondering differences between wants, needs, and values, clarifying undifferentiated "values" seems a step backwards. It trades in amoral obfuscation, not moral clarification.

Instead of trying to rehabilitate the reputation of this approach, let us credit this overblown critique. Despite it, nothing in the values-clarification con-ception precludes developing more morally salient and crafted classroom exercises fit for most reflect-ive students. Such exercises could dramatically highlight distinctions between interests and values, as well as among types of values. They can help students distinguish carefully between toleration and relativism, toleration and acceptance, accept-ance and endorsement. Specific practice can be provided in how to judge an act (wrong) while accepting its value (good intention) and author (person). Indeed, tasks can be designed to help students distinguish mindless value relativism from legitimate moral relativism themselves. This would move values clarification a giant step ahead of sup-posedly more sophisticated alternatives – moral dis-cussion and character education. Here students might practice separating subtle forms of moral contextualism and particularism from relativism. And they might seek clarity on the ways that we cooperate morally despite differences in the "universal principles" we actually hold. This would represent another step ahead of major rival approaches and the values-clarification critics they nurture.

If not straitjacketed by its label, the "clarifica-tion" process expands on its own to encompass most cognitive-moral processes. Even in the college classroom, sophisticated moral philosophy dwells most on clarifying (detailing) moral values or tenets. It labors over careful distinctions among types of values, noting that some moral values con-trast sharply with non-moral ones while others fall on a continuum. Such distinctions require explan-ation and justification, which leads to questioning and debate and the posing of alternatives. The moral-discussion approach fails to recognize the continuum-distinction, to the great detriment of its theory and practice.

Clarification is a form of description, which is a

type of interpretation. Interpretation blurs readily into explanation since interpretive renderings make values comprehensible. Clarifying depictions of this sort can become deep, broad, and multifaceted, tracing a value's form, content, and function, and its many relations within value systems.

Much of sophisticated moral theory focuses on just this sort of depiction. Indeed, the most prominent intellectual fads of the current decade – postmodernist narrativism and social constructionism – have philosophy doing little else. Here all types of philosophical explanation, justification, and argument are portrayed as different types of interpretation, none more fundamental or legitimate than any other. The values-clarification approach foreshadows philosophical ethics here, at its cutting edge of research.

In my experience, moral-dilemma discussions in high-school classrooms are dominated by clarifying processes, focused on value differences. So are student reactions to presentations on character traits. Critics from the character camp may believe that values can be clarified without being weighed and evaluated. Perhaps this is barely possible. But I'd like to see character educators confine discussion in this way in an actual classroom.

Values, by nature, imply their own importance and desirability. Stating one's values advances claims. It implies that certain underlying beliefs and associated value preferences have credibility – at least for the speaker. And forwarding claims brings comment, contrast, and challenge from others. In class, valuers are called upon to explain and justify themselves. This is especially so where values are not yet fully explicated or clarified. Here mutual misinterpretations and confusions usually abound. The same is true when values are complex. And there are few values or valued virtues, basic or not, that are not complex and open to interpretation. Ever self-expanding here, the values clarification blends into moral discussion.

*Anecdote*: recently in class I read the parable of the prodigal son from the New Testament (Luke 15). Then I showed Franco Zeffirelli's dramatization of the parable *Jesus of Nazareth*. (As noted, such readings and visual representations are recommended character-education strategies.) Predictably, students had great difficulty deciding which values and virtues were being communicated Parables, like any good moral story, foster this sort of difficulty. They are designed to make one ponder, question, wonder, and look deeper. But even the

traits exhibited by Jesus-as-storyteller seemed obscure to students. They did not come through loud and clear as supposedly sent.

Character advocates hold that virtues, even more than basic values, are widely shared and obvious (Bennett 1988, Wynne and Ryan 1993). But in practice this is clearly not the case. It is one thing to vaguely mention, label, or conceive a value. But it is quite another to pose or identify its proper expression in a situation. Consider our valuing of complex adult virtues such as personal integrity. Is it clear how and when this is shown in the complex and varied situations we face every day?

Once students in my class lighted on key themes of compassion, toleration, mercy, and forgiveness in the Jesus character, their takes on what these amounted to in the parable were quite diverse. Such diversity would have increased tenfold if I had posed apparent values and vices not noted. Critical theorists would cite three: (a) authoritarianism (rabbis like Jesus tell, listeners accept); (b) unfairness (in the father's different treatment of his prodigal son and faithful son), and (c) political; collaborationism. (Zeffirelli has Jesus tell the parable to bring a reconciliation between Simon-Peter and his brother Mathew – a "bloodsucking" tax collector for the Roman occupation in Judea.) Note how much you, as sophisticated reader, have to work on my three-part list above to interpret my meaning. I could have eased your task by packing the idea less densely, making each meaning, aspect and implication clear, and separating it from others. But moral values and principles do not come that way. Even the most "clear" and "basic" are densepacked and deeply ambiguous.

Thus character education cannot help but rely heavily on clarifying values. Moral literacy requires it – the first movement of character education. Internalizing virtue does as well – character education's second theme. Virtues may be moral habits, but their formation requires conceptual processing to have moral standing. (Repetitive behavior or habituation is not enough.) Clarifying values allows character-students to understand as they go through the behavioral motions, and understand why they are going through these motions. It helps them identify desirable traits in others, set goals for moral self-development, and monitor their progress toward these goals.

Still we must discover how character education can imbibe the crucial virtues of values-clarification processes without breaking out in their alleged vices. Alterations and safeguards are needed. In particular, students must be presented with certain immunizing clarification tasks. Consider a handful:

1 What are the differences and similarities among needs, wants, interests, tastes, preferences, values, and types of values? (Examples may include moral, non-moral, and quasi-moral values – practical, economic-material, aesthetic.)
2 Are certain values more basic and defining to value systems than others? Are some ultimately basic? How are these distinguished from less basic ones? And what is the importance of this difference?
3 How do these different types of values compare and rate? What places do they occupy in our lives? What are they for and what do they do?
4 How do moral values differ from moral principles? Consider difference in the value aspect and principle version of fairness, equality, benevolence, and group welfare.
5 What are the differences and similarities between the toleration, acceptance, and validation of each other's values? How should these different reactions be tailored to different types of values?
6 What are value relativism and moral skepticism? What different forms do they take? How does relativism differ from tailoring values or principles to different people in different situations at different times?

Obviously, such tasks must be simplified for younger children. And teachers have to be provided information on different ways to make the distinctions involved. Surely sample answers will be needed to get students going in class and guide their responses in constructive directions. This information can easily be extracted from introductory ethics texts or the *Encyclopedia of Philosophy*.

To the moral-discussion camp, stressing such content may raise prospects of indoctrination. But these can be avoided here in a direct, moral-reasoning way. Explanations can be provided for why basic values and virtues are considered non-relative and important. These can be criticized from alternative perspectives, with replies to the criticisms posed. Most important, the bases for preferring one view to another can be analyzed with students. Source materials from philosophical and theological ethics come well-packaged with all this supporting material.

## Reclaiming moral discussion

As suggested, the moral-discussion approach can be readily combined with values clarification. Discussion is the means to clarification and clarification is constantly needed for discussion to progress. Thus as students begin stating, interpreting, and questioning each other's values the two approaches join. Yet moral discussion adds distinctive components. First, it focuses on particular moral issues or problems and how we bring our values and moral rationales to them. It then focuses on figuring these problems out – posing varied solutions to them and comparing their relative merits. Finally, it asks teachers to reinforce more elaborate and well-developed thinking over limited and simplistic thinking.

This is where the approach appears controversial. How do teachers know which thinking is better, and what if teachers differ in their assessments? Are teachers simply to accept the lush theoretical claims of founders in this approach? Need they simply accept Kohlberg's moral-stage theory, on which the approach is based, preferring what he terms "higher"-stage thinking to lower?

Values-clarification advocates might baulk at such preferential treatment of certain "value systems" over others and the "indoctrinative" tendencies involved. (Ironically most character advocates feel comfortable with indoctrination – some straightforwardly advocate it – so long as it is not the Kohlbergian sort of "liberal" indoctrination, like "aberrations" such as humanism or "Eastern" meditative philosophies.)

In practice, however, the moral-discussion approach raises little cause for concern. The key to fomenting classroom moral discussion is to keep conversation flowing and insure that all opinions and rationales are *heard* as well as expressed. In peer discussion, views can only be recognized as superior as they contrast with less adequate ones raised in class. There is no authoritative, outside judge to pronounce on their validity here. Kohlbergians ask teachers to reinforce higher-stage reasoning *merely by orally repeating it*, not judging or advocating it besides. And they are to do this only when necessary – when this reasoning seems not to have been heard or appreciated. In short, the *positivity* of reinforcement here is to come from the quality of reasoning itself, not the teacher's endorsement. (Kohlberg joins values clarification in viewing any further reinforcement as partisan and indoctrinative.)

Moreover, in the moral-discussion approach, teachers are to reiterate higher-stage reasoning only when they can clearly identify it. In classroom discussion, this is very difficult and would rarely occur. (Indeed, a 977-page scoring manual is needed to link particular statements accurately to stages, even when they are written down (Colby, Kohlberg et al. 1987).) Thus, in educative practice, Kohlberg's particular stage theory exerts little influence. Only his main, commonsense assumption seems at work: the more we are exposed to others' thoughts and perspectives, thinking about them, the better our thinking becomes.

Still, to integrate moral discussion happily into a more encompassing approach, we do best to focus on its two main intended contexts and roles. The first keys in on history and social studies curricula. Here students take pro and con views on American practices and institutions. This helps them develop an unusually enlightened critical perspective on America's 300 years of domestic and foreign policy. And it avoids the tendencies of higher-moral-stage reasoning to distort personal decision-making by generalizing and abstracting moral rationales to fit large-scale, institutional contexts. The second key focus is in democratically constituted school (and prison) programs – so-called just communities. Here moral issues are taken up as they actually arise for students (or inmates) in the course of daily and fairly structured interactions. Moral discussions become a natural, non-violent part of group efforts to get along. As such, they aid in developing trust and loyal relationships, and in managing interpersonal fears, envies, and hostilities. Indeed, these discussions aid in simply thinking things out, and assessing where classmates (or fellow) inmates are "coming from." Character education neglects the first context and can only benefit from a helping hand in the second.

Again, critics claim that Kohlberg's moral-development theory is biased toward social-institutional morality. It downplays and distorts interpersonal and familial ethics. Many reject the whole Kohlbergian approach based on this alleged bias. Assuming these critics are correct, then confining the educational applications of this theory to history and social studies classes seems just what is called for. So does its confinement to constitutionally democratic classrooms.

The moral-discussion approach is unquestionably limited. And like values clarification, it is designed to be. The developmental theory from which it stems covers a small portion of moral cognition – that which arises naturally (spontaneously in all cultures) and coheres holistically in problem-solving systems. Because moral discussion only targets students' most basic reasoning ability, it cannot claim to promote highly detailed or interpersonally subtle decision-making. Indeed, it is remarkable how generally useful and adaptable such moral development has proven to be in classroom practice given its limited scope (Higgins and Powers 1984).

And just as character education must rely on clarifying processes for educating values, so it must rely on reasoning ability to achieve moral understanding and virtuous self-expression. Students cannot know how values or character traits apply in different situations without carefully figuring the specifics out. (Habits of virtue only go so far in guiding these applications, involving what went before, not what is to come.) To know what true honesty or courage come to in a situation requires thinking through which particular skills and attitudes to engage and how effectively to convey them to others. The virtue of honesty is not mere truth-telling, for example, which can be crude and hurtful and sometimes even misleading. (We communicate more subtly than "true–false" formats allow.) Sometimes honesty demands overall personal integrity, sometimes authenticity, sometimes emotional genuineness. Likewise, what counts as courage often can be foolhardiness, self-abnegation, or aggression. What is often discounted as mere "going along" and "muddling through" in life is sometimes truly heroic. Being a single mother, for example, often is a heroic role in itself. This takes ruminating reflection to see, especially for young people. Learning basic right from wrong ("moral literacy") is helpful in facing basic, clear-cut moral issues. But most moral matters are anything but.

The role of moral reasoning in good character goes even further. One of the most important dimensions of moral-reasoning development is cognitive role-taking. This is the ability to put oneself in another's conceptual space – to perceive problems and weigh interests from their perspective. Such role-taking is at the heart of the Judeo-Christian "golden rule" and the Confucian "measuring square." It is crucial to all moral deliberations and most moral choices. The moral-discussion approach outdoes values clarification and character education combined in nurturing this ability.

In history and social studies classes, moral-dilemma discussion provides students a crucial counterpoint to indoctrination. It is inherently questioning, challenging, critical. Character education desperately needs this counterpoint since it has collaborated throughout its history in equating Americanism with moral decency and enlightenment. Increasingly self-determined moral reasoning does not accommodate well to such crude equations and eventually questions them directly. It is on this point that moral-literacy approaches must put up or shut up. But without the support of detailed moral reasoning their lists of values or virtues cannot hold up.

More constructively, morally developed reasoning helps students validate for themselves the values America aspires to and, with Western culture generally, so often achieves. It also helps students value America's constant moral self-criticism as one of its greatest achievements. What better moral safeguard is there for students against the moral skepticism of Western adolescence? Yet a developing moral perspective also helps students broaden their moral horizons, overcoming ethnocentrism. It helps them seek out what is admirable in other cultures and sub-cultures and learn from their ways of doing things.

One of the greatest moral achievements of Western culture is constitutional democracy. This is America's "traditional value" supreme. Yet without the sort of moral development that Kohlberg and cognitive-developmental colleagues promote, American citizens may not fully participate in this achievement. How can we enjoy government of, by, and for the people if we cannot understand the US Constitution in its own terms – if we cannot truly agree to it and figuratively sign it? Jefferson conceived the purpose of public education in American democracy for this co-signatory purpose. And as we learn more about common moral understanding, we see that public education has not achieved it.

Repeated studies and surveys indicate that Americans do not really understand the democratic principles and the civil rights they enjoy. They opt continually for scrapping the First Amendment simply because some of its uses are unpopular or harmful. Yet political rights, by definition, tolerate immoral acts. At the same time many equate Supreme Court interpretations of the right to bear arms (against the soldiers of tyrannical governments) with the right to own hunting rifles, handguns, and AK-47s for the fun of it.

In principle moral discussion could help students transform our current aristocratic democracy (government by the elite) into a truly popular democracy. Habits of moral character and conformity, no matter how virtuous or excellent, can never serve this end. We must learn how to think and act for ourselves, creatively and self-determiningly. This requires perspectival and holistic thinking that steps outside the status quo of moral and political convention. No traditional or basic moral virtues possess this capacity. Nor do traditional intellectual virtues for that matter.

In Kohlberg's "just-community" approach, popular democracy becomes participatory democracy. And we see the thinking that upholds it at work in everyday functions – helping students understand and get along with each other better as equals, addressing the problems and prospects raised by mutual liberty in their lives.

Gilligan's (1982) research on relational caring, and its application to schooling (Noddings 1992) promises crucial additions to moral discussion here, increasing interpersonal focus. And to address this focus, a variety of perceptual, empathic, and relational skills are highlighted. Here caring transcends moral reasoning in precisely those virtue-oriented ways that character educators welcome.

But even with such circumscribed foci, preserving the strengths of moral discussion for character education is difficult given its attendant flaws. Recall that moral discussion may upgrade the capacity for artful self-deception, rationalization and hypocrisy. It may foment the kind of ethical relativism or skepticism engendered by applied ethics. (Debates over dilemmas can go on and on without resolution.) And in interpersonal interchange, reasoning skills can frustrate effective communication, negotiation, and accord. Reasoning often overlooks others' personal needs, worries, and emotional concerns. It delegitimizes such phenomena as well, viewing them as psychological problems of no moral import. Reasoning also sometimes contributes contentious argument and outside intervention when careful "insider" negotiation and a soothing of anxieties are called for. Where discussions should become light, laughing trivial problems off, reasoning is ever serious and picayune.

Well-nurtured virtues can mitigate some of these problems, but often not solve them. Thus when combining the two approaches, character strategies must be immunized against such flaws. The direct-warning approach seems best. To wit:

1 The discussion of moral issues helps us develop our abilities to analyze and understand them, also to deliberate about and resolve them. It plays crucial roles in explaining our views to others and showing their credibility. But reasoning alone is quite limited. It must be aided by moral sensitivity and perception and by moral feelings of compassion and courage. We need good interpersonal skills to get along with others, nurturing mutual trust and loyal relationships. And we need a sense of basic decency based on the moral facts of life.

2 The same abilities that help us explain and stand up for our positions can cause contention, undermining needed cooperation and meetings of the mind.

   (a) It can cause us to speak and advocate when we should be listening – to pressure others into agreeing with us, pushing our views on them.

   (b) It can be used to deceive ourselves as well, fueling hypocrisy. All too often we make up false reasons for not doing what we should – for excusing ourselves from promises and responsibilities that others depend on.

3 Moral debates on the most difficult issues go on and on, creating the impression that they cannot be resolved – that they are just a matter of opinion. Perhaps some cannot, though we often can agree to disagree. Most often, however, complex issues merely take a long time to resolve, and much effort. The process of criticizing and defending opposing views does not go on forever. And eventually either the sounder view wins, or the prospects for an accommodation become apparent. To see this, try to come up with more than the first two or three obvious reasons for supporting one side on an issue and its chief rival – one runs out of thoughts rather quickly.

Such warnings would have to be well-illustrated for teachers and students alike to work in class. While moral tragedies should be acknowledged (dilemmas allowing no solution), the value of keeping hope alive and struggling toward resolution should be highlighted.

## Reclaiming moral theory: a word to the wise

Saving moral theory for character education is a much more involved process, which I address elsewhere (Puka 1995). But a few observations may be useful here. First, to criticize moral theories for being too abstract, general, and impractical is misdirected. Why fault theory for being theory? Why use theories, or lay expectations on them, as if they were non-theories?

To seek an overarching conceptual account of morality is a legitimate enterprise. So is the more specific aim of seeking a fundamental logical explanation of the logic of moral reasoning. Such an overarching picture will be general and abstract as a matter of course, especially if it seeks coherence, unity, or holism. A logical explanation of reasoning will be rationalistic in focus. Such theories are only biased or impractical if they are applied to the whole domain of ethics, in every particular type or aspect. Logical explanation is not discursive or commonsense explanation and it does not produce commonsense understanding or knowhow. Theories do what they do, they focus where they focus, and they are limited (merely theoretical) by nature.

Theorists have long distinguished between general and specific theories (as in general and specific relativity theory) and between theories and theorizing. There is analytic, interpretive, justificatory, and applied theorizing, for example. Those who wish more applicable and concrete conceptions, born of theorizing processes, can rightly create them. The intuitionist and virtue traditions in ethics have done so for three millennia. But can general theories be faulted simply for not being such processes?

Second, the most general theories of ethics are filled with pointed and substantive insights. Utilitarianism holds views of what makes good things good, how good things differ, what gives goods more and less quality, and how we can tell. Ethical egoism offers views on prudence and self-responsibility. Kantianism offers respect and fairness rationales on why people and their traits have value. Many of these insights or views can be utilized independently of the abstracted structure and universal principles, surrounding them.

Third, in part, leading ethical theories contain enhanced versions of commonsense ethical views – the views that first gave rise to them. (Kant's theory of respect elaborates the everyday "golden rule," for example.) These enhancements can be added to our everyday moral ideology. But again, they must be located and extracted from theoretical super-structures to do so.

Moreover, the leading ethical theories provide perspectives or "moral points of view" for viewing the world and our place in it. These help answer questions of meaning and purpose in life. Question: Why am I here? Answer 1 (moral perfectionism): To fully develop my natural talents and help others reach their full potential as well. Answer 2 (utilitarianism): To contribute my share to human welfare, leaving the world a better place than when I arrived. Answer 3 (ethical egoism): To get as much out of my life and be the best version of me that I can.

Taking these perspectives can help us recognize and define the different roles we should play, the different considerations we should note, and the different aspects of a problem to be addressed. But these perspectives *really* have to be taken in life to see their use. These substantive insights and views have to be lived every day to determine their value. We can't be merely theoretical about theory.

Ironically, critical theorists are merely theoretical in their critiques. They trash traditional theories before actually trying them out in daily practice. As such, they take the same over-conceptual, abstract, general, and impractical approach *to* them that they criticize *in* them.

## Concluding with character: sin and salvation

With these preservative recipes we might begin folding "alternative approaches" into character education. Or more even-handedly, we might begin the process of integrating rival approaches into an inclusive moral-education strategy. But one giant step remains: cataloguing the sins of character education and rectifying them. Since these sins can "fill a book," I have analyzed them independently (Puka 1995, 1995a). But the deepest stains should at least be listed here with proposed remedies.

As noted, character education has a depraved past. It has promoted unnecessarily punitive measures in the classroom to promote virtuous self-discipline and combat student sloth – corporeal punishment, public humiliation, induced dread and self-blame. (Recall the use of dunce caps, of being

made to stand in the corner, being paddled with broom handles, having one's knuckles rapped with a ruler, being sent to the principal's office, or being labeled a "bad kid.") Traditional "moral literacy" included lessons endorsing racism, sexism, homophobia, and national chauvinism. All of these quite traditional American and Western values were upheld as basic moral values in the formal and informal curriculum. This was especially so in history and English classes.

In the schoolyard, students were taught that fighting solves problems and that might makes right. They also were taught that ridiculing or "ranking out" the weak, unpopular, effeminate, and disabled was acceptable. (At least such practices were not opposed or debunked, but given the tacit approval of observing faculty.) Isn't it the job of such people to be "good sports," after all, not our job to "baby them." The idea of regarding such people "different" or "differently abled" rather than "weird" would have seemed preposterous if suggested to students in this tradition. They would have been laughed out of the school by traditional (male) faculty – especially the gym or shop teachers among them.

Whether or not these evils express the traditional values of character education, they show the vulnerability of this approach to moralistic use, misuse, and abuse. Character education has a long and ignoble track record (paper trail) here. Thus they require current character advocates to provide firm and detailed safeguards against continuing or foreseeable outrages of the sort. Unfortunately, as noted, some current character advocates vaunt their long tradition relative to the recent "liberal aberrations" we've been reclaiming (Bennett 1988, Oldenquist 1993). They do not spurn, apologize for, or even mention this long tradition's prolonged obscenities. (At least I cannot find such account in the vast character literature despite asking leading character-education "gurus" to point me toward them.) Some advocates call for a return to punitive disciplining in class and want discrimination against homosexuals taught as a proper value.

Placing a "liberal" tag on alternative educational programs raises a second problem in the character approach: ideological bias. Character educators equate Western, Judeo-Christian values and virtues with basic moral values (Bennett 1988, 1993, Wynne and Ryan 1993, 1993a). They ignore the sorts of pagan or pre-Christian virtues (humor, sociability, bravura) and subjective values (material, experiential, or erotic) that attract their avowed target audience – inner-city teens. The values of "partying," "hanging out," and "talking trash" are given no mention at all. Neither are "being cool" or "flaunting an attitude." The founders of the Western character tradition – Plato, Aristotle – would have recognized their value orientations in these student practices, not in the restrictive, often humorless moralism of character faculty.

Moreover, the view these advocates present of basic Western, Judeo-Christian values bears suspicious similarities to the "family values" agenda of the New Right, Christian Right, and Republican conservative platform. Judge for yourself regarding the most prominent value profiles offered by notable character educators. For example, familial duties define three of the nine "moral facts" supposedly affirmed by all people, and especially Westerners (Wynne and Ryan 1993). Christian good-samaritanism and the property right define another three (two thirds of the list overall). Faith, hope, and charity constitute three of the eight shared ideals. The economic virtues of fortitude, prudence, and temperance occupy all but two of the remaining slots.

This last triumvirate is especially anomalous since such virtues can be used for moral good or evil. Adolph Eichman showed fortitude, being quite diligent and persevering in his extermination of Jews. Prudence has been a major traditional enemy of kindly virtues and practices. It makes inherent moral motivation (doing X because it is right) and self-sacrifice a vice. Placing the exemplars of such "virtues" – the Wright brothers, Jonas Salk, Christopher Columbus, and Telemachus – alongside Harriet Tubman or Martin Luther King extends the value skew (Bennett 1988).

To inculcate students in (such) partisan and questionable norms under the guise of basic moral values is morally objectionable. Indeed, inculcating them in *any* values is objectionable where the possibility of joint value inquiry and discussion remains live. This is especially so where accompanying explanation, justification, self-criticism, and comparison with alternatives can easily be provided. Indoctrination is not only the mortal sin of character education's "moral literacy" campaign, but one pointedly rationalized away as the carping of fussy critics (Bennett 1988).

## Savings

How can these apparent biases and injustices be overcome? First, clearcut criteria can be set out for identifying morally basic or defining values. (Samples of such criteria are readily available in the ethics literature.) These criteria can be distinguished from culturally shared and validated interpretations of such values. (Of course these also can be legitimate raw materials for moral education, but being shared obviously is not enough to establish validity. As noted, the Western tradition has rationalized racism and sexism, not to mention American slavery, as fitting and proper.)

Proper criteria can distinguish morality from merely conventional, traditional, or partisan norms. Using such criteria, in combination with the mutual-exploration techniques of values clarification and moral discussion, indoctrination can be overcome. If we help students think hard about value issues from varied perspectives – if we let them challenge each other's views – little more is needed. I suggest that indoctrination can be avoided by these measures even when the teacher explicitly favors certain views in class. This is because teaching a favored position in class is not indoctrination so long as comparative explanations and strong justifications are provided. The key is to assure that the basis for a view carries its own authority, not the teacher's authoritative position or authoritarian air. And where students are encouraged to challenge the teacher's authority in matters of substance, thus building children's own sense of authority, this air can be cleared.

Problems of Victorian moralism in our moral traditions can be mitigated by balance. Including benign "pagan" virtues in value profiles helps. So does including non-harmful, subjective values. As moral educators we can take our lead from these goods and abilities that so attract students, already piquing their interest. Even those felt-goods that lace the very evils we are trying to combat should be attended to. Here I mean the goods of drug "highs," gang membership, and teenage pregnancy. Students should be helped to identify and pursue the goods found here down less destructive paths. "Highs," belonging, mutual loyalty and enterprise and the like can be found in myriad constructive and self-affirming contexts. But most of these are not immediately accessible to children or adolescents. And they have bad/boring reputations. Students need to acquire the arts of appreciating these alternatives before they can compete with currently glamorous practices. The arts of appreciation may be the most neglected topic and set of abilities within moral education.

A fourth problem to be addressed in character education concerns the very existence of its moral ideals – traditional virtues and values. Also at issue is the moral propriety of traditional "virtues," should their psychological existence as traits ever be confirmed. Character advocates need to address well-known research that challenges the psychological reality of character traits. They also must address research that distinguishes the mere conventionality of virtually all common value judgments from the "truer" morality of principles (Hartschorn and May 1928, Turiel 1978, 1980, Kohlberg 1982 chs 1–3, 1984, ch. 1).

Emerging research on "local heroes" or "creative altruists" is especially challenging for the character-education program. It suggests that the exemplars character educators uphold in class do not actually show those traditional virtues they supposedly exemplify (Oliner and Oliner 1988, Puka 1991, Colby and Damon 1992). In fact, individuals who truly do extraordinary good, and practice the high ideals they preach, often show traditional (Christian) vices where virtues should be. For example, many real-world saints are more confrontational with others than understanding, more feisty and stubborn than accommodating or cooperative. They can be as critical and radically impatient as they are loving or generous, and more socially disruptive and practical-minded than they are "morally responsible" or ethereal.

Most surprising, many real-world exemplars consciously affirm these tendencies, preaching the mottoes of their practice: "Get angry at conditions in the world and do something about them. Be good *doers*, not do-gooders." Some exemplars explicitly disparage "childlike" virtues like temperance, faith, and hope, even *traditional* honesty and courage. They are readily willing to "bend" the literal truth to address desperate human needs. They are willing to proclaim that "some ends do justify the means." And they have no time to wish for better days or to rally a sense of bravery in confronting their fears: they are too busy to notice or bother with such ego-absorbed things.

Most of the exemplars we interviewed saw the moral key outlook, not virtue or extraordinary effort. This we found most surprising and profound. "Apparently we *see* things differently from most people. We look through the eyes of love or faith. We see ourselves as people who are here to love and live their faith. Then we act as anyone else would, with no greater effort or resolve." (Mother Teresa, a most unsentimental saint, was avid about this in forgoing systematic training for her helpers: "Come and see, then you'll know what to do.")

The majority of American moral heroes researched in the literature are religious. But they often disdain the traditional practice of Christian "charity." For them, it is not radical enough, not authentic enough. These people literally *love* their neighbors *as themselves* and *as God*, regarding everyone is their neighbor and their God. (Mother Teresa talked of interacting with the dying and the poorest of the poor in the filthy streets of Calcutta as going to Heaven. It was literally being with Jesus, facing one's God) in his distressing guise (Puka 1991, Colby and Damon 1992).

Character-education programs can easily build on the *actual* attitudes and perspectives of real moral exemplars, forsaking fantasy ideals. And they should do so. They might also forsake their current emphasis on historical figures and literary protagonists. There is often more fantasy than fact about these personages as well. Character education also can adjust its profile of values to the goals these exemplars set and the purposes they pursue.

At the least character educators should look to the observable realities of people's moral psychologies, not speculative human-nature categories like "virtue" or "character." These categories pre-date Socrates and Confucius. They likely reflect the pre-empirical (deeply superstitious) orientations toward "human nature" that then prevailed.

## Miscellaneous problems

Several questions can be raised with character education's classroom strategies. As asked above, is the use of literary and historical figures to exemplify moral traits realistic or myth-making? Will it set students in search of attainable and fulfilling moral lifestyles or author fantasies and personal frustrations? Are recommended classroom exercises and "morality plays" up to the level of street-sophistication possessed by inner-city teens – or even pre-teens? Might not current curricula seem a bit saccharine, idealistic, and "whitebread" to this target audience? Again, combining character education with other approaches and gathering morally raw materials from students themselves can address these problems.

More crucial questions arise in fitting high ideals to morally hostile environments. Should we push unvarnished honesty on students who could die from expressing it on the way home? (Answering a drug dealer or gang member honestly can get you shot.) Should families struggling to survive worry foremost about being fair and dutiful? By contrast, the ethics and political philosophy literature offer concepts of "justifiability." This involves doing what is least harmful or wrongful when doing the "right thing" isn't feasible. Character education might start with such minimal concepts – responsive to student realities – then work up.

## Postscript: culture and subculture

By focusing on Western and Judeo-Christian value traditions, character education explicitly endorses cultural influences on moral education. By raising problems of cultural indoctrination and bias, competing approaches challenge this endorsement. But these approaches pose blanket endorsements of "reasoning" and toleration of *individual* value differences that bespeak cultural biases of their own. For cultural critics, individualism and rationalism are the leading indicators of Western ethnocentrism. Ironically, these critics do not recognize similar tendencies in their casting of these cultural qualities as biases. (Is it not a peculiarly "Western" tendency to identify and oppose ethnocentrism?) And consider that rather strong cases have been made for moral individualism and rationality in ethics. Their assets have been detailed by research and theory in cognitive-developmental psychology, education, and philosophy. Thus these are anything but arbitrary prejudices. And it hardly makes sense to criticize such tendencies in Western culture while boosting comparable leanings (toward sociocentrism and intuitionism or mysticism) in non-Western cultures.

But peculiarly cultural sensitivity of a more subtle and pointed sort is fully warranted in moral education. My own role-models education experience provides an instance. In 'Be Your Own Hero', exemplary role-models are profiled and discussed by students as a prelude to investigating their own potential for socio-moral heroism. Following this "self-ideal clarification" component, a local hero or two that they study make surprise visits to students' classroom. This allows students to probe exemplary motivation and experience, finding great similarities with their own. Mentored service internships are then provided for students, within school or extending into the community. Here students are helped to practice what they see and admire. Finally, students are then counseled on how to gear their vocational or avocational aspirations to social benefit.

When piloting this program within Chinese-American subcultures we encountered fundamental difficulties. Individual heroes who stood outside and above their family or community were not admired – quite the contrary. The traditional (Confucian) model of exemplarism is based on playing one's part within defined role-relations and normative rituals. Focusing on extraordinary and groundbreaking individual accomplishment is abhorrent to traditionalists here – to some parents or grandparents of our students especially. Where students were taken with such models, and parents not, an already painful generation gap was exacerbated, threatening family unity.

We had foreseen this problem and addressed it by including exemplary groups and families in our heroic honor role. But these role-models did not usually fill the subcultural bill. In traditionalist eyes, activist groups represent artificial constructs. They are composed of strangers tied to willful causes. Such activists make an unseeming display of themselves in their community to get notice for their issue. They not only stand out, but stand against status quo practices in confrontative ways. Likewise, the heroic American families we cited showed a super-achiever orientation that failed to fit with Chinese conventions. And this was so despite the great entrepreneurialism shown by many Chinese-American immigrants.

More broadly, the "hero" notion shows a masculinist tendency. It overemphasizes a particular kind of courage and assertiveness, vaguely reminiscent of militaristic roots. But the obvious alternative theme of "saintliness" strikes students as unrealistic and overdemanding. It is off-putting as well, due to its "slavishness," placing emphasis on self-sacrifice, giving without getting, following inherent moral motivation while spurning material reward. Such "nobility" is a "hard sell" in the classroom. Consider its marketing message: "Here's something to strive toward, students: a life of deprivation, personal cost, and patient suffering. Now how can becoming instantly wealthy and respected among peers for dealing drugs ever compete with that?"

In any event, an inclusive approach to moral education should not merely address cultural biases. It must take a positive, multifaceted cultural approach emphasizing subcultural, ethnic, racial, and class factors. Such an approach focuses on the insitutionally mediated features of moral beliefs, norms, and practices including moral self-concept and character itself. Nothing is more enlightening (mind-bending) to students than reconceiving their most private, inner sanctum of self in socially "constructed" terms. This process can reveal what amounts to an alien inside us, "possessing" us, with which we would never consciously choose to identify. Conceptual clarification and reasoning can be extremely useful in revealing this socialized self to ourselves. But these approaches must focus on very particular metacognitive ways to do the job. And pointedly sociological and socio-economic modes of inquiry are required to get a true handle on the cultural influences involved.

Of course, such lessons should not be pushed too far. The distinctive cultural emphasis wrought by "social constructionism" is part of a faddish postmodern ideology currently gripping academe. It is more the brainchild of literary analysis (narrativism) than empirical anthropology. And it is unclear how much of its peculiar emphasis will be found credible as it is carefully scrutinized in theory and practice.

Ironically, Kohlberg's "just-community" approach may merit a second look here by postmodern, cultural critics. Its explicit aim is to embed moral reasoning, dialogue, and interpersonal interaction within a fair institutional environment. And it focuses primarily on student participation in the conscious creation of this environment. Over time, Kohlbergians recognized that moral-dilemma discussion alone could not sustain sizable moral development in an institutional (school) culture hostile to it. But more important, the process of creating and sustaining a more welcoming moral culture is the stuff of moral development itself. Even the cognitive component of moral development arises through interpersonal or social interaction, not conceptual struggle in the abstract. (This was a tenet of Piagetianism and Kohlbergianism from the start.)

The original virtue and character traditions of Aristotle and Confucius were in clear agreement on this point. And as a result centuries of culturally insensitive scholarship criticized them for ethnocentrism. The typical charge was that they built features of Athenian or dynastic Chinese culture into the form and function of moral concepts *per se*. These should be logically independent. To more culturally sensitive observers, the cultural biases involved seem more circumscribed, focusing on culturally conformist features of moral socialization at the expense of constructive ones. Current character education may be faulted for the same tendency. But there is great potential in each of these traditions for a more full-bodied cultural perspective that gauges the socially created and creatable features of moral personality or character. Its question: How might our culture design its institutions to better nurture our individual and joint potentials for virtue?

It is hardly difficult to imagine classroom projects fit to answer this question. One exercise might consist of a rudimentary anthropology lesson in which students compare the beliefs and practices of a radically different culture to their own. Stress would be placed on the relation between the key cultural purposes to be served in two different environments and the ways that moral norms served, frustrated, or functioned independently of them. A closely related project would focus on the impressive history of intentional American communities (large-scale communes) that flourished in the 1800s. These communities were invariably structured around conscious moral ideals that to this day contrast favorably with those of our dominant culture.

Students might also be helped to create science-fiction scenarios contrasting "alien" cultures guided by imaginary moral norms. Science-fiction texts (from *Brave New World* to *Star Trek*) could be consulted and analyzed in the process, emphasizing how different views of human nature give rise to different moral-cultural norms and vice versa.

The (non-harmful) socio-moral ways of life projected here could be acted out in class for a single period, day, or week. The relation would be noted between institution and norm, assessing their differences and similarities, pros and cons. Such projects could easily be "brought down to earth" through analogies to subcultures (cliques) within the school community and the community directly surrounding it.

# References

Bennett, W. (1988) "Moral Literacy and the Formation of Character", in *Our Children and Our Country*, New York: Simon & Schuster.

Bennett, W. (1993) *A Book of Virtues*, New York: Simon & Schuster.

Colby, A. and Damon, W. (1992) *Some Do Care*, New York Free Press.

Gilligan, C. (1982) *In a Different Voice*, Cambridge, MA: Harvard University Press.

Hartschorne, H. and May, M. (1928) *Studies in the Nature of Character*, New York: Columbia University Teacher's College Press.

Higgins, A. and Powers, C. (1984) "The Relation of Moral Atmosphere to Judgments of Responsibility", in W. Kurtines and J. Gewirtz (eds) *Morality, Moral Behavior, and Moral Development*, New York: Wiley Interscience.

Hoff Sommers, C. (1991) "Teaching the Virtues", *Imprimus*, 20.11.

Kohlberg, L. (1982) *The Philosophy of Moral Development*, New York: Harper & Row.

Kohlberg, L. (1984) *The Psychology of Moral Development*, New York: Harper & Row.

Likona, T. (1983) *Raising Good Children*, New York: Bantam Books.

Likona, T. (1988) "Four Strategies for Fostering Character Development in Children", *Phi Delta Kappan*, 69.6: 419–23.

Likona, T. (1992) *Educating for Character*, New York: Basic Books.

Noddings, N. (1992) *The Challenge to Care in Schools*, New York: Teacher's College Press (Columbia University).

Oldenquist (1993).

Oliner, S. and Oliner, P. (1988) *The Altruistic Personality*, New York: Free Press.

Puka, B. (1991) "Be Your Own Hero: Careers in Commitment", talk given at the annual convention of the Association for Moral Education, Notre Dame University (Nov).

Puka, B. (1995) "Taking the Moralism Out of Moral Education", submitted to the *Harvard Educational Review* 6/93).

Puka, B. (1995a) "Exemplar Education and Character Education: Pros and Cons", unpub. m.s.

Turiel, E. (1978) "The Development of Social Concepts: Mores, Customs and Conventions", in J. Glick and A. Clark-Stewart (eds) *The Development of Social Understanding*, New York: Gardner Press.

Turiel, E. (1980) "The Development of Social-conventional and Moral Concepts", in M. Windmiller, N. Lambert, and E. Turiel (eds) *Moral Development and Socialization*, Boston: Allyn & Bacon.

Wynne, E. and Ryan, K. (1993) "Curriculum as a Moral Educator", *American Educator* (Spring): 20–48.

Wynne, E. and Ryan, K. (1993a) *Reclaiming Our Schools*, New York: Macmillan.

# 14  Schemas, Culture, and Moral Texts

DARCIA NARVAEZ AND CHRISTYAN MITCHELL

In the midst of teaching, teachers make a dazzlingly quick series of judgments about what to do next or how to respond to unforeseen eventualities. These intuitive and immediate judgments are based not on calmly reasoned discussions that occurred months before but on viscerally felt, "gut" instincts concerning which actions best fit certain situations. They are informed by recollections of similar situations experienced in the past. Even as we react to a situation, we are scanning our memories for incidents that felt like the ones we face and that might provide some guidance on how to respond. This process occurs almost instantaneously so that reflection is perceived as concurrent with action.

(Stephen Brookfield, *The Skillful Teacher*, 1990)

Whether it's presidential dalliances, Taliban rulings, Teletubbies, altercations in the former Yugoslavia, individuals differ in their interpretations and evaluations of socio-moral events. Such moral conclusions vary according to the background knowledge and experience the interpreter brings to the situation. What are the factors that lead to these radically different understandings? What brought the Rev. Jerry Falwell to "besmirch" the reputation of the Teletubby, Tinky Winky? A cognitive psychological interpretation would be that Falwell has a general knowledge structure, or schema, for homosexuality (which he condemns) that Tinky Winky evoked (carries a purse, has a triangle on his head, and so must be gay).

"Schema," refers to a general knowledge structure in the mind, formed by repeated experience, and evoked by stimuli in the environment (Bartlett 1932). Repeating patterns in the world are encoded in memory as chunks of information, or schemas, that save repeated processing of previously experi-

enced material. Over time, toddlers learn that an object with four legs, a seat and a back is a chair and is used for sitting. This knowledge is automatized so that older children don't even think about the usage of such an object but automatically use it appropriately. What schemas do is enable the perceiver to identify stimuli quickly, fill in information missing from the stimulus configuration, and provide guidance for obtaining further information, solving a problem, or reaching a goal. Schemas are tacitly and automatically invoked, working "behind the scenes." The major tenet of schema theory is that people simplify reality by storing knowledge at a molar, inclusive level, rather than squirreling away, one by one, all the original individual facts of experience (Taylor and Crocker 1981, Fiske and Taylor 1991) for which there are not enough hours in the day!

Recently, our research in moral judgment has demonstrated the effects of schemas on moral decision-making. Rest, Narvaez, Bebeau, and Thoma (1999) have revised and reformulated Kohlberg's (1984) theory into a neo-Kohlbergian theory using three schemas instead of six stages to refer to developmental change. Research with tens of thousands of subjects using the defining issues test (DIT) indicates that individuals change over time in their preference for these global moral-judgment schemas (personal interest schema, maintaining norms schema, postconventional schema). Evidence for the existence and developmental sequence of these schemas is provided by means of seven validity criteria (see Rest et al., 1999). Among these are demonstrated relations to behavior.

Taylor and Crocker (1981) provide one of the most thorough descriptions of schemas in the social domain. They list seven characteristics (in italics below). We match each characteristic to research in moral judgment.

1   *Schemas lend structure to experience.* When a stimulus configuration is encountered in the environment, it is matched against a schema from the long-term memory store, and the order and relations among the elements of the schemas are imposed on the elements of the stimulus configuration. Thus the schema is "activated" (or triggered or evoked) from long-term memory in the perceiver. Similarly, moral schemas drive the interpretation of socio-moral events, as in the dilemmas of the DIT (see Rest, Narvaez, Bebeau, and Thoma, in press).

2   *Schemas determine what information will be encoded or retrieved from memory.* Which schema is activated makes a difference in the interpretation of stimulus events. Imposing a schema on a stimulus configuration increases overall recall, especially recall of schema-relevant material. In Narvaez (1998) moral schemas affected both accurate recall of moral reasoning in stories and the invention of reasoning that was not in the story. When subjects were asked to recall narratives about moral situations in which moral reasoning (at different Kohlbergian stages) was embedded, sometimes they introduced distortion in the form of invented arguments that were not in the story. Here is an example of an argument distortion. A neo-Kohlbergian Stage 4 excerpt from "Tom, the Manager" reads: "What had been keeping him tossing and turning sleeplessly every night for the last two weeks, however, was his feeling of responsibility to the business as well." Some subjects incorrectly recalled this passage as a Stage 1 concern: "He was afraid of losing his job." The type of moral-judgment schemas the reader has developed affects recall from the narrative of the moral arguments which are based on those schemas. In fact, those who had developed the higher schemas (as measured by the DIT) were significantly more likely to recall and even invent high-stage arguments for the story.

3   *Schemas affect processing time, speed of information flow, and speed of problem-solving.* A schema is an efficient means for moving information speedily through the human processing system. For example, chess experts can "read" and solve chess board configurations more quickly than novices (Chase and Simon 1973). This is one of the assumptions of the study of moral thinking that we describe below, whereby cultural schemas affect the speed of reaction to moral inferences.

4   *Schemas enable the social perceiver to fill in data missing from an input stimulus configuration.* Schemas supply missing information when there is a lack of information, or ambiguous data. In morality research, the DIT is a device that provides fragments of moral-judgment schemas which in turn activate the participant's existing moral-judgment schemas (not activating schemas the participant does not have). Once activated, the individual's moral schema fills in the gaps in the moral arguments presented in the stories and items on the DIT (Rest, Narvaez, Bebeau, and Thoma, in press).

5   *Schemas provide bases for solving problems.* As schemas provide an interpretation of events in the world, the interpretation suggests courses of action and lines of decision-making for solving problems. In our work at the Center for the Study of Ethical Development, we find that participants who lack the more sophisticated schemas have a more difficult time making decisions about social-policy issues (Rest, Narvaez, Thoma, and Bebeau, in press).

6   *Schemas provide a basis for evaluating experience.* A corollary to this proposition is that people with highly developed schemas make more confident and extreme evaluations. Our work indicates that when groups of people have different schemas that are highly developed, they polarize on ideological and public-policy issues (Rest, Narvaez, Thoma, and Bebeau, in press).

7   *Schemas provide a basis for anticipating the future, setting goals, making plans, and developing behavioral routines to deal with them.* Schemas don't just describe and catalogue experience; schemas also suggest prescriptions for action. In morality research, this has been best described by Thoma (e.g., 1994) in terms of the relation between responses on the DIT and behavior.

Whereas the neo-Kohlbergian schemas are worthwhile in predicting group developmental differences, they are not finely tuned enough to distinguish among other group differences, such as religious or political differences. Hence, further studies have been performed looking at other influences on decision-making between groups known for their differences. Narvaez, Getz, Rest, and Thoma (1999) looked at the effects of religious group differences on attitudes toward human rights. Fundamentalism, political orientation (conservative), and moral judgment score predicted over 60 per cent of the variance of attitudes towards human-rights issues (women's rights, homosexual rights, abortion, etc.)

One large-group difference that has been studied in cross-cultural research is orientation to relationships in terms of individualism or collectivism (Triandis 1995). Like religion and politics, difference in orientation to relationships can be a source of value conflicts. In an individualistic orientation everyone is expected to look after self and immediate family, whereas with an orientation to collectivism persons receive protection from a cohesive ingroup in exchange for loyalty (definitions are from Hofstede 1991). Triandis and his colleagues (e.g., Kim, Triandis, Kagitcibasi, Choi, and Yoon 1994) have studied this construct and postulate that it reflects cultural syndromes for which evidence at the individual level is accumulating. Triandis gives the following definitions:

> *Collectivism* may be initially defined as a social pattern consisting of closely linked individuals who see themselves as parts of one or more collectives (family, co-workers, tribe, nation); are primarily motivated by the norms of and duties imposed by, those collectives; are willing to give priority to the goals of these collectives over their own personal goals; and emphasize their connectedness to members of these collectives. A preliminary definition of *individualism* is a social pattern that consists of loosely linked individuals who view themselves as independent of collectives; are primarily motivated by their own preferences, needs, rights, and the contracts they have established with others; give priority to their personal goals over the goals of others; and emphasize rational analyses of the advantages and disadvantages to associating with others. (Triandis 1995: 2)

So, Triandis suggests, in a restaurant setting, waiters in places with different cultural orientations on individualism-collectivism will behave differently. For example, a waiter in Brazil (collectivist) takes the order from the senior member of a group because he assumes that the group will build bonds by sharing the same food. In contrast, most waiters in Western countries (individualist) will assume that each person will order according to individual preference. As cultural background individualism-collectivism can have such a strong influence on the way an individual approaches a social situation that it is an empirical question whether such orientations can influence the activation of moral schemas.

We were interested in studying the effects of the individualism-collectivism construct on moral judgment. First, we consider the methods of study previously used in moral-judgment research.

## Methods for studying moral judgment

Moral judgment has been studied in a variety of ways. The method that Piaget and Kohlberg used to measure how people make moral decisions was to directly interview individuals about their moral reasoning. Although both researchers spawned a great deal of important research in moral development, research in cognitive science is pointing out that the direct-interview method may not give us what we seek.

> A vast amount of research in cognitive science clearly shows we are conscious only of the content of our mental life, not what generates the content. It is the products of mnemonic processing, of perceptual processing of imaging, that we are aware of – not what produced the products. Sometimes people report on what they think were the processes, but they are reporting after the fact on what they thought they did to produce the content of their consciousness. (Gazzaniga, Ivry, and Mangun 1998: 532)

Gazzaniga has described the responses of patients whose linkage between the halves of the brain has been severed (for therapeutic reasons) when one side of the brain is shown a picture and they are asked to say what it was. If the non-verbal right side of the brain is shown a picture of someone laughing, the patient will laugh but when asked why will make something up, such as "I felt like it."

Similarly, Toulmin (1981) has noted that whereas expert bioethicists may agree on what should be done in a case, they are unlikely to agree on the principles by which the decision should be made. In other words, individuals can identify the product of their thinking but have difficulty describing the process by which they arrived at that conclusion. Therefore it is doubtful that a person interviewed about their moral reasoning is able to accurately know or convey their decision-making process. "Should Heinz steal the drug?" "Yes!" "Why?" "Well. . . (the subject makes up an answer that satisfies the interviewer).” Thus, if we ask people from different groups how they made a judgment from an individualist or collectivist perspective, we run the risk that they merely construct an *ad hoc* rationalization for the conclusions they reached.

Another way to study moral judgment is indirectly via recognition. The DIT has been successful in accessing the tacit knowledge of the individual as represented in moral schemas. A measure like the DIT is not easy to construct. Triandis (1995) and colleagues are developing multiple-choice tests of individualism-collectivism with some success. In the study described below, we used as the independent variable a scale of collectivism inspired by their work, a measure of a cultural schema.

A third method for studying moral judgment is to study the effects of unconscious processing on behavior, a process often used in cognitive science. This can be done in various ways. As responses to texts provide a microcosm of an individual’s response to events in the world, we describe below two methods that use texts: recall of moral texts (e.g., Narvaez 1998) and lexical decision. In lexical-decision studies, the reader is reading a story (typically) off a computer screen and is periodically interrupted with a string of letters such as “potato” or “ibsenah.” The reader decides whether or not the letters represent an English word or not. The time it takes to respond is assumed to reflect the accessibility of the letter string. Readers respond more quickly to words that have been activated by the reading context (see Haberlandt (1994) for a review). For example, if a reader sees “She carried in the groceries and began to prepare dinner” and then is interrupted with a decision about the word “kitchen,” the reader is quicker to indicate that “kitchen” is an English word than if the word presented were “engine.” The word “kitchen” is activated faster than the word “engine” because it is evoked in the context of the sentence about groceries and preparing dinner.

The lexical-decision task has been successful in measuring the activation of particular kinds of inferences during reading. For example, in van den Broek et al. (1994), readers of literary stories were asked to respond to inference words that represented knowledge they would need to apply in order to understand the story at that point. Van den Broek et al. were able to select words that represented inferences from general background knowledge as well as reinstatements of earlier text information, indicating particular activations in the minds of the readers.

## Studying schemas using texts

In general, as a reader reads and remembers text, he or she attempts to create a coherent mental representation of the text not only by integrating text information but also by elaborating on the text with prior knowledge about the world (van den Broek 1994) and by building a mental model (overall meaning structure) of the text (Van Dijk and Kintsch 1983, McNamara et al. 1991). Prior knowledge often comes in the form of general structures such as schemas, and has been shown to affect how readers comprehend a text (e.g., Anderson and Pichert, 1978; Bartlett, 1932; Bobrow and Norman, 1975; Rumelhart, 1980; Rumelhart and Ortony, 1977).

Two kinds of processing affect the comprehender’s understanding of discourse (Bower and Cirilo 1985). Bottom-up, data-driven processing (based on what the text says) initially activates cognitive structures which, in response, guide further processing according to the conceptual structures activated in the mind of the comprehender. Readers form a mental representation of the text using top-down processing – applying their background knowledge – and bottom-up processing – constructing word and phrase units by deciphering the cues in the text. For example, the processing of the sentence “Tristan threw his jeans into the washer” might proceed in the following manner. First, “Tristan threw his jeans” is processed as pieces of data involving a subject, an action, and an object. Second, “in the washer” might activate a high-level “laundry schema.” After the high-level structure is activated, it, in turn, activates accompanying subschemas or conceptually driven processing. Associations of “doing the laundry” are activated and would include, in an industrialized nation, laundry detergent, washer selections, and so forth. Processing, then, continues concurrently guided by expectations (“top-down” processing). The next sentence, “He sorted the rest of the items by color” is immediately coded as fitting into the “laundry” schema because of its context. Alone, this sentence would otherwise require additional elaboration to comprehend, because “the rest of the items” could refer to candy, toys, shoes, or any number of things. As processing continues, guided by expectations, it is an interaction between the two types of text processing – what the words of the text mean and what the reader expects.

Differences in text comprehension as a result of conceptually driven or top-down processing have been documented in various situations. For example, initial perspective plays a role in what is represented and later recalled due to the conceptually driven processing it elicits. Pichert and Anderson (1977) demonstrated that when readers are instructed to read a description of a home either as a potential burglar or a potential home buyer, recall is significantly influenced by the "biased" representation one has for the characteristics of the home. That is, recall is influenced by what is salient to the purpose of the perceiver. Anderson et al. (1977) postulated that a subject's schemas provide the interpretive framework for the understanding of a discourse. They instructed subjects to read and then describe a paragraph about a person escaping a situation in which he was trapped that could be interpreted in two ways. Physical education majors interpreted the story as a wrestling match, whereas non-majors interpreted it as a prison escape. Alexander and Judy (1988) describe research comparing good and poor readers as they studied a science lesson. Both groups of readers frequently distorted text content to conform with their pre-existing knowledge, in other words, with their expectations. In short, schemas can influence the reader's mental representation of a text and are demonstrated by the characteristics of what a reader recalls or does not recall from the text, including distortions, intrusions, and the elimination of information that does not match the schemas of the reader. Cultural differences are a mismatch of schemas.

What knowledge do people from different cultures draw on when they read culture-specific texts? When texts are inconsistent with the expectations or high-level knowledge structures of the reader, the reader will poorly understand (Bransford and Johnson 1972), misrecall (Steffensen et al. 1979), and even distort memory to fit with his or her mental schemas (Reynolds, Taylor, Steffensen, Shirey, and Anderson 1982). A classic example is Bartlett's (1932) seminal work with "The War of the Ghosts" folktale in which subjects had an increasingly distorted recall over time of this Native American story, making it conform to familiar story schemas. Bartlett was the first in this century to provide evidence for the influence of cultural expectations, a type of conceptually driven orientation, on narra-

tive recall. In subsequent research, Harris et al. (1988) found that routines from another culture were increasingly misrecalled over time by those from a different culture, indicating a conceptual influence during memory retrieval. Readers apply culture-based schemas to how they mentally represent the text (e.g., Reynolds, Taylor, Steffensen, Shirey, and Anderson 1982). For example, when Harris et al. (1988) asked subjects to recall texts about events in a different culture, they found distorted recall as in the following. The text said:

> Ted was eager to go downtown to do some shopping for Carnival. He needed to buy some gifts for his parents and some new costumes for himself and his friends . . . He got on the bus at the rear door and found a seat in the back. After getting settled, he pulled out his wallet . . . He then carried a stack of fifties up to the cashier in the center of the bus . . . Ted passed through the turnstile and found a seat just behind the driver . . . When he arrived, he scrambled out the front door of the bus.

Subjects from the United States tended to recall incorrectly that Ted got on the front of the bus, paid and sat down in the back. Subjects from Brazil did not make these errors because the bus experience was a familiar schema.

What knowledge do people draw on when they read moral texts? In the 1990s there has been widespread popular interest in reading moral stories to children in order to develop moral literacy (e.g., Bennett's bestselling book, 1993). Underlying this popularity, there seems to be an implicit assumption that individuals – for example, adult writers and child readers – extract the same themes from a moral text. However, text-comprehension research has demonstrated that readers do not comprehend (non-moral) texts in the same way, due to individual differences in skill and background knowledge (see for examples, Gernsbacher (ed.) 1994). In other words, a comprehender does not necessarily understand what the author intended. In addition, there is considerable empirical evidence for developmental and expert–novice differences in moral judgment (e.g., Rest 1986) that suggests individuals often view social events differently and, as a result, perform moral-comprehension tasks distinctively (e.g., Rest, Thoma, and Edwards 1997). Narvaez and colleagues (Narvaez, Bentley, Gleason, and Samuels 1998, Narvaez, Gleason, Mitchell, and Bentley 1999) have found developmental differences in moral-theme comprehension.

Young children are unable to select a moral theme for a children's story (11 per cent correct), being attracted to distortions based on lower-level reasoning. Older children are more likely to make the correct selection (45 per cent of the time) but still do not perform as well as adults (91 per cent). In short, people apply their moral-judgment schemas to how they represent the text.

## Influence of culture on moral-text processing

Not only is culture known to affect the recall of culturally relevant texts, as discussed earlier, it can also affect reaction time to personal questions (Kitayama and Markus 1996) in that collectivists may be slower at decontextualizing questions about the self than are individualists. Keeping this in mind, we designed a study to examine the influence of culture (individualism-collectivism) on the online processing of moral texts, an indirect, non-personal method.

In Narvaez, Mitchell, and Linzie (1998) we tested two groups: Asians/Asian-Americans and non-Asians, expecting that the Asian group would more reliably provide us with collectivists than other groups. Participants had native skills in English and read several stories on computer. Half of the stories were "filler" (non-moral) stories and half were moral stories. The moral stories were about individuals who were asked for help by a relative (aunt, uncle, cousin). In half of these stories, the protagonist sacrificed his/her own goals in order to help ("help" stories); in the other half he/she did not help ("no-help" stories). See the following sample story, with target probes.

---

### Leroy and the race ("no-help" story)

Every morning, Leroy got up early to run before breakfast and work. He was in good shape for his age. After running, he would shower and eat breakfast and then head out for work. He was a carpenter and would drive to many places around the city. Every other Saturday he wouldn't work so he could do a 10- to 15-mile-long run. He knew how important this run was for developing good endurance, so he rarely missed it. He liked to enter races and, even though he had never won, he usually finished in the top of his age group. He worked hard to better his times. For four months, he trained for the local "Grandpas'" marathon race, for men 55–

65. He logged nearly 60 miles a week. As a 57-year-old in good shape, his wife and friends were certain that he could win the local title.

When the day of the race finally arrived, he got up early for breakfast, pancakes and coffee. He drank lots of orange juice and water. The event started at 8 a.m. (PROBE FOR REINSTATEMENT: MARATHON) While he was getting dressed, the phone rang. It was Thomas, his cousin. Thomas had a family emergency, his father-in-law had had a heart attack during the night and was in the hospital. Thomas needed to drive the family to the small town hospital to see him. Thomas asked if Leroy would watch his corner grocery store for the day. The supply truck would be bringing the week's produce during the day. If no one was there to receive them, Thomas would miss getting the supplies for the week. Leroy was the only person he trusted with running the store. Leroy sympathized but told him that he had other plans. Leroy said he had a good chance at winning the race this year. He told Thomas he would call after the race. He wished him well and then hung up the phone. (PROBE FOR MORAL INFERENCE: DISLOYAL)

After he parked his car, he jogged around to warm up and then headed for the starting line. There were so many people on the narrow street that he could hardly move. As the race got underway, Leroy found that he wasn't able to reach his normal pace until more people fell behind him. Once he hit his regular pace, he felt comfortable. Although he was exhausted at the finish, he came in with a faster time than he ever had. But he didn't win. A 62-year-old came in first. He felt good about his personal record. After some stretching, he milled around with the crowd, picked up his marathon t-shirt and ate some bagels. That night, he went out to celebrate his accomplishment with some other racers.

---

While they were reading, the participants were interrupted with a lexical-decision task, as described earlier. Some of the letter strings were not (English) words, some were words irrelevant to what they were reading, and some of the words represented inferences assumed to take place by the reader at that point in the story. (See the following examples of inference types.)

| Category | Example |
|---|---|
| Reinstatement | Mary was looking for her car keys. She looked on the dining-room |

|  |  |
|---|---|
|  | table. Then she looked on the kitchen counter. She found them (MENTAL REINSTATMENT: KEYS) next to the sink. |
| Elaboration | Mary took her car keys and went out the door. She pulled out of the driveway. (MENTAL ELABORATION: SHE GOT IN THE CAR, PUT THE KEYS IN THE IGNITION AND STARTED THE ENGINE. SHE STARTED DRIVING.) |

In this study two kinds of inferences in the moral stories were tested: reinstatements of information from earlier in the text necessary to understand a current sentence, and moral inferences – elaborations on current text action based on background knowledge. (Look back at p. 150 for examples of probe words for "Leroy.") The moral inferences occurred after the protagonist decided to help or not help in the story. In the "help" stories the moral inferences were represented by words like "dutiful" or "loyal." In the "no-help" stories the moral inferences were represented by words like "self-centered" or "shameful." Using the non-relevant English words as a baseline, each subject served as his or her control. We expected there to be a significant response-time difference between the two groups for both kinds of moral stories. We also expected that the Asian group would react more quickly, especially to the moral probes in the "no-help" stories. We expected the violation of expectations (of the protagonist to help a relative) to create a greater reaction (immediate and negative) to the protagonist. Participants also took an inventory of their orientation to individualism or collectivism. Reading-skill differences were controlled.

Scores on the collectivism scale were split into high and low groups using a median split. As expected, there were no significant differences in reaction time for reinstatement (non-moral) probe words based on collectivism score, ($F_{(1,75)} = .79$, $p <.37$). But we did find significant differences in reaction time to moral probe words in the "no-help" stories based on collectivism scores ($F_{(1,76)} = 5.43$, $p <.022$, effect size $=.51$). Further, significant differences in reaction time to moral probe words remained after holding ethnicity constant ($F_{(2,75)} =3.98$, $p <.023$, effect size $= .71$). Similar results were obtained with the "help" stories. Collectivism scores, regardless of culture, were significantly related to reaction time for moral inferences but not for non-moral inferences.

We concluded that cultural-ideological background can influence which moral inferences are made while reading. The results also suggest that judgments about moral events can be successfully examined at the preconscious level. Online processing of moral events can be studied with activation measures used in discourse research. Rapid-fire, preconscious reactions to the moral or immoral actions of others may influence group and individual interaction, fuel prejudice, and contribute to disputes. Various cultural and moral schemas of interpretation may be examined with this technique and give insight into schema activations and their effects. Studies at this level may provide more insight into the sources for moral and cultural conflict.

While we process familiar things quickly to fit into our existing schemas, we process unfamiliar things slowly, often consciously. As a result, we tend to feel negatively towards the unfamiliar because it stops us in our flow of expectations and takes energy to figure out (Bargh 1989). We process familiar things more rapidly, which results in positive feelings (Zajonc 1980). Cultural differences are often processed negatively because they are unfamiliar and require extra processing. We tend to feel uncomfortable in situations in which our expectations are thwarted, inclining us to avoid such encounters or to shut out those who act "offensively" (not in accordance with our schema-driven expectations).

Returning to the quote by Stephen Brookfield with which this chapter opens, the quick-fire effects of cultural moral schemas occur also in the classroom. For example, the child who was raised in a culture in which respect is shown by not looking into the other's eyes offends the teacher whose cultural schema of "respect" requires direct eye-gaze. The student whose culture-based schema of 'authority' requires a commanding adult is not impressed with the teacher whose culture-based schema of 'authority' involves playing down power by asking for compliance rather than demanding it. As Brookfield points out, these judgments usually occur subconsciously and according to what "feels" right. The judgments occur so quickly that what is "right" seems directly perceived and coordinated simultaneously with action, making changes in these reactions difficult. After the first encounter, one party or both may feel a residue of discomfort that, unexamined, can build into blatant disregard over time. To circumvent this process and enable teachers to be effective with all students, we need to establish what kinds of preconscious culture-based inferences occur in which groups (Narvaez 1996). Then we will be able to design methods for preparing teachers to be interculturally adept for the multiple cultures of students they will encounter.

# References

Anderson, R. C. and Pichert, J. W. (1978) "Recall of Previously Unrecallable Information following a Shift in Perspective", *Journal of Verbal Learning and Behavior*, 17: 1–12.

Anderson, R. C., Reynolds, R. E., Schallert, D. L. and Goetz, E. T. (1977) "Frameworks for Comprehending Discourse", *American Educational Research Journal*, 14.4: 367–81.

Alexander, P. and Judy, J. (1988) "The Interaction of Domain Specific and Strategic Knowledge in Academic Performance", *Review of Educational Research*, 58.4: 375–404.

Bargh, J. (1989) "Conditional Automaticity: Varieties of Automatic Influence in Social Perception and Cognition", in J. Uleman and J. Bargh (eds), *Unintended Thought*, New York: Guilford, pp. 3–51.

Bartlett, F. C. (1932) *Remembering*, Cambridge: Cambridge University Press.

Bennett, W. (1993) *The Book of Virtues*, New York: Simon & Schuster.

Bobrow, D. and Norman, D. (1975) "Some Principles of Memory Schemata", in D. Bobrow and A. Collins (eds), *Representation and Understanding: Studies in Cognitive Science*, New York: Academic Press, pp. 131–49.

Bower, G. and Cirilo, R. (1985) "Cognitive Psychology and Text Processing", *Handbook of Discourse Analysis, Vol. 1*, New York: Academic Press, pp. 71–105.

Bransford, J. D. and Johnson, M. K. (1972) "Contextual Prerequisites for Understanding: Some Investigations of Comprehension and Recall", *Journal of Verbal Learning and Verbal Behavior*, 11: 717–26.

Brookfield, S. D. (1990) *The Skillful Teacher*, San Francisco: Jossey-Bass.

Chase, W. and Simon, H. (1973) "Perception in Chess", *Cognitive Psychology*, 4: 55–81.

Fiske, S. T. and Taylor, S. E. (1991) *Social Cognition*, New York: McGraw-Hill.

Gazzaniga, M. S., Ivry, R. B. and Mangun, G. R. (1998) *Cognitive Neuroscience: The Biology of the Mind*, New York: Norton.

Gernsbacher, M. A. (ed.) (1994) *Handbook of Psycholinguistics*, New York: Academic Press.

Haberlandt, K. (1994) "Methods in Reading Research", in M. Gernsbacher (ed.), *Handbook of Psycholinguistics*, New York: Academic Press, pp. 1–32.

Harris, R. J., Lee, D. J., Hensley, D. L. and Schoen, L. M. (1988) "The Effect of Cultural Script Knowledge on Memory for Stories over Time", *Discourse Processes*, 11: 413–31.

Hofstede, G. (1991) *Cultures and Organizations: Software of the Mind*. London: McGraw-Hill.

Kim, U., Triandis, H. C., Kagitcibasi, C., Choi, S., Yoon, G. (1994) *Individualism and Collectivism: Theory Method and Applications*, Thousand Oaks, CA: Sage.

Kitayama, S. and Markus, H. (1996) "Culture, Self, and Emotion: A Cultural Perspective to 'Self-conscious' Emotions", in J. P. Tangney and K. W. Fisher (eds), *Shame, Guilt, Embarrassment, and Pride: Empirical Studies of Self-conscious Emotions*. New York: Guilford.

Kohlberg, L. (1984) *Essays on Moral Development Vol.2: The Psychology of Moral Judgment*, San Francisco: Harper & Row.

McNamara, T. P., Miller, D. L. and Bransford, J. D. (1991) "Mental Models and Reading Comprehension", in R. Barr, M. L. Kamil, P. B. Mosenthal, and P. D. Pearson (eds), *Handbook of Reading Research, Vol. 2*, New York: Longman, pp. 490–511.

Narvaez, D. (1996) "Moral Perception: A New Construct?" annual meeting of the American Educational Research Association, New York (Apr.).

Narvaez, D. (1998) "The Effects of Moral Schemas on the Reconstruction of Moral Narratives in 8th Grade and College Students", *Journal of Educational Psychology*, 90.1: 13–24.

Narvaez, D. (1999) *Expertise Differences in Comprehending Moral Narratives: Recall and Thinking Aloud*. Manuscript submitted for publication.

Narvaez, D., Bentley, J., Gleason, T., Samuels, J. (1998) "Moral Theme Comprehension in Third Grade, Fifth Grade and College Students", *Reading Psychology*, 19.2: 217–41.

Narvaez, D., Getz, I., Rest, J. R. and Thoma, S. (in press) "Aspects of Moral Thinking: Moral Judgment and Cultural Ideology", *Developmental Psychology*.

Narvaez, D., Getz, I., Rest, J. R. and Thoma, S. (1999) "Individual Moral Judgment and Cultural Ideologies", *Developmental Psychology*, 35: 478–88.

Narvaez, D., Gleason, T., Mitchell, C. and Bentley, J. (1999) "Moral Theme Comprehension in Children", *Journal of Eduational Psychology* (in press)

Narvaez, D., Mitchell, C. and Linzie, B. (1998) "*Comprehending Moral Stories and the Influence of Individualism/Collectivism*", annual meeting of the Association for Moral Education, Hanover, NH.

Pichert, J. W. and Anderson, R. C. (1977) "Taking Different Perspectives on a Story", *Journal of Educational Psychology*, 69.4: 309–15.

Rest, J. (1986) *Moral Development: Advances in Research and Theory*, New York: Prager.

Rest, J., Narvaez, D., Bebeau, M. and Thoma, S. (1999) "A Neo-Kohlbergian Approach to Moral Judgment:

An Overview of Defining Issues Test Research", *Educational Psychology Review*.

Rest, J., Narvaez, D., Thoma, S. J., Bebeau, M. J. (in press) "DIT2: Devising and Testing a New Instrument of Moral Judgment", *Journal of Educational Psychology*.

Rest, J., Thoma, S. J. and Edwards, L. (1997) "Devising and Validating a Measure of Moral Judgment: Stage Preference and Stage Consistency Approaches", *Journal of Educational Psychology*, 89.1: 5–28.

Reynolds, R., Taylor, M., Steffensen, M., Shirey, L. and Anderson, R. (1982) "Cultural Schemata and Reading Comprehension", *Reading Research Quarterly*, 17: 353–66.

Rumelhart, D. E. (1980) "Schemata: The Building Blocks of Cognition", in R. Spiro, B. Bruce and W. Brewer (eds), *Theoretical Issues in Reading Comprehension*, Hillsdale, NJ: Erlbaum, pp. 33–58.

Rumelhart, D. E. and Ortony, A. (1977) "The Representation of Knowledge in Memory", in R. C. Anderson, R. J. Spiro and W. E. Matague (eds), *Schooling and the Acquisition of Knowledge*, Hillsdale, NJ: Erlbaum, pp. 99–135.

Steffensen, M., Joag-Dev, C. and Anderson, R. (1979) "A Cross-cultural Perspective on Reading Comprehension", *Reading Research Quarterly*, 15: 10–29.

Taylor, S. E. and Crocker, J. (1981) "Schematic Bases of Social Information Processing", in E. T. Higgins, C. P. Herman and M. P. Zanna (eds), *Social Cognition: The Ontario Symposium*, Hillsdale, NJ: Erlbaum, vol. 1, pp. 89–134.

Thoma, S. J. (1994) "Moral Judgments and Moral Action", in J. R. Rest and D. Narvaez (eds) *Moral Development in the Professions: Psychology and Applied Ethics*, Hillsdale, NJ: Lawrence Erlbaum, pp. 199–212.

Toulmin, S. (1981) "The Tyranny of Principles", *Hastings Center Report*, 11: 31–9.

Triandis, H. C. (1995) *Individualism and Collectivism*. San Francisco: Westview Press.

van den Broek, P. (1994) "Comprehension and Memory of Narrative Texts: Inferences and Coherence", in M. A. Gernsbacher (ed.), *Handbook of Psycholinguistics*, New York: Academic Press, pp. 539–88.

van den Broek, P., Rohleder, L. and Narvaez, D. (1994) "Cognitive Processes in the Comprehension of Literary Texts", in H. van Oostendorp and R. Zwaan (eds) *Naturalistic Text Comprehension, Vol. 53: Advances in Discourse Processes*, Norwood, NJ: Ablex, pp. 229–46.

Van Dijk and Kintsch, W. (1983) "Strategies of Discourse Comprehension", New York: Academic Press.

Zajonc, R. B. (1980) "Feeling and Thinking: Preferences Need no Inferences", *American Psychologist*, 35: 151–75.

# Part Three

## Moral Values

# 15 Values and Studentship in Post-compulsory Education and Training

TERRY HYLAND

As in other sectors of education in Britain, the domain of post-school education has experienced widespread and revolutionary structural change over the last 25 years. There has been a technical rationalisation of all aspects of provision in line with neo-liberal and instrumentalist doctrines which has resulted in a marginalisation of values in relation to curriculum, teaching and the ends of education. All this has brought about a centrally imposed and highly deterministic conception of education and training which is unduly economistic and concerned almost exclusively with employability skills and current industrial demands. Under the influence of this new technicism, values are either neutralised – implying a spurious consensus about education, society and nationhood – or marginalised as questions of educational purposes, processes of learning and the nature of studentship are overlooked in the drive to achieve national targets for education and training (NTETs).

I intend to offer a critique of these developments in the sector of post-compulsory education and training (PCET) along with the political, social and economic agenda which underpins them. The principal focus will be the area of vocational studies which, in recent years, has experienced more structural change and political attention than perhaps any other sphere of education in Britain. Finally, I will make recommendations for a renewed and reconstructed programme of vocational education and training (VET) which draws on Deweyan notions of vocationalism and pays due attention to the process of studentship, and to the values which underpin conceptions of work, learning and democratic citizenship in a period which has witnessed the globalisation of work, economics and capital.

## Vocationalism, vocationalisation and neo-Fordism

The reassertion of the economic and vocational function of education in Britain is typically dated from the time of the Great Debate and Callaghan's Ruskin College speech in 1976 (Whitty 1985). Chitty's recent reappraisal of this period with the hindsight of 20 years of educational legislation demonstrates forcefully that the 1970s 'signalled a clear public re-definition of educational objectives' which gave 'legitimacy to a largely utilitarian view of the purpose of schooling' (Chitty 1996: 15). In the years that followed, the role of education in helping to improve industrial performance was taken up by public figures and politicians and subsequently reflected in official publications of the then Department for Educational and Science (DES). Arnold Weinstock, then head of the General Electric Company, could be confident of a warm reception for his charges of 'anti-industry bias' and a preference for the 'life of the mind over the practical life' (Weinstock 1976: 2) levelled against the teaching profession in the 1970s.

Of course, there was nothing new about such claims; industrialists had been expressing similar sentiments from time to time (usually in times of economic recession!) at least since the time of Britain's relatively poor performance at the Paris Exhibition of 1867 (Musgrave 1966). However, this renewed call for a return to vocational basics coincided with massive youth unemployment, a world economic recession generated by massive increases in oil prices in the early 1970s, and a determination to deflect criticism for industrial and economic ills away from governments and towards the alleged failings of educational systems. Thus, the so-called 'new vocationalism' (Esland (ed.) 1990) which has influenced the development of PCET from the 1970s to the present, has been characterised chiefly by a scapegoating of the education system, school leavers and the teaching profession in conjunction with a wilful neglect of the complex reasons – such as the failure of investment policies, erosion of the manufacturing base and the dominance of finance capital – for Britain's relative economic decline since 1945 (Armstrong et al. 1984). The largely unquestioned assumptions supporting this view of the relationship between education and the economy have now acquired the status of a 'folk myth' (Esland, 1996: 46) which effectively precludes the consideration of alternative perspectives.

In the struggle for the curriculum in the 1970s and 1980s the vocational lobby gained a noticeable edge so that, by the time of the secretary of state's North of England Conference speech in 1984, Sir Keith Joseph felt the need to urge the adoption of a curriculum with a 'practical element' which was 'relevant to the real world' (Joseph 1984: 4). The green paper *Education in Schools* (DES 1977) had stressed the vital role of education in aiding Britain's economic recovery through the improvement of manufacturing industry, and the change of ethos is reflected clearly in the DES publication *Better Schools* which recommended a 5–16 curriculum which would encourage

> the qualities, attitudes, knowledge, understanding and competences which are necessary to equip pupils for working life. With this aim in view the Government has established the Technical and Vocational Education Initiative (TVEI) which explores how best to fit work-related skills within full-time education.   (DES 1985: 6)

From the outset, TVEI schemes were informed and guided by the Manpower Services Commission (MSC) definition of vocational education as that 'in which students are concerned to acquire generic or specific skills with a view to employment' and TVEI was intended ultimately to influence 'the whole curriculum' (Pickard 1985: 23). Following the abolition of TVEI and the MSC, the work of linking education with employability and industrial-skills training has been undertaken by the National Council for Vocational Qualifications (NCVQ) established in 1986 to 'improve vocational qualifications by basing them on the standards of competence required in employment' (NCVQ 1989:

2). The new National Vocational Qualifications (NVQs) – underpinned by a behaviourist strategy of competence-based education and training (CBET) based on employer-defined skills – are now central to the key objective of making education and training totally responsive to the needs of industry and the economy (Barnett 1994, Hyland 1994). Although NVQs have failed to meet, not only the officially stated objectives of the NCVQ, but also the needs and demands of employers, students, educational institutions and industrialists (Smithers 1993, Hyland 1996, Robinson 1996), the central role assigned to them in the government's National Targets for Education and Training (NACETT 1995) ensures that the narrow job-skills strategy remains at the heart of national policy on PCET.

In responding to the suggestion by Gray and Wilcox (1995) that the national curriculum 'over-emphasises the vocational dimension of education at the expense of its role as initiation into a cultural inheritance' (p. 27), Winch (1996) makes a number of interesting observations about the contemporary education scene. Chief amongst these is the claim that the work of schools and colleges must be accountable in terms of publicly agreed standards and criteria or education will be left 'vulnerable to the claim that it is a confederation of producer interests, unconcerned with whether or not resources are effectively deployed' (ibid.: 57). This point merits attention, as does the further one that, because of a historical ambiguity and tension between liberal/vocational traditions and a lack of clarity about aims in the British system, the grounding in core skills and attention to vocational aims is often at fault. However, as Winch notes, there is a crucial difference between vocational education in the sense of activities 'concerned with the development of knowledge, skills and understanding insofar as these fit people for a particular kind of employment or range of employments' and mere 'job training … which fails to take account of the wide variety of occupations that are available' (ibid.: 38). Barnett (1994) makes a similar distinction in higher education between 'vocational' aims which seek to ensure that graduates are 'adaptable to the changing demands of the world of work', and 'vocationalism' which stands for 'temporariness and a shallowness of commitment' (p. 68).

Such sentiments are reminiscent of Dewey's

approach to vocational education which was based on occupational activities – defined as the 'continuous organisation of power along general lines' (1965: 132) – and was highly critical of the rather narrow, rigid and specialised conception of vocational education based on the mechanical 'social-efficiency' philosophy (Lewis 1991) which influenced American education earlier this century. A similar, though reconstituted, form of social efficiency has informed contemporary VET developments in Britain based on behaviourist versions of CBET and narrow skills training leading to occupationally specific NVQs (Hyland 1994, Higham, Sharp and Yeomans 1996). What makes these recent developments all the more remarkable is that – unlike the overt utilitarian industrial policy which underpinned the system which Dewey was attacking (Wirth 1991) – contemporary VET policy is justified in terms of its function in promoting the 'skills revolution' and 'learning society' (Jessup 1991: 95, 98) necessary to the 'post-Fordist' industrial society.

As with many other aspects of contemporary VET policy, the vision of the multiskilled, flexible worker represents the yawning gulf which exists between rhetoric and reality. Edwards (1993), for example, has argued that the so-called flexibility and openness of the 'skills revolution' based on employer-defined competence approaches actually mask a reality in which 'discourses about open learning' come to be 'strategically ranged to normalize a view of the future of work – based in structural unemployment and underemployment – as not only inevitable but also preferable' (p. 185). CBET strategies, which are apparently accessible to all, superficially open as to means yet closed on ends defined largely by industrial needs, are ideal vehicles for ensuring that 'persons will be disciplined into certain forms of behaviour and more readily managed within a social formation of structural inequality' (ibid.). As Sieminski (1993) suggests, only a minority of core workers in the new flexible labour force will require high-level skills. NVQ strategies are designed to provide an essentially low-level training for 'those who will occupy an uncertain future being assigned to the periphery of the labour market' (p. 99).

The apparent contradiction between post-Fordist demands for high-level, multiskilled, flexible workers and the narrow low-level occupationalism which actually drives current VET policy – described by Avis as the 'myth of the post-Fordist society' (Avis 1996: 71) – may be explained by considering contemporary approaches as neither Fordist nor post-Fordist but as instances of 'neo-Fordism'. Brown and Lauder (1995) remind us that the organisational restructuring, applications of new technologies and 'flexible accumulation' commonly identified with post-Fordist enterprises do not 'necessarily lead to changes in the nature of skills and employee involvement which are said to be required in order to compete in "high value" production' (p. 20). Many economies, including Britain's, have really opted for 'neo-Fordist' solutions which can be 'characterized in terms of a shift to flexible accumulation based on the creation of a flexible workforce engaged in low-skill, low-wage temporary and often part-time employment' (ibid.).

The exposure of the post-Fordist myth makes nonsense of the official rhetoric about the need to foster a 'learning society' (Raggatt, Edwards and Small (eds) 1996) in Britain to produce the new flexible, multiskilled workforce. In fact, the emphasis on the accreditation of employer-defined skills and numbers of NVQ certificates awarded, as Ainley (1996) points out, marks the 'road to a certified not a learning society' (p. 91). More significant than these issues, however, from the standpoint of social values and justice, is the disastrous impact of such policies on the community and polity. Not only do those people in work face increasing controls over their working practices and scope for initiative (Field 1995), but also thousands of young people are subjected to low-level training which ill equips them for life in a highly uncertain employment future. The 'immorality' (Lee et al. 1990) of this approach to VET consists, not just in its disingenuousness and internal contradictions (Esland 1996), but in its effects on the lives of working people who, faced with increased redundancies and casual employment, are both alienated and at the same time denied the means and wherewithal of either understanding or dealing with their problems and the root causes of their alienation (Hutton 1995). Moreover, the social implications of such policies in terms of the massive increases in income inequality in Britain (much greater than in other European countries; (Atkinson 1996) and the continued rise of homelessness and relative poverty (Rowntree Trust 1995) need to be interrogated by students and teachers committed to the moral point of view (Hyland 1995).

## VET and the McDonaldisation of the post-school sector

The narrow skills training which characterises recent trends in VET has been linked with certain other political, economic and ideological trends in terms of the increasingly centralised role of the state in educational policy-making and the overriding commitment to 'market forces' as a means of controlling developments (Avis et al. 1996). An overarching metaphor used to describe many of these features is provided by Ritzer's (1993) conception of 'McDonaldisation', used to illustrate the increasing technical rationalisation of all aspects of social life in post-industrial economies. This incredibly fertile metaphor has extensive explanatory power and, when applied to post-school trends over the last two decades, serves to illustrate vividly the current malaise. The analysis offered by Hartley (1995) highlights a number of key characteristics of the 'McDonaldisation' of education and training which provide useful tools for understanding contemporary VET policy and practice.

The process is typically characterised by (Hartley 1995: 414–19):

*efficiency:* all educational aims and objectives are subjected to the managerialist conceptions of input/output efficiency (described by Avis as 'neo-Taylorism'; 1996: 110 ff.) measured against 'products' defined by the funding councils for further and higher education and the NTETs. Questions of curriculum content, learning processes and student autonomy are marginalised and subordinated to such 'outcomes'.

*quantification and calculability:* in order to enhance the efficiency model, all educational aims and objectives are reduced to the overtly measurable; hence the dominance of behaviourist competence outcomes assessed by checklist (Wolf 1995).

*predictability and control:* in spite of all the official rhetoric about consumer choice and diversity, all choices for post-school students and teachers are severely restricted by means of funding regulations which, in line with government policy, are arranged so that curricula are in line with NTETs and the 'technical rationality' of the national agenda for education and training (Hodkinson and Sparkes 1995).

*fake fraternisation:* in order to make the new dehumanised and deterministic system acceptable to consumers, students and teachers need to be persuaded that they have more control over their own learning. This is achieved principally through what Collins (1991) has called a 'technicist obsession' which has reduced learning to 'situations managed by technical formulations, such as standardized pre-packaged curricula and preconceived needs assessment instruments put together by experts' (p. 5). By means of computer packages, needs analysis, action plans, and modularised programmes students may be cajoled into thinking that they have autonomy over teaching/learning processes. The radical mismatch between means and ends, process and product cannot, however, be remedied by persuasive rhetoric. Even if the means are theoretically open (and there is ample evidence that this is illusory; (Edwards 1993, Hyland 1994), there can be no hiding the fact that the relentless determinism of centralised policy ensures that the ends remain unequivocally closed and non-negotiable (Avis et al. 1996).

The implications of such approaches and their impact on post-school education and training have already been referred to. Learning becomes commodified in an education and training market in which self-interested consumers seek to maximise their employability skills. Pragmatic values such as efficiency and control are to the fore, though the official version would have us believe that the whole system is in some sense 'value neutral' (Halliday 1996) and that it is simply a matter of determining the most cost-efficient means of achieving universally agreed ends concerned with improving economic competitiveness. Not only does all this marginalise debate about the nature and purpose of VET, the relationship between learning and community, education and the economy, it also results in a 'morally impoverished' (Fish 1993) view of vocational studies. Such an approach, if it allows for the discussion of values at all, generates a largely uncritical and mechanistic strategy in which something called 'moral competence' (Wright 1989, Hyland 1992) is recommended largely as a means of ensuring that young people develop the 'qualities and personal skills employers require' (Industry in Education 1996: 9).

## Values and studentship in post-school VET

Accepting Jarrett's (1991) suggestion that perhaps 'the single most important goal for a teacher to work towards has to do with the basic attitude towards work' (p. 206), I intend to outline some guidelines for morally justifiable vocational studies programmes in PCET which, following Dewey (1966), stress 'the full intellectual and social meaning of a vocation' (p. 316). Such an approach will also need to be underpinned by the 'shared values' which inform our 'common understanding of why productive work is a fundamental condition of human life' (Skilbeck et al. 1994: 50).

## A work-related curriculum

Instead of narrow job skills (which could be supplied by specific employment-based courses), a broad-based vocational curriculum would take seriously questions concerned with the nature and value of work in human life. Distinctions need to be made between work, labour and toil (Herbst 1973, Hyland 1995) and the positive value and life-affirming nature of all kinds of work needs to be closely examined. According to Wringe (1991), for example, a part of the 'morality of work' is to insist that 'work does not have to be sublime or spectacular . . . to be worthwhile. Many relatively mundane jobs can be challenging and varied, and involve standards of logic, efficiency, integrity, judgment and so on' (p. 38). In a similar vein Green (1968) argues that the 'meaningfulness of a task lies not in the work but in the worker' and that 'some people may find even cosmic significance in a task that, to others, would seem mean and inconsequential' (p. 25). As Jarrett (1991) suggests, all such discussions of work are ultimately connected with moral questions relating to human values, attitudes, motives and dispositions. The values connected with Buddhist 'mindfulness' – the seventh branch of the eight-fold path which seeks to wean us 'away from our usual habit patterns' in a way which 'sharpens and intensifies our powers of direct perception' and 'gives us eyes to see into the true nature of things' (Snelling 1987: 61) – are worthy of special emphasis in the sphere of vocational or technical pursuits in which activities are so often greatly undervalued (Williams 1994).

A particularly vivid illustration of the application of such spritual/aesthetic values to work is provided with penetrating insight and imagination in Pirsig's *Zen and the Art of Motorcycle Maintenance* (1974). At one point Pirsig's central character makes the following observation:

Precision instruments are designed to achieve an *idea*, dimensional precision whose perfection is impossible. There is no perfectly shaped part of the motorcycle and never will be, but when you come as close as these instruments take you, remarkable things happen, and you go flying across the countryside under a power that would be called magic if it were not so completely rational in every way . . . I look at the shapes of the steel now and I see *ideas*. . . . I'm working on *concepts*. (p. 102, italics original)

On perhaps a more pragmatic plane, Corson (1991) calls for a consideration of work as 'craft . . . pursued for its own ends . . . as unconstrained occupational work . . . similar to recreational work as having a value for its own sake' (p. 171). Similarly, Ainley (1993) reminds us of the history of craftsmanship and 'artisanship' (pp. 5 ff.), combining the work of artists and craftspeople, and its importance in determining the status of work and the divisions of knowledge and labour. Simple pride in achievement is worth stressing here, if only to combat the deskilling tendencies and belittling of underpinning practical and intuitive knowledge characteristic of current CBET approaches to VET (Hyland 1994). Moreover, re-emphasising such features can do much to enhance vocational studies and help to break down the damaging vocational/academic divide, in pursuit of the coherent and unified curriculum most educators and industrialists officially subscribe to (Dearing 1996, Higham, Sharp and Yeomans 1996).

Again, it is perhaps in the work of poets and novelists that we find the fullest expression of these notions of craft and artisanship. Seamus Heaney's poems provide vivid illustrations in this respect. The sheer joy of useful, productive and careful work is nowhere better described than in Primo Levi's *The Wrench* in which the central character, Faussone, tells stories about his work as a rigger on construction sites around Europe. In a similar vein, in *The Ragged Trousered Philanthropists* Tressell describes the work of painters and decorators in the early years of the century who, in spite of constant hardship and fear of dismissal, struggled to give meaning to their work by doing the best possible job in all areas. One of the workmen, for example, forced with his colleagues to constantly rush all the jobs in the interests of profit,

could not scamp the work to the extent that he was ordered to; and so, almost by stealth, he was in the habit of doing it – not properly but as well as he dared. He even went to the length of occasionally buying a few sheets of glasspaper with his own money.   (Tressell 1993: p. 162)

There are, of course, many negative aspects of the world of work and, in the absence of ideal conditions, vocational studies still has a vital role to play in helping students to make sense of a world of work in which toil may be a commonplace experience. Wringe (1991) has two key proposals to make in relation to the 'morality of toil and the division of labour'. First, since 'toil, regular, serious toil, cannot itself be a necessary part of the good life', the 'facts of human existence are such that a preparedness to undertake it may be regarded as a necessary part of a life that is just'. Secondly, if 'toil is a necessary evil, training which enables it to be done more efficiently . . . or enables it to be replaced by a more challenging or worthwhile form of work seems morally desirable' (p. 40).

In the light of such observations, both vocational (technical) and moral education (concerning the values of work and craft) are necessary components of a work-related curriculum – as, indeed, are those aspects of general education (art, humanities, science, sport) which give meaning to those aspects of life not taken up with work or toil.

## Work, social values and citizenship

The 'new vocationalism' described earlier is underpinned by a one-dimensional 'economistic' conception of vocationalism in which the only value ascribed to work is in contributing to employers' profitability and national economic competitiveness (Esland 1996). The post-Fordist myth paints a picture of flexible, multiskilled generic workers, moving from one contract to another in the self-interested pursuit of the fruits of gainful employment; we are all to 'become self-regulating enterprising subjects who will give of their all and are committed to the values and goals of the organisation in which they work' (Avis 1996: 76).

The glaring one-sidedness and monocultural nature of this conception of working life – its cavalier dismissal of the 'traditional work ethic which stressed the integration of work and personal development' (Carlson 1982: 135) – cannot be disguised by the rhetoric of the enterprise culture or the post-Fordist folk myth (often using fashionable postmodernist symbolism; see Gleeson 1996). Esland (1996) argues forcefully against the dangers

of the 'technical rationality' of this narrow vocationalism, asserting that

it is a system which renders both human labour and its skills as commodities to be utilized or discarded as circumstances – and profits – determine. There is at the heart of technical rationality an *ethical indifference towards the non-economic value of employment* and the social costs of an oppressive employment environment.   (p. 24, my italics)

This 'ethical indifference' – which typifies the narrow occupationalism of the new vocationalism and the thrust of current government policy on PCET – is responsible for the complete failure to capture the craft and aesthetic features of work mentioned above, and flies in the face of all the findings of the human-relations school of industrial psychology (Mayo 1945, Peters 1987) which stress the importance of creating a committed and self-motivated workforce by colonising the meanings that workers attribute to wage labour.

It is not just unethical, however, but also counter-intuitive to neglect the personal development and cummunicative-collaborative aspects of work. As Zuboff (1988) has suggested, the most successful and genuinely flexible industrial organisations have been those which have interpreted the new conditions as calling for 'relations of equality' in the working environment which can 'encourage a synthesis of members' interests' so that the 'flow of value-adding knowledge helps legitimate the organisation as a learning community' (p. 394). This idea of the learning community – whether it is in the public or private sector, education or industry – is dependent upon 'collective intelligence' (Brown and Lauder 1995: 28) and action generated by consensual understanding, and it is precisely such an approach which has enabled the 'social-partnership' models of education and training provision to produce such enviable VET systems in Europe (Green 1995).

Economic activity and working practices cannot exist in a vacuum which artificially excludes developments and consequences at the societal global and ecological level (Lipietz 1993). As Hart (1996) argues, the narrow technical industrial model of work concerned exclusively with productivity and economic growth

generates an interpretation of the current crisis which screens out the most important and troubling aspects of this crisis: the increase in precarious, unstable work relations, the growing North/South division, the feminization of poverty in conjunction with a new sexist division of labour, and the continued destruction of the environment. (p. 109)

A work-related curriculum will need to examine critically all such issues and, questioning the current post-Fordist paradigm, take note of alternative strategies and economic models. There are, after all, many other approaches to these issues which question the materialistic individualism of the enterprise culture, and point to the importance of linking economic considerations with social values, democracy and citizenship (Heelas and Morris (eds) 1992, Ranson 1994). Indeed, the dominance of the 'free-market' paradigm is being challenged increasingly by economists such as Ormerod (1994) who propose a new economics in which

> economic success can be achieved, and achieved more successfully within a broader and more beneficial framework than that driven by the pure, individual rationality of the economics textbooks . . . The power of markets needs to be harnessed to the wider benefit of society. (pp. 204–5).

Moreover, the globalisation of capital, markets and economic activity demands a global conception of work and citizenship instead of an 'increasingly narrow conception of national self-interest which bears a diminishing relationship to what is happening in the global economy (Esland 1996: 21). The values associated with learning – whether this is vocational, academic, institutional or work-based – are, as Ranson (1994) rightly observes, actually moral values inextricably linked with civic virtue, democracy and the rights and duties of citizenship. All this calls for a reconstructed model of PCET for the twenty-first century which 'acknowledges social and personal aims, values and needs and locates education and training goals in relation to the kind of society we wish to see develop and the qualities in people that are to be fostered and nourished' (Skilbeck et al. 1994: 46).

## Values and studentship in the post-school sector

In order to achieve the independence of thought, autonomy and capacity for critical analysis necessary for such a reconstructed model of VET and a work-related curriculum based on social values, models of student learning based on 'empowerment' (Hodkinson 1996) will be required. The concept of 'studentship' with its emphasis on the experimentation and activity of learning characteristic of the experiential tradition (Kolb 1993) can help to facilitate such strategies. Originally used by Stenhouse (Ruddock and Hopkins 1984) to refer to a capacity for independent study and for recognising the problematic nature of received knowledge, this approach goes beyond the merely descriptive, time-serving notions associated with vocational 'traineeship' (Dearing 1996) and takes seriously the idea of fostering in students the autonomy and independence characteristic of critical thinking and reflective practice (Barnett 1994).

Interpreting the notion of studentship in the broadest possible sense, Bloomer (1996) employs the term to refer to 'the variety of ways in which students can exert influence over the curriculum in the creation and confirmation of their own personal learning careers' (p. 140). Centralised state control and the economic determinism outlined in previous sections have resulted in a highly prescriptive curriculum with hardly any scope for creative engagement or input on the part of teachers and students. Not only does such a strategy fail to meet basic ethical and educational criteria connected with autonomy and the preconditions of genuine learning (Callan 1994), there is the danger that such a blinkered approach will leave unexamined the vital questions of citizenship, social justice and the future of work and employment which are integral to the values foundation of vocational studies.

Current conceptions of society, citizenship and the economy offer monocultural accounts based on individualism, market forces and nation-state economic competitiveness as straightforward and unproblematic descriptions of our current and future needs (Avis et al. 1996). Preparation for adult working life and for citizenship, however, require rather more than the nakedly utilitarian lessons in consumer rights and job training characteristic of recent government initiatives (NCC 1990, Hyland 1992). If such conformist views go unchallenged then, as Bloomer (1996) argues, the 'economic rationalism which treats people as objects, as human resources, for the economy – *as if the economy is an end in itself*' will remain dominant and will effectively 'obscure an active view of citizenship which, in a democracy, is the end-point for which all systems of society, including the economic, exist' (p. 143, original italics).

Moreover, the 'making through action' (ibid.: 141) aspect of studentship and independent learning not only enhances student motivation and effective learning (Haselgrove (ed.) 1994) but also promotes the generic critical-thinking skills which, in theory at least, educators and industrialists regard as essential for the 'learning society' of the twenty-first century (Raggatt, Edwards and Small (eds) 1996). If we are to move beyond the 'mechanistic metaphors and traditions' which delimit human agency and prevent us from escaping the inequities, violence, human wastage, and ecological damage which typify current socio-economic strategies, it will be necessary for teachers to foster what Hutchinson (1996) calls 'critical futurism' in our educational practices, through which all 'taken-for-granted ways of thinking about educational and other institutions' (pp. 20 ff.) are constantly challenged. The central challenge of our time is that 'of moving from violence-condoning, intolerant cultures to more tolerant and peaceful cultures' (ibid.: 3) and this challenge can only be met by fostering the critical examination of value assumptions referred to above.

There is no more important task than that of preparing young people for adult and working life and, if this is to amount to something more than the unquestioning endorsement of the status quo, vocational programmes must examine the wide-ranging moral underpinnings of working life and society in the late twentieth century. An indispensable element in this moral dimension of VET will be the recognition of its traditional tendency to monoculturalism coupled with the determination to remedy this shortcoming by emphasising the essential multicultural aspects of contemporary working life. There is more than enough evidence to suggest that ethnic minorities in Britain have been marginalised and severely let down by the education and training policies of the last two decades (Drew 1995). Similarly, the inherent racism of many of our post-school institutions has been vividly illustrated in a number of studies (Troyna and Selman 1991). Emphasising the values underpinning education for work within the framework of the empowerment offered by models of studentship must address the issues and challenges posed by such evidence.

In a telegraphic and uncharacteristically metaphysical section of Sir Ron Dearing's recent national review of 16–19 qualifications we are told that 'Education means preparing young people for life in the widest sense. As adults they will assume responsibility for the quality of our society and civil-isation. Spiritual and moral values must therefore be an essential element in education' (Dearing 1996: 4). Such a recommendation should be given pride of place and incorporated into all future reforms and proposals for post-16 education and training in Britain.

## References

Ainley, P. (1993) *Class and Skill*, London: Cassell.

Ainley, P. (1996) 'The Eternal Return of the Same: Dearing's Latest Review', *Forum*, 38.3: 90–2.

Armstrong, P. et al. (1984) *Capitalism Since World War II*, London: Fontana.

Atkinson, T. (1996) 'Why Do Britain's Have-nots Have Less', *Times Higher Education Supplement*, 12 Apr.

Avis, J., Bloomer M., Erland, G., Gleeson, D. and Hodkinson, P. (1996) *Knowledge and Nationhood*, London: Cassell.

Avis, J. (1996) 'The Myth of the Post-Fordist Society', in Avis et al. (1996).

Barnett, R. (1994) *The Limits of Competence*, Buckingham: Open University Press.

Bloomer, M. (1996) 'Education for Studentship', in Avis et al. (1996).

Brown, P. and Lauder, H. (1995) 'Post-Fordist Possibilities: Education, Training and National Development', in L. Bash and A. Green (eds) *Youth, Education and Work*, London: Kogan Page.

Callan, E. (1994) 'Autonomy and Alienation', *Journal of Philosophy of Education*, 28.1: 35–53.

Carlson, D. (1982) 'Updating Individualism and the Work Ethic: Corporate Logic in the Classroom', *Curriculum Inquiry*, 12.2: 131–42.

Chitty, C. (1996) 'Ruskin's Legacy', *Times Educational Supplement*, 18 Oct.

Collins, M. (1991) *Adult Education as Vocation*, London: Routledge.

Corson, D. (ed.) (1991) *Education for Work*, Clevedon, UK: Multilingual Matters.

Dearing, Sir Ron (1996) *Review of Qualifications for 16 to 19 Year Olds*, Hayes: School Curriculum and Assessment Authority.

DES (1977) *Education in Schools: A Consultative Document*, London: Department of Education and Science.

DES (1985) *Better Schools: A Summary*, London: Department of Education and Science.

Dewey, J. (1965) *The School and Society*, Chicago: University of Chicago Press.

Dewey, J. (1966) *Democracy and Education*, New York: Free Press.

Drew, D. (1995) *Race, Education and Work: The Statistics of Inequality*, Aldershot: Avebury.

Edwards, R. (1993) 'The Inevitable Future? Post-Fordism in

Work and Learning', in R. Edwards, S. Sieminski and D. Zeldin (eds) *Adult Learners, Education and Training*, London: Routledge/Open University.

Esland, G. (ed.) (1990) *Education, Training and Employment*, Wokingham: Addison-Wesley/Open University.

Esland, G. (1996) 'Knowledge and Nationhood: The New Right, Education and the Global Market', in Avis et al. (1996).

Field, J. (1995) 'Reality-testing in the Workplace', in P. Hodkinson and M. Issitt (eds) *The Challenge of Competence*, London: Cassell.

Fish, D. (1993) 'Uncertainty in a Certain World: Values, Competency-based Training and the Reflective Practitioner', *Journal of the National Association for Values in Education and Training*, 8: 7–12.

Gleeson, D. (1996) 'Post-compulsory Education in a Post-industrial and Post-modern Age', in Avis et al. (1996).

Gray, J. and Wilcox, B. (1995) *Good School, Bad School*, Buckingham: Open University Press.

Green, A. (1995) 'The European Challenge to British Vocational Education and Training', in P. Hodkinson and M. Issitt (eds) *The Challenge of Competence*, London: Cassell.

Green, T. F. (1968) *Work, Leisure and the American School*, New York: Random House.

Halliday, J. (1996) 'Values and Further Education', *British Journal of Educational Studies*, 44.1: 66–81.

Hart, M. (1996) 'Educating Cheap Labour', in Raggatt, Edwards and Small (eds) (1996).

Hartley, D. (1995) 'The McDonaldisation of Higher Education: Food for Thought?', *Oxford Review of Education*, 21.4: 409–23.

Haselgrove, S. (ed.) (1994) *The Student Experience*, Buckingham: Open University Press.

Heelas, P. and Morris, P. (eds) (1992) *The Values of the Enterprise Culture*, London: Routledge.

Herbst, P. (1973) 'Work, Labour and University Education', in R. S. Peters (ed.) *The Philosophy of Education*, Oxford: Oxford University Press.

Higham, J., Sharp, P. and Yeomans, D. (1996) *The Emerging 16–19 Curriculum*, London: David Fulton.

Hodkinson, P. (1996) 'Careership: The Individual, Choices and the Market in the Transition into Work', in Avis et al. (1996).

Hodkinson, P. and Sparkes, A. (1995) 'Markets and Vouchers: The Inadequacy of Individualist Policies for Vocational Education and Training in England and Wales', *Journal of Education Policy*, 10.2: 189–207.

Hutchinson, F. P. (1996) *Educating Beyond Violent Futures*, London: Routledge.

Hutton, W. (1995) *The State We're In*, London: Jonathan Cape.

Hyland, T. (1992) 'Moral Vocationalism', *Journal of Moral Education*, 21.2: 139–150.

Hyland, T. (1994) *Competence, Education and NVQs: Dissenting Perspectives*, London: Cassell.

Hyland, T. (1995) 'Morality, Work and Employment: Towards a Values Dimension in Vocational Education and Training', *Journal of Moral Education*, 24.4: 445–56.

Hyland, T. (1996) 'Why NVQs have Lost their Vocation', *Daily Telegraph*, 27 Mar.

Industry in Education (1996) *Towards Employability*, London: Industry in Education.

Jarrett, J. L. (1991) *The Teaching of Values: Caring and Appreciation*, London: Routledge.

Jessup, G. (1991) *Outcomes: NVQs and the Emerging Model of Education and Training*, London: Falmer Press.

Joseph, Sir Keith (1984) 'View from the Top', *Times Educational Supplement*, 13 Jan.

Kolb, D. A. (1993) 'The Process of Experiential Learning', in M. Thorpe, R. Edwards and A. Hanson (eds) *Culture and Processes of Adult Learning*, London: Routledge.

Lee, D., Marsden, D., Rickman, P. and Duncombe, J. (1990) *Scheming for Youth: A Study of YTS in the Enterprise Culture*, Buckingham: Open University Press.

Lewis, T. (1991) 'Difficulties Attending the New Vocationalism in the USA', *Journal of Philosophy of Education*, 25.1: 95–108.

Lipietz, A. (1993) *Towards a New Economic Order: Post-Fordism, Ecology and Democracy*, Cambridge: Polity.

Mayo, E. (1945) *The Social Problems of an Industrial Civilisation*, Cambridge MA: Harvard University Press.

Musgrave, P. W. (1966) 'Constant Factors in the Demand for Technical Education', *British Journal of Educational Studies*, 14.2: 173–87.

NACETT (1995) *Report on Progress Towards the National Targets*, London: National Advisory Council for Education and Training Targets.

NCC (1990) *Education for Citizenship*, York: National Curriculum Council.

NCVQ (1989) *Assessment in NVQs: Use of Evidence from Prior Achievement*, London: National Council for Vocational Qualifications.

Ormerod, P. (1994) *The Death of Economics*, London: Faber & Faber.

Peters, T. (1987) *Thriving on Chaos*, New York: Knopf.

Pickard, J. (1985) 'The Technical and Vocational Education Initiative', *Times Educational Supplement*, 3 May.

Pirsig, R. M. (1974) *Zen and the Art of Motorcycle Maintenance*, London: Corgi.

Raggatt, P., Edwards, R. and Small, N. (eds) (1996) *The Learning Society*, London Routledge/Open University.

Ranson, S. (1994) *Towards the Learning Society*, London: Cassell.

Ritzer, G. (1993) *The McDonaldisation of Society*, London: Pine Forge Press.

Robinson, P. (1996) *Rhetoric and Reality: The Evolution of the New Vocational Qualifications*, London: London School of Economics, Centre for Economic Performance.

Rowntree Trust (1995) *Income and Wealth*, Poole: Joseph Rowntree Foundation.

Ruddock, J. and Hopkins, D. (1984) *The Sixth Form and Libraries*, London: British Library.

Sieminski, S. (1993) 'The "Flexible" Solution to Economic Decline', *Journal of Further and Higher Education*, 17.1: 92–100.

Skilbeck, M., Connell, H., Lowe, N. and Tait, K. (1994) *The Vocational Quest*, London: Routledge.

Smithers, A. (1993) *All Our Futures: Britain's Education Revolution*, London: Channel 4 Television 'Dispatches' Report on Education.

Snelling, J. (1987) *The Buddhist Handbook*, London: Rider.

Tressell, R. (1993) *The Ragged Trousered Philanthropists*, London: Flamingo.

Troyna, B. and Selman, L. (1991) *Implementing Multicultural and Antiracist Education in Mainly White Colleges*, London: Further Education Unit.

Weinstock, A. (1976) 'I Blame the Teachers', *Times Educational Supplement*, 23 Jan.

Whitty, G. (1985) *Sociology and School Knowledge*, London: Methuen.

Williams, K. (1994) 'Vocationalism and Liberal Education: Exploring the Tensions', *Journal of Philosophy of Education*, 28.1: 89–100.

Winch, C. (1996) *Quality and Education* special issue of *Journal of Philosophy of Education*, 30.1 Mar.

Wirth, A. G. (1991) 'Issues in the Vocational–Liberal Studies Controversy (1900–1917), in Corson, (ed.) 1991.

Wolf, A. (1995) *Competence-Based Assessment*, Buckingham: Open University Press.

Wright, D. (1989) *Moral Competence*, London: Further Education Unit.

Wringe, C. (1991) 'Education, Schooling and the World of Work' in Corson, (ed.) 1991.

Zuboff, S. (1988) *In the Age of the Smart Machine: The Future of Work and Power*, New York: Basic Books.

# 16 What Value the Postmodern in Values Education?

JAMES W. BELL

## Values education and postmodernism: a critical perspective

In educational theory postmodern critiques are on the increase. This chapter explores some of the limitations of postmodernism while highlighting the strengths of certain strands of postmodern thinking towards more responsive values-education practices. In particular it argues that a critical and liberatory postmodernism as expressed by liberation theology is an important framework for enhanced moral education.

This chapter questions the value of some postmodern perspectives in relation to values education in a multicultural society. The focus will be on the problems involved in assessing the topic of values approaches in any educational activity, particularly when these values approaches are informed by postmodern perspectives. The concern will not be with formulating a specific postmodern values framework for education. Of greater concern are the challenges facing teachers who wish to create for their students (and themselves) an awareness that their values must be factored into any educational environment which is neither nihilistic nor sentimental and neither guilt inducing nor given to overly broad sweeps of value relativism.

I come to questions of modernity and postmodernity as a worker in 'critical pedagogy' and as an educator with particular value positions and agendas. For me, this perspective might be summed in the following questions: How might we, as educators, reduce unnecessary human suffering in this world? And further, how might we act together to increase human dignity and work towards a vision of a radically more responsible and democratic world community?

Further, I use the notion 'critical!' in a particularly value-laden sense, where I have a social vision with a particular agenda. This vision is inspired by Enlightenment sensibilities and intentions which hold that humans are capable of coming together to create a more just world.

A notion of the critical which is traditionally valued in formal teaching situations is less related to a social vision than it is to a well-developed 'critical rationality'. Svi Shapiro starkly describes this notion of critical ability:

> The critical capacities that are developed in that strictly cognitive sense can be put to use to build better hydrogen bombs, and indeed are. They can be put to use to produce better, more manipulative advertising on Madison Avenue. And indeed they are. They can be put to use to find better ways to market products that are destructive to the environment. And they are. I mean the fact of the matter is that the people who sit at the heads of our corporate board rooms and governmental agencies . . . often are extraordinarily great critical thinkers. They have highly developed critical powers. They have been to good colleges and universities. (in Kanpol 1994: 168)

Shapiro contrasts this with what he calls 'critical consciousness' in which we focus our critical abilities and our questioning capacities on the everyday world of our experience with specific moral purposes and vision. Shapiro continues:

> And that purpose is rooted in a moral vision. It has to do with looking at the world as to whether, in fact, it treats people with dignity and respect; whether the world is one in which certain groups of people or individuals are limited or dominated, or whether the world that we live in, in fact, lives up to its democratic and humanistic promises. (ibid.: 167–8)

It is from this latter perspective of the critical that I

address questions of the modern and the post-modern in relation to values education.

## Postmodernity as product and process

There is debate as to whether the postmodern is really an epochal shift or not, whether what is described as the postmodern period is really unique as an epoch or whether the postmodern period is better described as a stage of modernity (see Shapiro 1995). In either case the postmodern period marks an unprecedented global scepticism of Eurocentric rationality and confidence.

Charles Jencks, architect and postmodern critic, cites the beginning of the postmodern era as 3:32 p.m. 15 July 1972, the time when the Pruitt-Igoe housing project in St. Louis, Missouri was detonated and brought to the ground. Jencks viewed the demolition of this building as an agreement that the values and methods of abstract functionalist architects had been shown to be false, that 'machines for living', such as the Pruitt-Igoe building and other international-style high-rise dwellings built to warehouse poor people in cities around the globe, could not and would not serve the interests of their inhabitants (Papenek 1995). By locating the birth of the postmodern period in this way Jencks tacitly identifies the postmodern as both period and process. Jencks's logic portrays the postmodern as a period, as a temporal shift which marks a turning away from an Enlightenment confidence in technology and the possibility of absolute human triumph over social problems. The demolition of such 'machines for living' underscores how the reductive logic and value systems of late-industrial markets is miserably failing the very people it once promised to serve or even liberate. By signifying the advent of postmodernity this way Jencks also portrays the postmodern as process. He charges that architectural forms must redefine the ways certain human and cultural needs are met. His location of the advent of postmodernity at the moment of a housing project's demolition is value laden and represents new imperatives in addressing material social challenges.

## Limitations of modernist approaches to values education

It is clear that modernist approaches to ethics edu-cation are not adequate. Modernist ethical perspectives suffer from a patriarchal and Eurocentric lineage. This lineage oppresses various groups through structures of ideological privilege and corresponding imposed silences. Peter McLaren phrases our current condition in this way:

> We inhabit sceptical times, historical moments spawned in a temper of distrust, disillusionment, and despair. Social relations of discomfort and diffidence have always pre-existed us but the current historical juncture is particularly invidious in this regard, marked as it is by a rapture of greed, untempered and hypereroticized consumer will, racing currents of narcissism, severe economic and racial injustices, and heightened social paranoia. The objective conditions of Western capitalism now appear so incompatible with the realisation of freedom and liberation that it is no understatement to consider them mutually antagonistic enterprises. Situated beyond the reach of ethically convincing forms of accountability, capitalism has dissolved the meaning of democracy and freedom into glossy aphorisms one finds in election campaign sound bytes or at bargain basement sales in suburban shopping malls.   (1994: 192–3)

Within such a historical moment educators are often overworked and overwhelmed as they try to make enough sense of their own world that they might work out of some kind of desirable and achievable vision for themselves and for their students. The creation of a relevant values education, which embraces social difference, and which moves beyond many of the limitations of both modern and postmodern thinking, is a difficult and uncertain task. Such a values education will challenge educators with not only making major shifts in their thinking but also with reassessing many of their attitudes and beliefs.

## Modern problems and postmodern responses

Modernity has been under attack from almost every intellectual corner in the past few decades. Social modernity suffers what Matei Calinescu calls the 'bourgeois idea of modernity', which characterises as:

> the doctrine of progress, the confidence in the beneficial possibilities of science and technology, the concern with time (a measurable time, a time that can be bought and sold and therefore has, like

any other commodity, a calculable equivalent in money), the cult of reason, and the idea that freedom [should be] defined within the framework of an abstract humanism, [and] also the orientation toward pragmatism and the cult of action and success.   (in Giroux 1990: 6)

The modernist project of the Enlightenment has not however been entirely without its humanitarian benefits. Much of our contemporary well-being, comfort, longevity and security can be attributed to advances in science and technology. Such projects are incomplete, argues Jürgen Habermas, perhaps the great contemporary apologist for modernism. Habermas states that:

> The defects of the Enlightenment can only be made good by further enlightenment. The totalised critique of reason undercuts the capacity of reason to be critical. It refuses to acknowledge that modernization bears developments as well as distortions of reason.   (1984: 72)

Modernist imperatives have had significant influences on the development of public schools in the nineteenth and twentieth centuries. These phenomena have been chronicled in a number of studies, including the groundbreaking work of Foucault in *Discipline and Punish* (1977) and the critical educational work of Apple, Giroux and McLaren.

Schools have suffered from the onset of a positivism fuelled by managerialism, behavioural psychology and systems-management approaches. Joe Kinchloe makes the following observation:

> The forces of efficiency, productivity, and scientific management unleashed by Taylor and Thorndike have helped shape the twentieth century. Efficiency, productivity, science, and technology have achieved almost godlike status on the twentieth century landscape. The daily lives of educators attest to the power of these forces, as teachers teach subject matter that has been broken into an ordered sequence of separate tasks and 'factoids'. Trained to follow a pretest, drill, posttest instructional model, teachers efficiently follow a scientific pedagogy that has insidiously embedded itself as part of their 'cultural logic'.   (1993: 7–8)

Problems of modernity have been cited throughout this century and a history of critiques of modernity can be found in a number of sources. Berger and Luckman were in the vanguard challenging modernist notions of the march of progress to the certainty of knowledge and reality with the publication, in 1966, of *The Social Construction of Reality.*

This volume was perhaps the first to popularise constructivist notions preceding postmodern thinking in English-speaking contexts.

Modernism sees reality as objectifiable, observable and easily manipulable. It sees the end result of diligent observation and enquiry leading to a dependable and certain truth. The implications for values education is that a *best*-values approach can and should be developed.

From a postmodern perspective no such particular kind of truth or certainty is possible. Reality is something which is contingent, contestable, and constructed within particular historical and social discourses. Post or anti-modern reality, then, exists not so much 'out there' as a set of things to be discovered, but is more something which emerges from the kinds of discursive spaces we inhabit, the kinds of lives we have lived, our personal histories and our relationships to privilege, power, knowledge and oppression. With an acceptance that reality is socially constructed we are afforded a kind of radical hope; where there is injustice it is not 'natural' but rather a social construction. Similarly, social justice can be a viable project created out of responsible human actions.

A unifying feature of many, if not all, postmodern perspectives is the notion that truth, like all social reality, is socially constructed and relevant to particular historical moments. Truth, therefore, is always contextualised, always contingent, it is contestable and often it might be contradictory. Within every 'regime of truth' there are particular possibilities and limitations – in other words, in a democratic discourse justice will have certain characteristics. Similarly, justice in a Judeo-Christian sense will have very different, though perhaps overlapping, qualities, meanings and implications, as it will have in a totalitarian communist society or in other political and religious frameworks.

Postmodernism is often seen as a rejection of modernism which has elevated reason and progress, most specifically industrial and economic progress, to quasi-religious status. To end this section it may be useful to quote Patti Lather's description of postmodernism:

> Postmodernism can most simply be termed the advent of the end of certainty, the end of linearity, of a cause and effect world in which every observable and nameable outcome can be understood and described by objective analysis. To write postmodern is to simultaneously use and call into discourse, to both challenge and inscribe dominant

meaning systems in ways that construct our own categories and frameworks as contingent, positioned, partial. My struggle is to find a way of communicating these deconstructive ideas so as to disrupt hegemonic relations and received notions of what our work is to be and to do.   (1991: 1)

## Problems with the postmodern and ethics education

Postmodern critiques and perspectives are not without a complex range of difficulties and potential problems, some of which are related to corresponding problems of modernism. Terry Eagleton offers this disdainful but pointedly critical parody of postmodern thinking and research.

> There is no such thing as truth; everything is a matter of rhetoric and power; all viewpoints are relative; talk of 'facts' or 'objectivity' is merely a specious front for the promotion of specific interests. The case is usually coupled with a vague opposition to the present political set-up, linked to an intense pessimism about the hope for any alternative . . . Those who expound it tend to be interested in feminism and 'ethnicity' but not in socialism, and to use terms like 'difference', 'plurality' and 'marginalisation' but not 'class struggle' or 'exploitation'.   (1991: 165–6)

There is bite to this critique. In an obvious contradiction, relativism is held as absolute, facts and truth are relegated to the cosmetic obscurities of ulterior agendas. Perhaps more central to issues of a critical values education, Eagleton sees postmodern thinking as alien from socialist or other utopian visions and programmes towards a more just world, particularly as he contrasts postmodern notions of 'difference' and 'pluralism' with Marxist notions of 'class struggle' and 'exploitation'.

It is not particularly surprising that a great deal of postmodern perspectives have anti-Marxist qualities. Jean-François Lyotard, one of the key thinkers in the development of French postmodernism, broke with the radical French Marxist movement of the 1960s and chronicled this break in an essay entitled 'A Memorial to Marxism'. Indeed, the totalising narratives of Freud and Marx have been duly criticised for their Eurocentric monoculturist perspectives of self and society and for their presentation of a world which can be finally understood and then controlled through the elimination of repressed tensions for Freud or of false conscious-

ness for Marx. Of course this is an oversimplification of their work, which is arguably both important and relevant to our current social condition. Nevertheless, their work legitimates a modernist absolutism which has silenced the experiences of many while offering individual and social visions unachievable within their narrative framework.

In Rust's work on postmodern implications for comparative education an overview of Lyotard's disaffection with Marxism as a totalising metanarrative is presented. Lyotard views Marxism as no less problematic than the totalising narrative of Christianity, the Western metanarrative of racial and cultural superiority and dominance or the modernist metanarrative that knowledge and truth are most appropriately based on abstract rules and principles. Lyotard's work is a direct challenge to constructions of Marxism and threatens a deconstruction which replaces it with no particular agenda or framework (Rust 1991: 615).

Rust urges educators committed to a responsible cultural pluralism and to values education not to reject metanarratives altogether but instead to understand and engage with the variety of metanarratives through which they operate. He states:

> The solution should not be to reject all metanarratives, trapping us into localised frameworks that have no general validity, that disallow comparison, and that deny integration of cultures and harmonising values. Legitimate metanarratives ought to open the world to individuals and societies, providing forms of analysis that express and articulate differences and that encourage critical thinking without closing off thought avenues for constructive action . . . Our task is to determine which approach to knowing is appropriate to specific interests and needs rather than to argue some universal application and validity, which ends up totalizing its ultimate effect.   (ibid.: 616)

This statement positions Rust as a postmodern modernist. Such work is akin more to a 'critical postmodernism' than to certain reactionary postmodern work.

The deconstruction of texts, discourses and 'regimes of truth' is simultaneously a strength and weakness of postmodern work. Postmodernism has often been described as a process of peeling an onion, deconstructing a text, layer after layer. The problem arises as to when to stop peeling any particular discursive 'onion'. When is enough enough? For a number of people engaged in postmodern social critique the deconstructing is an end in itself.

Deconstructionists must remind themselves, however, of their creative powers for constructing more desirable, if imperfect, social realities.

I am reminded of the pea-counting character in Camus' *The Plague*, the metaphorical tale of a horrendous bubonic plague outbreak in pre-war Algeria which was claiming the lives of almost every other person in the city. This character was content, even happy, sitting in his local cafe with a bowl of peas which he carefully counted day in and day out, the stench of death all around him. Certain activities related to postmodernism, I fear, can become not much more than degenerate ends in themselves in which cynicism and despair are soothed by the intellectually entertaining work of analysis and deconstruction. Postmodernism, as an analytical technique, does not require any kind of radical hope. Indeed, for a variety of postmodern agendas radical hope can, at best, be just another discourse awaiting further deconstruction.

Pressures continue to mount toward the development of educational technologies which are increasingly dehumanised and which seek discreetly predictable and measurable outcomes. Such technologies often foster relentless competition, increased social divisiveness and an unreflective relation to knowledge and power in the world. Such pressures are more directed at providing flexible workforces for rapidly changing job markets than at developing the critical and moral capacities of children which might redress social problems. Within such pressurised educational systems well-meaning teaching professionals may succumb to the kind of pea counting described by Camus. Given professional and cultural pressures, teachers may have reason to find for themselves relatively safe or manageable activities which might bunker them from any direct moral or political 'firing line'. Postmodern critiques and work in education can be constructed in ways that are both 'interesting' and value-neutral or value-ambiguous and which are without any vision for a different world. Furthermore, postmodern educational practices can be constructed to fit with the values systems of managerial or other anti-critical educational settings.

Pluralism is another feature commonly attributed to postmodern perspectives and is also not without its problems. It is difficult to know what to do when we accept a meta-ideology for understanding and making sense of the world which is premised from its very roots on a pluralism which seeks to value in some significant ways all voices and interpretations of human experience. It is possible to argue a postmodern world in which there is no 'better' or 'worse', that there is, instead only 'difference'. Taken in many forms postmodern perspectives run risks of extreme and dangerous value relativism in which it is impossible to determine any right (responsible) or wrong course of action. It is no wonder that the postmodern thinkers Baudrillard and Lyotard have been accused of 'entirely vacuous' politics by both Terry Eagleton and Peter McLaren (Eagleton 1991, McLaren 1993).

Indeed, I meet an increasing range of students who are all in favour of the democratisation of voice. In other words, these students are keen that everyone's voice is presented and heard, but they also hold that all positions presented are of similar merit and value. When probed about people's opinions which are specifically racist or sexist some will state that these are private opinions and should not be open for debate or judgement. This shows me the extent to which personal belief is assumed to be private property and, even when invited into the public realm, should not be open to serious debate or criticism.

Postmodernism is also readily coopted by the marketing establishment. As with any other discourse which has disruptive and challenging elements, the postmodern is easily hegemonised, homogenised, sloganised, packaged, labelled and put on the shelf in order to sell any available commodity. This is a double-edged sword in which postmodern presentations are simultaneously accessible and dismissible as yet another commodity option to be window shopped and consumed. The knitwear company Benneton has used advertising campaigns which have been criticised for representations which link disturbing and potentially critical representations with their 'united colours' message. In these 'postmodern' ads Benneton presents a multicultural and pluralistic world which is devoid of any values position.

Another criticism of postmodern theory is that it is most frequently written by academics for academics. This presents two significant problems. The first has to do with the form through which postmodern discourse is transmitted. One of the most frequent criticisms of postmodern theory is that it is written in such a specialised language that it is inaccessible to most people working outside academic circles. The second problem is that this rich and potentially transformative body of theory may well become part of a ritualised process of academic advancement and prestige. In this situation postmodernism can become a reified sacrament which is not employed because of its particular relevance, but because it has become a currency involved in academic advancement.

Perhaps one of the most significant criticisms against postmodernism is that it contributes to the kind of plurality that turns individuals back onto themselves with neither centre nor foundation. All that is left, perhaps, is an ability to appreciate the myriad world of discourses which come into view. Christopher Norris raises such a problem as he has accused Michael Foucault of a 'private-aesthetic conception of social issues' with regard to postmodern thinking (1993: 79). This criticism is connected to the problems of value relativism described earlier.

Terry Eagleton states that no life can continue completely absent of meaning, even in advanced capitalism:

> No individual life . . . can survive entirely bereft of meaning, and a society which took this nihilistic road would simply be nurturing massive social disruption. Advanced capitalism accordingly advances between meaning and non-meaning, pitched from moralism to cynicism and plagued by the embarrassing discrepancy between the two.   (1991: 39)

From such a position, one of the strongest claims levied against postmodernism is that it colludes with a powerlessness and absence of moral and ethical anchorage. Without such anchorage how can any substantive and significant project toward social justice and vision proceed? Such questions are difficult to answer. When do we stop peeling layer after discursive layer of meanings in our world and get down to the work of redressing some of the inequities?

Part of the answer might be partially found in Freire's notion of 'concientisation' which combines activities of both developing our consciousness and of acting in relation to our deepest and best-informed conscience. In the first instance, consciousness is most postmodern-friendly in that it is about instructing our awareness in as broad a way as possible. Consciousness for Freire is about being involved in dialogues and discourses so that people become aware of their particular subject relations within society (Taylor 1993: 49). As people become aware of their particular subject positions, this places them in different positions with regard to the dialogues in which they might engage.

Freire's notion of consciousness is largely drawn from the work of Hegel and Hegel's three stages of consciousness: consciousness of the object, consciousness of the self and consciousness of reason. It is in this last stage, a stage in which people come to recognise their relationship to others around them, that the 'stoic or unhappy consciousness' in Hegel's terms, or the 'passive, intransitive consciousness', in Freire's terms, might be surpassed (ibid.: 50). It is through this most significant shift in consciousness that cynicism and nihilistic inactivity might be replaced by liberational actions related to informed conscience (Freire 1970). I see Freire's notion of concientisation as including and welcoming elements of postmodern discourse but also as refusing any such extreme value neutrality or relativity.

Here is a summary of some specific dangers associated with postmodern critiques. Postmodernism can be used to cultivate an extreme value relativism which can promote personal helplessness, immobility, apathy and despair. Further, postmodern thinking often encourages its own unique form of alienation and isolation in which people are situated in a world that is uncertain and bereft of stable foundations.

Postmodern thinking often carries with it either an implicit or an explicit assumption that the entire modernist/Enlightenment tradition is dangerous and no longer worthwhile and that it should be jettisoned from any project related to improvements in social justice. In such a way postmodernism can be presented as another totalising metanarrative. Further, presentations of postmodernism typically attain places of power and privilege within academic communities. This positioning has contributed to postmodernism's often inaccessible form for people outside these communities. Postmodern critiques are thus susceptible to particular forms of ritualised practices as they relate to career development and advancement within this and other professional cultures.

Postmodern thinking is easily coopted by advanced capital markets. It is readily hegemonised and made bereft of potentially subversive power, perhaps more conveniently so than other theoretical discourses due to its popularised culture presence. In this process of hegemony the liberatory potential of postmodern thinking can be drained and then distilled into trivialised representations used to sell the most recent crop of consumer goods.

Perhaps most significantly, postmodern thinking,

in and of itself, does not require any kind of radical hope nor any particular commitment to a vision of a more just and equitable world.

## Postmodernism and spiritual and religious discourses

Belief is one of the languages most often lost to postmodern critiques. Belief and meaning can even be seen as completely irrelevant in a world which is entirely socially constructed.

One of the most significant things that spiritual and religious discourses offer the postmodern is a tradition of explicitly addressing belief in terms which might be more accessible to a great diversity of audiences. I argue that the postmodern is primarily concerned with belief, the ways in which we come to our beliefs and how we act in relation to these beliefs. If postmodern thinking and theorising is about addressing a variety of discourses and their constructions, and if within any particular discourse there is a moral and ethical world, then it seems very appropriate to explore these discourses through the notion and lens of belief.

Appropriating discourses from spiritual and religious traditions toward enriched critical educational work is not without some significant limitations and problems. This work is not intended to advocate a sentimental or reactionary return to fundamentalist religious traditions. The current popularity and renaissance of often acritical and myopic religious sects is more a symptom of the pandemic hopelessness and despair of our time than a genuine response to these problems. I am arguing, rather, that there are a rich variety of discourses available to us which embody alternative and potentially liberatory responses to a host of overwhelming issues such as global multinational capitalism, the problems associated with hyper-real and hyper-fast global infotechnologies, and global environmental degradation which has advanced to the extent that human survival on this planet is seriously in question.

Furthermore, it would be absurd to argue that any single religion or group of religious traditions is unproblematic or disconnected from practices of oppression, silence or dehumanisation of particular groups of people. On the contrary, we are surrounded by ongoing legacies of pain and suffering directly related to specific religious beliefs and practices. Even though highly problematic, such discourses present educators with a number of critical opportunities. Liberation theology, for example, brings together concerns for both people's spirits and the material conditions of their lives. Here is a summary of some of the possibilities of appropriating discourses from certain spiritual and religious traditions toward enriched values-education work informed by critical postmodern perspectives.

- Spiritual and religious traditions and discourses are often more accessible and more meaningful to large communities of people than is the often abstract work of postmodern writers. These discourses are often more familiar and accessible to specific communities than many other forms of social discourse.
- Spiritual and religious discourses frequently emerge and are produced from 'below' and from communities that already know a great deal about solidarity and are engaged in social action.
- When other cultural discourses are increasingly bereft of a vision of hope or possibility, more often than not spiritual and religious discourses contain within them tangible visions of hope and justice.
- Many spiritual and religious traditions promote community life which is based on cooperation, mutual interdependence of members and personal and collective responsibility. Such commitments are anathema to the alienation and isolated nihilism often associated with both modernism and postmodernism.
- Many spiritual and religious discourses and traditions contain within them thinking which is not at odds with many postmodern ways of thinking, especially relating to issues of certainty, linearity of reason and history, the power and importance of narrative in people's lives and the role of scientific and technological progress.
- Spiritual and religious discourses offer a rich variety of metaphors with which we might address our deeper moral and social concerns, including among others: compassion, forgiveness, mercy, love and sacrifice – metaphors often absent from our educational work.

Religious and spiritual traditions and discourses are rich with possibilities for social justice but are at increasing risk of being generally dismissed by both modern and postmodern critiques. Liberation theology consists of a particularly dynamic body of contemporary religious discourse with challenging implications for critical postmodern work in education.

## Liberation theology and a postmodern values education

Work in liberation theology is diverse and has been developed from a number of religious, social and regional perspectives. There are active movements in Christian, Jewish, Palestinian, Asian, Black American and feminist liberation theology. Common to most all these movements is a belief or acceptance that God is on the side of those most oppressed and least powerful and that human action is the only way to eradicate or alter unnecessary human suffering. Although this work is generally informed through Marxist-materialist critiques of power and oppression, the work pushes beyond such perspectives in ways which view power relations as more than reproductive, as contingent upon particular social experiences and contexts. A common theme in liberation theology is a belief that the voices of the oppressed must be heard in any project for social transformation or liberation. Personal narratives, then, are essential to much of this work.

Mary Daly (e.g. 1973), a North American Christian feminist, describes liberation theology in a way which illustrates assumed connections between particular social constructions of reality and the suffering which occurs based on these constructions:

> Liberation theologians . . . do not try to discover and describe universal conditions for the possibility of sin; they try to unmask the myriad manifestations of particular forms of sin, particular forms of domination. They contend that this unmasking is necessary given the collective nature of sin. Our participation in structures of oppression is largely unconscious. Our complicity is unwitting and naive. The task of liberation theology is to break the facade of innocence and expose the impact of our social system.   (in Welch 1985: 49)

This passage emphasises an understanding that 'sin' is neither transhistorical nor necessary, but is contingent on the particular belief systems of people within any culture. Further, this position implies that structural oppression can only be redressed through dual acts of developing consciousness and conscience, an imperative which echoes Freire's notion of *conscientizacao* introduced in *Pedagogy of the Oppressed* (1970: 19).

Dorothee Soelle is a German writer in liberation theology who links spiritual issues with the material conditions of people's lives. She has worked for a number of years in Latin America and argues that:

> Christianity exists for slaves. It is the religion of the oppressed, of those marked by affliction. It concerns itself with their needs. People are pronounced blessed not because of their achievements or their behavior, but with regard to their needs. Blessed are the poor, the suffering, the persecuted, the hungry.   (1975: 159)

The implications for teachers are profound. Within such a specific needs-oriented framework academic achievements and well-managed behaviour can no longer be the singular goal of schools. Instead, students are worthy not because of their 'excellence' but in relation to their particular needs. Love, then, becomes a crucial component to such a needs orientation to worthiness. Love in this context is taken to be related to the alleviation of suffering rather than a way of determining how suffering originates. Furthermore this kind of love is directed to specific social goals and agendas. Soelle continues:

> Love does not cause suffering or produce it, though it must necessarily seek confrontation, since its most important concern is not the avoidance of suffering but the liberation of people. The more we love, the more people in whom we take an interest, the more closely we are bound to them, the more likely it is we get into difficulties and experience pain. . . . The hope for a better future must be firmly established in the present, as consolation for the people who are now suffering. God must also be thought of as present with those who are in misery, and thereby the truth even of love that has not yet achieved its goal remains certain.   (1975: 164)

While generally suspicious of a discourse for education which values love as a goal and guiding principle, I am encouraged that writing in liberation-theology addresses love in a more critical sense than is presented in a lot of popular media. From a liberation-theology position, expressions of love are never necessarily 'good'. Expressions of love must be challenged and open to rigorous critique. This assumes that expressions of 'love' are no more exempt from critical challenge than any other human construction and can create a range of oppressing or silencing experiences. Phylis Trible provides a particularly rigorous critique of biblical portrayals of violent and unjustifiable 'love' in her 1984 work *Texts of Terror*.

Sharon Welch's *Communities of Resistance and Solidarity: A Feminist Theology of Liberation* is an example of work in liberation theology which is particularly indebted to postmodern thinking in its presentation of forms of social praxis. Welch uses the work of Foucault to criticise modernist perspectives of the self as related to meaning and suffering. Her work is also suspicious of postmodernist critiques which do not lead to people coming to greater understandings of their own subject positions in relation to their particular social contexts. She states:

> These analyses 'dissolve' human being; they do not find in human being the foundation of meaning and representation, for what it means to be human is itself a particular, contingent 'effect of truth,' the creation of networks of power and knowledge. (1985: 12)

These are only a sample of a variety of narratives which might provide critical spaces for teachers and students in local communities. These critical spaces have grown out of the dynamic traditions of liberation theology and can connect students' desires for non-sentimental hopefulness with possibilities of social action. Because of the dual acknowledgement of the spiritual and the material, these traditions are particularly appropriate to postmodern approaches to values education.

## Conclusions

Postmodern practices and critiques in educational settings will continue to grow and develop. As we conceive and enact these postmodern pedagogies within our teaching practices we must challenge our own education attitudes. We must examine the extent to which these perspectives collude with disempowering, alienating and silencing practices or lead to more desirable social outcomes. Students and teachers alike are then set with the tasks of responsibly creating the liberating and democratic relationships they envision. Only by questioning and challenging our moral assumptions can we judge the value of postmodern perspectives in values education.

If such awareness causes us to question the kinds of critique we use in our work, then I am encour-

aged. Such critical work demands that we ask a range of questions. For instance:

How readily will we accept and incorporate managerial, corporate and economic rationalist discourses in our educational communities? What other kinds of discourse do we bring into our work? Are they primarily modernist and totalising? Whose voices are privileged within these discourses and whose voices are silenced? Are there other important discourses we could bring into our educational work and how do we choose these?

We know that education managers frequently make decisions based on economically rationalised 'bottom lines' rather than on the needs of students. This is consistent with the ongoing corporatisation of schools and is one of the educational by-products of 'globalisation'. These practices are contracting the opportunities teachers have with their students towards greater understanding of the political and moral structuring of society. As these opportunities contract we run the risk of leading students into the world without the ability to situate themselves, to identify themselves, as responsible and aware global citizens.

In the most extreme case we can use the incredibly rich and diverse body of theoretical work which falls under the category of postmodernism to chronicle the decline of human civilisation on our planet. Or, we can engage in particular postmodern discourses in ways which will allow us to become more keenly aware of our deepest moral convictions and how these convictions might be brought into transformative action towards a viable and sustainable future which values the presence and contributions of its citizens in ways we have yet to experience. It may well be that by connecting a number of carefully chosen elements of spiritual and moral discourses and certain religious traditions with some of the alienating and anchorless postmodern thinking which currently abounds, our students and ourselves might stand in a much-improved position of turning such socially emancipatory visions into reality.

A great strength of critical postmodern perspectives is that from their outset such perspectives are wrestling with issues of belief and personal subjective positions as they are related to, or inscribed within, particular social discourses and practices. Any postmodern discourse which somehow separates practices related to the material conditions of people's lives from discourses or texts which are put to the deconstructionist scalpel can only lead to a dangerous nihilism which is no less alienating than certain totalising modernist frameworks. Perspectives from liberation theology may well serve to remind us in our educational practices of the connections between the material conditions of people's lives and the discourses of their cultural and political environment. It is our duty to attend to the struggles and experiences of our students – the weakest and most vulnerable partners in education activity, and those for whom dispossession and marginalisation is a growing international reality.

# References

Apple, M. (1982) *Education and Power*, Boston, Mass: Routledge & Kegan Paul.

Berger, P. L. and Luckman, T. (1966) *The Social Construction of Reality*, New York: Anchor Books.

Daly, M. (1973) *God the Father: Towards a Philosophy of Women's Liberation*, Boston: Beacon Press.

Eagleton, T. (1991) *Ideology: An Introduction*, London: Verso.

Foucault, M. (1977) *Discipline and Punish: The Birth of the Prison*, trans. A. Sheridan, London: Allen Lane.

Freire, P. (1970) *Pedagogy of the Oppressed*, trans., M. B. Ramos, New York: Continuum Publishing Corporation.

Giroux, H. A. (1990) 'Rethinking the Boundaries of Educational Discourse: Modernism, Postmodernism, and Feminism', *College Literature*, 17: 2/3.

Habermas, J. (1984) *The Theory of Communicative Action, Vol. 1*, trans. T. McCarthy, Boston: Beacon Press.

Kanpol, B. (1994) *Critical Pedagogy: An Introduction*, London: Bergin & Garvey.

Kinchloe, J. (1993) *Toward a Critical Politics of Teacher Thinking: Mapping the Postmodern*, London: Bergin & Garvey.

Lather, P. (1991) *Getting Smart: Feminist Research and Pedagogy With/in the Postmodern*, London: Routledge, pp. 1–18.

Lyotard, J-F. (1988) 'A Memorial to Marxism', for Pierre Souyri, *Peregrinations: Law, Form, Event*, New York: Columbia University Press.

McLaren, P. (1993) 'Multiculturalism and the Postmodern Critique: Towards a Pedagogy of Resistance and Transformation', *Cultural Studies*, 7.1.

McLaren, P. (1994) 'Multiculturalism and the Postmodern Critique: Toward a Pedagogy of Resistance and Transformation', in H. A. Giroux and P. McLaren (eds) *Between Borders: Pedagogy and the Politics of Cultural Studies*, London: Routledge.

Norris, C. (1993) *The Truth About Postmodernism*, Oxford: Blackwell.

Papenek, V. (1995) *The Green Imperative: Ecology and Ethics in Design and Architecture*, London: Thames & Hudson.

Rust, V. D. (1991) 'Postmodernism and its Comparative Education Implications', *Comparative Education Review*, 35.4 (Nov.).

Shapiro, S. (1995) 'Postmodernism and the Challenge to Critical Pedagogy', in P. McLaren (ed.) *Postmodernism, Postcolonialism and Pedagogy*, Albert Park, Australia: James Nicholas Publishers.

Soelle, D. (1975) *Suffering*, Philadelphia, PA: Fortress Press.

Taylor, P. V. (1993) *The Texts of Paulo Freire*, Buckingham: Open University Press.

Trible, P (1984) *Texts of Terror: Literary-Feminist Readings of Biblical Narratives*, Philadelphia, PA: Fortress Press.

Welch, S. D. (1985) *Communities of Resistance and Solidarity: A Feminist Theology of Liberation*, Maryknoll, NY: Orbis Books.

# 17 Authenticity, Teachers and the Future of Moral Education

JAMES C. CONROY AND ROBERT A. DAVIS

> If to do were as easy as to know what were good
> to do, chapels had been churches and poor
> men's cottages princes' palaces.
> (Shakespeare: Portia in *The Merchant of Venice*, Act
> 1 Scene 2)

It is axiomatic that if 'good' actions naturally flowed from the human encounter concerns about moral education would be redundant. It is equally clear that reflections on 'the good' are as important today as in the sixteenth century. For advanced industrial societies questions surrounding action and reflection have become increasingly vexed in recent times, the difficulties compounded by the disappearance of any clear moral narrative to which the many peoples and cultures inhabiting the same geographical and historical space can jointly subscribe. It is partly for this reason that the activity of an educational framework aimed at nurturing sympathetic and empathetic moral engagement has been placed under increasing strain by an alternative vision of educational purposes. Primary relationships are redefined in terms of globalised systems of exchange and control which banish serious moral consideration of the 'other.'

In this chapter we trace the evolution and consequences of this process in three stages. We begin by reflecting on some of the conditions which have given rise to and sustain this model of exchange. We then explore the consequent displacement of authenticity as a central feature of contemporary moral life. We conclude by discussing the connection between the recovery of authenticity and the cultivation of moral feeling.

Questions as to the nature of the good are rendered ever more complicated by the regular and simplistic insistence on the part of many of those who exercise political and social power that moral reflection and action are actually quite straightforward.[1] In the modern democratic utopia, personal morality and political economy, it is argued, are to all intents and purposes discrete domains.[2] The individual lives in a privatised and atomised world of moral action where the validity of moral choices is to be measured according to personal feeling, dispositions and attitudes,[3] with the only caveat that any consequent action does not obviously or overtly transgress the feelings, dispositions and attitudes of others. Such decisions themselves partake in no coherent personal narrative, but tend to be momentary, fragmentary and disconnected.

The engine of political economy, on the other hand, harnesses the immense social energies released by the personal autonomy generated by modern industrial society. Such political economy, however, is seen to possess no extrinsic moral character other than that yielded by the sum of the many private and individual transactions which constitute the life of the market in action. The belief that political economy can provide a communal moral nexus is hence very narrowly defined, restricted to a minimalist account of the ethical interactions and conventions required to ensure maximum efficiency in the trading of goods and services in the marketplace. In his analysis of the marketisation of the state, Pierre (1995: 67) suggests that the underlying purpose of recent politico-economic moves is to remove all barriers to the direct relationship between provider and consumer: 'The marketization of the state . . . means the depoliticization of the state (enabling) . . . citizens/customers to send signals to service suppliers without having to go through political channels.' Thus the market resists any more ambitious moral claims on the grounds that they might prove inimical to the functioning of its financial and incentive mechanisms and interfere with the free play of social exchange on which it depends.[4]

A further element in the current composite social reality is the illusion of 'majority' heteronomy. One of the most pervasive and pernicious manifestations of this syndrome is the drive towards moral populism – a trend which reaches its zenith in the phone-in poll and spurious dilemma industry promulgated by the mass media and supported by the increasingly 'interactive' potential of our information technologies. This has culminated in widely publicised television 'events' such as Carlton Television's monarchy debate[5] which prompted over 2 million responses.

Surveying this contemporary moral landscape, we can thus identify three conflicting forces shaping our lives and circumscribing our choices: personal autonomy in individual moral decision-making, the subordination of public morality to political economy, and the manipulation of public opinion by the appeal to a superficial populism (cf. Campbell 1993: 60–8). The social reality which emerges from this experience impacts dramatically on the ways in which key collective projects such as education can be carried out. For all three forces described above exhibit the singular absence of what has been the cornerstone of moral reflection across many cultures[6] and throughout the Western tradition, and which remains central to moral dialogue in our schools: authenticity.

What do we mean by authenticity? Any usable definition of authenticity must include a recognition of it as a moral discourse, the salience of which is directed from the fullest possible comprehension of the self, to the fullest possible comprehension of the other. It is therefore immediately and categorically sequestered from all notions of subjectivism and relativism, because it compels us to attend ineluctably to its essentially *dialogic* character (cf. Taylor 1991: 32 ff.).

Authenticity is not merely concerned with 'me' and 'my dispositions'. For although these are forms of introspection which certainly betoken a self-validating sense of *sincerity*, sincerity itself ought to be clearly separated from authenticity. Jacob Golomb's analysis of Lionel Trilling's reflections on sincerity and authenticity provides an illuminating distinction, based on the perception of sincerity as congruence between an individual's avowals and their public actions (Golomb 1995: 8 ff.). Authenticity, by contrast, requires the individual constantly to renegotiate and recreate the self in ever changing contexts and ever shifting relationships. The obligation placed on the authentic self is to act out of an understanding and empathy with the other's needs and realities, and not simply from adherence to an inwardly constructed sense of principle. The teacher may avoid, for example, the discussion in class of particularly 'hard' issues (such as drug abuse) as a consequence of a deeply held and sincere belief that young children need to be protected from such realities. To do so is, however, inauthentic. It is a decision which may indeed protect the teacher but which does disservice to the children's moral education because it refuses to connect the lifeworld of the classroom to the needs of the children in the wider communities they inhabit.

A more contentious if no less important example is provided in a robust account of black masculinity by Sewell (1995: 21–41). In his fascinating and sometimes brutal study of the sexual politics in inner-city-school subculture, Sewell analyses the nature and power of sexually violent rap lyrics and their interplay with attitudes to schooling. Such discomfiting attitudes and their consequences are largely ignored in education and therefore go unchallenged by teachers in the school setting because acknowledgement carries the threat of chaos and disorder – or so the teachers believe. This ignores the existence of an already subsisting low-level threat which ensures significant dysfunctionality within parts of the educational system. In his conclusions, Sewell challenges educators and researchers to move beyond 'additive models of oppression and look at complex matrices of power relations, bringing together critical sociological and psychological frameworks. This will also mean schools giving up their coyness when it comes to looking at Black male sexuality' (ibid.: 41). This lack of authenticity is replicated at all levels of social exchange, no more visibly than in the relationship between the moral rhetoric of political economy and the moral task of the teacher (Carr 1996: 5).

While this account of authenticity is undoubtedly characterised by inwardness and self-determination it is an inwardness which recognises its interdependence and consequently seeks to deal with the other as one who influences and shapes radically the formation of our subjectivity. We define our identity always in dialogue with, sometimes in struggle against, the identities others want to recognise in us. As Taylor notes, 'The genesis of the human mind is in this sense not "monological," not something each accomplishes on his or her own, but dialogical' (1991: 33). The interplay of the classroom, by contrast, is too often a context in which the teacher acts as a 'soft relativist' (ibid.: 13 ff.), engaging in a subjectivism which – while appearing to root itself in interiority – is in fact narcissistic, embodying superficiality, absence of genuine dialogue and an inability to utilise the resources of the curriculum traditionally associated with the promotion of authenticity in, for example, language, arts and philosophy.

Here we begin the process of rehabilitating a hermeneutic of authenticity which confronts some of the key concerns raised by the spectre of contemporary fragmentation, while at the same time avoiding the moral paralysis associated with postmodern relativism. In attempting this, we draw on the insights of just-community schools as one means of re-imaging the classroom as a site of organic community.[7] This implies challenging the current ossification of much contemporary moral discourse and the contrived artifice of putatively mutually agreed roles and boundaries – not only between persons, but also in the very structure of the curriculum.

The structure of British schooling and the image of childhood upon which it is predicated have largely failed to recognise the vast changes which have occurred in childhood thought and language. Much of current moral discourse rests on models of the child and models of virtue which have not taken and cannot take proper account of the impact of cultural and technological change on the management of knowledge, power and the community.[8]

When we juxtapose the hallmarks, or cultural indices, of the past with those of the present we end up with two very different languages which have had a profound shaping impact on the structure of learning, and consequently on moral development. These are by no means definitive or wholly differential categories, but rather an indicative taxonomy of social and cultural change. In sketching such differences there is no desire to valorise uncritically the past and/or denigrate the present but, in the first instance, the intention only to plot linguistic changes as a prolegomenon to discussing some possible moral responses to cultural change.

| *PAST* | *PRESENT* |
| --- | --- |
| Organic communities | temporary, fragmented, goal-oriented liaisons |
| consensus (eco/social) | special/sectional interests |
| cultural particularity | multiculturalism/pluralism |
| cultural hegemony | cultural heteronomy |
| hierarchy of power and knowledge | 'democratic' access |
| involvement | isolation |
| collective | individual |
| relationship | networks |
| duties | rights |
| deferral | immediacy |
| service | enterprise |
| market-as-means | market-as-end |
| knowledge/skill | information |
| reason | nihilism |
| moral command culture | subversion |
| virtue | pragmatism |
| lifeworld patterns | life-world insecurity |

The dialectic of past and present represented in these two columns is now deeply embedded in current critiques of the project of neo-liberal or laissez-faire economics and the social practices which underpin it. From *fin-de-siècle* doom-mongers to the intellectual histories advanced by thinkers such as Isaiah Berlin (1996) and the late Christopher Lasch (1995a), it has become axiomatic to assert that the transformations of the late-capitalist administrative state and the emergence of complex structures of narcissistic consumerist individualism mark the postmodern condition as a decisive break with the assumptions of the Enlightenment.

Lasch's claim that the chief victims of the shift represented in our two columns have been traditional moral communities such as the family and the school house deserves special attention by virtue of its originality and subtlety of thought. Like Oakeshott's (Oakeshott and Fuller (eds) 1996) before him or John Gray's (1996) after, Lasch's analysis resists appropriation by either conservatives or liberals, the twin adversaries who have disputed this territory most vociferously. For conservative moral thinkers who demand a restoration of the full moral competence of traditional social institutions, there is small comfort in an argument which identifies the relentless forces of free-market capitalism as the principal destabilising influence unravelling the customary ties of family, profession, neighbourhood and school.[9] Equally, there is only anxiety for the liberal optimist, wedded to the ideology of progress and the march of individual rights, who learns that the fragile principles of liberal rationalism survive almost parasitically on those older forms of social life and civic virtue which liberal theory either ignores or downgrades in the name of freedom.[10] The school, for example, whether negatively conceived by liberal theory as a contingent social unit colluding with the mechanistic processes of socialisation, or positively, as a state institution expressly focused on engineering egalitarian outcomes, cannot either way be accorded the independent moral weight which accrues to authentic communities through the human investment of time, custom and convention.

To overcome this impasse in a manner which establishes real commerce between the characteristic forms of past and present, while resisting the fragmentary sensations and meretricious superficiality of postmodernism, Lasch and his disciples propose an ethics of *hope* (Lasch 1995b). Hope is to be distinguished from progressivism principally in its moral scepticism and recognition of limits. Unlike liberal progressivism, hope is a virtue securely anchored to the historic experience of a people and the forms of life and community emergent from that experience – particularly the family, the neighbourhood, the school, the trade or profession, the voluntary association, the church. Its roots are local and ancient, its aspirations reasonable, its judgements balanced. Moral dialogue evolves in this kind of community from the bottom up, and not from the top down, which is another key feature of moral authenticity across cultures.

It is noteworthy that in many Western societies, where the process of modernisation has effaced traditional bonds of home and community, it is in the experience of immigrant and ethnic minority cultures that the continuing reality of rootedness and collective identity is frequently most visible. Faced with the dominant 'monologic' discourse of often hostile majority cultures, ethnic minorities define themselves, and create a validating matrix of socialisation, by reliance upon precisely those features of local organisation and coherence which many social commentators wish to see revived throughout industrial society: religious affiliation, economic interdependence, informal welfarism and self-help, artistic celebration, extended family support. Undoubtedly, these networks and social patterns do not endure unchanged in the context of advanced industrial democracies. Indeed, there is ample evidence of their systematic erosion by the moral and economic forces at work in a pluralist society geared to permanent change. Nevertheless, the creation of a climate of authenticity in the moral

exchanges between peoples, and in the complex interactive environments of schools, obliges us to enfranchise a more subtle and nuanced language which empowers the individual and the group to create and recreate, as well as describe their living experience. In his study of the essentially dialogic character of identity formation, Sampson points out that these communities recognise implicitly that identity is in large part a function of communal talk. 'The other is a vital co-creator of our mind, our self and our society. Without the other we are mindless, selfless and societyless . . .' (Sampson 1993: 109). Consequently it is impossible to conceive of communities emerging by edict!

Nowhere is the need for this more evident than in the contemporary school, which in recent times has seen its primary responsibility to the wider community redefined almost exclusively in terms of instrumental accountability.[11] Hence governments insist upon measurements of school effectiveness which rely on subordinate categories of what is to count as a good school: league tables, truancy rates, bullying figures and so on. Schools are in danger of becoming institutions driven by measurements rather than by hope.

This last observation serves to illustrate how Lasch's moral populism furnishes itself as a powerful rejoinder to the intellectual fashions of communitananism.[12] In his later works, Lasch makes clear that the moral vision of authentic communities is founded upon specific and stable forms of material production, and the social relations between groups and individuals which develop out of these forms. Contemporary communitarianism frequently appears to derive from no particular material production, no class of people, and no way of making a living. Hence the sometimes crippling nostalgia with which it describes an arcadian past, in a range of endeavours from architecture to education (Lasch 1995b: 112–35). Hence, also, its regular resort to statist prescriptivism, and its top-down rhetoric. The failure of communitarians so far to address and make sense of real communities is largely the consequence of an academic movement possessing no 'lived' organic base, reliant, instead, upon an appeal to the fears postmodernism evokes in certain elements of the cultural elite and in the wider civil polity.

The gap between the virtual lifeworlds posited by the communitarians and the *felt*, authentic experience of genuine moral communities can be discerned in the imagined locations and recaptured *zeitgeist* of David Guterson's novel *Snow Falling on*

*Cedars* (1995). Part of the appeal of this narrative lies in its evocation of an authentic moral community striving to heal and make sense of divisions which menace its coherence and identity. The values and insights of imaginative writing, of *story*, press themselves urgently on to our deliberations when given such moral and imaginative form. *Snow Falling on Cedars* exhibits a moral intelligence beguiled by neither the politics of nostalgia nor the postmodern irony which places the supremacy of individual desire over personal and collective morality. Guterson is therefore able to carry us to the centre of at least one vital truth in the search for moral communities which is too frequently elided in the manifestos of communitarians: *ambiguity.*

The community of the small 1950s Pacific Northwest island Guterson delineates possesses coherence, continuity and identity. The death of a young fisherman, however, apparently murdered by a Japanese-American interned in the recent war, exposes the complex local and particular interactions – many of them coercive and unjust – which lie beneath seemingly organic continuities of time and place. The lifeworlds of two peoples claustrophobically interlocked on one small island are exposed, as is the intricate series of exchanges and negotiations by which these lifeworlds establish links within and between themselves, and generate a shared civil polity in which the experience of individual meaning and choice is vouchsafed (cf. Kahn 1995).

Guterson's novel reveals that in crisis a community's true and ambiguous nature is exposed. This does not result in the simplistic exposure of hollowness and hypocrisy – though elements of each of these may be present. Rather, it issues in a moving and authentic sense of human encounter, marked intermittently by misunderstanding, suspicion and prejudice, but leading also to compassion and love. Behind any real or imagined vision of a community, Guterson suggests, lies an ambiguous contact zone remote from liberal contractual theory, where smaller, more local, provisional and fissiparous groupings constantly renegotiate the terms of their shared existence in a dialogue that is at once painful and tender, and from out of the material and moral conditions of which emerges a functioning context for the shaping of the human person.[13]

Returning to the classroom with the insights gleaned from Guterson, we are able to recognise the continuing influence of those subsisting tensions between old and new, established and innovatory. Indeed, just as the novel discloses racial and cultural tensions which subsist in that community as a necessary precondition of accommodation and ultimately reconciliation, so the school must do likewise in respect of its own processes and procedures. Ideally, classrooms evolve as organic forms; good teachers nurture a living, hope-filled reality rooted in notions of justice which moves beyond its own confines to inform the life of the school. This in its own turn affects the community in which the school is located, contributing to the moral fabric and plurality of discourses which constitute its being. It is therefore not government's role to *prescribe* a moral curriculum but to create the conditions which optimise the potential for human flourishing. However, politicians are apt to confuse their role here and valorise a moral prescriptivism at the expense of creating optimum conditions. When they do so it is almost inevitable that the values of the dominant culture (usually the politicians' own) are privileged at the expense of other important cultural influences in the life of the school.[14]

We nevertheless need to acknowledge that much of the *classroom's* actual moral discourse remains predicated on the assumptions of the older elements within the taxonomy we have outlined above. Given that these elements no longer obtain in their historic forms, the question arises as to how we create opportunities for moral growth in our classrooms which recognise – without uncritically embracing – the cultural changes that have taken place? Can we go back or re-establish a meaningful commerce between the insights and understandings of the older model, with all of its paradoxes, and the challenges of the new? Can our present moral discourse be nourished by some of the language of the older model while at the same time being aware of at least some of the hypocrisy, delusion and confusion embedded in it – not least its limited understanding of human freedom and its lack of multicultural awareness?

One pathway worth exploring is the development of a pedagogy rooted in the rediscovery of the poetic and imaginative spirit (Norton 1996) as it manifests itself in a range of cultures, and the consequent drive to mature moral understanding through attending to and living with *ambiguity.* In this approach can be found the seeds of wisdom, and indeed we believe that the present moment of multicultural encounter holds real opportunities for moral growth. Structurally, these are only sustainable if we are prepared to modify our allegiance to a conception of curriculum and indeed of knowledge rooted in British empiricism. The provision of such a rethought curricular framework underpins all our endeavours to understand what an authentic moral engagement between teacher and student might look like.

In the current climate, curriculum development and construction is characterised by skills and outcomes which are manifestly to do with behaviours and external responses.[15] It concerns itself increasingly with the demonstration of *competence*. At its crudest this practice aims to produce citizens who can deliver to, and on behalf of, society uses of language and mathematical skills which are almost entirely instrumental, in the support of means of production which are themselves widely perceived to be temporary and transient. In Britain, public rhetoric unashamedly promotes education as an integral part of the industrial infrastructure,[16] even when the traditional validating patterns of that industrial infrastructure are in flux. It was once understandable – if not exactly commendable – that such a close link be made when clear continuities existed between education and work. In a globalised economy, which no longer sustains these links, it is neither understandable nor rational. Once again, in Britain the service rendered by educational enterprise to the industrial superstructure has culminated in the merger of the state departments for education and industry.

Curriculum policy in Britain similarly shows widespread evidence of having been colonised by a mode of perception which privileges the apparent skills needs of the industrial complex. In the curriculum framework for students aged 5–14 in the Scottish educational system, for example, the structure of the English-language guidelines document places an artificial emphasis on the development of language for vocational or 'life-skill' purposes, which are defined in terms seemingly incommensurate with the imaginative and creative potential of children's language use. This leads to a contrived separation of the 'strands' in reading and writing associated with personal and expressive language use from those identified with the expository and functional, driving a wedge, for example, between 'reading for information' and 'reading for enjoyment' (SOED 1991). In recent debates in Scotland over post-16 language teaching certain interested parties ('stakeholders', we might now

fashionably term them) went so far as to suggest that imaginative literature be withdrawn from the upper-school curriculum because of its irrelevance to the economy's putative training needs.[17]

In other, parallel developments within the post-16 Scottish curriculum, the mode of study formerly entitled 'religious and moral education' has recently been supplanted by 'religious, moral and philosophical studies' (HSDU 1996). *Prima facie* this seems to be a perfectly sensible innovation. On closer scrutiny, however, what may actually be occurring is the substitution of the creative, expressive and culturally reflective opportunities embodied in the synoptic study of religion by the skills-driven approach to knowledge. Many of the programmes planned to be on offer derive from older SCOTVEC components which have regarded philosophy as concerned with little more than training the mind in cognitive skills, with a consequential loss of attention to the centrality of the person. Philosophy is of course central to thinking about religious and cultural meanings. In this proposed model, however, it is in danger of being reduced to a component in the operation of the economy.

None of the above is intended to imply that a functioning economy does not have legitimate claims on a publicly funded education system; it is rather to argue that such facile instrumentalism and reductionism necessarily undermines any and every attempt to establish a common morality. It is further to suggest that in so doing it undermines that which it purports to support. Indeed it is in these movements within curriculum planning that the flaws inherent in our earlier discussion about the role of morality in contemporary political economy become most apparent. Just as ethical considerations pertaining to the identity of the individual within the life of political economy are offered only in a truncated and debilitating form so too in recent curriculum construction the implied understanding of the person is diminished and mechanistic.

On the basis of the trends we have described, it is clear that the place of moral dialogue in the educational structures of late capitalist society is highly problematic. It is correspondingly unclear how the educational establishment can incarnate its rhetorical claims to be concerned with the whole person while constructing a curriculum almost exclusively driven by the instrumentalism (even to the principles underlying timetable construction) of our time. We shall demonstrate a little later that this instrumentalism has appropriated even the language and the forms of the poetic and the imaginative in an attempt to domesticate the feelings and sense which are their life blood (SOED 1991).

We do not believe that it is either possible or desirable to throw into reverse historical and social forces which have been unfolding irresistibly over several generations; to believe so is to fall prey to a moral and intellectual amnesia which would abolish rather than reinterpret modernity. Neither do we aim merely to ratify unquestioningly the rapid processes of change and dislocation represented in the postmodern condition. We seek instead to encourage in schools the establishment of a pattern of organised and just relationships which addresses not only the structures and management of schools but also the nature of the curriculum and its modes of delivery. Such a vision of schooling requires that the members of the community be drawn into a world where the transcendental imagination is seen as the principal means of entering into the life-worlds of others.

The realisation of such an aspiration begins in determining what is to be understood by the notion of childhood or studenthood in the postmodern experience, and in re-imaging what might be termed the *anthropology of learning* that arises out of this. Running through the operations of the economic and instrumental view of education adumbrated above lies a set of assumptions about the nature of childhood and the position of being a student in contemporary society.[18]

Clearly, to be a child continues to be seen in our society as being in some sense different from being an adult. Morally and psychodynamically, this difference can reasonably be expressed in the perception that a child, or indeed a student of any age, is in a state of *becoming* rather than a state of *being*. Children are *to become* adult; they are *to become* moral agents; they are *to become* effective contributors to the economic infrastructure. Always the assumption is that they have not yet *become* full contributing members of the common weal. As Matthews (1994) among others has demonstrated, such a view of childhood is untenable in terms of the potential contribution which very young children can make to this common social good.

This may be clearly seen in the type of situation where, for example, a small number of children aged between 10 and 13 become increasingly aware of the grief, tragedy and suffering caused by war in central Africa.[19] They decide in the course of a discussion (without any reference to any adult group

standing outside their own boundaries) to organise a number of charity events because they are so moved by such suffering. Their being moved does not represent an incomplete understanding of human tragedy, but is a fulsome though contextualised response to a situation where the content of their inner emotional lives resonates meaningfully and critically with their appreciation of, and engagement with, the external 'facts'. The contextualisation is provided by their geographical, personal-historical, and power locations in the world.

As Thomson (1986: 8 ff.) points out, there is a compelling requirement for us to acknowledge that our moral judgements originate outside intersubjective agreement. This strengthens the argument that even for young children moral reflection is rooted in the definition of what it is to be human. Such a conclusion is a long way from endorsing the view of Kohlberg and a number of his disciples that children's responses in the type of example cited above are 'sub-moral' or 'pre-moral'. Indeed, we would argue that what motivates their moral response is a recognition that *people matter* (cf. Rorty 1989: 189–98). This vital recognition derives immediately from the individual's personal sense that 'I matter' and the concomitant ability to transfer one's own feelings of 'mattering' to other persons. We shall return to the centrality of feelings to our thesis a little later.

As suggested earlier the linkages between self and other upon which the capacity for transference depends originate in the imagination. This is revealed in the examination of the children's innermost motives. When asked to explain their reasoning, the children in our example responded initially by simply suggesting that it was wrong for people to suffer. Probed further, they began to talk about what it might feel like to be in a similar situation. They can only make such comments because (a) they have felt the pain of hunger or illness in no matter how limited a way, and (b) they are able to deploy their analogical powers so as to know what it could be like to suffer substantially, even though they themselves are unlikely to have actually suffered pain in any manner remotely comparable.

This can be extended by attending to another scenario, in which a 4-year-old is watching the film about the life and death of Steve Biko in South Africa, *Cry Freedom*. Early in the movie there is a brutal depiction of the Sharpville school massacre. The small child sits quietly crying. His parent notices and asks if the child is all right; the child responds by asking, in a voice charged with incredulity and horror, Why are those men doing that? It's not fair.'[20]

What explanation are we to offer for such events? That these particular children are the products of a form of socialisation which enables them to cultivate their sense of empathy at an early age? Or that all human beings innately have such a sense? Either way, here at least there are some intimations of the principle of universalisability. It is noteworthy that even the most recent rigorously scientific and *evolutionary* accounts of human virtue recognise that the capacity for moral judgements and consequent behaviour is located in fundamental predispositions of human consciousness acquired in the process of natural selection and found across all cultures.[21] As Wilson has it, 'the moral sense must have adaptive value; if it did not, natural selection would have worked against people who had such useless traits as sympathy, self-control, or a desire for fairness and in favour of those with the opposite tendencies . . .' (Wilson 1995: 23).

Let us, for a moment, look at the converse and explore what happens when feelings are discounted. If a child were to watch the events of the Sharpville massacre and communicate that she felt nothing, we would be likely to think of her, and maybe even describe her, as 'a heartless little brute'. Worse still, were she to sit laughing and claim to be enjoying the suffering depicted we would think her inhuman. In either event, we would be likely to suggest that she was 'unfeeling'. Clearly, used in this way 'feeling' and 'unfeeling' carry moral overtones. We do not dissociate feelings from actions. We regard some feelings as appropriate and others as inappropriate whether or not they lead to specified and entirely congruent action. It is not simply a matter of publicly displaying feelings. Camus' Mersault in *L'Etranger* (1992) makes us wary of suggesting that in the education of feelings it is all show.[22] What the reader of Camus' text recognises, but the players fail to see, is that Mersault does display sensitivity and integrity in relation to the world in which he finds himself. None the less it is precisely here that we have the key to the inclusion of feeling as a central feature in the moral curriculum.

In her essay, 'The Objection to Systematic Humbug' (1981), Mary Midgley effectively critiques Stuart Hampshire, among others, for suggesting that feelings are at best parasitical on external actions and at worst unimportant in moral life. She charges him with having too limiting a notion of what it is to be a human being engaged in the world of lived experience. Hampshire's error has its roots in yet another core Enlightenment belief – that the application of the processes of rationality always leads to the appropriate action. This finds its fullest expression in Ryle's (1993) condemnation of the 'ghost in the machine' kind of philosophy, and of course Ryle would be right if one were to assume some kind of correspondence between particular feelings and their consequent actions. To limit feelings in such a way is fundamentally to misunderstand their complexity. Feelings derive from our experiences and shape our actions in a generic way.

By and large individuals do not have a single experience which gives rise to a particular feeling which, in turn, is incarnated in their day-to-day living; rather they come to their *modus operandi* gradually, drawing on and integrating whole sets of experiences. These families of experiences give rise to and interact with our feelings. Thus a given behaviour is shaped not by a particular individualised feeling but by the interplay between feelings, deductive reasoning and engagement, and ongoing experiences. When the 10-year-old 'feels' compassion as she watches the graphic pictures of destitution on her television screen and decides to do something about this state of affairs she is not responding to a singular, dislocated feeling. She is responding out of her total worldview.

In his reflections on the massacre of the Tutsi population by Hutus in Rwanda in 1995, Fergal Keane manages to point us to one of the ways in which we, *qua* human groupings, can visit the most hideous barbarities on each other. This is done, he suggests, by controlling and shaping the language by which we describe both ourselves and our relationships with others, so that the other is demonized and consequently dehumanised. The result is manifest not primarily in individual acts of butchery but in the totality of the self's disposition towards the other, an attitude which is learned and inculcated in the language used to describe the other. In retelling how a priest locked Tutsi children in a church at their own behest and of the priest's evident distress at the likelihood that they had already been murdered, Keane writes (1996: 232), 'And so I think to myself yet again. What kind of man can kill a child? A man not born to hate but who has learned hatred. A man like you and me.'

The fundamental belief that an individual

operates out of a worldview is intelligible only if the individual has a coherent, integrated and singular worldview, but we know that children in schools do not, any more than adults, operate out of such a platonically integrated worldview. Their feelings and their actions are demonstrably different from one context to another. The playground sees a largely different set of relationships and actions from the classroom; children 'feel' differently towards different people or even the same individual from one context to the next.

Thus it is that we return to the impact of postmodernity on the moral enterprise in the school or classroom situation. The feelings which children wish to give expression to or articulate in the classroom are often deemed by the teachers to be inappropriate. (We are using the word 'inappropriate' as it is commonly used by teachers and do not want to pursue what it might mean for a feeling to be inappropriate.) As we have argued in an earlier paper (Conroy and Davis 1994), children learn to play according to the rules of the game very quickly so that they can engage with the worlds in which they find themselves. They learn to avoid giving linguistic form to a range of feelings which will be deemed inappropriate since the teacher is ultimately the arbiter of the acceptable and the permissible.

The arrangement of the curriculum and the patterns of being and relating in the school freely employ the rhetoric of choice, of freedom, of authenticity, but they are, in fact, frequently artifice. This of course is an empirical point but one which is extremely important. We can take an example from outside the moral domain to illustrate this. In her study of PE teachers in an east-coast American school, Ennis (1995) recognises that the central difficulty in running an effective PE programme is the lack of student motivation. This lack of motivation she traces back to the absence of emotional support and a poor definition of common goals. The students were not involved in curricular decision-making and the programme, with the exception of basketball, reflected white, male, middle-class preoccupations with using sporting encounters to clinch deals. Not surprisingly many of the students felt alienated from this process but, more importantly, teachers placed the responsibility for non-participation with the students. Ennis regards the teachers as having deflected the problems of motivation and insulated themselves from accountability for designing and teaching a meaningful curriculum. A different perspective on the same thing may lead us to say that problems of real engagement are a derivative of the failure to attend to the actual attitudes of students towards their place in the school enterprise, and their feelings that the entire exercise is both futile and irrelevant.

So what then is meant by suggesting, as we do, that the construction of the curriculum is frequently artificial? In the Scottish elementary curriculum we have guidelines for expressive arts which embody a substantial set of outcomes under the heading 'Expressing feelings, ideas, thought and solutions' (SOED 1992). At Level D (for 11-year-olds) it is intended that pupils 'show attention to authenticity, based on personal observations of everyday situations' (ibid.: 3). What does 'authenticity' mean in such circumstances? Does it mean that children engaged in a role-play should use the language of the street? Will children be allowed to introduce such adjectival language? If a student responds to a particular stimulus in a manner not approved of by the teacher, will it be deemed to lack authenticity, or if it is thought to reflect an authentic but marginal viewpoint will it be ruled out of order? Indeed, is it possible for one to have an *authentic* role-play? (ibid: 178.) Given these and other questions, the point at issue is surely whether or not 'authenticity' is acceptable in one set of curricular or school relations and not in another. What is at stake here is the subjugation of feelings![23] Within contemporary curriculum development all is directed towards acquiring a set of appropriate and centrally approved feelings which will inevitably lead students to 'work co-operatively' (Kerr 1997). Ambiguity is eased out of the picture and the source of these denuded feelings is the thrust towards becoming more efficient members of society. The very attempt to reduce the expression of feelings to a curriculum outcome inevitably leads to its disengagement from the lifeworlds of the students it purports to serve.

It is here that we find the fullest incarnation of postmodernity, in which the traditionally valued qualities of depth, meaning, coherence and authenticity are evacuated or dissolved in the random deployment of empty signals. Consequently the process of curriculum planning recycles the images and ideas of the past but with attachment to neither their original meaning nor the existence of the pupils.

Let us return then to Guterson's novel to bring together the central claims of this chapter. In *Snow Falling On Cedars*, as we have suggested, what is at stake is not hypocrisy versus authenticity in any simple or purist way; rather the community is faced with two competing accounts of feelings, their moral and social import and what to do with them. One image is of feelings as things to be controlled and which have little or nothing to do with civic society; the other is where feelings constitute the very life blood of social action and interaction. They cannot be ignored or removed from the living context. To do so is to fall prey to the kind of post-Enlightenment solipsism which results in the claims of transactional analysts, among others, that my feelings are entirely private and that your actions have indeed nothing to do with them. Guterson's depiction of the dilemmas of intercultural communication also crystallises many of the issues facing postmodern, multiethnic societies (cf. Walzer 1997).

It is clear that:

1 'hope' in the sense understood by Lasch embodies the conjunction of feeling and rationality
2 feelings remain a constant in human relations
3 feelings are riven with ambiguity
4 the good society, post-Enlightenment, has to find ways of embodying such ambiguity without falling victim to its potential for moral paralysis
5 the good society which acknowledges the cultural, religious and social diversity of its members must seek harmony without uniformity.

The implication for such a position is that the classroom, indeed the school, has to provide the possibility of negotiating and renegotiating the ways in which our feelings are to be engaged in and by the moral discourse. Schools have to be permitted to begin with and return to the real lives of students, but through the development of the moral imagination need also to be constantly open to transcending their own limitations. And we, as teachers, must be prepared to follow where that enterprise leads.

*My Name is Asher Lev*, Potok's fascinating study of the tensions that exist between a traditional community and an artist's need to express the truth as he experiences it, provides us with some final insights into this dilemma. In the early part of the novel Asher Lev is seen to be a sensitive young man entirely immersed in American Jewry. The ongoing tension which exists in the relationship between the young artist and his father culminates in the cre-

ation of a painting depicting his mother stretched cruciform across the window of their New York apartment, her head in balanced segments; tormented she looks to the street below, to where Lev and his father stand on opposite sides of the window, he with his palette, his father with his brief case. It is a portrait rooted in profound anguish and despair, a painting which in the artist's own words is done

for the unspeakable mystery that brings good fathers and sons into the world and lets a mother watch them tear at each other's throats . . . For the Master of the Universe, whose suffering world I do not comprehend. For dreams of horror, for nights of waiting, for memories of death, for the love I have for you, for all the things I remember, and for all the things I should remember but have forgotten, for all these I created this painting – an observant Jew working on a crucifixion because there was no aesthetic mould in his own religious tradition into which he could pour a painting of ultimate anguish and torment. (Potok 1974: 277)

The narrative evokes the tension not only between the old and new but also between our liberal and conserving instincts. It is reflected more generally in our political, economic and social lives. Here we are collectively self-divided and thus prey to the Leviathan-like forces of global competition which press us into an ever-diminishing account of educational values. To reinvent our educational processes in ways which fit us for the future we must embrace ambiguity rather than suppress it. To stimulate an authentic moral dialogue with the next generation we must offer hope as well as technological achievement.

As we have attempted to demonstrate in this chapter, such hope must be rooted in an understanding of the politico-economic context; the range of cultures that comprise our educational life; the moral lives of the young and the relationships between feelings, understandings and actions.

## Notes

1 See p. 7 Susan Young, report in *Times Education Supplement Scotland* (12 July 1996) where she quotes Nick Tate, Chief Executive of the School Curriculum and Assessment Authority for England and Wales on their initiative for developing common values as saying that 'the intention is to provide a series of moral absolutes; things are wrong because they are rather than because of their consequences'.

2   For recent analyses of these arguments see Hutton 1996: 13–36 and Gray 1995 *passim*.

3   For a recent analysis of this trend as an unforeseen and unwitting consequence of the Kantian tradition see especially Berlin 1996: 176–9.

4   For a recent example see C. Barrie et al. 'The Day they Pull the Plug', *Guardian* 31 Dec. 1996 and ensuing correspondence in the *Guardian* 3 Jan. 1997. The article explores the nature and extent of moral responsibility which may be attached to electricity providers in a market environment.

5   This programme, entitled '*Monarchy: The Nation Decides*', was broadcast on Tuesday 7 Jan. 1997.

6   For a contemporary example see Pawar 1993: 99–110. There are of course many other examples in ancient collections such as E. Mellor, *Value of Friends: Jataka Tales*, USA: Dharma Publishing, 1990.

7   Accounts of the just community in philosophy abound. See for example Leming 1986: 247–50.

8   Cf. Postman 1985. Postman famously argues that the predatory intrusions of the mass media (especially television) into the patterns of family life have abolished the many traditional and validating boundaries between adulthood and childhood.

9   For a useful representative study of the moral and economic conservative envisaged here see Himmelfarb 1995. Himmelfarb wishes to restore a nineteenth-century social and political order based on stolid middle-class virtues rooted in a strong capitalist economy.

10  Rawls 1993: 48 ff. Rawls holds out hope that the well-ordered society of the present and the future will be rooted in and sustained by a 'reasonable' consensus. Such a consensus is only made possible, of course, by its attachment to older and more abstracted notions of the relationship between reason and appropriate or indeed good behaviour.

11  This is evident in a wide range of reports emanating from central government and its agencies. See for example Nick Tate, "Two Worlds One Purpose", *Times Educational Supplement Scotland* 29 Nov. 1996, p. 49.

12  See as a currently popular advocate of the 'communitarian' ideal Etzioni 1995. It is worth noting that prior to Etzioni's appearance on the British political scene analyses of community regeneration and redefinition as *organically* rooted forms were being commented upon. See Sedgwick 1992: 61 ff.

13  Cf. Giroux and McLaren 1994 for a critical discussion of the politics of the local.

14  For a useful recent discussion of this in relation to decisions made by the then secretary of State for Education, John Patten, see Hayden 1997. Hayden points out that potency analysis of moral education fails to reflect the complexity of the plural cultures in which it is to be enacted.

15  A position adopted in even so influential a document as the CERI/OECD *Prepared for Life? How to Measure Cross-curricular Competencies*, Paris. OECD, 1997.

16  DFEE 1995. Cf. Geoffrey Holland, 'Education: A Marriage Toast', *Guardian* 18 July 1995.

17  Authors' private source.

18  For a recent discussion of changing representations of contemporary childhood and their impact on professional practice see Davis 1993: 117–39.

19  Example taken from authors' direct classroom experiences.

20  Example taken from authors' professional experience.

21  For a recent important discussion of this thesis see Ridley 1996.

22  In his recent work on literary theory Stanley Cavell applies similar criteria to the representation of authentic self-definition in a literary text. The actions of fictional characters command our attention insofar as they partake of authentic ontologies of feeling, for these are the essence of freedom. Cf. Cavell 1995.

23  For a valuable discussion of feelings as the originating power of moral and theological reflection see Kerr 1997.

# References

Berlin, I. (1996) 'The Romantic Evolution: A Crisis in the History of Modern Thought', in *The Sense of Reality: Studies in Ideas and Their History*, London: Chatto & Windus.

Campbell, B. (1993) *Goliath: Britain's Dangerous Places*, London: Methuen.

Camus, A. (1992) *The Outsider* (*L'Etranger*), London: Hamish Hamilton.

Cavell, S. (1995) *Philosophical Passages: Wittgenstein, Emerson, Austin, Derrida*, Oxford: Blackwell.

Carr, D. (1996) *The Moral Role of the Teacher*, Dundee: Consultative Council on the Curriculum.

Conroy, J. and Davis, R. (1994) 'Meaning and Value: An Exploration of the Dialogics of the Classroom', unpub. paper delivered at the Association for Moral Education, Banff, Alberta.

Davis, R. A. (1993) 'Some Themes in the Representation of Childhood', in P. Donnelly (ed.) *Excellence in Training: Proceedings of the Dundee Childhood Conference*, Ithaca, NY: Cornell University Press.

DFEE (1995) *Comparison of the Estimated Demand for Skilled Employees and Skilled Supply from FE Sector*, London: DFEE.

Ennis, C. D. (1995) 'Teachers' Responses to Noncompliant Students: The Realities and Consequences of a Negotiated Curriculum', *Teaching and Teacher Education*, 11.5: 445–60.

Etzioni, E. (1995) *Spirit of Community: Rights, Responsibilities and the Communitarian Agenda*, London: Fontana.

Giroux, H. and McLaren, P. (1994) *Between Borders: Pedagogy and the Politics of Cultural Studies*, London: Routledge.

Golomb, J. (1995) *In Search of Authenticity: From Kierkegaard to Camus*, London: Routledge.

Gray, J. (1995) *Enlightenment's Wake: Politics and Culture at the Close of the Modern Age*, London: Routledge.

Gray, J. (1996) *After Social Democracy: Politics, Capitalism and the Common Life*, London: Demos.

Guterson, D. (1995) *Snow Falling on Cedars*, London: Picador.

HSDU (1996) *Arrangements for Religious, Moral and Philosophical Studies*, consultation document, Edinburgh: Higher Still Development Unit, Scottish SCC.

Himmelfarb, G. (1995) *The De-Moralization of Society: From Victorian Virtues to Modern Values*, London: IEA Health and Welfare Unit.

Hayden, G. (1997) *Teaching About Values: A New Approach*, London: Cassells.

Hutton, W. (1996) *The State We are In*, London: Vintage.

Kahn, J. S. (1995) *Culture, Multiculture, Postculture*, London: Sage.

Keane, F. (1996) *Letter to Daniel: Despatches from the Heart*, Harmondsworth: Penguin.

Kerr, F. (1997) *Immortal Longings: Versions of Transcending Humanity*, London: Society for the Promotion of Christian Knowledge.

Lasch, C. (1995a) *The Revolt of the Elites and the Betrayal of Democracy*, New York: W. W. Norton.

Lasch, C. (1995b) *Haven in a Heartless World: The Family Besieged*, New York: W. W. Norton.

Leming, J. (1986) 'Kohlbergian Programmes in Moral Education: A Practical Review and Assessment', in S. Modgil and C. Modgil (eds) *Lawrence Kohlberg: Consensus and Controversy*, London: Falmer Press.

Matthew, G. B. (1994) *Philosophy of Childhood*, Cambridge, MA: Harvard University Press.

Midgely, M. (1981) 'The Objection to Systematic Humbug', in *Heart and Mind*, London: Methuen.

Norton, D. D. (1996) *Imagination, Understanding and the Virtue of Liberality*, Lanham, NJ: Rowman & Littlefield.

Oakeshott, M. and Fuller, T. (eds) (1996) *Politics of Faith and the Politics of Scepticism: Selected Writings of Michael Oakeshott*, New Haven: Yale University Press.

Pawar, U. (1993) 'Justice', in G. Dharmarajan (ed.) *Separate Journeys*, London: Mantra Press.

Pierre, J. (1995) 'The Marketization of the State: Citizens and the Emergence of the Public Market', in B. G. Peters and D. J. Savoie (eds), *Governance in a Changing Environment*, Montreal: McGill-Queen's University Press.

Postman, N. (1985) *The Disappearance of Childhood*, London: W. H. Allen.

Rawls, J. (1993) *Political Liberalism*, New York: Columbia University Press.

Ridley, M. (1996) *The Origins of Virtue*, London: Viking.

Rorty, R. (1989) *Contingency, Irony and Solidarity*, Cambridge: Cambridge University Press.

Ryle, G. (1993) *Aspects of Mind*, ed. R. Meyer, Oxford: Blackwell.

Sampson, E. (1993) *Celebrating the Other*, Hemel Hempstead: Harvester Wheatsheaf.

Sedgwick, P. (1992) *The Enterprise Culture*, London: Society for Promoting Christian Knowledge.

Sewell, T. (1995) 'A Phallic Response to Schooling: Black Masculinity and Race in the Inner City Comprehensive', in M. Griffiths and B. Troyna (eds) *Antiracism, Culture and Social Justice in Education*, Stoke on Trent: Trentham.

SOED (1991) *Curriculum and Assessment in Scotland: National Guidelines: English Language 5–14*, Edinburgh: Scottish Office Education Department.

SOED (1992) *Curriculum and Assessment in Scotland: National Guidelines: Expressive Arts 5–14*, London: HMSO.

Taylor, C. (1991) *The Ethics of Authenticity*, Cambridge, MA: Harvard University Press.

Thomson, A. (1996) *The Growth of Moral Understanding*, MOSAIC Monograph 6, Bath: University of Bath Press.

Walzer, M. (1997) *On Toleration*, New Haven: Yale University Press.

Wilson, J. Q. (1995) *The Moral Sense*, New York: Free Press.

# 18 "E Pluribus Unum": American Educational Values and the Struggle for Cultural Identity

CHRISTOPHER R. L. BLAKE AND JAMES B. BINKO

The epithet *E Pluribus Unum* ("one, from many"), minted on the nation's currency, is a signpost to the American Dream of unity from diversity. The same hope also underpins much talk in the USA currently surrounding values in education. A groundswell of public desire is discernible for American society to cohere around common, core values that will bring consensus of ideas and actions, rather than the cultural fragmentation and diversification that is perceived as prevalent. One main stage on which this play is now being enacted is that of the public school system.

This is intriguing in itself. On face value one might surmise that since religious education has never featured in the public school system, on the basis of the constitutional separation of religion and state, so schools would avoid getting entangled in the risky business of social values and morals. But such is not the case. Currently from conservative and liberal voices, public organizations, individual citizens, the popular media and civic institutions, comes a united call for school action in the moral domain, and a strident claim that education should be leading the way in reforming the hearts, minds and lifestyles of today's youth (Bloom 1987, Bennett 1995, Wynne and Ryan 1997).

The response of the education system to this "hot" issue has, however, been uncertain and tentative. Lickona (1992) notes that the summons to education has been initiated from outside the school walls, and has been borne from broad public perception of societal and individual decline, for which schools are being required to provide suitable correctives. This post-Deweyan idea of school accountability has often left the teaching profession in America feeling ill-prepared and uneasy. Instead of leading the debate on societal values and their relationship to education, the teaching profession

has found itself frequently listening and reacting to the rhetoric and ideas of others (Coles 1997). We were starkly reminded of this by a teacher-educator colleague and former school principal, who remarked despondently that "there aren't any values left in American education, at least none that could be called educational."

This skepticism exemplifies the problematic nature of values education in the USA, where even the term itself is confusingly synonymous with character education, values clarification, moral education, citizenship education and other titles used in recent years (Harmin 1988, Lawton 1995). The constitutional divide between religion and state has reinforced for several decades an uncertainty within the public school system regarding the place of morality in education. Coupled to this is now an increased sense of substantive and accelerating changes in cultural reality, a rush toward what Kincheloe (1993) calls "postmodern hyperreality," that have thrown into doubt many of education's "sacred cows" and challenged American certainties about educational priorities.

In this chapter we shall engage with the current values education debate in the USA from a position that shares much with reconstructionist and critical theory (Gutek 1984, Giroux and McLaren (eds) 1989, Kanpol 1994, Sleeter and McLaren (eds) 1995). In so doing our goal is to affirm the primacy of pedagogy within any discussion of values in schools, and also to recognize the culturally-laden discourse of values education. By this we mean that honest discussion of values education is sterile and counter-productive without robust reflection on the potential of teachers and their host institutions, schools, as change-agents, and that the search for values education is ultimately part of a broader discourse of cultural conflict and growth (Hunter

1991). For our basic contention is that values in education are not simple, objective cultural artefacts, providing curricular paradigms or inputs for schools that assemble, as Lawton (1989) puts it, "a selection from culture." Instead, we propose that values are basic, necessary qualities of human growth, and are existentially forged within the ambiguities and conflicts of societal living, of which schooling provides a paramount example (Hirsch 1987, Goodlad et al. (eds) 1990).

Our prognosis is, we hope, far from gloomy. In what follows we shall attempt to show that values education can exemplify key enduring qualities, both contentious and successful, of American historical democracy. Moreover, it embodies the same tensions between cultural consensus and diversification that have repeatedly characterized American life and its institutions, and have been a source of tension and creativity within those institutions. This is not a glib or simplistic outlook. Indeed, the kind of values education that is desirable in the USA should be creatively contentious and dialectical, on the "cutting edge" of complex and sustained debate about the optimal ways for free individuals and institutions to grow in thought and action within a pluralist, developing democracy. Any form of values education that fails to engage in such a creative enterprise would either be unworthy of attention, or, more dangerous still, serve ulterior purposes of ideology and social manipulation that are anathema to the moral precepts of both education and democracy.

In what follows we shall sketch a general overview, since that large picture gives context and meaning to the current state of American values education. Furthermore, our panorama is intended as a corrective to the myopia and relativism that characterises much contemporary discussion about morality and education. Put simply, we feel that many of the lessons of history and legacies of tradition are in danger of being sidelined in an emotive clamour for simple institutional solutions in the perilous field of morality.

Our analysis and argument follows three paths, leading to a rationale for values education. The first sets out an historic relationship between culture, values and education that has been intrinsic to the public education system of the USA since its birth (Goodlad et al. (eds) 1990). The second offers a brief case study of one major initiative currently in values education, that of Baltimore County in the state of Maryland. We are fortunate in being close

to this initiative, allowing us insight into problems and possibilities of values education that are sometimes oversimplified in the public debate. And lastly, we set out a philosophical position on values education, seeing it as one vital voice in the discourse of cultural studies, highlighting the awkward conjunction between education and culture. To establish that argument, we need to consider first what we can learn from history.

## Values and American education: a historical perspective

An understanding of both the context and current state of values education needs to begin by recognizing the historic reliance of American education on certain perennial values and practices that have immeasurably shaped its unique development (Gutek 1991, Rippa, 1992). The thread that unites these and has characterized the development of the USA is unparalleled cultural diversity (Takaki 1993).

Without this perspective the current values-education movement makes little sense. One main weakness in the ideas of those who currently perceive a social crisis and demand school action through values education against such a crisis is an oversight of this historical legacy. Sensationalized by the media and adopted by short-term political strategists as a popular motif, the public face of values education has often been that of a newly discovered first-aid to societal ills. This "apocalypse" mentality not only falls into the trap of historical relativism, but more importantly ignores the potential of values-oriented traditions that have successfully been nurtured for over two centuries in American education (Jervis and Montag (eds) 1991). Those traditions, emerging within a context of cultural plurality, provide the essential backdrop to current thinking in values education. They can be described as frontier egalitarianism, pragmatic utilitarianism, participative democracy and citizenship, and secular morality.

These traditions were not, however, created from a homogeneous cultural experience in the new colonies, nor did they act initially in a monocultural fashion. Instead, the diversified experiences of the early settlers provided the basis for socio-economic growth and the governance of public life during the colonial era. Education, as an example of the latter, has since its roots in seventeenth-century

Massachusetts been subject to these dialectical tensions of contrary and competing cultural forces. Many of the early colonial experiences, in which educational tradition was encultured by specific priorities, have provided legacies that still resonate today (Tyack and Hansot 1990).

The colonial era saw at its base level the adaptation of diverse European heritages and worldviews to a new environment. In the New England colonies, the region that gave rise to public education, the dominance of Puritanism and traditions of shared, local governance sustained a principle of frontier egalitarianism. The most enduring outcome and example of this was the town school, with its common curriculum of reading, writing, arithmetic, catechism and religious singing. This landmark institution represented a shift away from the elitist and religiously oriented European antecedents and the beginnings of egalitarian views of social policy in the "New World" (Morrison 1956). The New England pattern, however, was not common elsewhere. The Mid-Atlantic experience of religious, cultural, and linguistic pluralism meant that education was initially marginalized to the private work of the various denominations, giving rise to the rapid growth of parochial and independent schools. In the South the trend was again different, based on its particular demographics and economics. Its rural vastness and disparate populations acted as a brake against the formation of a coherent educational system. For white landowners the use of private tutors was commonplace, at least until the use of Anglican boarding schools in the eighteenth century. For poor white labourers, and for the increasing slave populations, no formal education was provided, nor was it even permissible for the latter group (Anderson 1988).

Two legacies of importance in terms of educational values were left by the colonial period. First, the concept of education was based on popular diversity: education would mean different things to different people, not least in its available forms. Second, the variety of systemic *forms* did not mean a variety of systemic *functions*. In other words, education throughout the colonies shared a utilitarian function, remote from the lofty scholasticism of European heritage, and instead geared toward colonial survival and integrity, based on a new sense of egalitarian needs. Since the colonies were diverse, the necessary forms to attain such ends would also be diverse.

Systemic pluralism was adequate only in as far as the different colonial cultures retained introspective identities and aspirations. Once those had matured into aspiring to nationhood, the die was cast for a radical transformation of education. With the birth of the United States after the War of Independence, the urgent need to nurture a unified nation, with new cultural ramifications, meant that colonial antecedents in education gave way to a larger vision and plan. This vision proposed, in Ornstein's and Levine's (1997: 138) words:

> that education should prepare people for republican citizenship; should include the utilitarian and scientific emphases that would aid in developing a nation with vast expanses of frontier land and abundant natural resources; and should be divested of European cultural residues and create a uniquely American culture.

The education of the new republic was to embody more strongly than ever the principles of egalitarianism, utilitarianism, and civic democracy and participation. The form in which it did this was essentially the common school (Cremin 1951). The intention of its founder, Horace Mann, was explicitly to forge a link between public schooling and participative democracy. Like Webster and Jefferson before him, Mann perceived cultural pluralism, especially in the immigrant communities of the nineteenth century, as a threat to a unified nation (Messerli 1972). The common school, therefore, was the conduit both for promoting a sense of national identity and purpose and for realizing the goal of participative democracy, by placing its governance in the hands of the local public. And to seal its consensual, public nature, Mann protected the Common School from sectarian and church influence. Here was the cornerstone of an assimilationist society, in which the individual's cultural heritage was recast within the overarching context of the new American national identity. The self-labeling of groups today as Italian-American, African-American, Irish-American, etc. is testimony to the powerful effect of Mann's creation.

The moral basis to this model of schooling was fundamental. Although devoid of religious influence, the inculcation of character and virtue was axiomatic to the work of the Common School. Egalitarianism and civic duty could only be attained if certain values were popularly accepted, a fact fully recognized by the school leaders of the nineteenth century. The centrality of values in this respect was clear. The publication series known as the *McGuffey*

*Readers*, named after clergyman and educationalist William Holmes McGuffey (1800–1873), testifies to the importance of moral education in the emerging school experiment. Over 120 million editions of the *McGuffey Reader* were published across the States between 1836 and 1920, the largest circulation of any book in the world other than the Bible, thus ensuring the nurturing of certain values across several generations. McGuffey's message was ideal for the newly expanding republic, where individualism in the service of the greater good was prized above diversification and collectivism. Westerhoff (1978) notes that the *Readers* celebrated a protestant work ethic, and esteemed an Anglo-Saxon heritage that emphasized the individual's duty in moral virtue and patriotism.

Here the vision of cultural and moral conformity was at its zenith. American education was able to solidify its values basis around a specific nationalistic vision, secular in form but rooted in protestant, Anglo-Saxon traditions, and egalitarian in its privileging of conformity and disregard for difference. For commentators such as Takaki (1993), in this narrative the history of morality in American education is bound to ideology and racial domination, with the goal of eroding cultural diversity. Schlesinger (1992) and others, however, contend otherwise. For them, American history is meaningless without the privileging of certain values and beliefs. The United States only exists since certain choices were made, and reflected in its public institutions such as schools, because the search for national survival and identity required a selection of values that could foster that particular political end. In this picture, the decisions and actions of history are not determined primarily by ideology but by pragmatism. In Schlesinger's (1992: 16–17) scheme ideology is dangerous, especially in relation to cultural issues, focusing erroneously on "ethnic and racial criteria . . . that fragment a unifying American identity."

These contrasting perspectives reflect a broad division and generalization about cultural pluralism in the States, that have far-reaching implications for values education in today's school. Broadly speaking, egalitarian and pragmatic values in socioeconomic and public life empowered the trend in the nineteenth and early twentieth centuries toward enhanced access and greater participation in the educational sphere. Yet with these values also came an increasingly partisan view of what counted as desirable culture and a perception of identifiable character and morality traits which might serve the emerging cultural hegemony. The function of education in this respect was axiomatic, providing the stage on which morality and culture could openly be harmonised. The result was that American education came to reflect a broad bias toward white European heritage, and reinforced this bias by inculcating particular notions of the virtuous character and moral life. This effectively served the nineteenth-century expansion of the new nation's economic and geographic frontiers, but at a price of cultural dominance. For indigenous, immigrant, and slave minorities, that price was high (Cohen 1990).

Twentieth-century history has largely seen that hegemony maintained, but weakened. The practice of cultural domination has remained, but increasingly the exclusion of minority cultures and dysfunctionality of traditional values has impinged uncomfortably on societal consciousness. The initial response was ambivalent. On the one hand, the drive to assimilate more fairly and comprehensively became a priority (Berry and Blassingame 1982). But while this comprehensive and consensual voice was strengthened, so also was that of a new trend, that of pluralism. For advocates of the latter, the lesson of two centuries was a cultural powerplay in which America had tried "to have its cake and eat it." The reality noted by the latter group was that national identity was not achieved by consensus, but through domination (Kammen 1995). For pluralist thinkers, monoculturalism via a policy of assimilation was not a realistic model for future aspirations. Instead a revisionist view of diversity was both necessary for democratic change and a meaningful consequence of pluralist society. In the pluralist paradigm, an education for all Americans did not mean broadening access to cultural homogeneity, but instead providing a vision of a just cultural pluralism in a changing context.

The power behind this alternative perspective lay in the historical reality that the values that had sustained cultural hegemony were, for the first time, now in doubt. Here lies the crux for any theory of values education in today's democratic societies. In the same way that a relationship existed in the eighteenth and nineteenth centuries between the ascendancy of cultural homogeneity and the values of egalitarianism, utility, and secularism, so an inverse relationship can be discerned increasingly in the twentieth century between personal values and cultural discourses of heterogeneity and diversity.

This fundamental relationship, the contingency or interdependency between values education and cultural discourse, is underscored by the history of school-based values-education programs in recent decades.

By the mid-twentieth century the accelerated pace of social and technological change, underpinned by epistemologies such as logical positivism, saw a recession of traditional school norms in moral and character education. Much psychological theory raised doubts about character as a meaningful notion, and Hartshorne's and May's (1928) famous "doctrine of specificity" gave an empirical rationale for a review of morality as contingent on specific contexts. This combination of social change and new knowledge was to effect a fallout that, in Lickona's (1992: 8) words, "fell like a cold ash on moral dialogue."

By the 1960s this lack of confidence in the epistemological basis to morality had infused popular culture. The priority of individual worth and fulfillment reached a new level of societal consciousness, bringing in its wake the call for freedoms and struggles against various injustices. Here morality was not absent, but socio-politically oriented toward individual self-expression and legitimacy, over against forms of authority and governance, whether just or not. The knock-on effect in schools was initially in the development of an approach coined by Louis Raths et al. (1966) as "values clarification," and later in the ideas of "moral development and reasoning" proposed by Lawrence Kohlberg (1978).

The former relied on a proximity between espoused values and personal actions, and encouraged students to reflect on how their actions might reflect their values. Critics were quick, however, to pounce on the limitations of this approach, in particular its replacement of moral content with value-oriented volitions and feelings, needing simply to be "clarified" in the learner. For many this represented a curricular endorsement of superficial moral relativism in society at large, which as Lickona (1992: 11) puts it:

> made no distinction between what you might *want* to do . . . and what you *ought* to do . . . There was no requirement to evaluate one's values against a standard, no suggestion that some values might be better or worse than others . . . In the end, values clarification made the mistake of treating kids like grown-ups.

Values clarification ultimately had a moral methodology but little moral theory. This shortcoming, however, could not be said of Kohlberg's ideas of moral development, which offered a more sophisticated and robust theory for values education. Kohlberg's emphasis on stages of moral reasoning was evidence of the use of contemporaneous epistemology, in this case empiricism, combined with a model of developmental psychology that cohered with the dominant child-centered teaching of the 1960s and 1970s. Kohlberg provided an impressive rationale for moral education in cognitive terms and grounded it within an educational process oriented toward "thinking skills." But however persuasive his approach may have been in terms of pedagogy, it lacked broader conviction in a changing moral climate. Put simply, Kohlberg, like the earlier advocates of values clarification, steered clear of moral *content* in education, in preference for moral *process*. Increasingly this liberalism was unable to withstand or assuage a growing societal dissatisfaction with the moral legacy of the 1960s and its relativism, or seemingly provide an adequate model of values education capable of dealing with the postmodern era.

Several themes emerge from this brief and selective historical sketch. The most important is that values have featured as an external source of cultural struggle and consolidation. In short, the values that the education system has embodied and transmitted have been part of a wider struggle about cultural survival and identity. In this sense, their function has been *utilitarian*, promoting a sense of cultural progress, and *epistemological*, reinforcing a concept of cultural identity, rather than *moral* in any metaphysical sense. Secondly, this process has inevitably involved a clash of ideas about the dominant cultural discourses in America. As part of the dialectics of democracy, values education has been a mode of conversation between diverse and contrary cultural viewpoints. In recent decades, as with the early colonial period, this conversation has refocused the debate about the extent to which heterogeneity or homogeneity is the natural state of affairs in American cultural life. Values education has thus been one conduit or cipher by which a broader dialogue and struggle has taken place. And thirdly, the use of values education as one means of ensuring this dialectic says much about views of education in a participative democracy. The function of school in this context is responsive or reactive, rather than reconstructionist or initiatory. Such a function certainly sees school as a mode of social change, but primarily as a servant rather than an initiator. In other words, far from elevating school to the role of change agent, it presents a reductionist view of the potential of contemporary schools by envisaging them as servants rather than agents of change.

The new wave of values-education initiatives can be viewed as an emotive reaction to the disturbing passage to societal postmodernity. It aims to rediscover the moral (and hence cultural) certainty contained in the character-education programs of the early century, and looks to core moral *content* that schools can institutionalize and curricula can deliver. Such a desire revisits traditions of old: the aspiration for cultural identity and consensus, the shoring up of participative democracy against trends of disempowerment and fragmentation, and the seeking of shared consensus, even identity, in the moral fabric of our cultural lives. In this sense the values education of today is impressively pragmatic: it is geared toward social survival, in the same way that the founders of the nation had to ensure similar basic goals rather than academic ideals. How such an initiative demonstrates this, and confirms the absolute relationship between values in schools and deeper questions of cultural struggle and identity, can be seen in the case of the Baltimore County initiative in values education.

## The case of Baltimore County's values-education initiative

The issue of values came to a head in the USA in the 1970s, when the confidence of the modern era began to wane rapidly. Several key events of that period crystallized a broad anxiety at the popular cultural level: the engagement in the Vietnam war; changing family structure; Watergate and other instances of government impropriety; alarming increase of drug use; violence among the nation's youth; and Civil Rights struggles. These trends led to the widespread conviction that America's public schools were failing to emphasize a core set of values that would provide a panacea to the turmoil in norms of ethics and behavior besetting the nation.

In response to these national trends the Maryland state legislature in 1978 passed a bill mandating a Values Education Commission, thereby reinforcing the real or at least perceived view that greater community support was necessary if values were to become an integral part of the state's school curricula. Maryland legislators perceived that societal problems, such as delinquency, vandalism, drug abuse, and increased sexual activity among youth, should impel educators to examine present methods for teaching values in the schools. The issue stated succinctly was this: disturbing trends within the nation demand that schools actively engage in promoting values which, while recognizing the importance of diversity, enable us to maintain order in a democratic and pluralistic society.

The urgency of this issue was reflected in the consensus view of those Americans who responded to the twelfth annual Gallup poll. Eighty-five percent of the respondents with children in public schools favoured instruction in values, whilst only 4 percent opposed such instruction. Researchers Burkholder et al. (1981: 484) summarized the dilemma facing America's schools and communities: "Many U.S. citizens today appear to believe that the public schools neither reflect nor support the values held by their clients. Nor do they see public schools exerting a sufficiently positive moral influence on young people." The example of one Maryland school system is useful in illuminating the issue. The public school system in Baltimore County had traditionally placed strong emphasis on values education and prided itself on developing positive ethical values among its students. Amongst the tangible evidence of the system's efforts in values education was a student handbook which had articulated the rights and responsibilities of students, and in doing so had established a core set of values for students in the public schools (Baltimore County Committee on Student Behavior 1968). At every grade level from elementary through high school, the handbook reinforced fundamental values such as respect for self and others, tolerance of diversity, and respect for learning.

Responding to the broad national trends and the 1978 state legislation, the Baltimore County Public Schools Board of Education created a Task Force on Values Education and Ethical Behavior in 1981. This 21-member committee was to review the status of values education in the public schools and make recommendations within a year. In his charge to the task force Superintendent Robert Dubel cited the results of the Gallup poll as evidence that the public expected schools to exercise responsibility for teaching students about values, and that the task force should review current efforts within the school system to meet its moral objectives.

To begin its work the task force surveyed 475 teachers and administrators in 13 schools within the system to determine the present perceptions of the role of values in education. A summary of the survey yielded the following generalizations:

1 The majority of teachers agreed that the school has a responsibility to teach values.
2 The great majority (80 percent) of teachers agreed that they should be expected to serve as role-models for students.
3 The great majority of teachers (85 percent) agreed that values should be taught as part of the planned curriculum.
4 The majority of teachers agreed that the school system's efforts to teach values were insufficient.

It is worth noting that a similar survey addressed to a sample of parents yielded results virtually identical to those in the survey of educators. That is, parents agreed that the school should teach values, that teachers should be role-models for students, and values should be taught as part of the curriculum. They also agreed that schools' current efforts in teaching values were insufficient.

When asked to define values, teachers' replies typically identified the following: standard of living; personal responsibility; citizenship; integrity; honesty; acceptance of consequences for one's actions; and knowing right from wrong. To the same request, parents in the survey responded: knowing right from wrong; citizenship; honesty; moral development; work ethics; responsibility; and respect.

As part of their deliberations, the task force invited representatives from various community and professional groups to share their views on values and the school role in teaching values. Discussions included principals of independent schools, representatives from liberal and conservative political groups, media professionals, judges, and business leaders. Questions raised by the task force during these discussions included:

1 What do you do with pluralistic values?
2 Who or what is the moral example?
3 What is the ultimate value?
4 How do we teach values without indoctrinating students?

5 What values should schools teach, and how?
6 Should values regarding religion or political party be prohibited in schools?

A central issue for the task force was how to reconcile respect for diversity, heightened by America's extraordinary mix of ethnic and cultural groups, with the search for a set of core beliefs, or values, which these same groups could recognize as vital to their common heritage as Americans.

This is a challenge identified earlier by Bartlett Giamatti (1984), then president of Yale University:

Pluralism does not mean the absence of standards. It signals the recognition that people of different ethnic groups and races . . . and personal beliefs have a right to coexist as equals under the law and have an obligation to forge the freedoms they enjoy into a coherent, civilized and vigilant whole.

After much investigation and study, the task force did, in 1984, reach agreement on a common core of values to be used as the centerpiece of the school system's values-education program. These are here presented in alphabetical order, reflecting the task force's conclusion that their interdependency prevented them from being prioritized: compassion; courtesy; critical inquiry; due process; equal opportunity; freedom of thought and action; honesty; human worth and dignity; integrity; justice; knowledge; loyalty; objectivity; order; patriotism; rational consent; respect for others' rights; responsibility; responsible citizenship; rule of law; self-respect; tolerance; and truth.

Nearly a decade later (1991) the task force reaffirmed this list of values while attempting to develop strategies for teachers and administrators for implementing the study of values in their schools. The initiative was formally evaluated as being successful in terms of highlighting public awareness and illustrating the function of values education as beneficial in three ways: in curriculum enrichment, showing that values and ethics are natural domains of disciplinary and interdisciplinary teaching; in pedagogical theory, highlighting the potential of teacher as role-model and the classroom as an environment where certain cultural values should dynamically prevail; and in institutional reflection, revealing how the school's hidden curriculum transmits, reinforces and institutionalizes key values, both positive and negative, amongst its students.

## Conclusion: toward a new rationale for values education

In this final section we aim to establish a new rationale for values education, by outlining some problems and possibilities it faces, and offering some principles for its continued presence and enrichment. In essence we are concerned that the historic themes which have long endured and provided the context for moral education are no longer fit for the purpose. Earlier we suggested that those themes – egalitarianism, utilitarianism, participative democracy and secular morality – have prevailed in different forms through most periods of American educational history. The current state of societal development requires education to recognize these, but also to go further and embrace a distinctive role for the critical educator in contemporary society. The search for moral identity in our diversified and fragmented world demonstrates this need, but also the limitations of our current resources to this end. For no longer can moral *conformity* be legitimized, given the cultural ramifications that such a goal implies and requires. Instead a new capacity for moral dialogue, a sense of shared, participative moral *inquiry*, is the essential need of education in the postmodern condition. This requires a new vision of critical pedagogy and of the place of education in the conscious reconstruction of democratic, civilized society. Education in this picture does not give us the clarity of solutions that the current technicist orthodoxy purports (whether in values-education projects, information technology or other simplified fads), but offers clues for moral growth and participation in the face of societal and moral disarray. What scope then might values education offer?

First, it should be absolutely rooted in the relationship between moral growth and the reproduction of democratic society. This Deweyan principle, overshadowed in recent decades, recalls that in such matters both students and teachers are seekers and that once this is acknowledged a radically different view of pedagogy follows, firmly rooted in traditions of critical and reconstructionist thought. Aristotle once defined teaching as an activity that is done "as to a friend." This means that a teacher is more than a good role-model, or curriculum developer, or representative of a moral institution. It is rather a vision of a personal inquirer, seeking to find with others the potential for growth and healing in the face of individual uncertainty and societal

ambiguity. Students long for this, but because of its enormous risk and demand in personal terms most teachers are not equipped to be that "friend." Teachers can hardly be blamed for such reluctance. As a society we have striven our hardest to eradicate personal, subjective, and moral enterprises from the public educational domain and to sanitize all moral matters to the objective, sterile, soulless functions of teacher modeling, curriculum planning, and institutional ethics. Such a reductionist view of a moral pedagogy is patently inadequate to the task at hand, though frankly it still prevails in most values-education initiatives. In Purpel's (1989: 68) words, "our responsibilities are not to promulgate visions but to inquire into them, not just to study them but to be critical and discerning of them."

From this it follows that values education should be perceived as a *resource* rather than a *directive* or a *goal* for education. This point is in real danger of being lost at present. The trend within values education, clearly visible in the Baltimore experience, is to objectify a consensual level of consciousness, albeit arrived at through a sensitive and democratic process. But precisely in arriving at an agreed core of moral interests do we do a disservice to education, cutting it adrift from the inconsistencies and inadequacies of society's dominant discourses, which urgently require an educational, moral critique. For the real potential of inquiry and growth lies not in acquiescing to agreeable ideals, but in contemplating disagreeable realities. The danger of consensus in values education is that it elevates an ethereal moral core to educational privilege, whilst failing to engage learners in the critical act of deconstructing the fragmented and arbitrary codes of the postmodern age. Put simply, it gives us a moral fantasy, a calm hallucination, to help shut out the experience of our present disjointed condition, which increasingly requires a penetrating moral analysis.

Here then lies the diversionary danger of current values-education thinking. By celebrating the consensual it runs the risk of indulging the vacuous. For all sane, rational individuals and cultures acknowledge the legitimacy of such principal values as honesty, knowledge, and justice. The role of education, however, lies in its capacity to help us maneuver from the quiet backwaters of consensus into the unsettling undercurrents of real life, where our interpretation of principal values in the human situation confronts us with dilemma, turmoil, and disagreement. This challenge of taking us outside of our points of certainty is the task currently facing values education.

Such a challenge has not yet been fully appraised. This shortfall on the potential of values education undermines the power of education to provide a robust moral critique of the current order and thus risks the requisite moral input for the full growth of democratic society. Instead we need to ensure that values education gives free rein for teachers and students to participate in what Kincheloe (1993) calls a "pedagogy of consciousness." Such consciousness starts from a recognition of both the failure of "totalizing" perspectives to provide meaning to our human condition, and the ambiguities of our own cultural and personal experiences. But it also goes on to take as axiomatic those experiences as we make moral sense of the dilemmas of daily living. This "relativism" of sorts is not meant to negate the possibility of moral growth, but just the opposite. Only by recognizing the shared crisis of cultural and individual identity can we hope to share in the pained but hopeful task of recreating a just, democratic society in the information age. As Kincheloe (1993: 229) puts it: "Educational visions that simply attempt to reveal fixed eternal truths or the great ideas of America . . . fail to engage students with living arguments and with practical forms of understanding that move us to acts of democratic courage."

This approach to values education is not novel or untried. It recalls the insight of Dewey (1916), who understood that becoming a participatory citizen meant being enabled to think critically and engage actively with culture's dominant assumptions and symbols. This relationship between curriculum and cultural tradition is brought up to date in Mikhail Bakhtin's (1981) concept of dialogism. Bakhtin asserts that cultural tradition can be seen as a "text" in which the public's many voices and multiple perspectives intersect. We can grow to comprehend this "heteroglossia" and in so doing will expand our capacity to think critically as citizens – and to uncover new dimensions for education and the curriculum, in particular. For Bakhtin such an educational process reveals where tacit forces of oppression and injustice occur, and allows for individual empowerment and societal growth through enhanced participative democracy.

Such participation is, critically, resistant to totalizing views or consensual pictures. Instead it takes seriously the arbitrariness of the postmodern condition, but goes on to equip each individual to seek a

vision and meaning in its face. This is a grander task than identifying core themes in morality of educational interest. It is about utilizing all our capacities – mental, emotional, personal and social – in the quest for becoming moral change-agents. Such a quest goes beyond even the worthy processes of critical *thinking*, because it needs to recognize that moral inquiry is about affective and personal investment, as well as cognitive awareness. This is the reality of human experience that led Lenin (1960) to assert that "truth is concrete." In this he meant that morality does not abide in metaphysical ideals, but in the hopes, struggles, and achievements of our personal and collective lives.

The school and its culture provide such a concreteness. In such a community we come across what Benhabib (1992) calls an "interactive universalism," or the coming together of conflicts between experiences, traditions, ideas, and practices in our diversified culture. This has been evident throughout the history of American education. The reality is that public education has always been the arena for cultural contestation, negotiation, and regeneration, rather than the homogeneous system that modernism has sought through ideologies such as egalitarianism and utilitarianism. This is the crux for any education in morality. The real strength of such education lies in its potential to awaken and empower us in the face of the arbitrariness of our cultural condition. But simultaneously its weakness lies in its susceptibility to reinforcing objectified, totalist visions of a metaphysical nature and cultural identity that simply do not square with everyday experience.

This is why advocates of the religious right have been so successful recently in the public sphere, in "the guts of American politics," as Shapiro (1995) puts it. They alone have provided a moral vision that encompasses the breadth and depth of human experience: put simply they treat all our life experiences very seriously. But with their vision also comes a totalizing dogma that is willing to trade in intolerance and closed-mindedness in order to achieve a communal life secure from daily insecurities. Here lies the challenge for the moral educator today. What we must do is articulate for our students and our society a morally and spiritually rooted communal vision as the motif for progressive social change and individual participation. This role for spirituality and morality at the heart of our educational discourse is not about safeguarding the "truth" but about identifying how we can and should image and reimage the world, and envisage human potential in ways that can give meaningful, worthy existence to individuals and cultures. Educational theory, distracted by the onslaught of technicist values and the criticism of established traditions from the right, has simply missed this in recent years. As Giroux and McLaren (eds) (1989: foreword) note:

> It (educational discourse) has lost sight of its fundamental mission of mobilizing public sentiment toward a renewed vision of community; it has failed to recognize the general relevance of education as a public service and the importance of deliberately translating educational theory into a community-related discourse capable of reaching into and animating public culture and life.

Of course such a vision puts education precariously on the line. On the one hand education urgently needs to find a moral imperative geared to a participatory, compassionate, and communal society. On the other it must do so without proposing a monolithic, straitjacketing vision that appeases consensus at the expense of meaning and challenge. This is precisely the tightrope that a community-sensitive initiative such as that in Baltimore walks. The task of finding such a moral vision is also made more difficult by the frameworks we commonly adopt in American educational discourse. We conceptualize our work in terms such as curriculum planning, pedagogical techniques, classroom models, etc., as though somehow these are objective entities with reified status. Such thinking is both obscure and obtuse. It loses the point that education is bound to dynamics that speak to our existential selves, that unite with the transformation of cultural reality, and that provide an environment for the connection of our intersubjectivities.

For values education this cannot be more pertinent. It should be a major contributor to our schools' capacities to offer vision and meaning, rather than supplying a curriculum model or moral content. Such a role would save values education from the domain of single-issue politics, where it receives regular acclaim, or from the type of segregation that educational bureaucracies envisage. Instead it would find a radically inclusive role aligned to the basic question of what it means to be an educated individual in the postmodern era. Such an inclusiveness needs a broader picture of educational opportunity than we currently portray. The tasks we set education, such as critical thinking,

socialization, citizenship, multidimensional skills, and so on, are necessary but insufficient. A deeper educational cause is called for that touches teachers' and students' spiritual, emotional, existential, and cultural lives. Such a need is indeed heightened by America's present sense of societal dislocation and cultural insecurity.

This need for a radical values pedagogy must not be ignored, since our basic human quest for existential meaning will be answered by one value source or another, be it ideological, political, psychotic, or narcotic. Here lies the ground for values education, especially fertile since the encoded cultural mores of former generations are of waning power. What is needed to accomplish this is a more radical and risky enterprise than teaching core moral values on which we agree, in an otherwise alienated and differentiated world. Indeed, the danger of the latter is two-fold: it falsifies morality by giving it an opaqueness, or an independent identity, that tends toward a Cartesian-type rationality; and it relegates education in morality to the simplistic, the uncontroversial, and the inconsequential by anaesthetizing it from the very anguish that confronts us as moral beings and that calls for moral wisdom.

Education in our present social condition needs to act like a prism, enabling us to see ourselves, our limitations, our potential, our lifestyles, our communities, our cultures, and our society, and empowering us to struggle together for justice and meaning in our lives. This lesson is not new. It recalls the origins of public education in America, where education and morality were synonymous and absolutely bound with societal survival. In such a context morality is not a separate part of life, capable of discrete identity, but totally bound to our human consciousness and thus to every act deemed educational. Such a priority needs rediscovering. In America's historical passage from modernity to postmodernity, we need to revisit and reformulate that insight, without accepting the inevitability of cultural hegemony that came in its wake. Values education can offer this hope, that positive cultural conversations can occur across our societal divides and that citizens be morally empowered to build their futures together.

In this sense, despite being an artificial construct of curriculum and school, values education can harness morality to the experiences and hopes of our individual and cultural autobiographies, and thus point to the reality that we are not educated persons unless we are moral persons. In so doing, it may help us forge a reconstituted society, and remind us that all educational quests are ultimately about being human and how we should live as free individuals in the broad human community. This paradoxical hope for shared living in a diverse world – "one, from many" – is ultimately the same ideal on which democracy in general, and American society in particular, rests its legitimacy and aspirations.

# References

Anderson, J. D. (1988) *The Education of Blacks in the South, 1860–1935*, Chapel Hill: University of North Carolina Press.

Bakhtin, M. (1981) *The Dialogic Imagination*, Austin: University of Texas Press.

Baltimore County Committee on Student Behavior (1968) *Student Behavior Handbook*, Towson, MD: Baltimore County Public Schools.

Benhabib, S. (1992) *Situating the Self: Gender, Community and Postmodernism in Contemporary Ethics*, London: Routledge.

Bennett, W. (1995) *The Children's Book of Virtues*.

Berry, M. F. and Blassingame, J. W. (1982) *Long Memory: The Black Experience in America*, Oxford: Oxford University Press.

Bloom, A. (1987) *The Closing of the American Mind*, New York: Simon & Schuster.

Burkholder, S., Ryan, K. and Blanke, V. (1981) "Values: The Key to a Community", *Phi Delta Kappa*, 62.7: 483–5.

Cohen, R. D. (1990) *Children of the Mill: Schooling and Society in Gary, Indiana*, Bloomington: University of Indiana Press.

Coles, R. (1997) *The Moral Intelligence of Children: How to Raise a Moral Child*, New York: Bantam Books.

Counts, G. S. (1932) *Dare the School Build a New Social Order?*, New York: John Day.

Cremin, L. A. (1951) *The American Common School: A Historical Conception*, New York: Teachers College Press.

Dewey, J. (1916) *Democracy and Education*, New York: The Free Press.

Giamatti, B. (1984) Unpub. address, cited in Task Force on Values Education and Ethical Behavior 1984.

Giroux, H. A. and McLaren, P. (eds) (1989) *Critical Pedagogy: The State and Cultural Struggle*, New York: State University of New York.

Goodlad, J. I., Soder, R. and Sirotnik, K. A. (eds) (1990) *The Moral Dimensions of Teaching*, San Francisco: Jossey-Bass.

Gutek, G. L. (1984) *George S. Counts and American Civilization: The Educator as Social Theorist*, Macon, GA: Mercer University Press.

Gutek, G. L. (1991) *An Historical Introduction to American Education*, 2nd edn, Prospect Heights, Ill.: Waveland Press.

Hartshorne, H. and May, M. (1928) *Studies in the Nature of Character*, New York: Macmillan.

Hirsch, E. D. Jr. (1987) *Cultural Literacy: What Every American Needs to Know*, Boston: Houghton Mifflin.

Hunter, J. D. (1991) *Culture Wars: The Struggle to Define America*, New York: Basic Books.

Jervis, K. and Montag, C. (eds) (1991) *Progressive Education for the 1990s*, New York: Teachers College Press.

Kammen, M. (1995) *Contested Values: Democracy and Diversity in American Culture*, New York: St. Martin's Press.

Kanpol, B. (1994) *Critical Pedagogy: An Introduction*, Westport, CT: Bergin & Garvey.

Kincheloe, J. L. (1993) *Toward a Critical Thinking of Teacher Thinking: Mapping the Postmodern*, Westport, CT: Bergin & Garvey.

Kohlberg, L. (1978) *Essays on Moral Development, Vol. 1: The Philosophy of Moral Development*, San Francisco: Harper & Row.

Kohlberg, L. (1984) *Essays on Moral Development, Vol. 2: The Psychology of Moral Development*, San Francisco: Harper & Row.

Lawton, D. (1989) *Education, Culture and the National Curriculum*, London: Hodder & Stoughton.

Lawton, M. (1995) "Values Education: A Moral Obligation or Dilemma?", *Education Week*, 17 May, pp. 1–11.

Lenin, V. I. (1960) *Selected Works, Vol. 2: Notes to Hegel*, London: Lawrence & Wishart.

Lickona, T. (1992) *Educating for Character: How Our Schools Can Teach Respect and Responsibility*, New York: Bantam Books.

Messerli, J. (1972) *Horace Mann: A Biography*, New York: Knopf.

Morrison, S. E. (1956) *The Intellectual Life of Colonial New England*, New York: New York University Press.

Ornstein, A. C. and Levine, D. U. (1997) *Foundations of Education*, 6th edn, Boston: Houghton Mifflin.

Purpel, D. E. (1989) *The Moral and Spiritual Crisis in Education*, New York: Bergin & Garvey.

Raths, L., Harmin, M., and Simon, S. (1966) *Values and Teaching*, Columbus, OH: Charles E. Merrill Publishing Co.

Rippa, S. A. (1992) *Education in a Free Society: An American History*, New York: Longman.

Schlesinger, A. M. (1992) *The Disuniting of America*, New York: W. W. Norton.

Shapiro, S. (1995) "Educational Change and the Crisis of the Left: Toward a Postmodern Educational Discourse", in B. Kanpol and P. McLaren (eds), *Critical Multiculturalism: Uncommon Voices in a Common Struggle*, Westport, CT: Bergin & Garvey, pp. 19–38.

Sleeter, C. and McLaren, P. L. (1995) *Multicultural Education, Critical Pedagogy, and the Politics of Difference*, Albany, NY: State University of New York Press.

Takaki, R. (1993) *A Different Mirror: A History of Multi-cultural America*, Boston: Little, Brown.

Task Force on Values Education and Ethical Behavior (1984) *1984 and Beyond: A Reaffirmation of Values*, Towson, MD: Baltimore County Public Schools.

Task Force on Values Education and Ethical Behavior (1991) *How to Establish a Values Education Program in Your School*, Towson, MD: Baltimore County Public Schools.

Westerhoff, J. H. (1978) *McGuffey and his Readers: Piety, Morality, and Education in Nineteenth Century America*, Nashville: Abingdon.

Wynne, E. A. and Ryan, K. (1997) *Reclaiming Our Schools: Teaching Character, Academics and Discipline*, 2nd edn, New Jersey: Merrill/Prentice Hall.

# 19 Values in Education: Definitely: 'Your Feet are Always in the Water'

ISABEL MENEZES AND BÁRTOLO PAIVA CAMPOS

The issue of values in education is probably as old as education itself. In fact, educational theories have always emphasised, more or less openly and more or less intentionally, the idea that education is not only about making people more knowledgeable, in a strictly 'intellectual' sense (whatever this may be!), but also about making people more ready for citizenship, in a broad sense. However, the meanings of this are clearly divergent and sometimes even conflicting, depending on perspective. For some, education should be concerned with transmitting the dominant values that constitute the core of civilisation, thus aiming to make people 'good' (e.g., Ryan 1989, 1993, Lickona 1991, 1993); for others, the issue of values is too controversial for the school to interfere in, and they stress the importance of neutrality (e.g., Raths, Harmin and Simon 1978); others still argue that it is more important to promote students' competence to make autonomous and principled personal choices, by developing the flexibility, reciprocity and complexity of their self-organisation processes (e.g., Piaget 1977, Beane 1990, Sprinthall 1991). These different perspectives have relevant implications in educational *praxis*, with attention being called to various practices such as exhortation and example, interaction and self-expression, and action and critical reflection.

In this chapter we aim to analyse how these various perspectives on values in education have been influential in Portugal, taking into account that the country has experienced severe structural changes in these last 20 to 30 years, namely the transition from dictatorship to democracy, and the development towards a full 'European status'. Along the way, education has clearly been expected not only to accompany but also to participate in these changes, with obvious (and sometimes huge) fluctuations in what values should be stressed and how schools should do it.

## The 'Southern European story': from dictatorship to democracy in Europe

In a recent study by an international agency, democracy was considered to be the most frequent option for political regimes all over the world. However, Southern European democracies are quite recent: only during the 1970s did Portugal, Spain and Greece experience the fall of dictatorial regimes under which they had lived for most of twentieth century. The Portuguese experience during that century included monarchy, until 1910, and a short and agitated experience of a republican regime until 1926, when a military coup gave way to a dictatorship that survived the Second World War. Not until 1974, once again by the initiative of the military, did a revolution restore democracy. These convulsions in our recent history clearly determine educational options and are instrumental for understanding how values in education are conceptualised and discussed today.

During the First Republic (1910 to 1926), the school was viewed as a relevant instrument for societal change: education should contribute to the development of a 'republican ethic' and teachers were seen as moral agents at the service of the republic. Even then, however, Sérgio (1984 (1915)), argued against education as mere instruction and defended its role in the formation of students' 'personality, initiative, responsibility, creative will, self-restrain and citizenship' (Godinho 1984: 4); he criticised the value of exhortation as an educational technique and, following Dewey's experience (1966 (1916)), he argued for self-government in schools. However, the rise of an authoritarian regime resulted in stressing the teaching of 'basics': love for God, fatherland and the family. Naturally this implied an absolute respect for authority, a subservient attitude towards those in power and obedient behaviour in work and other social institutions (Mónica 1978). These basic principles were present in every instance of educational organisation, either in the curricula and the official textbooks, or in the classroom setting (which had to display a crucifix and a photograph of the president and the prime minister) and school organisation; additionally, compulsory education was the shortest in Europe (four years until 1964, and six years afterwards), drop-out rates and absenteeism were extremely high, and teacher training was almost non-existent. In the words of the dictator, Portugal was 'proudly alone' in Europe, turned towards the African colonies and conscious of its glorious past as an old nation.

During the 1960s, under the influence of economic and social changes such as increasing commercial trade, external investment, tourism and emigration (emigrants to European countries represented 12 per cent of the population), 'European re-orientation' (Barreto 1994: 1051) began: Europe 'was almost a metaphor or a symbol of democracy and freedom' (ibid.: 1054). The consequences in education planning involved the extension of compulsory education, the reorganisation of teacher training and the reform of polytechnic and university education; however, the majority of these changes were not implemented.

Following the 1974 revolution there was clearly a shift in educational goals: the aim was now to foster a democratic and socialist society by promoting personal development and national progress and reinforcing social cohesion (Grácio 1981). Curricular innovations involved new textbooks, and the creation of new subjects (such as politics in grades 10 and 11) and curricular areas that implied the students' active participation in their own community (for instance, a mandatory year of civic service before entering higher education). These latter experiences were severely criticised on the grounds of risks of ideological inculcation (Brederode Santos 1981, 1984, Bettencourt 1982, Bettencourt and Brederode Santos 1983) and were suspended in 1976 by a socialist government. Simultaneously, the debate on the role of the school in preparing students for democratic citizenship was more or less abandoned until entry to the European Economic Community (EEC).

Integration in the European Community in 1985 was a national project that generated a large consensus, viewed – both nationally and by the member states – as instrumental to the economic and political development and stability of the new Southern democracies. The 'European option' meant the political and economic support of a democratic parliamentary regime, free elections, a free-market economy and technological and cultural progress. And, from a Portuguese point of view, Europe also had important symbolic functions, working as a 'buffer of losses and grievances (such as) the defeat in the colonial wars, the disappearance of the empire, the shortening of the fatherland and the loss of its historical sense' (Barreto 1994: 1060).

European membership brought about important economic, technical, scientific and cultural developments; the Portuguese even experienced a relative economic prosperity, especially during the late 1980s and early 1990s (Almeida 1994, Barreto 1994). An important sign of the general satisfaction with the formal integration in Europe is that only recently, with the emergence of some social and economic difficulties such as increasing unemployment, have there been signs of opposition to the European project, with the reappearance of a nationalistic political discourse (Barreto, 1994). But, in general, research on political socialisation shows that there are positive attitudes towards the European Union (Figueiredo 1988, França (ed.) 1993) and that people – 46 per cent of the Portuguese sample in the European Values System Study Group survey – are 'convinced of the advantages of the European Union in preserving national identity' (Reis and Dias 1993: 27). Therefore, the European space has been a context for 'expectations and confidence rather than rejection and distrust' (Almeida 1994: 63).

The consequences of these changes for Portuguese society are also detectable at the level of value tendencies, which should be taken into account in a discussion of values in education. Almeida (1994) identifies four major trends, namely, moderate individualism, pragmatic orientation, conviviality and tolerance, and ideological eclecticism; these are particularly visible in urban, well-educated and younger-generation groups. However, these global trends could be subject to erosions originating in several factors such as the rapid growth of social exclusion, unemployment and immigration or regional inequalities; and tolerance could, according to Almeida (1994), be the first to fall.

Portuguese 'soft-individualism' is characterised by the importance given to personal fulfilment as a life principle: the primacy of family and affect, of personal pleasure within the work context, of personal projects and of concerns with personal goals and well-being.

The search for pragmatism, the commitment only to close, immediate and controllable goals, is also a current trend, accompanied by scepticism towards idealistic and long-term aims such as those involving social and political participation (Almeida 1994). This pragmatic orientation is visible in areas such as national identity: 'there is an overall decline in the rituals of nationality, giving way among youngsters to a nationalism more pragmatically rooted, closely linked to and stimulated by the country's tangible dynamics' (Conde 1989: 39), such as a good reputation for sports, a beautiful landscape, conviviality, a capacity for enterprise. The tendency to be non-associative and non-participative in political and social domains was detected in various studies, together with a low interest in political and social issues (Correia Jesuíno 1983, Braga da Cruz, 1985, Reis 1985, 1986, Vala 1985, 1986, Brederode Santos and Dias 1993; França 1993). However, Braga da Cruz (1985) relates these phenomena to the relatively low level of political development and culture of the Portuguese, mainly due to the lack of democratic experience. And a recent study (Cabral 1995) reveals that if 40 per cent of the population do not identify with political parties, those who decide to become members are predominantly under 35 years of age. Therefore, it remains to be proved whether this Portuguese pragmatism derives from a sceptical attitude or from lack of participatory experience and culture.

The openness and more complex nature of Portuguese society led, according to Almeida (1994), to a growing tolerance towards others and to an emphasis on conviviality; this flexibility is diminishing the differences between religious and political groups, even if there are no signs of a strong value relativism. It should be stressed that this positive perspective is particularly visible in younger generations, since tolerance towards personal options and 'deviations' has increased significantly; unfortunately, when it comes to religious and ethnic prejudice and intolerance, even if not high in Portugal, younger people are no different from older generations (Brederode Santos and Dias 1993). Therefore, the trend towards tolerance appears to be more evident in some areas of life than in others.

Finally, Almeida (1994) refers to important changes in the way the Portuguese consider different ideologies: an instrumental and eclectic attitude towards the different political and religious systems seems to be dominant; being left- (or right-) wing, some years ago, implied clear-cut options in terms of behaviour, ethics, values, lifestyles, which are now increasingly interpenetrating and cross-sectional. Therefore, Portuguese citizens seem to value a more individualised and autonomous process of choice of ideological elements which are then personally organised into an idiosyncratic meaning-making system.

These social trends in value orientations signify a significant closeness with Europe. In fact, as Reis and Dias (1993: 305) conclude, 'the distance between Portugal and Europe is less important than we could expect. [The existing research reveals] that Portugal is part of a larger socio-cultural universe: the European universe'.

Looking back on this 'Southern European story', the expression 'times are changing' seems apt, especially if one adds 'rapidly, profoundly and (sometimes) violently'. And these changes undoubtedly had a strong influence in determining today's educational options, particularly when it comes to values.

## Educational change and the issue of values in education

The climate of social stability generated since 1985 allowed for the political consensus that was necessary for defining a new Education Act (Law 46/86 of 14 October 1986) and implementing curricular reform (1989–91). However, reminiscent of past experiences, the Education Act begins by stating (probably with some naivety) that education should not be determined by state ideological tendencies and clearly favours both value diversity and social cohesion, emphasising the need to promote students' adaptation to society and simultaneously their capacity to change it. The new aims are the development of citizens who are free, responsible, autonomous and capable of commitment to social progress and transformation; a democratic, pluralist spirit that respects others and their ideas, and is open to dialogue and the free exchange of opinions; and a national identity that is open to diversity in a spirit of universal humanism, solidarity and international cooperation. Schools must also provide experiences that promote civic awareness and emotional maturity, and attitudes and practical habits of cooperation within the family or the community (Articles 2 and 7). To fulfil these objectives schools must function as democratic institutions and the curricula shall 'include at all levels an area of personal and social education, possibly comprising ecological education, consumer education, family education, sex education, health education, accidents' prevention and citizenship education' (Article 47).

This emphasis on students' personal development and social and political participation is understandable, given the main results of psychological, sociological and educational research during the 1980s and early 1990s (see Campos and Menezes 1996 for a review) which portrayed Portuguese youngsters as revealing low levels of reciprocity and committed personal choices, the primacy of individualistic and conformist processes in personal development, and feeble signs of political interest and participation (Correia Jesuíno 1983, Braga da Cruz 1985, Reis 1985, 1986, Vala, 1985, 1986, Coimbra 1991a, Coimbra and Campos 1991, Costa 1991, Costa and Campos 1991, Brederode Santos and Dias 1993, França (ed.) 1993). Furthermore, data on curricula, teaching methods and school organisation was also disappointing, with primacy given to cognitive aims, and even harmful effects on students' democratic learning (Bettencourt and Brederode Santos 1981, Brederode Santos and Roldão 1986, Soares and Abreu 1986, Bettencourt and Marques 1987, Lima 1988, Marques 1990, 1991, 1992, 1993).

The curricular reform (1989–91) was accompanied by great expectations on the part of teachers, school administrators, educational scholars, parents and even political leaders. Public and scholarly debate was also intense, stressing the need for a 'new school' that would provide success experiences for all rather than failures, teachers' and students' participation rather than passivity, innovation rather than routinised practices. The reform involved new curricula, new subjects, new evaluation mechanisms and new organisational devices. However, the centralised nature of the educational system was not challenged and the majority of the decisions concerning educational practices remained with the ministry of education, even if school autonomy was emphasised at the discourse level. This centralisation implies that the main decisions concerning curricula, evaluation and management are defined at the government level with only limited power being granted to teachers and school administrators – a practice that has been shown to have perverse effects, with teachers and administrators complaining about their limited autonomy but still managing the centrally defined constraints according to their own interpretation (Lima 1992). The exception to this centralised panorama was the creation of a mandatory curricular space for project development, the 'school area', with three major aims: the practical application of knowledge, closeness within the school community and emphasis on personal and social education; in academic terms, the development by students of specific projects, selected and implemented with the support and cooperation of the various subject teachers.[1]

The issue of values in education was particularly relevant when discussing what personal and social education (PSE), as defined in the Education Act, should be. While some considered that it should be primarily concerned with the transmission of values, others favoured a broader and more processual approach, stressing the need to promote students' psychological development. This debate was so lively that the Catholic church decided to interfere, before the government's decision on how PSE was to be operationalised, by declaring that the intention to create a 'mandatory subject' offends the Catholic ethic, since the optional subject of 'Catholic moral and religious education' already addresses the issue of universal values and Catholic ethics (see Campos 1991 and 1992a for a description of this process). This idea of a new subject mainly concerned with values education had been, until then, rejected by those involved in the curricular reform, for several reasons such as the need for specific teacher training (which might interfere with its generalization) and hostility to the proposed subject-like organisation. The tendency was to prefer a curricular space that could be coordinated by the class tutor. However, the minister's decision was to create a specific subject of 'personal and social development', alternative to 'moral and religious education' (Catholic or based on other creeds); additionally, all subjects, the school ethos and extra-curricular activities should also be concerned with personal and social education.

This political decision gave rise to an important

and public debate on values in education. For some, the alternative status was clearly a 'misunderstanding', since personal and social development should be broader than ethical and moral education (Brederode Santos 1992, Campos 1992a, Castro 1992, Lourenço 1992, Roldão 1993, Carita and Abreu 1994, Reis and Salgado 1994); for others, it was the proof that this new subject was ultimately (and exclusively) about values (Cunha 1993, 1994). Moreover, Portuguese authors diverged on how values should be addressed: should it be, as Lourenço (1992) puts it, an 'education for justice' or an 'education for holiness'? Underlying this debate is the issue of what role students, through personal and social education, are expected to play in the process of values construction. Marques (1994) explicitly argues that personal and social education should inculcate certain values (courage, goodness, etc.) that are considered basic. Campos (1991) considers that this is only a problem in the absence of social consensus; when unanimity about values exists, it is probably not necessary for the school to make an explicit effort to transmit such values; when these values are still under discussion and far from reaching a social agreement, perhaps the school should not take sides; and perhaps more important is the role that formal education can play in empowering youngsters to be active participants in the ongoing process of personal and social construction of values.

The significance of this discussion is not exclusive to Portugal; on the contrary, the major contemporary theoretical proposals on values education simply vary in relative emphasis over these issues. Therefore, the assumptions of these proposals, as well as their legitimacy and effectiveness, should be carefully analysed if one aims to make progress with the fundamental issue in values in education: the fact that, as Mosher (1978) puts it, 'your feet are always in the water'.[2]

## Theoretical proposals on values in education: an exploratory typology

The concern with values in education has given rise to a multiplicity of theoretical proposals and intervention strategies, which vary greatly in their epistemological assumptions and practical considerations. Recently, Coimbra and Campos have proposed a typology for analysis of the rationality, aims and processes of various strategies in the area

of interpersonal development (Coimbra 1991b) and vocational guidance (Campos 1992b) which can be useful in analysing the main contemporary theories on values education. These authors identify two major types of intervention strategies: one that is informative-instructive and one that involves reconstructive exploration. The former emphasises the acquisition of specific skills, dispositions or behaviours through training in artificial situations, mainly by the use of information transmission and role-playing techniques; the latter stresses the need to take into account real-life experiences in order to transform idiosyncratic processes of meaning-making.

Informative-instructive strategies in values education include character education and skills-training approaches in the moral domain. A common assumption is the imposition of an alien rationality that is considered to be the 'good rationality': the aim is to teach the students more 'adequate' ways of behaving and 'better' values to guide their actions, presupposing that the students' values or behaviours are inadequate or wrong. However, little or no account is taken of the processes involved in the development of dispositions or behaviours and, through directive techniques, the student is expected to acquire this 'better' way of functioning, generally in artificial contexts, and to act accordingly in real-life situations. This emphasis on students' adaptation to society generally does not include an analysis and critique of the social conditions: as Beane (1990: 99) puts it, 'character education is yet another case of implying that young people should be made to adapt to present conditions without questioning the morality of the conditions themselves'. Therefore the intervention assumes a function of social control (Sultana 1992). This is sometimes clearly stated by some authors in the field: Ryan (1989: 15) considers that 'the public pays teachers not to devise schemes to change the social order, but to educate the young to a much more demanding idea, to teach the young the best of the past so that they might preserve it and build on it and thus extend it and improve on it'.

The movement for character education (Wynne 1985/1986, 1989, Walberg and Wynne 1989, Ryan 1989, 1993, Lickona 1991, 1993, Kilpatrick 1992, Wynne and Ryan, 1992) is paradigmatic of these type of strategies. Its fundamental aim is to promote students' 'good character', defined as a three-dimensional concept involving knowledge, affect and action (Ryan 1989). Knowledge implies acquiring skills of ethical reasoning, affect refers to 'help(ing) the young learn to love the good' (p. 10), and action includes the will to pursue justice, the skills and behaviours to act effectively and the habit of using such behaviours in life situations. The educational practices suggested comprise:

1   example, considering that teachers should be models of ethical behaviour, and that the study of history and literature should be a source of high moral standards
2   exhortation, appealing to the students' 'best instincts' (Ryan 1989: 12) in order to change their feelings and behaviours
3   environmental expectations, emphasising the need to create a moral classroom environment
4   experience, through the involvement of the students in projects that include helping those in need.

Recognising the importance of the school ethos, Ryan (1989) also suggests that there should be high expectations concerning the ethical behaviour of the school staff and older students, stresses the value of school codes, mottoes and rituals that emphasise good character and deeds, and evaluation procedures that reward 'good discipline, contributions to the life of the classroom, service to the school and the community, respect for others, and good sportsmanship' (Ryan 1993: 18).

It seems clear that authors in this domain consider that moral choices in real-life situations are always clear-cut, that moral principles can be reduced to a bag of virtues and that there is a direct relationship between values and behaviours (Lockwood 1985/86, 1991, 1993). Based on these, at the least, doubtful assumptions, the theorists of character education define inventories of values – kindness, honesty, respect for authority, self-restraint, self-discipline, 'the right to private property' (ibid.: 16), etc.[3] – that should be inculcated, therefore imposing their rationality upon the students. Underlying these proposals is the conception that young people are mere passive recipients of adult messages, denying the fact that the meaning of values can depend on the individual's developmental characteristics and results from a process of active construction on the part of the subject (see Menezes and Campos 1997 for an empirical validation of this assumption). Moreover, as Lockwood ironically observes, 'to be effective, it appears that we must not only persuade teachers to be moral

educators but also persuade young people to pay attention to them' (1993: 75). Finally, but not least important, evaluation of the effectiveness of educational interventions that aim for the acquisition of specific skills and behaviours reveals small and not enthusiastic results, generally with rare and erratic effects in real-life situations (Barker 1984).

Reconstructive exploration strategies rest on psychodynamic, humanist, structural-cognitive and ecological perspectives of human development, especially in their more recent conceptualisations (Bronfenbrenner 1979, 1986, Mahoney and Lyddon 1988, Beane 1990, Sprinthall 1991, Campos 1992b, Mahoney and Patterson 1992, Campos et al. 1994). Their main assertion is that individuals have an active role in the process of meaning-making which results from confrontation with relevant life-experiences, in context, and critical reflection on these experiences. The individual's relationship with the world, which involves mainly affect and emotion and not knowledge, is indissociable from action (Campos 1992b); that is why these strategies place such a strong emphasis on action opportunities as a means to the construction and reconstruction of the subject's relationship with the world, which is achieved through interaction with others in a specific social context. And the meanings thus produced are necessarily different according to the quality of those experiences and interactions and to the social context in which they occur. Therefore, the intervention must 'provide people with experiences that can help them question and transform their current relationship with the world and create the conditions that will allow them to live, express and integrate those experiences' (ibid.: 13–14). There is 'a basic respect of the individual's right to determine the direction of their own destiny' (Campos 1989: 161), aiming to promote their capacity to participate in the process of social transformation (Campos 1991, Sultana 1992). These perspectives take into account the psychological processes that underlie personal change (Coimbra 1991b) and the fact that human action is, by definition, 'action-in-context' (Orford 1992). Therefore, the aim is not to impose meanings and norms but to support the individual's efforts to reconstruct personal meanings and his/her current relationship with the world. Another relevant aspect is the ecological dimension of change, recognising the importance of transforming 'transpersonal structures' such as moral climate, social support networks, organisational features and power relations within a given context, if the intended changes at the individual level are to endure (Bronfenbrenner 1979, 1986; Weissberg, Caplan and Sivo, 1989, Campos et al. 1994). Finally, evaluation of the effectiveness of these approaches has revealed positive results (Barker 1984, Sprinthall and Scott 1989, Silva and Miranda (eds) 1990, Powell et al. 1991).

A paradigmatic proposal of reconstructive exploration strategies is the deliberate psychological education model developed by Norman Sprinthall (1980, 1991). Sprinthall considers that the effectiveness of deliberate psychological education depends on four major components:

1  role-taking, that is, meaningful, challenging and in-context experiences, generally involving interpersonal relationships with others
2  balanced reflection on experience
3  support, since 'growing to new levels of cognitive-development is painful' (Sprinthall 1991: 37)
4  continuity, since no change is to be expected from discontinuous or brief experiences.

The intervention must give students opportunities for assuming significant roles in real-life situations (such as the development of supportive relationships with small children, older people, or others); these experiences are challenging and disturbing, in the Piagetian sense, therefore allowing cognitive conflict to emerge, a necessary condition for evolution through more complex levels of self-organisation. However, this emphasis on action should not be interpreted as mere 'activism', which would have adverse consequences (Schultz and Selman 1990), but as an organised opportunity for meaningful action that must be accompanied by systematic reflective enquiry. In fact, the balance between action and reflection is mandatory if the aim is personal integration and the construction of personal meaning from experience. Obviously, this implies the need for the other two components, continuity and support: long-term and continuous projects are necessary for changes in personal development to arise, and teacher support is fundamental, since confrontation with challenging experiences can arouse negative emotions and the development of new ways of conceiving the world implies dealing with loss; a safe context and supportive relationships are crucial for taking the risk involved in personal growth (Marcia 1991).

Evaluation of the effectiveness of deliberate psychological education has revealed significant results in the area of personal development, including relevant improvements in moral reasoning (e.g., Thies-Sprinthall 1984, Sprinthall and Scott 1989). Its effects in other than processual dimensions, such as the individual's skills or values and attitudes, have not been emphasised, although positive results have been detected (Kessler, Ibrahim and Kahn 1986; Reiman et al. 1995); however, although direct effects are not to be expected, the attention given to real-life experiences probably facilitates the transference of the student's learning to daily-life situations. Additionally, other research has proved that the promotion of the complexity, flexibility and reciprocity of self-organisation processes also increases the individual's autonomy and power to act, diminishing the influences of environmental characteristics and the need for an outside-imposed structure (Moos 1987). The result is, therefore, not a 'better person' according to someone else's criteria, but the promotion of the individual's competence to deal, according to personal criteria, with the challenges of ethical action.

The main interest of this typology is that it clarifies the assumptions that underlie the various proposals on values education, a necessary endeavour in a domain that is clearly characterised by many confusions, both from an epistemological and ideological point of view. Additionally, there is a frequent tendency to expect interventions in values education to achieve results that are either improbable under, or even incompatible with, the assumptions of their theoretical models; for instance, to expect changes in students' behaviours as a result of participating in values-clarification programmes or moral-dilemmas discussion (e.g., Niles 1986). Therefore, in order to achieve effectiveness in educational practice, teachers should be able to select interventions that are appropriate to their aims and to the needs of their students and school context, instead of asking for 'miraculous' results from supposedly 'inspired' intervention proposals, without taking into account their assumptions and predictable effects.

Furthermore, analysis of contemporary theories in values education also permits us to identify common factors that are associated with effectiveness, namely:

1  the importance of *time in task*, since episodic and discontinuous or short-term interventions

have been proved irrelevant for changes to emerge

2 the recognition of the relevance of the *hidden curricula* as an intentional target of educational change

3 the need to provide opportunities for *real-life experiences or actions*, with a disbelief in merely rhetorical approaches

4 the usefulness of strategies such as *community action or service* to operationalise the need to transform and diversify the contexts in which values education occurs

5 the relevance of involving *teachers, school administrators and staff, parents and the school environment* if the aim is to promote the ethical development of students

6 the validity of a conception of the individual that integrates, in theory and in practice, *cognitive, affective and behavioural dimensions*, rejecting the rationalistic bias that characterised values-education proposals in the past.

These commonalities include formal characteristics which are useful in the design of effective interventions by stressing the factors that educational research has validated. Acknowledgement and definition of these is fundamental in values education, if one aims to avoid ambivalence and equivocal practices. But still, a major question remains: is the final objective of values education to help students become 'better' individuals performing 'good' deeds or more autonomous and developed persons with more possibilities and alternatives for principled action?

This question is frequently reduced, by adherents of the former perspective, to whether or not we agree that students should follow certain rules and conform to specific attitudes and behaviours, such as addressing teachers with respect or treating their colleagues fairly and in non-violent ways. The denial of these adequate aims of values education would, according to them, imply a dangerous value relativism, which means accepting that all attitudes and behaviours are similarly 'good'. However, as Audigier (1996) has recently proposed in analysing civic education, underlying this argument are different conceptions of what values education is about: the difference between civility education and civic education, i.e., an education aiming to enable students to learn the good manners, courtesy and politeness that are necessary for social interaction, or an education that empowers the individual to

critically reflect on his/her society and to participate in social transformation.

## Values education in Portugal: current challenges and constraints

The implementation of values education in Portugal, as proposed in the 1986 Education Act and the subsequent curricular reform (1989–91), faces some major challenges and constraints. In a social context characterised by a large consensus on the importance of values education, recent innovations have given schools formal instruments with which to address values education within both the curriculum and the school as an organisation. However, dealing effectively with the implementation of values education demands a strong emphasis on resources, namely on:

1 *teachers' in-service training*, aiming at the development of reflexive professionals, committed to excellence in every aspect of their educational practice (and not merely emphasising subject matter and cognitive dimensions of their work)

2 *the production of curricular materials* that could serve as examples for educational practice, giving teachers access to relevant materials but simultaneously discouraging 'package' or 'recipe' approaches

3 *the diffusion of values-education experiences in other countries*, thus challenging teachers and significant others with the diversity of proposals in this domain and allowing the identification of relevant criteria for practice

4 *educational research*, since studies on the curriculum, schools' organisation, curriculum materials, teachers' attitudes and practices are scarce since the curricular reform; moreover, existing studies on political socialisation do not focus on the effectiveness of school education in promoting students' development and citizenship; finally, there is no research on students' representations of citizenship or their attitudes towards the law and authority, and no national assessment of values education has ever been undertaken.

An additional challenge has to do with the fact that democracies have not yet resolved effectively the gap between discourse and practice, even if its importance is generally acknowledged. A common example in Western countries has to do with voting behaviours, since it does not seem adequate that a democratic regime should be supported – as Western democracies frequently are – by only a small percentage of its citizens. Unfortunately, in educational interventions this is also true, and while students are exposed to formal opportunities for democratic messages they frequently experience, either within or outside the schools, a quite different reality.

Therefore, and even assuming that the school is not (and probably should not be) functioning artificially as an ideal 'just community' (Kolhberg 1985), the gap between discourse and results can be quite disturbing: while stating our 'good intentions' for promoting free, autonomous and tolerant citizens we may only be giving students opportunities for egocentrism, conformism and scepticism.

Finally, we strongly believe that the quality and effectiveness of values education in Portugal will depend on the assumption of an ecological-developmental approach (Campos et al. 1994), emphasising (i) a holistic approach to individuals or personal systems, (ii) changes in personal and transpersonal structures, empowering both individuals and their communities by transforming social-support resources, organisational features and psychosocial climates (Beane 1990, Gottlieb 1988, Moos 1987, Orford 1992, Vaux 1988) and (iii) the structuring of 'real-life opportunities where they can be practiced and reinforced' (Weissberg, Caplan and Sivo 1989: 266), instead of relying on segmented programmes, thus addressing real-life problems and situations (Sprinthall 1991) of the kind that students face within and outside the school.

## Notes

1 Curious, but not surprising, given the very centralised nature of the whole educational system, was the initial reaction of some teachers, who kept asking the ministry what they should do in the new area.

2 Mosher (1978) is quoting D. W. Brogan, who states: 'Democracy is like a raft. It never sinks, but damn it, your feet are always in the water.'

3 Curiously, the values included in these inventories are not necessarily the same across different proposals (see Beane 1990: 99–100), revealing that the universality criterion frequently used as an argument for the validity of character education is doubtful.

## References

Almeida, J. F. (1994) 'Evoluções recentes e valores na sociedade', in E. Ferreira and H. Rato (eds), *Portugal Hoje*, Lisboa: INA, pp. 55–70.

Audigier, F. (1996) '*Civics Education, Human Rights Education and the Council of Europe. Summing up the outlook*,' paper presented at the consultation meeting on the project Education for Democratic Citizenship, CDCC, Council of Europe, Strasbourg, 24–5 June.

Barker, J. R. (1984) 'Primary prevention and assessment', *The Personnel and Guidance Journal* (Apr.) 475–8.

Barreto, A. (1994) 'Portugal, a Europa e a democracia', *Análise Social*, 29. 129: 1051–69.

Beane, J. A. (1990) *Affect in the Curriculum. Towards Democracy, Dignity and Diversity*, NY: Teachers College, Columbia University.

Bettencourt, A. M. (1982) *La Liaison École-millieu-production à l'École Secondaire Portugaise*, Paris: University of Paris V.

Bettencourt, A. M. and Brederode Santos, M. E. (1983) 'O serviço cívico estudantil: proposta para uma discussão', *O Professor*, 51: 4–20.

Braga da Cruz, M. (1985) 'A participação política da juventude em Portugal', *Análise Social*, 21 (87, 88, 89): 1057–88.

Brederode Santos, M. E. (1981) 'Inovação educacional', in M. Silva and M. I. Tamen (eds), *Sistema de Ensino em Portugal*, Lisboa: Fundação Calouste Gulbenkian.

Brederode Santos, M. E. (1984) *Education for Democracy: A Developmental Approach to Teacher Education*, Boston: Boston University.

Brederode Santos, M. E. (1992) 'Educação cívica', in *Formação Pessoal e Social*, Porto: SPCE, pp. 99–104.

Brederode Santos, M. E. and Dias, M. (1993) 'Bem-estar individual, relações interpessoais e participação social' in L. França (ed.), *Portugal. Valores Europeus. Identidade Cultural*, Lisboa: IED, pp. 43–74.

Bronfenbrenner, U. (1979) *The Ecology of Human Development*, Cambridge, MA: Harvard University Press.

Bronfenbrenner, U. (1986) 'Ecology of the Family as a Context for Human Development: Research Perspectives', *Developmental Psychology*, 22. 6: 723–42.

Cabral, M. V. (1995) 'Grupos de simpatia partidária em Portugal: Perfil sociográfico e atitudes sociais', *Análise Social*, 30. 130: 175–205.

Campos, B. P. (1989) *Questões de Política Educativa*, Porto: Asa.

Campos, B. P. (1991) *Educação e Desenvolvimento Pessoal e Social*, Porto: Afrontamento.

Campos, B. P. (1992a) 'A formação pessoal e social na reforma educativa portuguesa', in *Formação Pessoal e Social*, Porto: SPCE.

Campos, B. P. (1992b) 'A informação na orientação profissional', *Cadernos de Consulta Psicológica*, 8: 5–16.

Campos, B. P., Costa, M. E. and Menezes, I. (1994)

'The Social Dimension of Deliberate Psychological Education', in G. Musitu, M. Gutierrez and J. Pons (eds), *Intervención Comunitaría*, Valencia: Set i Set Edic, pp. 31–40

Campos, B. P. and Menezes, I. (1996) 'Personal and Social Education in Portugal', *Journal of Moral Education*, 25. 3: pp. 343–57.

Carita, A. and Abreu, I. (1994) *Desenvolvimento Pessoal e Social. Programa para o 3º Ciclo do Ensino Básico*, Lisboa: Instituto de Inovação Educacional.

Castro, L. B. (1992) 'A comunicação na sala de aula e a formação pessoal e social', in *Formação Pessoal e Social*, Porto: SPCE, pp. 111–116.

Coimbra, J. L. (1991a) '*Desenvolvimento de Estruturas Cognitivas da Compreensão e Acção Interpessoal*', PhD thesis, Porto University.

Coimbra, J. L. (1991b) *Estratégias Cognitivo-desenvolvimentais em Consulta Psicológica Interpessoal*, Porto: ICPFD.

Coimbra, J. and Campos, B. P. (1991) 'The Relationship between the Interpersonal Understanding and Interpersonal Negotiation Strategies in Adolescents: A Cross-Sectional Study', in B. P. Campos and C. Vandenplas-Holper (eds), *Interpersonal and Identity Development: New Research Directions*, Porto and Louvain-La-Neuve: ICPFD and Academia.

Conde, I. (1989) *A Identidade Social e Nacional dos Jovens*, Lisboa: Instituto da Juventude e Instituto das Ciências Sociais.

Correia Jesuíno, J. (1983) 'Valores finais da juventude portuguesa em 1983', in *Situação, Problemas e Perspectivas da Juventude em Portugal*, Vol. VIII, Lisboa: IED, pp. 121–39.

Costa, M. E. (1991) *Contextos Sociais de Vida e Desenvolvimento da Identidade*, Lisboa: INIC.

Costa, M. E. and Campos, B. P. (1991) 'Social Context and Identity Development: The Case of University Area of Study', in B. P. Campos and C. Vandenplas-Holper (eds.), *Interpersonal and Identity Development: New Research Directions*, Porto and Louvain-La-Neuve: ICPFD and Academia.

Cunha, P. O. (1993) 'Objectivos, conteúdos e métodos da disciplina de desenvolvimento pessoal e social', *Inovação*, 6. 3: 287–308.

Cunha, P. O. (1994) 'A formação moral no ensino público. (Evolução de uma ideia)', *Brotéria*, 130: 59–80.

Dewey, J. (1966 (1916)) *Democracy and Education*, New York: Macmillan Publishing Co., Inc.

Figueiredo, E. (1988) *Conflito de Gerações. Conflito de Valores*, Lisboa: Fundação Calouste Gulbenkian.

França, L. (ed.) (1993) *Portugal, Valores Europeus, Identidade Cultural*, Lisboa: IED.

Godinho, V. M. (1984) 'A educação, a transformação de Portugal e a mudança de civilização', in A. Sérgio, *Educação Cívica*. Lisboa: ME.

Gottlieb, B. H. (1988) 'Support intervention: a typology and agenda for research', in S. Duck (ed.), *Handbook of Personal Relationships: Theory, Research and Interventions*, Chichester: Wiley.

Grácio, R. (1981) *Educação e Processo Democrático em Portugal*, Lisboa: Livros Horizonte.

Kessler, G. R., Ibrahim, F. A. and Kahn, H. (1986) 'Character development in adolescents', *Adolescence*, 21(8): 1–9.

Kilpatrick, W. K. (1992) *Why Johnny Can't Tell Right from Wrong*, NY: Simon & Schuster.

Kohlberg, L. (1985) 'The Just Community Approach to Moral Education in Theory and Practice' in M. W. Berkowitz and F. Oser (eds), *Moral Education: Theory and Application*, Hillsdale, NJ: Erlbaum.

Lickona, T. (1991) *Educating for Character: How Our Schools Can Teach Respect and Responsibility*, New York: Bantam Books.

Lickona, T. (1993) 'The Return of Character Education', *Educational Leadership*, 51. 3: 6–11.

Lima, L. (1992) '*A Escola como Organização e a Participação na Organização Escolar*', PhD thesis, Braga: Universidade do Minho.

Lockwood, A. L. (1985/86) 'Keeping Them in the Courtyard: A Response to Wynne', *Educational Leadership*, 43: 9–10.

Lockwood, A. L. (1991) 'Character Education: The Ten Per Cent Solution', *Social Education*, 55. 4: 246–8.

Lockwood, A. L. (1993) 'A Letter to Character Education', *Educational Leadership*, 51. 3: 72–5.

Lourenço, O. M. (1992) 'Desenvolvimento pessoal e social: Educação para a justiça ou educação para a "santidade"?' *Revista Portuguesa de Educação*, 5. 2: 129–36.

Mahoney, M. J. and Lyddon, W. J. (1988) 'Recent Developments in Cognitive Approaches to Counseling and Psychotherapy', *The Counseling Psychologist*, 16: 190–234.

Mahoney, M. J. and Patterson, K. M. (1992) 'Changing Theories of Change: Recent Developments in Counseling', in S. D. Brown and R. W. Lent (eds), *Handbook of Counseling Psychology*, New York: Wiley, pp. 665–89.

Marcia, J. (1991) 'Counseling and Psychotherapy from a Developmental Perspective', in B. P. Campos (ed.), *Psychological Intervention and Human Development*, Porto: Instituto de Consulta Psicológica, Formação e Desenvolvimento da FPCEUP and Louvain-La-Neuve: Academia.

Marques, R. (1994) 'Modelos curriculares de educação pessoal e social', in J. Tavares (ed.), *Para Intervir em Educação. Contributos dos Colóquios CIDInE*, Aveiro: CIDInE.

Menezes, I. and Campos, B. P. (1997) 'The Process of Value-Meaning Construction: A Cross-Sectional Study', *European Journal of Social Psychology*, 27: 55–73.

Mónica, M. F. (1978) *Educação e Sociedade no Portugal de Salazar*, Lisboa: Presença.

Moos, R. (1987) 'Person-environment congruence in work, school and health care settings', *Journal of Vocational Behavior*, 31: 231–47.

Mosher, R. L. (1978) 'A Democratic High School: Damn It, Your Feet are Always in the Water', in N. A. Sprinthall and R. L. Mosher (eds), *Value Development as the Aim of Education*, New York: Character Research Press, pp. 69–116.

Niles, W. J. (1986) 'Effects of a moral developmental discussion group on delinquent and predelinquent boys', *Journal of Counseling Psychology*, 33. 1: 45–51.

Orford, J. (1992) *Community Intervention. Theory and Practice*, Chichester: Wiley.

Piaget, J. (1977) *Études Sociologiques*, Genève: Librairie Droz.

Powell, R. E., Locke, D. C. and Sprinthall, N. A. (1991) 'Female Offenders and their Guards: A Programme to Promote Moral and Ego Development of Both Groups', *Journal of Moral Education*, 20. 2: 191–203.

Raths, L., Harmin, M. and Simon, S. B. (1978) *Values and Teaching*, Columbus, OH: Merrill.

Reiman, A. J., Bostick, D., Lassiter, J. and Cooper, J. (1995). 'Counselor- and teacher-led support groups for beginning teachers: A cognitive-developmental perspective.' *Elementary School Guidance & Counseling*, 30.2: 105–17.

Reis, I. B. and Salgado, L. (1994) 'O contexto escolar e a formação pessoal e social', in J. Tavares (ed.), *Para Intervir em Educação. Contributos dos Colóquios CIDInE*, Aveiro: CIDInE.

Reis, M. L. B. (1985) *Inserção e Participação Social dos Jovens*, Lisboa: IED.

Reis, M. L. B. (1986) 'Tendências recentes da atitude dos jovens portugueses face à política: análise comparativa com os indicadores europeus', *Desenvolvimento*, special issue: 67–8.

Reis, M. L. B. and Dias, M. (1993) 'Grupos e valores de referência sócio-políticos', in L. França (ed.), *Portugal. Valores Europeus. Identidade Cultural*, Lisboa: IED, pp. 261–306.

Roldão, M. C. (1993) 'Desenvolvimento pessoal e social: contradições e limites de uma área curricular, *Inovação*, 6. 3: 337–43.

Ryan, K. (1989) 'In Defense of Character Education', in L. P. Nucci (ed.), *Moral Development and Character Education: A Dialogue*, Berkeley, CA: McCutchan Publishing Corporation, pp. 3–17.

Ryan, K. (1993) 'Mining the Values in the Curriculum', *Educational Leadership*, 51. 3: 16–18.

Schultz, L. H. and Selman, R. L. (1990) 'Relations among Interpersonal Action-related Thought, Self-reported Social Action and Emotional Maturity in Early Adolescents', in C. Vandenplas-Holper and B. P. Campos (eds), *Interpersonal and Identity Development: New Directions*, Porto: Instituto de Consulta Psicológica, Formação e Desenvolvimento and Louvain-La-Neuve: Academia.

Sérgio, A. (1984 (1915)) *Educação Cívica*. Lisboa: ME.

Silva, M. J. and Miranda, G. (eds) (1990) *Projecto Alcácer*, Lisboa: Gulbenkian.

Sprinthall, N. A. (1980) 'Psychology for Secondary Schools: The Saber-tooth Curriculum Revisited?', *American Psychologist*, 35. 4: 336–47.

Sprinthall, N. A. (1991) 'Role Taking Programs for High School Students: New Methods to Promote Psychological Development', in B. P. Campos (ed.), *Psychological Intervention and Human Development*, Porto: Instituto de Consulta Psicológica, Formação e Desenvolvimento and Louvain-La-Neuve: Academia, pp. 33–8.

Sprinthall, N. A. and Scott, J. R. (1989) 'Promoting Psychological Development, Math Achievement, and Success Attribution of Female Students through Deliberate Psychological Education', *Journal of Counseling Psychology*, 36. 4: 440–6.

Sultana, R. G. (1992) 'Personal and Social Education: Curriculum Innovation and School Bureaucracies in Malta', *British Journal of Guidance and Counselling*, 20. 2: 164–85.

Thies–Sprinthall, L. (1984) 'Promoting the Developmental Growth of Supervising Teachers: Theory, Research Programs, and Implications, *Journal of Teacher Education*, 35. 3: 53–60.

Vala, J. (1985) *Representações Sociais dos Jovens: Valores, Identidade e Imagens da Sociedade Portuguesa*, Lisboa: IED.

Vala, J. (1986) 'Identidade e valores da juventude portuguesa uma abordagem exploratória', *Desenvolvimento*, special issue: 17–28.

Vaux, A. (1988) *Social Support: Theory and Intervention*, NY: Praeger.

Walberg, H. J. and Wynne, E. A. (1989) 'Character Education: Toward a Preliminary Consensus', in L. P. Nucci (ed.), *Moral Development and Character Education: A Dialogue*, Berkeley, CA: McCutchan Publishing Corporation, pp. 37–50.

Weissberg, R. P., Caplan, M. Z. and Sivo, P. (1989) 'A New Conceptual Framework for Establishing School-based Social Competence Promotion Programs', in L. A. Bond and B. E. Compas (eds), *Primary Prevention and Promotion in the Schools*, Newbury Park, CA: Sage Publications, Inc.

Wynne, E. A. (1985/1986) 'The Great Tradition in Education: Transmitting Moral Values', *Educational Leadership*, 43: 4–10.

Wynne, E. A. (1989) 'Transmitting traditional values in contemporary schools', in L. P. Nucci (ed.), *Moral Development and Character Education: A Dialogue*, Berkeley, CA: McCutchan Publishing Corporation, pp. 19–36.

Wynne, E. A. and Ryan, K. (1992) *Reclaiming our Schools: A Handbook of Teaching Character, Academics and Discipline*, NY: Merrill.

# 20 Valuing Being

ANTHONY J. GRAINGER

In our current emphasis on 'doing' – on achieving goals and meeting targets – the need 'to be' and to 'reflect' is easily overlooked. Winnicott's observation, 'after being – doing and being done to. But first, being', focuses on the importance of who we are and not simply on what we do. And for James Hillman (1974: 99) the most important of all the 're-'; words is 're-spect', meaning to look again; this for him is the whole of psychology in a single word (1991: 118–19). The need 'to be' and to 're-spect' deserve to be valued.

The prefix 're-', with its general sense of 'back' or 'again' is an invitation to stop in our tracks, to pause and to re-view, which is why for Hillman it is the most important syllable in psychology. He reflects on such words as remember, return, revision, religion, respect and respond. Psychotherapy invites us to re-spect, to look again at ourselves, but with respect, and to give time to ourselves since without time there is no relationship.

To say that 'I've no time for' or can't give 'the time of day to' either myself or another person is to have no respect; a patient in therapy, echoing Groucho Marx, said, 'If I were someone else I wouldn't want to know anyone like me'. And another commented that, 'I'm a thing what does, not a person who is'. Feeling that she had never been given the time to be, or to have her own life, she remained outside herself; she could 'act' but not 'be'. Someone who sees herself primarily as a functionary – 'a thing what does' – may *act* 'correctly' but does not do so from the centre of 'a person who *is*'.

As a teacher of English in a secondary school in the early 1960s I tried to create a class setting in which children could for about one hour each week find a time to be and to reflect; in all I worked in these groups for a total of about 135 hours. This was not group therapy, but it was a situation in which 30 or so young adolescent boys and girls, sitting in a circle face to face, studied their own behaviour as it occurred. Since I also taught these classes in normal lessons, I had a dual role. Once or twice a term I would ask them to write about – to reflect on – what, if anything, they had learnt. Ticking boxes and five-point assessment criteria were not in vogue then, so the children responded in, more or less, continuous prose which accommodates reflection better than tick boxes.

These meetings were nicknamed 'The Bullring' because, as one girl said, 'the speaker and the person being spoken to are all alone, like the bull and the matador in a bullring'. Professor Anthony noted that the title suggests 'excitement and violence, attack and counter-attack, cruelty and courage, and, somewhere along the line, perhaps a dreadful moment of truth'.[1] My aim of providing 'a safe area in which young adolescents could find out for themselves what sort of persons they and their friends and enemies were in relation to one another' had unforeseen consequences. I concluded the Preface to my book by saying that

> the risks taken were justified by results, and that unless we, as adults, will risk being personally involved in the moral education of children, such education is likely to remain an affair of the head without ever touching the heart.   (Grainger 1970: XV)

Since the psychological framework was loosely based on W. R. Bion's (1961) theories which, with inevitable modifications in the course of time, are still used by the Tavistock and the Grubb Institutes, the theoretical base remains more or less intact. But because children act out more readily there have to be rules which are unnecessary in comparable adult groups. There were therefore rules against causing physical harm, damaging school property, making excessive noise, and being 'disrespectful' to children or teachers coming into the room on school business. Additionally, without a rule against breaking the circle, which was generally obeyed, the children wandered about the room and split up into small uncontrollable groups with which it was impossible to communicate except by my reverting to an authoritarian role. Winnicott remarked that 'spontaneity only makes sense in a controlled setting', and that content has no meaning without form (Davis and Wallbridge 1981: 144). The rules enforced by my authority were part of the 'controlled setting', but the hope was that the children would eventually internalise their own 'form' or authority. The rules were to be obeyed in the spirit rather than to the letter.

The Bullring was therefore 'free' but not so formless as to be terrifying in its absence of structure, and the teacher tried to represent and re-present those attitudes of stillness, reflection and respect through which understanding might grow. A girl wrote that when they first discovered that they 'could say anything to anyone', the insults began to fly, 'most of all' to 'Mr Grainger who just sat still and did not seem to mind'. In an accurately remembered summary, she continued:

> According to Mr Grainger and his psychology, this all alarmed us and in one discussion this all came to light by us discussing bull fights and fox-hunting. In the fox-hunting discussion we said that if the farmer had locked up his chickens the fox wouldn't come after them . . . so it all boiled down to the fact that it was the farmer's fault that the foxes got out of control. This meant that it was Mr Grainger's fault that we got out of control, because he didn't use enough disciplinary action. But this was Mr Grainger's psychology again, and one of the reasons why the group turns 'aggressive' towards him, is because he always interprets everything we say psychologically, and not many in the group agree with him.
>
> Then we come to a phase where everyone criticises Mr Grainger in one way or another, either his dress, his manner or something else . . .
>
> After this phase, we began to get some quite sensible discussions going, and . . . began to talk freely to one another quite sensibly.
>
> But this state of affairs was not to last . . .
>
> The next Bullring was only about four weeks from the end of the term and we somehow got around to talking about death, and this, according

to Mr Grainger's psychology meant that in our subconscious we were aware that our Bullrings had almost come to an end; they had almost died in fact.

And this week we had another Bullring, but we did not discuss at all. In fact we realised that the Bullring had DIED the week previous.

Although some children said my comments were 'just right, for others I was a 'psychological Nit Wit' who talked 'Freudian hogwash'. I would still want to defend my comment about the farmer and the foxes; in a sense it was my 'fault' for allowing a situation to develop in which the children could be – though need not only remain – aggressive foxes rather than docile chickens. How to manage their own aggression, of which they could become victims, was a recurring topic. However, this writer has understood and remembered a way of interpreting even if she doesn't agree with it, although she seems to accept my comment that the Bullring had 'DIED' the previous week.

The following thought intelligently expresses approval of my 'psychology', but with qualifications: I ought to explain that I'm talking about *unconscious* motivation, and although they want to remain independent and I make 'the right number of comments', the Bullring could be improved by my not sitting there like a 'dummy':

> I seem now to find myself in complete agreement with your psychology views which most other people in the Bullring laugh at. I think that the Bullring could be improved . . . by making it a lot more clear that your psychology views are not in the conscious mind. The way you give your views it sounds as if we deliberately and consciously think these things. Perhaps the Bullring could be improved also by you not sitting there like a dummy.

Another boy was less restrained: 'Teachers should not go gassing and boring everyone with their speeches and psychology as nobody likes it and most people think it's mad.'

In spite of these protestations I had to resist demands for extra Bullrings, not primarily, I think, because the children wanted to avoid lessons. Once there was a note on my desk signed by all 32 members of a class saying that, 'without another Bullring tomorrow, our efforts will be wasted. . . . With the aid of you and our double lesson we think we can safely sort ourselves out'.

Since moral condemnation oppressses rather

than liberates, the Bullring approach is one of trying to understand, something which Andrew attempts:

> But I think the main reason for the lack of interest in the Bullring is that we now feel that we must tackle the more grown-up and adult subjects and that we are completely at a loss to know how to start and because of this I feel we start to talk and begin the childish habit of throwing paper, as a means of disguise to cover up our embarrassment. I was surprised we had started to throw paper, and I think that this has revived from our two previous years at the school. I also think that in the past four weeks we have been able to make much progress and I don't think that anyone would want to throw paper anymore.
>
> I don't think Mr Grainger speaks his mind enough on the topics we put forward and that if he did a lot more of the members of our group would feel more inclined to speak.
>
> I disagree entirely with our group when they say that members of our group refuse to listen or act awkward. I do not think these actions are performed on purpose as they seem to imply. I think it is partly from embarrassment and partly from our difficult age that makes everybody act so.
>
> I do not think that SEX is a good topic to start the group off with as some weeks have shown and VIOLENCE and WAR should be given a try-out.

When Andrew is 'surprised' by the paper-throwing he tries to understand, or to stand under *the fact*, rather than to find *fault*. The group regresses to this 'childish habit' out of anxiety: it is a 'disguise to cover up our embarrassment'. However, this is not an ideal response and he believes that the progress of the last four weeks would make it unlikely that anyone would want to throw paper again.

'The main reason for the lack of interest', according to Andrew, is that they are at a loss to know how 'to tackle the more grown-up and adult subjects'; or, in other words, they feel defeated by the responsibility of having to find the personal authority to act in a truthful and civilised way. Andrew's wanting me to speak my mind more on 'the topics' is an invitation to intervene with advice and leadership. And his idea that violence and war should be 'given a try-out' in preference to sex, might suggest that he feels that until the group has dealt with its aggressive feelings it is premature to 'talk about' sex, that is about having relationships with classmates of the opposite sex.

The next two writers refer to an occasion when a girl – breaking one of the rules – left her place in the circle, walked across the open space and slapped a boy's face. A boy wrote:

> one of our greatest moves backwards was when Helen hit another member which was a pitiful creature under the name of Collins. I don't really blame Helen for getting really aggressive towards him but obviously if we are all going to go about hitting people because they are dumb and can't help what they do we are eventually going to kill each other. We should ignore them or entirely differently, shout them down. We *must not* encourage them or laugh with them; it will make them worse.

And Helen herself wrote:

> The *worst* thing about the ring is the lack of trust. Nobody really expresses their feelings for fear of it getting out. . . . The thing that *irritated* me is Collins. He tries to be funny, but on the whole he is pathetic. I know it sounds nasty to say that about somebody, but in his case I really mean it. . . .
>
> I have learnt that our class is very interested in the ring. It is that they want the ring to go on. As a class they are not shy, as individuals they're bashful. Many are too shy to express any of their views. As time goes by I think this will pass.

The teacher does not try to change the group's behaviour for the 'better', but to reflect aloud about what he thinks is going on in the group as a whole. These reflections *may* in turn lead to a recognition that if we 'go about hitting people because they are dumb and can't help what they do we are eventually going to kill each other', but on the other hand they may not. *Generally* when people become aware of the possible consequences of their destructive behaviour, and have time to reflect, they will pull back from it, but if disillusionment is to be avoided 'generally' has to be stressed. Helen at least writes honestly about her feelings.

Subsequently in an interview recorded by two of the children, Helen described the Bullring as 'just a dodge to get out of lessons . . . it was a complete and utter failure . . . It's just been larking about and learning how to throw paper darts'. However, she thought it ought to continue and that it could 'succeed', because,

> I think you learn to accept, if of course you get a decent discussion going, I think you learn to accept people that you're with, even though you don't get on with them very well, and anyway people who you do get on well with, I don't think that you really do understand them until you have had a good discussion with them.

The Bullring, then, is not only about learning to 'accept' the shadow, but also about 'really' understanding people you do get on with because you can have 'a good discussion'. As with Andrew's reference to 'topics', 'discussion' here refers not to a subject but to the embodiment of an experience.

Becoming conscious of the shadow, which is an essential aspect of self-knowledge, means recognising as real those shame-inducing drives and values which consciousness rejects; someone who glimpsed her shadow for the first time said, 'I don't like to think I'm that sort of a person'. But where the shadow's existence is denied it becomes projected onto others, something which Laurie Lee appreciated when in an imaginary letter to his newly born daughter (1964: 11), he asked her 'never to persecute others for the sins hidden in herself'.

The children in the Bullring could learn to be moral because in Winnicott's phrase (1958: 270) they were 'healthy', did not need to be taught to feel guilty and could develop concern for one another.[2] It would have been different had they been disturbed and 'psychopathic'. Nevertheless some children are more healthy than others, some naturally feel more concern, and many, particularly if treated with respect, can learn to become *more* concerned. In this they are no different from adults, who, however, since they are more powerful, may project their own shadows onto children. Since adults can easily seek both the cause and cure for their own difficulties in children, Jung (1954: para. 286) recommended that 'if there is anything that we wish to change in our children, we should first examine it and see whether it is not something that could be better changed in ourselves'.

But the shadow not only comprises obviously bad feelings like hatred and envy, but also causes of shame like shyness and anxiety. More positively it represents what remains undeveloped within us, and is therefore 'for each individual what the individual might have been but has not had a chance to be'; consequently it raises problems of 'identity' (Humbert 1988: 49). When they have 'a chance to be', the children make both pleasant and unpleasant discoveries about their identity – 'what I'm really like'. Since repression of the shadow leads not only to the projection of our 'sins' onto others, but also to a weakening of our own personality and the loss of personal energy and 'weight', it needs to be accepted and integrated.

Having referred to being all alone like the bull and the matador, Jane, aware of her own shadow, continued:

> One thing I think the group must do is to learn to accept Jones. It is no good telling him that he cannot join the group . . . He is all right when he is on top but when he is underneath it is a different story. The best thing to do with people like Jones is to ignore them altogether. I don't like Jones and I never will. . . . I could write a lot more about him but I mustn't. The group must learn to accept him. Another reason is that whenever he wants to say anything somebody makes a comment and so he has to reply and the noise starts up again. If we stopped making these comments he might be more sensible. We must learn to accept him.

Jane, like Helen, hasn't solved her problem with a boy whom she will never like, but three times she writes that the group or we 'must learn to accept (him)'; and she rejects the idea of exclusion – 'it is no good telling him that he cannot join the group'. She knows what she feels but also what 'we' must do. She avoids the possibly sanctimonious 'I' and does not temper her dislike with false generosity. Problems which in the 'real' world are often dealt with by 'exclusion', 'getting round' or 'getting on top of' have to be 'faced' in the Bullring. No group ever seriously believed that excluding someone would solve their difficulties. Whether consciously or not, the children understood that 'they' – the awkward ones – were also our shadow, a part of 'us'. The nearest anyone came to being excluded was when my shoes were taken off and placed outside the room in the corridor.

Where acceptance is encouraged personal ambivalence can be expressed. A boy with a lively sense both of his own and the group's shadow, did not like 'these yelling sessions much although I am often involved . . . they make everybody hate everybody else and waste time', but then he was also 'irritated by the people who are always good in the groups'! Again, although he wants 'a little bit more control by the teacher', he 'would like more meetings as (he) believe(s) a lot can be learnt in them that could not be learnt in normal lessons'.

The complaint that if we start to hit people 'we are eventually going to kill each other' recalls the fateful experiment in democracy in William Golding's *Lord of the Flies*. The boys are only 'rescued' from their island by a naval officer, who is a representative of a world as much at war with itself as is the boys' own. When the officer interrupts the boy Ralph with – 'I know. Jolly good show. Like the

Coral Island' – Ralph 'looked at him dumbly'. Unlike the naval officer, Ralph has seen the choirboys' shadows and can weep for 'the end of innocence and the darkness of man's heart'. When 'the other little boys began to shake and sob', 'The officer, surrounded by these noises, was moved and a little embarrassed. He turned away to give them time to pull themselves together; and waited, allowing his eyes to rest on the trim cruiser in the distance'. (Golding 1953: 248). In this, the concluding paragraph of the novel, although he is 'moved' by the boys' sobbing, the officer is also a 'little embarrassed'. Not knowing or perhaps not wanting to know what has been happening on the island, 'he turned away' and found 'rest' in the reassuring symbol of the cruiser, hoping in the meantime that the boys would 'pull themselves together'. Although his life has been saved and order re-established, Ralph is struck 'dumb' by the officer's readiness to believe that it has all been like the Coral Island. Reliance on the power of 'the trim cruiser' may be a regrettable necessity, since as well as being persons we are also 'things' who have to obey the rules and meet targets, but the cruiser mentality is as irrelevant to meeting 'the darkness of man's heart' as is the sentimental denial of its existence.

The issue of 'trust' in the Bullring centres on whether the group believes that the teacher can maintain a non-punitive, non-vengeful role; problems of confidentiality are secondary and I never made promises about this, leaving it to them to decide whether or not I was trustworthy. At the end of one rather turbulent Bullring, a senior teacher who had been present as a visitor, said, on leaving the room, 'I feel very sorry for you, Jones, you've got a lot of growing up to do'. This vengeful response, no doubt hiding the teacher's own anxiety and hurt, destroyed trust and caused the children to be understandably angry with me for allowing it to happen.

But the senior teacher, who shamed Jones, and the naval officer also represent that part in all of us, including the children, which withdraws from the exploration of our own darkness, and prefers repression to consciousness. Nevertheless by their understanding of the difference between acting from a persona and from what Winnicott called 'a true self', the children showed how it was possible, given time, to move to greater consciousness and a deeper moral sense. A girl challenged one group to say what they thought the headmaster would do if he came in, to which a boy replied amid sympathetic laughter, 'He'd just faint'. One alternative to not being able to control the unfamiliar is to black out (or pretend to) and to retreat into unconsciousness.

Children's feelings of inferiority and their vulnerability to being criticised and shamed are not so easily hidden as those of adults. They often react to humiliation by becoming 'cocky, aggressive, and attention-seeking or shy and subdued' (Grainger 1970: xii), all of which responses are encountered in the Bullring, although here in a setting where honesty and respect are encouraged it is easier for individuals to accept these feelings. With trust comes the courage to bring out the truth, and where this does happen, it leads to growing self-confidence and feeling 'better'. As the truth is allowed to emerge in its own way and in its own time, self-respect and generosity seem to flourish; as one boy put it, 'I have learnt a lot about myself because of the ring. I find I can talk more easily (that is when someone listens). It seems to have given me more confidence, I feel better for it'.

True self-confidence encourages objectivity and tolerance; conversely where the pain of inferiority is acute – whether consciously recognised or not – concern for others tends to be eclipsed by the compulsive need to prove one's superiority. In the extracts below the writers are learning to trust the situation and themselves, the last admitting to being both 'a bit shy' and trying to show off, though trusting me enough to pull my ear and talk in 'a funny way'. [Author's additions in square brackets.]

> We have lear'nt that we can trust the teachers because I do not think they will tell anyone.
> Things I have learnt about teachers is that they don't mind you talking about sex and noddy (my nickname) never talks and sometimes never pays attention to the discstion. (Sex Bomb) [a girl]
> I have learnt that i am a bit shy to speak to. i join the noisey lot. I speak to my next door nabourgh and he speak to me. We have confersaions which I dere not speak out – also I have learnt that also i throw things about and try to show of a bit like going up to the teacher and pulling his ear or talking to him in a funny way.

Again, trust opens the way to learning and the exploration of feelings the following comments concern self-knowledge and the 'hidden truth':

> A lot of hidden truth comes out in the descution and to name one would not be fair but everybody has something to hide.

I think what I have learnt about myself should be kept as a personal thought, therefore I don't wish to discuss it.

I have found out what I am really like

I have found some people in the group mentioning no names suddenly show their hidden qualities e.g. they turn against you etc.

There is no pressure to reveal 'personal' thoughts, and although a lot of hidden truth comes out, there is a reluctance to mention names: 'everybody has something to hide'. If the Bullring implies 'face to face', it should also preserve, and allow others to preserve, as much private space as they need. Although the group is not completely a safe space, since some people may 'turn against you':, it is mostly safe enough. 'Frankingstone' below, for example, is surprised to find that he is not as shy as some of the others and that he can trust people.

I can know ['now'] get on with things better (it has gave me courage).

Myself I have learnt to express my own feelings and not to be scared to talk about them.

I am not scared to say what I like to the group or to the teachers. (Pugatha)

I learnt that I was not Shy as Some and I didn't know I cude trust people in the class. (Frankingstone)

But even where these confident claims to have found courage cannot be made, an admisssion of weakness – if only to oneself – is maybe an act of courage which increases self-respect:

They make me feel out of place when surjestive things are said (I am) to quiet I don't let myself out enough to speak and so I sit there, board.

As a member of the class I am quiet and rather shy. I like to listen to what they say but am too shy to join in.

For Jill, who showed an intuitive understanding of what the Bullring meant, 'sex and friendship' was the basic topic; again, she says little about the actual topic, but is able to describe an 'atmosphere' which is 'interesting' and in which respectful conversations are possible.

I think the Bullring has grown in development and has turned out for the best. Through these past weeks I've enjoyed the Bullrings because there is a spark of life and a down to earth atmosphere as well as being interesting because people have started to speak their minds. Some people behave stupidly and try to show off by their silly remarks but these

people do not get anywhere in the world because they forget the Bullring's moral.

I've learnt that the basic subject in our discussion is sex and friendship . . . sometimes (the children) mention this subject to elder people such as teachers and the teachers pretend (*sic*) the children speak stupidly, but this is not so. The teachers think that youths are thoughtless but they are sensitive towards this subject. The class as a whole react quite sensibly towards the Bullring because our class is mature enough to realise the meaning of the Bullring to them and their friends . . . I have learnt a lot from myself . . . I get along with people mainly because I have time (like in the Bullrings) to talk to them. I know I play a big part in the ring to agree and disagree with people, and to bring out the facts about life.

The teacher has no control, so everyone goes crackers – but do they? I don't think so because 3A1 is settling-down now knowing that no teacher is in control. Our comments are good ones and steady. There should be more frequent meetings.

The Bullring 'has grown in development' and 'turned out for the best', and is 'interesting' because people have started to speak their minds. In appreciating both the 'spark of life' and the 'down to earth atmosphere' Jill identifies those elements of spirit and matter which must be held in tension if *depth* is to be generated and play is not either to become leaden or to evaporate in unrelated fantasy. She is impatient with those who show off, who 'do not get anywhere in the world because they forget the Bullring's moral'.

Although neither the 'moral' nor the 'meaning' of the Bullring is defined both are important. Jill has learnt that the basic subject of their discussions is 'sex and friendship', and that they do not speak 'stupidly' about it. She has also learnt a lot about herself because she has time to talk, and 'to agree and disagree with people and to bring out the facts about life'. People don't go 'crackers' because the teacher has 'no control', and there ought to be 'more frequent meetings'.

Since freedom was valued and the rules were self-evidently there to protect that freedom, they were usually obeyed. But it was also recognised that the freedom itself had a serious purpose and was more than simply an opportunity to let off steam and 'go crackers': it was an opportunity to find the self-discipline by which they could live together without needing to destroy, exclude, or tyrannise one another. But this depended on there being *real* situations where students could know anarchy and authority, love and hate, acceptance and rejection, and personally learn the need to put themselves in 'the other person's shoes'.

Since there were no black children in the Bullring groups, scapegoating on racial lines did not become an issue. Difference in colour could, however, be one symbol of 'strangeness', along with other differences such as cultural background. Furthermore, blackness because it is 'dark' can more easily carry the projection of the shadow – of what is unknown, 'other' and felt to be inferior and unreliable. Jung (1963) believed that 'coming to terms with the Other *in us* is well worth while' (my italics) because it led to self-knowledge; failure to acknowledge this other does not mean that we cease to be fearful of it or fascinated by it but simply that another person or group carries our unconscious otherness for us. R. L. Stevenson, for instance, believed that the essential darkness or 'harm' in *Dr Jekyll and Mr Hyde* lay not, where popular imagination locates it, in Hyde, but in Jekyll, who was estranged from himself: '*the harm was in Jekyll*, because he was a hypocrite' (quoted in Saposnik 1947: 98; my italics).

A group may deny attributing 'difference' to someone who arrives late, yet their behaviour may imply that he is in fact perceived as strange and different. When someone arrived 15 minutes late, with suitable apologies, for a one-and-a-half-hour meeting, a group spent the next 35 minutes insisting that they felt no differently towards him than towards anyone else there. Moreover when the latecomer was finally released from being the explicit *object* of their attention, the group became obsessed with topics relating to lack of commitment, poor time-keeping and 'draft-dodging' while at the same time denying that these concerns might suggest that at some level their resentment at his lateness still smouldered.

Mature relationships depend upon our being able both to identify consciously with others and also consciously to value our own difference: when this necessary tension between being both like and unlike others is not properly sustained, or is too unconscious, it may slacken into sentimentality or cruelty, or both. It is 'cruel', for example, to discuss a latecomer as if he were an object, and sentimental to assert that 'our group' is generous enough to forgive lateness.

If an apparently trivial 'difference' like lateness can provoke such resentment that a group has even to deny that there is a problem, it would be naive to imagine that the difference and strangeness represented by *the fact* of ethnic differences could be ignored. The integration of black members or other sub-groups might require as much effort as or more effort than the integration of the latecomer before the shadow projections of, say, an envied or feared otherness were withdrawn.

Individuals and minority groups need not only to be protected from mob rule but have themselves to find a way of not colluding in the victim role. But the victimiser also who projects his own shadow, be it blackness, lateness or disability is himself a victim, threatened to such an extent by these aspects of himself that he has to externalise them. Those children in the Bullring who, following Blake (1946: 190), could feel that 'opposition is true friendship' – that is, those could *use* difference – could also say 'I have learnt a lot about myself'.

The shame of being unable to live up to a personal ideal of, for example, being racially unprejudiced, may lead to the truth of our feelings having to be concealed. Such concealment, however, only preserves what Lawrence (1932: 247) called 'an evil, bad, separating spirit under the warm cloak of good words', where in the gap between professed ideals and what is actually felt, insincerity flourishes.

But since 'we cannot become truthfully related until we have first been properly divided' (Howe 1965: 20) ways of articulating the 'bad separating spirit', behind the warm words, have to be found if truer relationships are to emerge. As Jill saw, the Bullring becomes 'interesting' only when 'people (begin) to speak their minds', but people will only speak their minds when trust has developed by accepting that 'everybody has something to hide'. One of the lessons of the Bullring is that being 'truthfully related' depends upon having first been 'properly divided', and of having worked through some of the divisiveness and aggression of the early meetings.

A black counsellor has recently detected a further complication which she describes as the phenomenon of 'internalised racism' whereby a black person identifies with white as good and rejects their own blackness as bad (Rose 1997). If, say, a subgroup of black children within a larger group were to identify with whiteness as good and to victimise their own blackness, then the group as a whole would be denied what was specifically valuable in the black experience. White children in a predominantly black culture might similarly feel forced to abandon their whiteness.

Black children in a minority within a group would be obvious 'pegs' on whom projections of the stranger, the enemy or the intruder could be hung, and these projections might be intense. But the Bullring tries to create a new, though of necessity temporary, educational institution with its own learning culture, where 'acceptance' is valued and where exclusion is not regarded as a desirable option.

In the course of the creation of this new society black children would no doubt at some stage feel 'different', whether or not this was consciously intended. But only when the projections of the dangerous stranger are withdrawn and the other members of the group search within themselves for their own 'difference' is new life generated. In the macrocosmic world, too, the monotheisms with their 'one-sided perception of a God in whom there is no darkness' (Dourley 1992: 67) – and nations which identify exclusively with their own purity – denounce their enemies as 'Satanic' or the incarnation of 'absolute evil'. The demonisation of an opponent, however, ensures that nothing can be learnt from him since he is held to be totally 'other' and therefore to be finally excluded. But if he is put beyond the pale, he cannot contribute, as the Catholic theologian Dourley puts it, to the discovery of 'one's own totality through the painful processes of integration' (ibid.).

Within the security of the Bullring separateness can be experienced as the necessary complementary opposite of togetherness. Difference, diversity and opposition need not be a prelude to Armageddon in which 'the demons' are finally slain – and we end up killing one another – but can be perceived as 'friendly', that is, as indispensable to our completion both individually and collectively. The opportunity offered by the group to respect, to reflect and to withdraw projections would remain whatever its composition.

As with all rituals the Bullring consecrated time and space to a particular purpose, providing the possibility of, but not guaranteeing, a transformation from one state of being to another. Rituals enact myths and, as Campbell says in his significantly entitled *The Power of Myth* (the significant word being 'power'), 'by participating in a ritual, you are participating in a myth' (Campbell 1989: 82). When, therefore, a girl in a small informal group said 'out of the blue', 'Is it the Bullring today?' it was as if a powerful mythological idea had been fitted to our experience of what had hith-

erto been described dully as 'free discussions'. Yes, of course, she was right: it is as if this were a Bullring.

Ritual settings meet the needs of the unconscious by providing a space which encourages the imagination and marks off, like the frame of a picture, 'a different kind of reality that is within it from that which is outside it' (Milner 1955: 86). The ritual thus functions as a 'container' to 'discipline' the very serious kind of 'play' that becomes possible within its confines – play which can be both enjoyable and frightening (Winnicott 1974: 58–9).

Participants in rituals are engaged at both conscious and unconscious levels and often experience a heightened sense of meaning, or are surprised.[3] Within the circle what was enacted and said could be re-spected and looked at symbolically – what is the meaning and implication of a girl slapping a boy's face, of the paper-throwing, the fox-hunting discussion, my shoes being put outside the door, and so on? By guaranteeing a time to be and supporting the symbolic life or a 'symbolical attitude' (Jung 1977: para 627)[4] ritual encourages the creation of new and significant connections; it is an invitation to fantasy. People are allowed to behave differently – to sit there 'like a dummy' – or wear funny clothes, use peculiar words and express bizarre sentiments – 'Let's castrate Noddy' – and act in exaggerated ways.

Within the ritual, life can be viewed differently; the teacher's having 'no control', for example, is both real and not real, but certainly a cause for concern. Andrew correctly saw the paper-throwing as a symptom of anxiety. But if the group's regressive 'illness' of paper-throwing is understood as a *communication*, then it is to be related to rather than suppressed. Within the symbolic context it is a psychological symptom or 'a measure toward healing that doesn't quite work and yet points to what is needed' (Moore 1990: 127). When viewed like this the *exchange* of darts, pellets, and crumpled balls of paper – sometimes friendly, sometimes not so friendly – points inchoately to a wish for relationship. As relations within the group improve, this symptomatic acting-out of frustration is replaced by subtler verbal exchanges.

The ritual act of sitting in a circle expresses equality, relatedness, safety, imprisonment, and so on; its practical value was given added significance by the children's moving their desks aside and sitting on chairs expectantly before I arrived, and never needing to be told to put them back afterwards. Since I never used the teacher's padded chair on these occasions, much was expected of anyone who usurped this symbol of authority; sometimes the occupant would defend his or her choice on the questionable grounds that it was 'more comfortable'. Another boundary was marked by there being tacit agreement that what had occurred in the Bullring should not be discussed elsewhere – at least with me. I neither marked nor commented on the written reports.

The Bullring probably functioned for most children as a symbol in the sense that it pointed towards a complicated cluster of ideas to which no final definition or meaning could be given: it's about being alone like the bull and the matador; it's a place where you find out what you're really like, where everybody has something to hide; it's where you admit to not being able to like people, where mostly you learn to trust, and where in the end there is probably more friendship than hatred, a place where there are rules but even these can be broken, and a place where you may find courage and confidence, a place where there may be many metaphorical deaths, a place with a morality and a 'meaning', and so on.

Where the shadow is accepted and weakness can be tolerated healing becomes possible. Anthony wrote of there perhaps being 'a dreadful moment of truth' and of it never being clear who or what in 'the elaborate metaphor' is dominating the proceedings; often when it looks as if chaos will triumph 'the magic of the transactional process takes over (Grainger 1970: xi and xii). And in an essay on bullfighting (1990: 62) Rafael Lopez-Pedraza, from a polytheistic perspective, also writes of a 'moment of truth when the soul and a god . . . are fused in confusion'. These indescribable moments which cannot be separated from conflict, ambiguity and paradox are all to be found in the children's comments.

Although within the circle there is no escape from conflict, the ring is also a home protected by the teacher for the most part against the outside world. Neville (1992: 350) refers to a class of people in organisations who have 'no commitment to the substance of what they do (because) they are all on the way to somewhere else'; they refuse, in other words, to be bound within the circle. But commitment to the 'substance' of the present, rather than escape from it, is liberating and sustaining, and it's a nice paradox that those who are always on the 'way to *somewhere else*' '*do not get*

*anywhere in the world* because they forget the Bullring's moral'.

Studying their behaviour in the 'here and now' encourages the group to tolerate frustration and to live with things as they are. To a boy who said, 'I reckon we ought to close the Bullring for this week . . . it'll be better next week', another replied, 'It'll be just the same won't it?' The optimistic assumption that 'it'll be better next week' is a way of circumventing the frustration and anxiety of the present, only *through* the suffering of which will change come about. Being with others who even in their own muddled ways are trying to be 'real' and suffer the present, can become a source of inspiration and hope to supplant the false optimism that next week it will be like the Coral Island.

By staying *with* events and reflecting on them they can become 'experiences'. For Hillman, 'soul', which is a 'perspective' rather than an entity, brings about the '*deepening* of events into experiences' (Hillman 1985: 16). However, soul not only deepens events into experiences, but is itself deepened by experiences, a reciprocal movement expressed at its simplest in the children's language as 'I learnt a lot'.

With the proliferation of SATs, league tables and targets much is being 'done', but this paperthrowing may sometimes, like the children's, be a substitute for reflecting on the more 'grown-up' subjects of values and relationships. Likewise the priority we give to teaching stratagems and inculcating techniques and skills may be better at producing functionaries 'what do' than persons who 'are'. The Bullring opposed the neglect of soul implicit in putting the meeting of targets before the meeting of people by giving an opportunity for the children to find their humanity and relate cooperatively as persons within a group.

Recently the Bishop of Monmouth spoke of there being 'kinds of rivalry and individualism we can't any longer afford', and against the background of 'a barbarised educational system with its passion for quantifiable output' he concluded that 'our corporate life can only either fragment further or be purified' (Williams 1996). I have tried to describe one way in which in an ordinary school setting it may be possible to bring about some diminution of rivalry and competitiveness and in a small way to purify the 'corporate life'.

Having had professional contact only with adults since the Bullring ended, I am struck by the similiarity of their behaviour, both in groups and as individuals, to that of children. This is not surprising since there is a child in every adult as much as an adult in every child. Anthony suggested that teachers too needed a Bullring where they could understand and be understood, where they could learn to accept and be accepted and where they could tolerate and be tolerated, and it is hard not to agree. Teachers also need time to be and to reflect and to fall back into a truer relationship with one another in community.

## Notes

1  Foreword by E. J. Anthony to Grainger 1970. I was very grateful for the encouragement of E. J. Anthony, who was Ittleson Professor of Child Psychiatry at the Washington University School of Medicine, and a group psychoanalyst.
2  Winnicott 1958: 270: '*The healthy child has a personal source of sense of guilt*, and need not be taught to feel guilty or concerned' (his italics).
3  See entry under 'Ritual', Samuels et al. 1986: 131.
4  Hobson 1985: 40: 'A symbolical attitude means, at first, a passive waiting to see what emerges from experiencing.'

## References

Bion, W. R. (1961) *Experiences in Groups*, London: Tavistock.

Blake, W. (1946) *The Poetry and Prose of William Blake* (ed.) G. Keynes, London: Nonesuch.

Campbell, J. (1989) *The Power of Myth*, New York: Doubleday.

Davis, M. and Wallbridge, D. (1981) *Boundary and Space: An Introduction to the Work of D. W. Winnicott*, Harmondsworth: Penguin.

Dourley, J. P. (1992) *A Strategy for a Loss of Faith*, Toronto: Inner City.

Golding, W. (1953) *The Lord of the Flies*, London: Faber.

Grainger, A. J. (1970) *The Bullring: A Classroom Experiment in Moral Education*, Oxford: Pergamon.

Hillman, J. (1985) *Archetypal Psychology*, Dallas, TX: Spring Publications.

Hillman, J. (1991) *Inter Views*, Dallas, TX: Spring Publications.

Hobson, R. F. (1985) *Forms of Feeling*, London: Tavistock.

Howe, E. G. (1965) *Cure or Heal? A Study of Therapeutic Experience*, London: Allen & Unwin.

Humbert, E. (1988) *C. G. Jung: The Fundamentals of Theory and Practice*, Wilmette, IL: Chiron.

Jung, C. G. (1963) *Mysterium Coniuntionis*, trans. R. F. C. Hull (*Collected Works*, vol. 14), London: Routledge & Kegan Paul.

Jung, C. G. (1954) *The Development of Personality*, trans. R. F. C. Hull (*Collected Works*, vol. 17), London: Routledge & Kegan Paul.

Jung, C. G. (1977) *The Symbolic Life*, trans. R. F. C. Hull (*Collected Works*, vol. 18), London: Routledge & Kegan Paul.

Lawrence, D. H. (1932) *The Letters of D. H. Lawrence*, ed. A Huxley, London: Heinemann.

Lee, L. (1961) *The Firstborn*, London: Hogarth.

Lopez-Pedraza, R. (1990) *Cultural Anxiety*, Einsiedeln, Switz.: Daimon.

Milner, M. (1955) 'The Role of Illusion in Symbol Formation', in M. Klein, P. Heimann and R. Money-Kyrle (eds) *New Directions in Psychoanalysis*, London: Tavistock.

Moore, T. (1990) *Dark Eros*, Dallas, TX: Spring Publications.

Neville, B. (1992) 'The Charm of Hermes', *Journal of Analytical Psychology*, 37.3 (Jul.): 350.

Rose, E. (1997) 'Daring to Work with Internalised Racism', *Counselling* (Journal of the British Association for Counselling), 8.2 (May).

Samuels, A., Shorter, B. and Plunt, F. (1986) *A Critical Dictionary of Jungian Analysis*, London: Routledge.

Saposnik, I. S. (1947) *Robert Louis Stevenson*, New York: Twayne Publishers Inc.

Williams, R. (1996) 'Commemoration of Benefactors', address in Peterhouse Chapel, Cambridge, 2 Feb.; repr. in *Peterhouse Annual Record 1995/1996*.

Winnicott, D. W. (1958) *Collected Papers*, London: Tavistock.

Winnicott, D. W. (1974) *Playing and Reality*, Harmondsworth: Penguin.

# 21 Values in Multicultural Education: Whose Ethics?

MARK MASON

Given that the challenges of teaching in a multicultural classroom face most teachers in late modern society, this chapter considers the questions of values and moral relativism in multicultural education. Specifically, it considers the question whether, in a multicultural classroom characterised by numerous competing values and moral norms, we must accept moral relativism, or whether there are any values and ethics to which we can expect all participants in the educational process, whatever their cultural background, to be committed.

Contemporary Western society is characterised by a plurality of voices. The aspirations of modernity to universal epistemological and ethical norms have given way to a cultural pluralism which makes space for those voices previously occluded by marginalisation and the denial of their identities or by assimilation and the dissolution of their identities. These voices include those of the colonised, of ethnic groups who are not white or European, of women, of religious groups previously excluded by their minority status or otherwise, and of the rural and urban poor. Many have referred to this culturally plural world as 'postmodern', and have sought to understand in terms of 'postmodernism' its diversity of epistemological and axiological claims, where the status of science and the claims of the Enlightenment (and some would say its hubris) have been radically questioned. Kuhn (1962) and Feyerabend (1975) offered some of the most radical epistemological challenges to modernity's scientific metanarratives; Bauman (1993, 1995) has offered one of the most consistent challenges to the moral narratives of both traditional and modern society.

This chapter is concerned with values and ethics in the educational context of such a plural or multicultural society. As such it considers the analyses of contemporary 'late modern' society offered from a postmodern perspective, briefly with respect to epistemological considerations and more substantially with respect to ethical considerations. While our chief concern here is with values and ethics, a brief consideration of these epistemological issues is useful because some of the problems attendant on 'postmodern' epistemology parallel and hence highlight some of the problems associated with moral issues in a multicultural context. The chapter is structured as follows: after a brief characterisation of postmodernism in terms of its non-foundational orientation, the chapter considers the problem of instrumentalism as a potential consequence of strong relativism, since relativism becomes a possibility in a plural world and in some accounts of postmodern ethics. I then situate the chapter in the context of research beyond postmodernism, much of which articulates a reassertion of value in the face of the potentially nihilistic implications of some postmodern theory. After a careful consideration of postmodern ethics, principally as articulated by Bauman, I derive what I call *the ethics of integrity* from postmodern ethics in an attempt to answer this most difficult question arising from a consideration of values in multicultural education: in a multicultural classroom characterised by numerous competing values and moral norms, must we accept moral relativism, or are there any values and ethics to which we can expect all participants in the educational process, whatever their cultural background, to be committed? The ethics of integrity is then postulated as a dialectical morality beyond postmodern ethics, a dialectic that seeks to avoid both the relativism associated with a non-foundational morality, and the fundamentalism and colonialist exclusionary practices of a foundational ethic.

## A characterisation of postmodernism in terms of its non-foundational orientation

While traditional and modern ethics sought moral frameworks that could be expressed in universalist terms of foundational principles, postmodern theory has challenged this metaphysical commitment to universals and the consequent occlusion of race, class and gender identities. In postmodernism the commitments to intrinsic notions of beauty in aesthetics, to Truth in epistemology, or to a foundational morality in ethics mistakenly based in 'objectively verifiable' human distress and torment, are dismissed as just logomachy over what are merely contextually specific and unstable linguistic constructs and metaphors. In this regard Benhabib has written that 'postmodernism, in its infinitely sceptical and subversive attitude toward normative claims, institutional justice and political struggles, is certainly refreshing' (1992: 15). But she has also cautioned us with respect to the debilitating consequences of this position, which give rise to the major concerns of this chapter. Soper (1993: 19) caricatures the situation thus:

> On the one side [are] the dogged metaphysicians, a fierce and burly crew, stalwartly defending various bedrocks and foundations by means of an assortment of trusty but clankingly mechanical concepts such as 'class', 'materialism', 'humanism', 'literary merit', 'transcendence' and so forth. Obsolete as these weapons are, they have the one distinct advantage that in all the dust thrown up by the flailing around with them, their wielders do not realize how seldom they connect with the opposition. On the other side stands the opposition, the feline ironists and revellers in relativism, dancing lightheartedly upon the waters of *différance*, deflecting all foundationalist blows with an adroitly directed ludic laser beam. Masters of situationist strategy, they side-step the heavy military engagement by refusing to do anything but play.

Each of these paradigms, the metaphysical and the postmodern, invites us to a position contrary to that of the other:

> [The metaphysical] asks us to keep a grip on the horror and ugliness of our world, never to forget the extent to which it is beset by war, famine, torture, loss of nature, grotesque inequalities and intolerable oppressions, and which therefore calls upon us to analyse all practice and historical process in terms of the degree to which it promotes or detracts from the realization of greater peace, equality, democracy, ecological well-being and the future flourishing of our species and its planet. The [postmodern] is the invitation to view history as littered with the victims of such well intentioned visions and utopian projects, and in the light of that to give ourselves over to a pragmatic acceptance of the loss of values. (ibid.: 20)

In stronger versions of postmodernism, then, ideas about value and associated terms such as justice or freedom in ethics, beauty or judgement in aesthetics, and objectivity or truth in epistemology, are construed as contextually specific and indicative of nothing beyond the limits of the discourse specific to each. According to this position, there are no foundational or universal qualities, ideals or experiences beyond the discursive in which we can ground questions of value. Texts are all there is. All is constructed in discourse.

## The problem: instrumentalism as a potential consequence of strong relativism

The question, again, which we are considering is whether in a multicultural classroom characterised by competing values and moral norms, we are bound to accept moral relativism, or whether there are any values and ethics to which we can expect all participants in the educational process, whatever their cultural background, to be committed. Moral relativism, the position that all ethical judgements are contextually – historically and socio-culturally – dependent and hence that a universal ethics not bound by time or space is an illusion, is a distinct possibility in a multicultural classroom. Whose ethics are to prevail? The school's, by virtue of its inertial momentum in defining the normal? The teacher's, by virtue of her authority in the classroom? Those of the pupils who enjoy a cultural majority in the classroom? The ethics of those who were previously marginalised and who may demand recognition of their claims, perhaps simply because they are different or because of the prior occlusion of their identities? Or nobody's, where the equal validity of all claims is assumed and 'anything goes'?

Moral relativism is of course not immediately to be feared: recognition of the worth of moral perspectives other than those of one's own culture is certainly a well-documented potential advantage of multicultural education. The problem is that instrumentalism is a potential consequence of strong relativism, and this is the deeper issue that underlies our question. In the paragraphs that follow my intention is to sketch why this should be so, and a brief consideration of the consequences of epistemological relativism will serve to illuminate our moral concerns.

Echoing Nietzsche's reference to truth as little more than the solidification of culturally specific metaphors,[1] Lyotard's (1984) characterisation of a mood of 'incredulity towards grand narratives' – principally towards the ideals of the Enlightenment and modernity – signals a ubiquitous conferring of legitimacy on previously marginalised positions. The normative practice of education as the institutionalised transmission of canonical disciplines and ethical norms is implicitly identified by Lyotard (ibid.) as such a 'grand narrative'. In terms of the prevailing mood, positions previously marginalised by the metanarrative of education claim legitimacy, often simply on the basis of prior marginalisation or on account of their being different. The concomitant blurring, and sometimes the collapse, of ethical (and epistemological) boundaries in education leaves teachers and other participants in the educational process potentially defenceless in the face of a moral relativism where, in Feyerabend's (1975) terms, 'anything goes'.

The obvious advantages of perspectivism notwithstanding, a generalised non-foundational orientation potentially produces a pervasive moral and epistemological relativism with unfortunate and destructive consequences. Muller and Taylor (1995), in Gramscian vein, highlight the recycling of deprivation that comes from students' lack of engagement with the canon consequent on a mood of strong epistemological relativism. Taylor (1991) demonstrates how the possibility of an authentic identity, an important goal of education, is frustrated by a moral relativism which denies the validity of our 'horizons of significance' and which underlies an instrumental attitude towards human relationships. Identified as 'postmodern' in much recent theory, dominant modes of ethical comportment in contemporary society are orientated in terms of a culture of 'self-fulfilment' and what Taylor (ibid.) has called a 'self-determining freedom'. Neither the process nor the ends of education are served by a moral relativism where anything goes: a *carte-blanche* ethics can quickly lead to an instrumental approach to moral decisions.

Bhaskar (1986) draws a distinction between an ontological realm of 'intransitive' objects, processes and events – those which exist independently of our formulations – and an epistemological realm of 'transitive' knowledge-constitutive interests – in whose construction we are implicated. Conflation of these realms is according to him the source of much confusion in strong relativist positions. The ontological cannot be reduced to the epistemological, which is a mistake typical of much postmodern theorising. Wittgenstein's assertion in Proposition 5.6 of the *Tractatus Logico-Philosophicus* that 'the limits of my language mean the limits of my world' (1961: 115) coincides with much postmodern confusion in taking 'the sheer variety of truth-claims advanced (and very often subsequently abandoned) down through the history of scientific thought as evidence that no truth is to be had' beyond 'whatever form of discourse – or *de facto* regime of instituted power/knowledge – happens to prevail in some given discipline at some given time' (Norris 1995: 111). Conflating the realms of ontology and epistemology in a constructivist move weakens the possibility of critical scholarship.

In like manner, much confusion in moral relativism results from the conflation of the ontological and the axiological. The danger of strong moral relativism is that the ontological is reduced to the axiological: it is arrogant and reactionary to ignore the very real privations of the exploited in the name of relativism. At least a minimum level of ontological commitment is critical if we wish to sustain any coherent discussion about values.

The problems consequent on a generalisation of postmodern scepticism to all moral foundations are particularly acute in education. The evident absence in many schools of a 'culture of learning', of a 'culture of teaching', and of mutual respect among teachers and students, are indicative of and partly consequent on the non-foundational orientation of the contemporary mood. While this mood and the concomitant 'culture of entitlement' (Morrow 1994) prevail, participants in the educational process find themselves unable even to begin to define what is worthwhile in education, let alone defend it.

This is not, however, to gainsay the progressive potential of postmodernism: the legitimacy claimed by and accorded to those previously excluded by the logic of the 'grand narrative' constitutes recognition of these voices in a celebration of identities previously denied by assimilation or exclusion. This chapter acknowledges and is situated in the aporetic tension between the progressive and reactionary potential of the postmodern turn. Faced with the exclusionary injustices of established educational practices on the one hand, and the ubiquitous claims to legitimacy by those previously marginalised by such metanarrative practices on the other, the question is whether it is possible to develop an ethics within the framework of which educational communities can engage in dialogue over these competing claims.

In answering our central question, then, we should be mindful of the problem that the 'anything-goes' relativism and non-foundational orientation associated with strong postmodern positions, while celebrating a plurality of previously marginalised voices, will potentially, by virtue of their retreat from a foundational moral position, perpetuate cycles of deprivation and instrumentalism, and minimise the possibility of realising a key goal of education, an authentic identity. This is the illusion of relativism construed as unambiguously progressive, and these are the difficulties consequent on an unreflective celebration of difference and diversity.

## Beyond postmodernism: the reassertion of value

My concern in this section is very briefly to situate my argument in defence of a moral principle in the context of research beyond postmodernism, much of which articulates a reassertion of value in the face of the potentially nihilistic implications of some postmodern theory. This defence of principle beyond postmodern ethics is consonant with recent research reasserting value beyond strong postmodern relativism. Derrida (1990) asserts that deconstruction is committed to 'the ethico-politico-juridical question of justice' and to 'the sense of a responsibility without limits'. Taylor's (1991) 'ethics of authenticity' assert the impossibility of constructing an authentic identity without accepting a non-instrumental commitment to our relationships and without acknowledging our 'horizons of significance' which generate moral demands from outside ourselves. Norris (1994) identifies in the recent work of Said (1993) and Kristeva (1991, 1993) a shift towards a reconstruction of the Enlightenment goals of justice and liberty, and away from their erstwhile positions which exalted difference and otherness and ultimately

equated notions of truth, reason and critique with a discourse of oppression. Benhabib (1992) is cautious of the debilitating consequences of postmodern relativism. Mouffe (1993) argues in defence of 'a new type of articulation between the universal and the particular'. Weeks (1993) seeks to balance relativism with 'some sense of minimum universal values'. Soper (1993) suggests that any vacillation in the comfortable position of postmodern cynicism is logically to be committed 'to certain political principles and values'. Squires ((ed.) 1993) calls for 'normative expressions of value', Hirst (1993) for a foundational ethics. Harvey (1993) is sceptical of an appeal to 'unassimilated otherness' and the celebration of all difference; Young (1993) suggests that a recognition of difference 'will also at the same time involve an assertion of some form of solidarity and agreement'. Smeyers (1995) offers a justification for an educational project in terms of 'what one cares for', rejecting the nihilism of strong postmodernism and its denial that 'anything is worthwhile'. Kane (1994) is concerned to search for 'absolute values in a pluralistic world', McCance (1996) to 're-address the ethical' in a move that reflects the current trend away from the focus on aesthetics in social theory under the influence of postmodernism, and the renewed interest in philosophy in the field of ethics.

## Postmodern ethics

Before going on to derive from postmodern ethics what I refer to as the ethics of integrity, in which we will be able to situate the question of competing moral claims in multicultural education, my concern here is to consider the most articulate statement of postmodern ethics, that of Bauman. The context of a non-foundational ethics is articulated in Bauman's (1993, 1995) postmodern ethics, characterised by the intuitionist position of 'morality without ethical code' (1993: 31) and marked by his return to Kant's 'mystery of morality inside me'. Bauman suggests that while the moral thought and practice of modernity may have been 'animated by the belief in the possibility of a *non-ambivalent, non-aporetic ethical code*', what is *post*modern is the '*disbelief*' in such a possibility' (ibid.: 9, 10). The postmodern insight into morality is that in an era when the range of our moral choices and the consequences of our actions are more far-reaching than ever before, we are unable to rely on a universal ethical code which would yield unambiguously good solutions:

> Human reality is messy and ambiguous – and so moral decisions, unlike abstract ethical principles, are ambivalent. It is in this sort of world that we must live. . . . Knowing that to be the truth . . . is to be postmodern. Postmodernity, one may say, is *modernity without illusions.*   (ibid.: 32–3)

Bauman's response to the ambiguity of human reality is based in his position that it is our *moral capacity* that essentially defines us as human beings. While Kant's categorical imperative to 'act only according to that maxim by which you can at the same time will that it should become a universal law' (1990: 38) is suggestive of universalism, Bauman's assertion – while seeking to avoid foundationals and universals – that 'if in doubt – consult your conscience' (ibid.: 250) is surprisingly close to deontological ethics. Postmodern ethics could almost be characterised in terms of an intuitionist deontology: of course not quite as deontological as Kant's classical statement since Bauman's conscience-guided morality would be more sensitive to the contextual specifics of a particular dilemma than would Kant's transcendental position.

Bauman (1993) outlines the following characteristics of the moral condition in the light of postmodernism. First, humans are morally ambivalent: they are neither essentially good nor essentially bad. Postmodern ethics holds that it is therefore impossible to design a logically coherent ethical code to accommodate our essentially ambivalent moral condition. Second, moral phenomena are inherently pre-rational: they cannot be construed instrumentally, since they are defined as moral phenomena 'only if they precede the consideration of purpose and the calculation of gains and losses' (ibid.: 11). Bauman actually uses the term *non*-rational because he wishes to construe moral phenomena non-instrumentally: this assumes an instrumental definition of rationality. I prefer to describe this position using the term *pre*-rational because it is consistent with Bauman's position that the essence of our existence, what defines us as human, is our moral capacity. While accepting Bauman's position, I will argue further in defence of the possibility of a reflective morality in terms of a non-instrumental understanding of rationality by which moral argument is possible. What defines us as human is also our rational capacity: it is our moral *and* rational capacities which make us capable of

moral reflection. Third, morality is incurably aporetic: it is always fraught with irreconcilable contradictions, since few choices (other than the relatively trivial and the existentially uninteresting) produce unambiguously good consequences. Modernity's quest for ethical certainty is therefore impossible. Fourth, morality is not universalisable: attempts to universalise morality merely substitute 'heteronomous . . . ethical rules for the autonomous responsibility of the moral self, . . . [resulting in] the incapacitation, even destruction of the moral self'. Attempts to universalise morality merely silence moral impulse (ibid.: 12). Fifth, from the perspective of the 'rational order', the order legislated by society's ethical custodians, morality is and is bound to remain irrational. Totalitarian visions of ethical universality are thus threatened by individual moral autonomy and committed to its domestication. Sixth, moral responsibility – being *for* the Other before one can be *with* the Other – is the first reality of the self: a starting point rather than a product of society. This is consistent with Bauman's assertion that the essence of our existence, what defines us as human, is our moral capacity. Seventh, and rather surprisingly, Bauman claims that the postmodern perspective on moral phenomena does not reveal the relativism of morality: an assertion quite contrary to the 'anything goes' triumphalism of some postmodern writers. Interestingly, his negation of the universalisability of morality is not an endorsement of moral relativism: agreeing that ethical relativism has nihilistic implications, he places his faith in our essentially human moral capacity. It is, he suggests, 'the ethical codes which are plagued with relativism', and not the ' "uncodified" moral condition' (ibid.: 14). Although Bauman doesn't specifically delineate the following (eighth) characteristic of the moral condition in the light of postmodernism, what is self-evident in his and other postmodern writing is that postmodern morality is non-foundational: there exist no *a priori* foundations of morality on which ethical codes can be built.

## Beyond postmodern ethics: the ethics of integrity

Faced with competing moral claims in the multicultural classroom, Bauman's non-foundational 'morality without ethical code' leaves us with little more than the injunction to 'consult your conscience' and an unbridled claim of 'responsibility for the other'. This reliance on conscience will help us in dealing with our question, and I will shortly pursue that further. But a retreat from a foundational moral position leaves us vulnerable to the instrumentalism potentially consequent on moral relativism. For despite Bauman's assertions to the contrary, the culturally plural classroom does face us with competing moral claims codified in the ethical paradigms of different cultures, a difficulty not easily resolved by the unclear status and source of his claim of an unlimited 'responsibility for the other'. In this section I will derive from Bauman's postmodern ethics the principles of respect for the dignity of our and each other's being, and of responsibility for moral choices. These principles, constituting the ethics of integrity, will, I shall show in the concluding section, provide us with a framework within which we can wrestle more productively with the vexed question of competing moral claims in the multicultural classroom.

Bauman's position that it is our pre-rational and pre-social *moral capacity* that essentially defines us as human beings, marked by his return to Kant's 'mystery of morality inside me', is ultimately an intuitionist argument which claims that moral capacity lies intuitively in all of us and not in some ethical code external to ourselves which is universally applied.

However, underlying an intuitionist position is an assumed principle: that we respect the dignity of our and each other's being as a prerequisite for the confidence we place in our and in others' moral positions. Acceptance of this obligation implies a willingness to take responsibility for the moral choices we make. As we strive continually to grow morally, it is towards this goal of taking responsibility for the moral choices we make because we respect the dignity of our and each other's being. This process constitutes what I postulate as the ethics of integrity: a life identified by commitment to growth towards integrity is a life that is inescapably responsible for moral choices made, and inextricably connected to respect for the dignity of being and the ensuing moral commitments. Conversely, a life respectful of the dignity of being and responsible for that commitment's moral consequences, is a life whose identity is defined first and last in terms of integrity. The three elements of the triunity exist in a relationship of equivalence: each is a *sine qua non* of the others, and the absence of any immediately implies the absence of the others. *The ethics of*

*integrity, then, imply respect for the dignity of being, and responsibility for moral choices.*

To clarify the logical derivation of my position from postmodern ethics, consider the statement that 'if it is raining, then the streets are wet' (if *a*, then *b*; or *a→b*). In other words, *a* is a *sufficient* condition for *b* (note, not a *necessary* condition for *b*, since broken fire hydrants may also wet streets). Now the only statement that can be derived from 'if *a*, then *b*', is ' "*not b*" implies "*not a*" '; or 'the streets are not wet implies that it is not raining'. Likewise, the only statement that can be derived from ' "*not b*" implies "*not a*" ', is 'if *a*, then *b*'.

Now, refer to my statement of respect for the dignity of being as *b*, and to Bauman's statement of postmodern morality's injunction to trust your conscience as *a*. Clearly, having no respect for the dignity of our and each other's being gives us no grounds to trust our consciences; or ' "*not b*" implies "*not a*" '. From this we logically derive that 'if *a*, then *b*'; or, if we are to trust our consciences as a moral resource, then it implies that we respect the dignity of our and each other's being.

From this respect for the dignity of being I derived the principle of responsibility for the moral choices we make. This is more simply derived by the observation that respect is not a *necessary* condition for responsibility (we may act responsibly for reasons other than respect, such as fear of eternal damnation), but it is a *sufficient* condition for responsibility. In other words, respect for the dignity of our and each other's being implies that we take responsibility for the moral choices that we make.

Bauman's (ibid.: 242) assertion that 'moral proximity, responsibility, and the uniqueness – irreplaceability – of the moral subject are triune; they will not survive (or, rather, would not be born) without each other' is consistent with the position I am advocating: for Bauman, 'being for Others [is the] cornerstone of all morality' (ibid.: 244), and 'moral responsibility is the most personal and inalienable of human possessions' (ibid.: 250). Also consistent is Taylor's (1991) argument that an authentic existence is not possible unless we recognise the validity of moral demands emanating from outside of ourselves as well as the demands of our commitment to others: to deny the first is to collapse Taylor's horizons of significance and to trivialise our more significant decisions by imbuing them with meaning solely on account of their having been freely chosen; to deny the second is to negate the possibility of meaningful identity construction given the politics of identity recognition in an age of flexible identity.

Although space prohibits my doing so in this chapter, from this moral principle of respect for the dignity of being it is possible to derive logically the five moral principles posited as widely accepted by Thiroux (1986):

> the value of life principle
> the principle of goodness or rightness
> the principle of justice or fairness
> the principle of truth-telling or honesty
> the principle of individual freedom.

The derivation of further moral principles such as those sketched by Thiroux, and the possibility of moral reflection, depend on a rational capacity which Strike and Soltis (1985) assume as a further distinguishing characteristic of humanity. We therefore have to draw on both our *moral* and our *rational* capacities if the potential of moral reflection is to be realised. Strike and Soltis invoke the possibility of moral reasoning as a defence against relativism. In this respect the crucial question has to do with the origins of our moral intuitions, since they are assumed to be the basic data for moral reasoning. Some positions assert them as innate, some as a way of seeing moral phenomena, some as culturally shaped. If the last is true, moral relativism is indisputable. But just as Bauman asserts that relying on moral intuition does not necessarily entail relativism (it is the competition among ethical codes for paradigmatic status, and not our moral intuition, that gives rise to relativism), Strike and Soltis take a less decisive position with regard to the origins of our moral intuitions, pointing to the commonalities of humanity, particularly at the broad level of intuitions. Strike and Soltis are content with the establishment of 'a provisional reflective equilibrium' (1985: 60) that is tolerant of a mild degree of social constructivism with respect to intuitional morality: 'we can be objective without being certain, and we can be tolerant and open to other points of view without being relativists' (ibid.: 61). Reflective equilibrium between members of radically different cultures may not be easily attained, but we are not so far apart that it is impossible. What is assumed is both our moral capacity – which is acknowledged in 'affirmative' postmodern positions (Rosenau 1992: 14) such as Bauman's – *and* our rational capacity – which has been celebrated in modernity. But both capacities, albeit in various

forms and to differing extents, have for centuries been identified as the essence of humanity, and both are essential resources for an ethics *beyond* postmodernism.

## A dialectical morality for multicultural education

We have now derived from Bauman's postmodern ethics the principles of respect for the dignity of our and each other's being, and of responsibility for moral choices. These principles, constituting the ethics of integrity, provide us with a framework within which we can situate and consider more sensitively the competing moral claims of the multicultural classroom.

All moral judgement and action, and particularly for us, moral judgement and action in multicultural educational contexts, exists, I suggest, within the span of the dialectic constituted by the tension between commitment to a foundational principle and the face-to-face demands of a particular situation. The two aspects of the ethics of integrity may be understood as constituting the two poles of this dialectic. The first constituent of the ethics of integrity is the principle of respect for the dignity of being. It is certainly true that we are moved to act morally by a commitment to a principle which we understand as foundationally constitutive of our identity. But our moral judgements and actions are motivated by more than purely a principled commitment: we are also moved to act morally by the demands of a particular situation in which we are involved at a Levinasian (1989) 'face-to-face' level. Such face-to-face interaction moves us, whether in solidarity, in empathy, or in horror, to take responsibility for our actions. This responsibility is the second constituent of the ethics of integrity which I have posited. Moral judgement and action exist always within the dialectical span of these two constituents: principled commitment and face-to-face responsibility. We understand our feelings of empathy or solidarity as significant (and hence they demand that we act) by reference to our 'horizons of significance', to the moral obligations which emanate from beyond ourselves, some of which – respect for the dignity of being, for example – we may understand as foundational. The immediate move to act, spurred by the face-to-face demands of the situation, is contextualised within a broader framework: it is by reference to this broader framework, which includes the obligation to respect the dignity of being, that we are able to recognise certain practices as enhancing or demeaning of dignity and are accordingly moved to act in support of or against them.

Conscience spans the continuum, but defined differently towards each end. Towards the pole of solidarity, conscience is understood in terms of Bauman's and Levinas's face-to-face responsibility, and Rorty's solidarity. Towards the pole of objectivity, conscience is understood in terms of Kant's respect for persons by virtue of the categorical imperative, and in terms of a principled commitment to a respect for the dignity of being that expands Taylor's horizon of significance to a universal horizon. Both understandings of conscience are consonant with the ethics of integrity. And the ethics of integrity in turn both celebrates and is constituted by both poles of the dialectic.

The ethical projects of modernity are motivated, according to Bauman, by the desire for certainty, for a non-ambivalent and non-aporetic ethical code. As such the ethics of modernity aspire, as is the case with ethics in traditional societies, to foundationality and universality. Postmodern ethics, according to Bauman, is convinced of the futility of this exercise, and is accordingly content to leave moral decisions to the specifics of a particular situation. Each of these orientations tends to ignore the potentially productive tension between them as each tends towards its own pole: modern ethics towards the goal of foundationality, risking the cruelties associated with colonialism and fundamentalism as it ignores postmodernism's celebration of the other and of difference; postmodern ethics towards the ambit of the local, the specific and the immediate, risking the cruelties associated with strong relativism in its denial of commitment to a foundational principle. What is lost is the potential of the dialectical tension between them.

This dialectical perspective highlights the challenges and advantages of multicultural education, and the importance of teaching both for a critical awareness of the moral norms of one's own culture that are taken for granted and for a sensitivity to the moral norms of different cultures. Beyer and Liston (1992: 375) argue for a more dialectical relationship between the local and the global, suggesting that 'the local can illuminate the more general', and that 'the global can heighten our sensitivity to the more particular'. According to Beyer and Liston, 'local efforts frequently require insight attainable only through the examination and critique of non-local sources of exploitation and oppression, and necessitate directions that are ascertainable through cultural and moral visions that may transcend the immediate situation' (ibid.: 375). What is established, then, is a tension between moral action as motivated by foundational principles and by face-to-face situation-specific responsibility and solidarity. Rorty's (1985) descriptions of objectivity and solidarity reflect the poles of this dialectic. Dynamically within this tension are *discursive moral principles*, moral obligations that are wrought simultaneously by the bipolar demands of a foundational respect for the dignity of being (associated with Rorty's objective pole) on the one hand, and by the demand that we take responsibility for our moral decisions by virtue of a Levinasian face-to-face solidarity (associated with Rorty's pole of solidarity) on the other. Ever situated within this dialectic, such discursive moral principles acknowledge the tension between universality and community, between objectivity and solidarity. For Rorty, 'the desire for objectivity is not the desire to escape the limitations of one's community, but simply the desire for as much intersubjective agreement as possible' (1985: 5). Moral judgement and action are wrought by this tension between objectivity and solidarity, between foundational commitment and face-to-face responsibility, as we strive towards 'as much intersubjective agreement as possible', towards a discursively principled morality. We become moral, asserts Greene (1990), as we come together in our educational communities and wrestle with the moral choices that we face. Such interaction is moral only insofar as it is based in the ethics of integrity. We are viscerally motivated by the Levinasian and Rortyan pole of face-to-face solidarity and responsibility, by Bauman's moral responsibility as the 'first reality of the self' (1993: 13), and we may avoid the potentially cruel consequences of a strong relativism and its *carte-blanche* morality consequent on a withdrawal of commitment by reference to the opposite and more objective pole, with which is associated the principle of respect for the dignity of being.

To return to our question by way of conclusion: in a multicultural classroom characterised by numerous competing values and moral norms, must we accept moral relativism, or are there any values and ethics to which we can expect all participants in the educational process, whatever their cultural background, to be committed? In terms of the arguments offered here, we can expect all of those present in a multicultural classroom to be sensitive to the different ethical norms that will inevitably be present in such a context, and to be tolerant of different moral perspectives. We should certainly defend a mild version of moral relativism which accepts that our ethical norms are at least partly dependent on our cultural background. But a strong moral relativism which insists that all ethical norms brought to bear in a multicultural context are equally valid cannot be defended in terms of these arguments. Practices which may be viewed in modern Western urban perspectives as sexist, for example, would be excluded on the grounds that they do not respect the dignity of women.

In the multicultural classroom, the discursive moral principles which I have posited will acknowledge the tensions among the values and ethics of the different voices present in such a plural context. But we can insist, by virtue of the justifications and arguments I have presented here, that all participants both respect the dignity of each other's being and take responsibility for their moral choices. Values and moral practices that violate these constituents of the ethics of integrity may thus justifiably be excluded from the multicultural classroom. Likewise, we may defend our moral judgements and actions in multicultural educational contexts if we are respectful of the dignity of all those present and if we take responsibility for the moral choices we make.

## Values and ethics in multicultural education in post-apartheid South Africa: a coda

Education in post-apartheid South Africa has produced some interesting issues with respect to our central question of whether there are any values and ethics to which we can expect all participants in the educational process, whatever their cultural background, to be committed. Classrooms in South Africa are slowly developing more heterogeneous populations. Apartheid's classrooms, typified by an astounding level of homogeneity within each, be it white English-speaking urban middle class, black Xhosa-speaking rural poor, coloured (mixed race) Afrikaans-speaking urban lower middle class, and the like, are slowly giving way to classrooms that are more diverse in terms of race, class, ethnicity,

religion, language and culture. And of course, these classrooms are sites of numerous competing value claims and moral norms, a situation exacerbated by generations of racial stereotyping and prejudice.

The case I am defending here is that we should acknowledge in a meaningful sense the differences among the values and ethics of the heterogeneous voices in such a plural context, but that we can insist that all participants both respect the dignity of each other's being and take responsibility for their moral choices. At the most basic level, this implies that we may quite justifiably exclude violence from our schools. While this may seem trite to some, apartheid's brutalisation of South African society has contributed to, in some senses, an acceptance of violence as a means of solving problems. The toughness of the scar tissue branded by decades of violence by the apartheid state has rendered us almost indifferent to the shocking level of violence prevalent in our transitional society. The widespread rape of young black women by HIV-positive men, particularly prevalent in KwaZulu-Natal Province, and the indiscriminate taking of life in political and gang-related or other criminal violence have spread into our schools. In the midst of the gang and factional strife that has been plaguing Cape Town recently, a pupil in a Cape Flats high school was cold-bloodedly executed by a shot to the head fired by a balaclava-hooded assassin walking brazenly into a classroom full of pupils at their desks.

That such behaviour is unacceptable goes without saying. There can be no more horrifying violation of the principle of respect for each other's being than rape or murder. Less appalling, but still in the realm of violence in our schools, is the issue of corporal punishment. The post-apartheid South African constitution, probably the most progressive in the world, has been interpreted by legislators to outlaw the caning of pupils. In terms of the arguments I have presented here, we cannot justify the use of corporal punishment. And yet, I have had reported to me by one of my students in his journal where he reflected on his practical teaching experience, that he had lined up an entire class and systematically caned them until the pupil responsible for the disappearance of a ruler, standing thirteenth in line, owned up. In fairness to everybody, reported my student, he caned the rest of the class to ensure equal treatment for all. That corporal punishment is a deeply ingrained practice in the culture of historically black schools is no reason, in terms of the case I have defended, to allow it to continue. It may justifiably be excluded, and legitimately so in terms of the constitution.

A potentially horrifying incident took place recently in a rural school in the South African province of Mpumalanga. A news broadcast on 19 September 1997 on SAfm radio reported that pupils at a school near Nelspruit had banded together to demand that the principal release R5000 (some £700, a considerable sum of money in a poor educational community) from school funds to pay for the services of a *sangoma* (a traditional healer) to come to the school and sniff out those responsible for the deaths of some pupils at the school. The children had died in various incidents over a period of time, and their fellow pupils were convinced that a witch was responsible. That witchcraft should be held responsible for the deaths of children is risible. That fellow pupils might be accused by a witchdoctor of culpability and pay with their own lives is sinister indeed. But the principal of the school was subjected to mass action by his pupils, and latest reports held that the Department of Education had not intervened. Are we to put the pupils' belief in witchcraft down to cultural relativism and, in the spirit of cherishing difference, to allow the consequences of a witchdoctor's placing of blame on some other children to run their course? Or are we to assert norms that demand that scientific evidence be tested before a constitutionally sanctioned court? The latter course of action would be justified in terms of the arguments I have presented here. The course of action demanded by the pupils violates the principle of respect for the dignity of being, and in terms of the ethics of integrity, we would be justified in proscribing those actions.

The issue of racial stereotypes and prejudice runs deeply in our previously divided schools. Some pupils at schools which were previously homogeneously white or coloured are wont to refer to newly enrolled black pupils as *kaffirs*, a racist and deeply hurtful epithet: a pupil who suffers this indignity recently reported that

> We feel very bad when people call us 'kaffir' because we are all the same. It's just the skin that differs, everything underneath is the same. Last year in my class, someone said to another girl: 'Don't sit by me, your blackness will rub off on me.' It was so painful for me to hear someone say that to another one. I thought about it and couldn't get it over my heart. But later on I

> thought I'll just take it as it is because it's apartheid that had such an effect on the children and so on. But it's very painful to see someone breaking down someone else. (Fakier, 1997b: 4)

Teachers have been exasperated by the refusal of coloured or white pupils to share desks with black pupils. Others have been derided by their pupils when they insisted that they should respect people of other cultures (Fakier, 1997c). Some teachers have expressed the wish that no tolerance should be shown to pupils who taunt their fellow pupils with the word *kaffir* (ibid.). In terms of what I have argued here, such teachers would be entirely justified, no matter what the contemporary demands are that we should be accepting of a wide range of behaviours because of our newly found sensitivity to difference, in showing no tolerance for such behaviour. It violates the principle of respect for the dignity of being, and of taking responsibility for our moral choices.

While the word *kaffir* is undisputedly a vile and racist term, the term *coloured*, referring in South Africa to people of mixed racial origin, is rather more complex. It used to be seen as pejorative, an apartheid epithet, and the progressive response was always to preface the term with the participial phrase, 'so-called'. In asserting their identity in a post-apartheid South Africa, many coloured people have now dropped this preface, but the use of the term and debates around it remain sensitive and complex. South African school pupils continue to be wary of the term. Fakier (1997a: 4) reports pupils as being content if the term is used descriptively and respectfully, while being hurt if the term is used pejoratively: 'If you used the term like [I] was nothing then I would feel bad, but if you use the term just to describe my mixed-cultural personality, then I won't feel bad.' Similarly, white pupils are hurt by a disrespectful use of terms such as 'whitey' or 'honkey' (ibid.). In being sensitive to deep-seated racial prejudice and stereotyping, teachers would, in terms of the arguments I have offered, be quite justified in taking a hard line with pupils who use these terms disrespectfully.

A problem faced by South African educators in this respect is that the issue of competing values and ethics in a multicultural classroom is new to most. Dealing with diversity is not something for which South African teachers have been prepared:

> We as teachers haven't been taught about how to deal with cultural diversity in the class. You have to

work on your instinct sometimes and sometimes you have to work on the skills you've acquired over the years in teaching and solving little conflicts.

Coloured teachers also come from a system that has told them they are better than Africans – and many of us teachers, we ourselves haven't been exposed to African people and their culture. The system isn't there, the in-service training isn't there to teach people how to deal with diversity and some of us are not yet equipped for the changes that are happening around us.   (Fakier, 1997c: 4)

A local high-school principal acknowledges that 'while teachers [are] not sufficiently skilled at the moment to deal with diversity, . . . the expectation is that schools need to take the initiative in developing such programmes themselves' (Fakier, 1997d: 10). These programmes will need to encourage teachers to acknowledge the tensions among the values and ethics of the different voices present in a multicultural classroom, but also to insist that all participants both respect the dignity of each other's being and take responsibility for their moral choices. Meaningful acknowledgement of difference implies the kind of exemplary level of tolerance for cultural differences shown by pupils at a formerly coloured Cape Town high school, where

African initiates with their particular kind of dress signifying manhood are accommodated – within limits, of course – along with Rastafarians with their distinctive dreadlocks. But, in deference to pupils of other faiths, the 'Rastas' have, in turn, elected to cover their 'dreads' with woollen caps. (Fakier, 1997e: 4)

This school has been careful to integrate, for example, the African choral tradition into the cultural life of the school. Included in the curriculum is the study of literature dealing with apartheid's forced mass removals and the destruction of different communities, black and coloured. A teacher reports that she uses her lessons to 'break down or unlearn certain myths': 'With that comes the realisation that there's a difference in our traditions and in our cultural practices. It brings with it a certain richness of experience . . . (and) an enormous amount of understanding and respect growing for each other's differences' (ibid). At the same time, she and other teachers point to our 'common humanity which makes people more trusting and trustworthy of each other' (ibid.). A dreadlocked black African pupil, claiming his common humanity with the coloured students around him, reports, 'I try to be serious with them and tell them they

mustn't treat me with disrespect and I try to explain to them what the problem is that I have with that' (Fakier, 1997b: 4).

The point is that South African teachers, and surely all teachers, while learning the skills of coping with and indeed valuing the tensions among the different moral claims in a multicultural classroom, should be sufficiently courageous to insist, by virtue of the case I have defended here, that all participants both respect the dignity of each other's being and take responsibility for their moral choices. These are the claims that an ethics of integrity makes on all of us in a diverse and plural world.

## Note

1 See 'Origin of Reason and Logic', 'Judgement. True-False', 'Thing-in-Itself and Appearance', and 'Science' in *Book Three: Principles of a New Evaluation* of Nietzsche's *The Will to Power*, where his arguments on truth are typified by his claim that 'The categories of reason . . . collected together . . . represent nothing more than the expediency of a certain race and species' (1967: 278).

## References

Bauman, Z. (1993) *Postmodern Ethics*, Oxford: Blackwell.
Bauman, Z. (1995) *Life in Fragments: Essays in Postmodern Morality*, Oxford: Blackwell.
Benhabib, S. (1992) *Situating the Self*, Cambridge: Polity Press.
Beyer, L. E. and Liston, D. P. (1992) 'Discourse or Moral Action? A Critique of Postmodernism', *Educational Theory*, 42.4: 371–93.
Bhaskar, R. (1986) *Scientific Realism and Human Emancipation*, London: Verso.
Derrida, J. (1990) 'Force of Law: The Mystical Foundation of Authority', *Cardozo Law Review*, II(5–6): 919–1045.
Fakier, Y. (1997a) 'Tomorrow's Leaders Bury the Past', *Cape Times*, 25 June.
Fakier, Y. (1997b) 'Schoolroom Battle to Change Hearts and Minds of Pupils', *Cape Times*, 30 July.
Fakier, Y. (1997c) 'Teachers Explain Their "Frustration"', *Cape Times*, 30 July.
Fakier, Y. (1997d) 'Getting to Grips with Racial Diversity', *Cape Times*, 6 Aug.
Fakier, Y. (1997e) 'A Tale of Two Cultures at Pioneering High School', *Cape Times*, 13 August 1997.
Feyerabend, P. (1975) *Against Method*, London: New Left Books.
Greene, M. (1990) 'The Passion of the Possible: Choice, Multiplicity, and Commitment', *Journal of Moral Education*, 19.2: 67–76.

Harvey, D. (1993) 'Class Relations, Social Justice and the Politics of Difference', in J. Squires (ed.) *Principled Positions: Postmodernism and the Rediscovery of Value*, London: Lawrence & Wishart.

Hirst, P. (1993) 'An Answer to Relativism?' in J. Squires (ed.) *Principled Positions: Postmodernism and the Rediscovery of Value*, London: Lawrence & Wishart.

Kane, R. (1994) *Through the Moral Maze: Searching for Absolute Values in a Pluralistic World*, New York: Paragon House.

Kant, I. (1990) *Foundations of the Metaphysics of Morals*, New York, Macmillan.

Kristeva, J. (1991) *Strangers to Ourselves*, Hemel Hempstead: Harvester-Wheatsheaf.

Kristeva, J. (1993) *Nations Without Nationalism*, New York: Columbia University Press.

Kuhn, T. (1962) *The Structure of Scientific Revolutions*, Chicago: The University of Chicago Press.

Levinas, E. (1989) *The Levinas Reader*, (ed.) Sean Hand, Cambridge: Blackwell.

Lyotard, J.-F. (1984) *The Postmodern Condition: A Report on Knowledge*, Minneapolis: University of Minnesota Press.

McCance, D. (1996) *Posts: Re Addressing the Ethical*, Albany, NY: State University of New York Press.

Morrow, W. (1994) 'Entitlement and Achievement in Education', *Studies in Philosophy and Education*, 13.1: 33–47.

Mouffe, C. (1993) 'Liberal Socialism and Pluralism: Which Citizenship?' in J. Squires (ed.) *Principled Positions: Postmodernism and the Rediscovery of Value*, London: Lawrence & Wishart.

Muller, J. and Taylor N. (1995) 'Schooling and Everyday Life: Knowledges Sacred and Profane', *Social Epistemology*, 9.3: 257–75.

Nietzsche, F. (1967) *The Will to Power*, New York: Random House.

Norris, C. (1994) *Truth and the Ethics of Criticism*, Manchester: Manchester University Press.

Norris, C. (1995) 'Truth, Science, and the Growth of Knowledge', *New Left Review*, 210: 105–23.

Rorty, R. (1985) 'Solidarity or Objectivity?' in J. Rajchman and C. West (eds) *Post-Analytic Philosophy*, New York: Columbia University Press.

Rosenau, P. M. (1992) *Postmodernism and the Social Sciences*, Princeton: Princeton University Press.

Said, E. (1993) *Culture and Imperialism*, London: Chatto & Windus.

Smeyers, P. (1995) 'Education and the Educational Project II: Do we Still Care about It?' *Journal of Philosophy of Education*, 29.3: 401–13.

Soper, K. (1993) 'Postmodernism, Subjectivity and the Question of Value', in J. Squires (ed.) *Principled Positions: Postmodernism and the Rediscovery of Value*, London: Lawrence & Wishart.

Squires, J. (ed.) (1993) *Principled Positions: Postmodernism and the Rediscovery of Value*, London: Lawrence & Wishart.

Strike, K. and Soltis, J. (1985) *The Ethics of Teaching*, New York: Teachers College Press.

Taylor, C. (1991) *The Ethics of Authenticity*, Cambridge, MA: Harvard University Press.

Thiroux, J. (1986) *Ethics: Theory and Practice*, New York: Macmillan.

Weeks, J. (1993) 'Rediscovering Values', in J. Squires (ed.) *Principled Positions: Postmodernism and the Rediscovery of Value*, London: Lawrence & Wishart.

Wittgenstein, L. (1961) *Tractatus Logico-Philosophicus*, London: Routledge & Kegan Paul.

Young, I. M. (1993) 'Together in Difference: Transforming the Logic of Group Political Conflict', in *Principled Positions: Postmodernism and the Rediscovery of Value*, Judith Squires (ed.), London: Lawrence & Wishart.

# Index